Addressing Difficulties in Literacy Development

This book outlines and critiques international strategies and programmes designed to address difficulties in literacy development. The high-profile team of contributors consider programmes for encouraging the development of literacy which operate at family, school, pupil and teacher levels. They argue that school is not the only legitimate location for literacy learning, and show how difficulties in literacy can be addressed sequentially, or simultaneously, both in and out of the school context.

Issues addressed include:

- the dilemmas facing practitioners in choosing between multiple approaches to practice;
- the factors which must be addressed in strategies which operate at the level of the family and the community;
- ways of conceptualising inclusive literacy practices in the classroom;
- approaches of putting theory into practice in programmes designed for use with individual students.

This book will be of interest to postgraduate students, teachers, researchers, education professionals and policy makers who are looking for well-researched, practical strategies to address difficulties in literacy development.

Janice Wearmouth is a Lecturer in the Faculty of Education and Language Studies at The Open University.

Janet Soler is a Lecturer in the Faculty of Education and Language Studies at The Open University.

Gavin Reid is a Lecturer in the Department of Educational Studies at the University of Edinburgh.

The companion volume in this series is:

Contextualising Difficulties in Literacy Development: exploring politics, culture, ethnicity and ethics, edited by Janet Soler, Janice Wearmouth and Gavin Reid.

Both Readers constitute part of a course jointly developed by The Open University and the University of Edinburgh. The Open University course is E801 *Addressing Difficulties in Literacy Development* (E801). The University of Edinburgh's course is the Postgraduate Certificate in Difficulties in Literacy Development.

The Open University Course E801 *Addressing Difficulties in Literacy Development*
E801 *Addressing Difficulties in Literacy Development* aims to raise the standard of all students' literacy levels. It is designed to increase teachers' awareness of the difficulties experienced by some students and will support teachers and others to explore and reflect on appropriate curriculum responses. Successful course completion, including the dyslexia component, enables students to apply to the British Dyslexia Association (BDA) for the award of Associate Membership (AMBDA).

This module is offered within the Open University Masters Programme in Education. The MA is modular and students may select modules from the programme which best fit their personal and professional interests and goals. Specialist lines of study are also available and include special and inclusive education, management, applied linguistics and life-long learning. The attainment of an MA entitles students to apply for entry to the Open University Doctorate in Education Programme. The Doctorate in Education degree combines taught courses and a dissertation designed to meet the needs of professionals in education and related areas who are seeking to extend and deepen their knowledge and understanding of educational issues.

How to apply
If you would like to find out more information about available courses, please write for the *Professional Development in Education* prospectus to the Call Centre, PO Box 724, The Open University, Walton Hall, Milton Keynes, MK7 6ZW, UK (telephone 0 (0 44) 1908 653231). Details can also be viewed on our web page http://www.open.ac.uk.

The University of Edinburgh Postgraduate Certificate in Difficulties in Literacy Development
This programme forms part of the Modular Masters Scheme which is offered by the Faculty of Education. The programme, which will lead to the achievement of credit equivalent to 60 Masters credits, will be available through part-time class contact at the University of Edinburgh over a 2 year period. The objectives of the programme are to develop an understanding of the issues relating to dyslexia within the broader context of literacy development. This will enable students to develop an awareness of the range of teaching approaches to difficulties in literacy development, and an awareness of the curricular difficulties experienced by students with dyslexia. Students successfully completing the programme are eligible to apply for the award of Associate Member of the British Dyslexia Association (AMBDA) from the British Dyslexia Association.

The programme will consist of two double modules each equivalent to 30 Masters credits. The modules are 'Literacy and Dyslexia: Identifying Individual and Contextual Needs' and 'Literacy and Dyslexia: Curriculum Access: Planning and Designing Interventions'. The modules will cover the following areas: conceptualising the barriers to literacy within the curriculum; equity issues, inclusion and the law; dyslexia as a syndrome; assessment, planning and intervention; reflecting on practice.

How to apply
Further information on the academic content of the programme can be obtained from Dr Gavin Reid, Gavin.Reid@ed.ac.uk. Applications or enquiries should be made to the Faculty of Education, Postgraduate Office, University of Edinburgh, Old Moray House, Holyrood Road, Edinburgh, EH8 8AQ, UK (telephone + 44 (0) 131 651 6139. The application form is available at the following URL: www.postgrad.ed.ac.uk/applicat/form.htm.

Addressing Difficulties in Literacy Development

Responses at family, school, pupil and teacher levels

Edited by Janice Wearmouth, Janet Soler and Gavin Reid

RoutledgeFalmer
Taylor & Francis Group

LONDON AND NEW YORK

The Open University

First published 2002
by RoutledgeFalmer
11 New Fetter Lane, London EC4P 4EE

Simultaneously published in the USA and Canada
by RoutledgeFalmer
29 West 35th Street, New York, NY 10001

RoutledgeFalmer is an imprint of the Taylor & Francis Group

© 2002 Compilation, original and editorial matter, The Open University

Typeset in Goudy by
Florence Production Ltd, Stoodleigh, Devon
Printed and bound in Great Britain by
MPG Books Ltd, Bodmin, Cornwall

British Library Cataloguing in Publication Data
A catalogue record for this book is available from the British Library

Library of Congress Cataloging in Publication Data
A catalog record has been requested

ISBN 0–415–28902–5 (hbk)
ISBN 0–415–28903–3 (pbk)

Contents

Preface   ix
Acknowledgements   xii

Introduction   1

1 Dilemmas in the choice of responses to students' difficulties
   in literacy development   3
   JANICE WEARMOUTH

PART I
Family and community   19

2 Parents and teachers   21
   PETER MITTLER

3 Collaboration between teachers and parents in assisting
   children's reading   39
   J. TIZARD, W. N. SCHOFIELD AND JENNY HEWISON

4 Pause Prompt Praise: reading tutoring procedures for home
   and school partnership   58
   TED GLYNN

5 Dyslexia: parents in need   71
   PAT HEATON

6 Rhetoric and research in family literacy   89
   PETER HANNON

7 Developing literacy in families with histories of reading
   problems: preliminary results from a longitudinal study of
   young children of dyslexic parents   111
   BENTE E. HAGTVET, ERNA HORN, LIV M. LASSEN,
   KIRSTI LAUVÅS, SOL LYSTER AND SIDSEL MISUND

8 Partnership approaches: new futures for Travellers   121
ELIZABETH JORDAN

PART 2
School and classroom   **133**

9 Using Soft Systems Methodology to re-think special needs   135
NORAH FREDERICKSON

10 Case studies of individual classrooms   153
E. C. WRAGG, C. M. WRAGG, G. S. HAYNES AND
R. P. CHAMBERLIN

11 Contradictory models: the dilemma of specific learning
difficulties   174
ALAN DYSON AND DAVID SKIDMORE

12 The National Literacy Strategy and dyslexia: a comparison
of teaching methods and materials   189
JUDITH PIOTROWSKI AND REA REASON

PART 3
Individual pupil   **203**

13 Examinations, assessments and special arrangements   205
NICK PEACEY

14 Learning to understand written language   224
JANE OAKHILL AND NICOLA YUILL

15 Specific developmental dyslexia (SDD): 'basics to back' in
2000 and beyond?   243
PETER PUMFREY

16 Multisensory teaching of reading in mainstream settings   269
MIKE JOHNSON

17 Researching the social and emotional consequences of dyslexia   282
BARBARA RIDDICK

18 An examination of the relationship between labelling and
stigmatisation with special reference to dyslexia   303
BARBARA RIDDICK

19 The long-term effects of two interventions for children
with reading difficulties   320
QUALIFICATIONS AND CURRICULUM AUTHORITY

20 Teaching spelling: some questions answered   340
DIANA BENTLEY

21 Spelling   354
REA REASON AND RENE BOOTE

Index   381

Preface

Janice Wearmouth

The issue of difficulties in literacy development has assumed a growing importance in many countries in recent years. This has occurred as a reaction partly
to the increasing focus on literacy standards at national level and partly to
an awareness of competence in literacy to individuals' life chances. Across the
world there is a very wide range of teaching programmes used to support the
literacy acquisition of those students who experience difficulties. Some
programmes or approaches operate exclusively at one level: family, school,
pupil or teacher. Others may be designed to operate at different levels, or
across levels. This book is designed to offer theoretical rationales for, and clear
descriptions of, a range of programmes operating at each of these levels.

Both internationally and across the UK teachers in classrooms have varying
degrees of opportunity to make their own decisions about what to teach pupils
and also how to teach it. Some countries have legally required National
Curricula with close prescriptions of content, modes of teaching and forms of
assessment. There may be less flexibility for decision-making at school or classroom level about how to implement the curriculum in such countries compared
with the greater freedom elsewhere. However, as Wragg (1997, p. 23) notes,
even in those countries which have a prescriptive National Curriculum, it is
impossible for central government to prescribe every detail of a school's
curriculum. Teachers often still have the opportunity to make decisions which
may have a profound effect over the quality of pupil learning.

The level at which a programme is designed to operate is clearly an important consideration in decisions about which programme or approach to use to
support the literacy learning of students who experience difficulties. However,
there are a number of other considerations which must also be taken into
account in the decision-making process if programmes and strategies are to be
tailored to fit the needs of students in real-life situations. Finding the best
method of teaching reading to students who experience difficulties is not
straightforward. Every method appears to work for some children. New
methods often work well at the beginning as a result of the 'Hawthorne effect',
that is the increased attention and interest they stimulate.

The book opens by considering some of the dilemmas facing practitioners
in choosing between multiple possible approaches to practice. Sometimes it

requires a great deal of reflection on problematic issues faced by students with literacy difficulties and, sometimes, their families, in order to gain new understandings of uncertainties, complexities and conflicting viewpoints inherent in the real world situation before informed decisions can be made.

The chapters in Part 1 *Family and Community* outline factors which must be addressed in approaches to literacy development which operate at the level of the family and community and then offer descriptions and evaluations of a number of such strategies both in the UK and elsewhere. In Chapter 2, Mittler outlines a number of concerns with regard to the whole basis of home–school relationships for pupils. He advocates devising new ways to bring teachers and parents into a more positive working relationship for the benefit of everyone involved. Work seminal to the development of home–school partnerships to support children's reading in the UK is described in the research associated with the Haringey Project in Chapter 3. In Chapter 4, Glynn outlines a New Zealand-based initiative, Pause Prompt Praise, which originated as a home–school literacy project in South Auckland and has been developed to take account of cultural contexts. Heaton writes from personal experience in Chapter 5 where she focuses on the issue of family responses to the needs of children identified as dyslexic. Hannon goes on to examine the rhetoric surrounding family literacy programmes and draws out implications of this for policy, practice and research in Chapter 6. In Chapter 7, Hagtvet *et al.* report on a longitudinal study which explores the developmental links between early linguistic and emotional factors and later problems with written language, and discuss preliminary findings on early precursors of reading difficulties and the attitudes of parents to the literacy development of children. Finally in this part, Jordan discusses issues related to the literacy development of students from families of Travellers.

Part 2 *School and Classroom* discusses issues related to initiating change in schools in order to support programmes designed to improve the literacy learning of those with difficulties. It also outlines factors identified in research studies as the hallmarks of effective classroom teaching of literacy. In Chapter 9, Frederickson introduces a practical strategy, 'Soft Systems Methodology', supported by theory, that can be used to reflect on practice and bring about improvement in the area of special educational provision, including that related to difficulties in literacy development. Wragg *et al.* in Chapter 10 focus on observation of six primary teachers identified as effective teachers of literacy to explore factors that appear to be significant in improving levels of literacy acquisition in primary classrooms. In Chapter 11 Dyson and Skidmore go on to discuss the dilemmas presented to schools in catering for pupils identified as 'having specific learning difficulties', which is, as they point out, an inherently problematic concept, while in Chapter 12 Piotrowski and Reason continue the theme of the challenges presented to schools in catering for individuals with difficulties in literacy within a curriculum designed for the majority of pupils in their examination of the suitability of teaching methods and materials for dyslexic pupils in the National Literacy Strategy.

Part 3 *Individual Pupil* goes on to discuss theory into practice in programmes designed for use with individual students and describes and critiques a range of such programmes. Peacey opens this part with discussion of the issues involved in seeking special dispensation for examinations for students who experience difficulties in literacy. In Chapter 14, Oakhill and Yuill take an approach from cognitive psychology in discussing reading comprehension and practical strategies that might be used to support those students with difficulties in this area. Four chapters on issues related to dyslexia then follow. Pumfrey in Chapter 15 addresses questions related to the nature and incidence of dyslexia and discusses how difficulties of a dyslexic nature might be addressed. Johnson then summarises and discusses an evaluation study of three schemes designed to promote phonological awareness in dyslexic students through a structured, multisensory approach. In the two following chapters, Riddick first outlines some of the social and emotional consequences of dyslexia from the research literature, and then, in Chapter 18, discusses the issue of labelling and stigmatisation as it relates to dyslexic students. Chapter 19 contains a summary of the findings of a study investigating the long-term effects of two interventions to improve reading levels, 'Reading Recovery' and 'Phonological Awareness Training', and compares the outcomes of these programmes against their aims. The final two chapters, 20 and 21, address the issue of spelling, first from a consideration by Bentley of issues relating to school spelling policies and the way in which they may impact on individual students with difficulties, and then from a consideration by Reason and Boote of practical strategies to improve spelling.

Reference

Wragg, E. C. (1997) *The Cubic Curriculum*, London: Routledge.

Acknowledgements

We are indebted to the following for allowing us to make use of copyright material:

Chapter 2: Mittler, P. (2000) 'Parents and teachers', in *Working Towards Inclusive Education: Social Contexts*. London: David Fulton. Reproduced by permission of David Fulton Publishers.

Chapter 3: Tizard, J., Schofield, W. N. and Hewison, J. (1982) 'Collaboration between teachers and parents in assisting children's reading', in *British Journal of Educational Psychology*, 52, pp. 1–5. Reproduced by permission of the *British Journal of Educational Psychology* © The British Psychological Society.

Chapter 4: Glynn, T. (1992) 'Pause Prompt Praise: reading tutoring procedures for home and school partnership', in S. Wolfendale and K. Topping (eds) *Family Involvement in Literacy*. London: Cassell Education. Reproduced by permission of Continuum International Publishing Group Ltd, The Tower Building, 11 York Road, London.

Chapter 5: Heaton, P. (1996) *Dyslexia: Parents in Need*, pp. 15–36. London: Whurr. Reproduced by permission of Whurr Publishers Ltd.

Chapter 6: Hannon, P. (1999) 'Rhetoric and research in family literacy', in *British Educational Research Journal*, 26 (1), pp. 122–137. Reproduced by permission of Taylor & Francis Ltd, 11 New Fetter Lane, London, EC4P 4EE. www.tandf.co.uk.

Chapter 7: Hagtvet, B., Horn, E., Lassen, L., Lauvås, K., Lyster, S. and Misund, S. (1999) 'Developing literacy in families with histories of reading problems: preliminary results from a longitudinal study of young children of dyslexic parents', in *European Journal of Special Educational Needs Education*, 14 (2), pp. 135–143. Reproduced by permission of Taylor & Francis Ltd, 11 New Fetter Lane, London, EC4P 4EE. www.tandf.co.uk.

Chapter 9: Frederickson, N. (1993) 'Using Soft Systems Methodology to re-think special needs', in A. Dyson and C. Gains (eds) *Rethinking Special Needs in Mainstream Schools*. London: David Fulton. Reproduced by permission of David Fulton Publishers.

Chapter 10: Wragg, E. C., Wragg, C. M., Haynes, G. S. and Chaplain, R. P. (1998) 'Case studies of individual classrooms', in *Improving Literacy in the Primary School*. London: Routledge. Reproduced by permission of Taylor & Francis Ltd, 11 New Fetter Lane, London, EC4P 4EE. www.tandf.co.uk.

Chapter 11: Dyson, A. and Skidmore, D. (1996) 'Contradictory models: the dilemma of specific learning difficulties', in G. Reid (ed.) *Dimensions of Dyslexia*. Edinburgh: Moray House. Reproduced by permission of Moray House Publications.

Chapter 12: Piotrowski, J. and Reason, R. (2000) 'The National Literacy Strategy and dyslexia: a comparison of teaching methods and materials', in *Support for Learning*, 15 (2), pp. 51–57. Reproduced by permission of Blackwell Publishers Ltd.

Chapter 14: Oakhill, J. and Yuill, N. (1995) 'Learning to understand written language', in E. Funnell and M. Stuart (eds) *Learning to Read: Psychology in the Classroom*. Oxford: Blackwell. Reproduced by permission of Blackwell Publishers Ltd.

Chapter 15: Pumfrey, P. (2001) 'Specific developmental dyslexia (SDD): "basics to back" in 2000 and beyond?', in M. Hunter-Carsch (ed.) *Dyslexia: A Psychological Perspective*. London: Whurr. Reproduced by permission of Whurr Publishers Ltd.

Chapter 17: Riddick, B. (1996) 'Researching the social and emotional consequences of dyslexia', in *Living with Dyslexia*. London: Routledge. Reproduced by permission of Taylor & Francis Ltd, 11 New Fetter Lane, London, EC4P 4EE. www.tandf.co.uk.

Chapter 18: Riddick, B. (2000) 'An examination of the relationship between labelling and stigmatisation with special reference to dyslexia', in *Disability and Society*, 15 (4), pp. 653–667. Reproduced by permission of Taylor & Francis Ltd, 11 New Fetter Lane, London, EC4P 4EE. www.tandf.co.uk.

Chapter 19: Qualifications and Curriculum Authority (1998) *The Long-term Effects of Two Interventions for Children with Reading Difficulties*. London: QCA. Reproduced by permission of the Qualifications and Curriculum Authority.

Chapter 20: Bentley, D. (1990) *Teaching Spelling: Some Questions Answered*. Reading: University of Reading. Reproduced by permission of the University of Reading.

Chapter 21: Reason, R. and Boote, R. (1994) 'Spelling' in *Helping Children with Reading and Spelling*. London: Routledge. Reproduced by permission of Taylor & Francis Ltd, 11 New Fetter Lane, London, EC4P 4EE. www.tandf.co.uk.

While the Publishers have made very effort to contact copyright holders of the material used in this volume, they would be grateful to hear from any they were unable to contact.

Introduction

Chapter 1

Dilemmas in the choice of responses to students' difficulties in literacy development

Janice Wearmouth

Introduction

Across the world there is a very wide range of teaching programmes and peda-gogic approaches used to support the literacy acquisition of those students who experience difficulties. Some programmes or approaches operate exclusively at one level: family, school, pupil or teacher. Others may be designed to operate at different levels, or across levels. The level at which a programme is designed to operate is clearly an important consideration in decisions about which programme or approach to use to support students' literacy learning. However, there are a number of other considerations which must also be taken into account in the decision-making process.

The task of choosing an appropriate programme or strategy to address an individual student's learning needs is not straightforward. This chapter sets out to explore the notion that there exists a considerable dilemma in choos-ing between multiple possible approaches to practice. This results from the multiplicity of conflicting values and goals and the degree of uncertainty in the area of difficulties in literacy and the underlying assumptions of programmes designed to address these difficulties. The chapter goes on to exemplify this notion with two specific instances of relevance to considera-tions both of the level at which it might be appropriate to introduce a literacy initiative and also of the underlying assumptions about the reading process on which literacy programmes or strategies rest.

Dilemmas in decision-making

Both internationally and across the UK teachers in classrooms have varying degrees of opportunity to make their own decisions about which programme or approach to use to encourage literacy acquisition among students who experience difficulties. Schools' and teachers' autonomy over decision-making in the curriculum is a particularly important issue where students experience difficulties in learning such as in the acquisition of literacy. In some countries there are protocols specified by statute for identifying and assessing 'special' difficulties in learning, including difficulties in literacy, which predispose to particular modes of assessment and individualised types of provision that can be quantified for accountability purposes. In some, for example as currently in England, targets for the raising of students' literacy levels are expressed in terms of reading scores referenced against the norm for a particular student cohort. Some countries have legally required national literacy curricula with close prescriptions of content, modes of teaching and forms of assessment. There may be less flexibility for decision-making at school or classroom level about how to implement the curriculum in such countries compared with the greater freedom elsewhere.

The setting of targets for individual pupils on individual education plans, records or profiles, and for whole cohorts of pupils by central government as well as the close prescription of curriculum content may give the illusion that there is a simple cause-and-effect relationship between the ends to be achieved and the means to do it. One implication to be drawn from the setting of simple targets is that these targets are fixed and unproblematic and that there is common agreement about how to achieve them. With agreement about ends, the question of how to act becomes merely one about which particular means achieve the ends most efficiently.

The assumptions underpinning an approach of this kind may be interpreted as closely reflecting the 'technical rational' model of management. Schön (1983, p. 21) defines 'technical rationality' as 'instrumental problem-solving made rigorous by the application of scientific theory and technique'. From a technical rational argument it should be possible for teachers to ground themselves in a scientific approach to accumulating empirical knowledge about the means most suited to raising literacy levels of all students, including those with difficulties. However, as Wragg et al. (1998) note, finding the best method of teaching reading to students who experience difficulties is not straightforward. He identifies three of the problems with which it is complicated:

- every method appears to work for some children;
- those who initiate new methods often have a significant personal stake in their success in improving reading levels and therefore believe that they work better than previous approaches;
- new methods work well at the beginning as a result of the 'Hawthorne effect', that is the increased attention and interest they stimulate.

Additionally, the choice of provision made for individual pupils which has resulted from the formulation of assessments for statutory purposes has often been led not by the pupil's learning needs but by available resources (Cline, 1992).

A number of writers (Habermas, 1974; Schön, 1983) have been very critical of the 'technical rational' approach. In real-world situations there is often confusion and conflict about both means and ends and, therefore, no possibility of viewing the issue unproblematically as a technical problem to be solved through instrumental means. The assumptions underpinning the technical rational approach are particularly problematic if we take seriously the phenomena of complexity, uncertainty, uniqueness and conflicting values (Schön, ibid., p. 14) which are inherent in the real world situation of addressing difficulties in literacy development in schools. As Schön (ibid.) notes, 'situations of practice' are characterised by 'uncertainty, disorder and indeterminacy' (ibid., p. 16) since practitioners are 'frequently embroiled in conflicts of values, goals, purposes, and interests' (ibid., p. 17). Each student with literacy difficulties is an individual. Each situation is unique. Each requires its own solution. Those professionals charged with choosing programmes or strategies to support the literacy acquisition of those students who experience difficulties in schools are often enveloped in uncertainty, indeterminacy and value conflict in their own work situations. Often, both the ends to be achieved and the process to be used are best clarified 'through the non-technical process of framing the problematic situation' (ibid, p. 41).

In order further to exemplify the dilemmas facing those charged with responsibility for choosing programmes or approaches to support the literacy acquisition of students who experience difficulties two particular issues are discussed below. These issues are especially significant as they are associated with both the level at which the programmes and approaches operate and also the assumptions underpinning reading programmes designed to address difficulties. The first is connected with issues surrounding family involvement in supporting improvement of students' literacy levels, the second to the underlying model of reading on which the programme is based.

The involvement of parents and carers

The first issue relates to the fact that, embedded within different approaches and strategies, are different underlying assumptions about the ability and right of families and/or carers from a diversity of backgrounds and cultures to support the literacy development of their children. The attitude of educators to the role of families as prime educators of children is of significance in planning programmes which will address difficulties in literacy development within the context of respect for the students' family and cultural backgrounds. Differences in views about difficulties in literacy learning within the context of family background and cultural environment obviously impact upon literacy teaching and interpretations of how to interpret and implement best research-based practice.

Until comparatively recently the homes of poor working-class and ethnic minority-culture families were commonly assumed to be less good literacy-learning environments than those of dominant-culture, middle-class families. A number of studies in the 1970s and 1980s suggested that achievement on standardised tests of reading is strongly related to social class, for example the National Child Development Study (Davie, Butler and Goldstein, 1972) which followed all the children born in one week in 1958 through from birth. The children of semi-skilled manual fathers were more than twice as likely to be poor readers than those students whose fathers held professional or technical posts.

Families with little tradition of formal literacy may be viewed as 'literacy-deficient' and unable to support their children's literacy acquisition. Hannon (1999) notes some of the consequences of a deficit perspective of the ability of some students' families to support the improvement of students' literacy:

- the school is absolved from responsibility for addressing the literacy difficulties of those students from 'literacy-deficient' families;
- the families themselves cannot be viewed as a source of positive support for the student's developing literacy until and unless their deficiency in literacy in addressed.

As Hannon (ibid.) notes, the assumption of a necessarily reciprocal relationship between low levels of parental literacy and the poor literacy development of their offspring is not fully supported by research findings. Studies have shown that parents from every social class are often very keen and able to help their students with reading at home (Newson and Newson, 1977). An example of such an initiative is the Haringey project (Hewison and Tizard, 1980) which might be interpreted as empowering families in its recognition of the social system of the family with a right to make choices. Hewison (1988) speculates that the crucial factor in its success may have been the motivational context of the home itself in which the opportunity for extra reading practice occurred. A further example of a well-known study of family involvement with the improvement of children's reading is the New Zealand-based 'Pause, Prompt and Praise' (PPP) procedures. PPP was developed, initially, in South Auckland in 1977 to train parents to tutor their children in oral reading in order to raise the poor reading achievement of older (10–12-year-old) pupils in schools. Amongst the considerations set out by McNaughton, Glynn and Robinson (1981) in their rationale for involving parents were:

> a growing concern for parental involvement in the education of their children . . . parents, while still feeling and being held responsible for their children, are becoming more and more powerless to influence their own children's development. . . . The parents in our research certainly felt keenly the segregation of home and school. . . . We felt that parents, as well as being willing and able to help their low progress children, have a right to take part in their children's schooling.
>
> (McNaughton, Glynn and Robinson, 1981, p. 4)

There is a great deal of heated debate about which is the most appropriate way to support the learning of students who experience difficulties in literacy development in ways which take account of a diversity of family and cultural backgrounds. Part of the reason for this is that there are important differences in views about the power relationship that should exist between schools and the families of students experiencing literacy difficulties. In a wide-ranging review of the literature on parent–professional partnerships, Dale (1996, chapter 1) identified a number of different partnership arrangements between schools and parents/carers which clearly reflect different kinds of power relationships in some of the common home–school literacy programmes. Among them are:

- The traditional 'Expert Model' where the parent is expected to rely on the expertise of the professional in making judgements and taking control of what needs to be done.
- The 'Transplant Model' where the role of professionals is to transplant skills to the parents to help the parents to become teachers. The professional still has the ultimate responsibility for decision making.
- The Empowerment Model where the right of the parent to choose as a consumer is combined with a professional recognition of the family as a social system. Here the job of the professional is to help empower the family to meet its own needs rather than to make judgements and decisions about those needs.
- The Consumer Model where there is a shift of power from the professional to the parent based on the view of the parents as consumers of services who draw upon their expertise in deciding what services they need and want for their child. In many countries legislation gives parents the right to express a choice in provision made for their child.

One of the motivating factors for the way in which PPP was initially conceptualised was an intention amongst the researchers to address the apparent growing sense of powerlessness over children's education among parents (McNaughton, Glynn and Robinson, 1981) together with the existence of research to suggest that early educational initiatives that produced lasting effects were those where parents were trained to teach children who had fallen behind (Bronfenbrenner, 1974; Chilman, 1976; Donachy, 1979).

In recent years, the introduction of PPP into different settings, for example the 'Rotorua Home and School Project' (Glynn, Berryman and Glynn, 2000), has led to a greater awareness of the importance of the cultural context of the family and community for children's learning:

> While it is clear that home and school exercise joint influences on children's literacy, facilitating learning across the two contexts depends on home and school knowing and understanding what literacy values and reading and writing practices are operating in the other.
>
> (Glynn, Berryman and Glynn, 2000, p. 9)

PPP may be seen as developing from a 'transplant model' with the transfer of skills to parents by teachers into an 'empowerment model' in the way in which it encapsulates respect for cultural background through the sharing of understandings and actions that are reciprocal between school and home.

There are many other examples of successful initiatives involving parents in the reading development of their students where the emphasis is much more upon the model of the teacher as expert. Topping (1992, 1995), for example, has prescribed a method for 'training' parents in the techniques of the 'Paired Reading' programme to support students' literacy development. He warns against assuming that 'any old thing that two people do with a book' constitutes 'Paired Reading' (Topping, 1996, p. 46). Having said this, however, the choice of home-based programme may need to be pragmatic as well as philosophical. There is no one 'right' approach. Some parents prefer and, for various reasons, 'need' expert direction from teachers. Others do not. This is part of the uncertainty and indeterminacy of a context in which conflicting views and values abound but with which those choosing literacy support programmes and approaches must deal.

Models of reading

Conventionally there are two contrasting theoretical perspectives on the act of reading which have each led to a different approach to the teaching of reading to students who experience difficulty. From one, reading comprises the process of decoding of the abstract and complicated alphabetic code, and through this the simple reconstruction of the author's meaning. This perspective sees reading as a series of small steps to be learned one by one, the 'bottom-up' approach to skill development. In order to learn how to do this, children must go through a staged process. First children must learn the letters of the alphabet and establish the principle of sound–symbol identification. Then they must learn to apply this in order to decode words. It implies teaching methods which emphasise the mastery of phonics and word recognition. With adequate practice, children will be able to understand written text. As Adams (1994) notes, the bottom-up approach was the earliest method of teaching reading which:

> followed a straightforward two-stage process:
>
> Teach the code then have them read.
>
> Teaching about the code was based directly on the alphabetic principle. Students were first required to learn the alphabet. The phonemic significance of the letters was instilled, for example, through the presentation of key words (e.g. G is for glass), practice in reading simple syllables, and exercise in spelling.
>
> (Adams, 1994, p. 21)

Reading matter for children in the early days was predominantly the Bible and this in itself helped to dictate the purpose of reading. There was very little need to be concerned about reading comprehension since the text was predetermined.

> This approach reflected an uncomplicated translation of the nature of the writing system: Teach the means and get on with the purpose. And thus it pretty much remained through to the middle of the nineteenth century.
>
> (Adams, 1994, p. 21)

In a major US report commissioned by the Center for the Study of Reading in Champaign, Illinois, to review all aspects of phonics and early reading instruction Adams argues that there is a great deal of research to support the conclusion that skilful readers of English thoroughly process the individual letters of words easily and quickly because they are well acquainted with the sequences of letters they are likely to see to automatic level (Adams, 1994, p. 108). Indeed, the difference between 'good' and 'poor' readers is a function of the differential ability in word recognition:

> proficient reading depends on an automatic capacity to recognise frequent spelling patterns visually and to translate them phonologically. Differences in this capacity are principal separators of good from poor readers. Only those prereaders who acquire awareness of phonemes (the sounds to which graphemic units map), learn to read successfully. Programs explicitly designed to develop sounding and blending skills produce better word readers than those that do not . . . synthetic phonics is of special value for young readers.
>
> (Adams, 1994, p. 293)

Adams' conclusions about the place of phonics in competent reading has a number of implications for teachers' practices in the teaching of reading. Firstly, from her perspective, beginning readers should learn to recognise individual letters before they are taught to recognise whole words. Secondly, beginning readers must learn to recognise individual letters quickly in order to optimise their ability to recognise whole words. It is logical to assume that difficulty at the level of single letter recognition will impede the recognition of strings of letter patterns. Thirdly, beginning readers need to pay attention to the sequence of letters in a word, not simply the whole word:

> Many of the most common practices of reading programs – including synthetic phonics, writing, exercise with frequent blends and digraphs, and practice with word families – seem ideally suited to this end. In this context, the allure of phonics, or the exercise of discovering a word by sounding out its spelling, is that it inherently forces the child to attend to each and every letter of the word, in left-to-right order . . . phonic activities that direct the child's attention to individual letters rather than sequences of letters do not seem useful to this end.
>
> (Adams, 1994, p. 131)

Adams sees writing and spelling of whole words as valuable in strengthening the 'perceptual integrity in recognition' of newly-learned words (Adams, 1994, p. 131). She also advocates exercises on frequent digraphs, letter blends and word families. When beginning readers encounter difficult words in their reading they should examine their spelling patterns and sound out their pronunciations:

> Overall, the best instructional strategy for orthographic development is to induce children to focus on the likely sequences that comprise syllables, words and frequent blends and digraphs. As the children become familiar with these spelling patterns, their ability to syllabify will naturally emerge along with the automaticity with which they will recognise the ordered spellings of single syllables.
>
> (Adams, 1994, pp. 134–5)

Despite her advocacy of the importance of phonics in initial reading instruction, it should be noted that Adams (1994, p. 422) also acknowledges the importance of semantic cues in reading and other 'critical sources of information':

> In the reading situation, as in any effective communication situation, the message or text provides but one of the critical sources of information. The rest must come from the readers' own prior knowledge. Further, in the reading situation as in any other learning situation, the learnability of a pattern depends critically on the prior knowledge and higher-order relationships that it evokes. In both fluent reading and its acquisition, the reader's knowledge must be aroused interactively and in parallel. Neither understanding nor learning can proceed hierarchically from the bottom up. Phonological awareness, letter recognition facility, familiarity with spelling patterns, spelling–sound relations, and individual words must be developed in concert with real reading and real writing and with deliberate reflection on the forms, functions and meanings of texts.
>
> (Adams, 1994, p. 422)

Semantic and syntactic skills and knowledge operate in parallel with word-processing skills. Cues from the context of the text are very helpful in suggesting to the reader what an orthographically difficult word might be. However, individual word recognition is paramount:

> Depending on the situation, they (*reading skills*) operate in dominance, complement, or deference to each other. Such coordination is possible because they are commonly anchored in the knowledge and processes involved in individual letter recognition.
>
> (Adams, 1994, p. 106)

The second perspective views reading as the active *construction* of meaning. This perspective is influenced by psycholinguistics with its emphasis on how we make sense of our world through the use of language.

> as we read, our minds are actively busy making sense of print, just as they are always actively trying to make sense of the world. Our minds have a repertoire of strategies for sense-making. In reading, we can call these psycholinguistic because there's continuous interaction between thought and language. We start with the text, written language, and use the cues from the various language levels to construct our own parallel text and meaning. We draw on our sense-making strategies all the time we're reading, but some of the cycles draw on some strategies more than others. All of these strategies have their counterparts in making sense of what we hear (listening), and in making sense of the world.
>
> (Goodman, 1996, p. 110–11)

The reader is seen to have expectations of what a text might be about, and then to test these expectations and confirm or reject them as s/he proceeds, the so-called 'psycholinguistic guessing game' (Goodman, 1967).

> By calling reading a psycholinguistic guessing game, I wanted to empha-size the active role of the reader in making sense of written language as a new key element in our understanding of the reading process. 1 wanted people to take distance from the view that reading is the accurate, sequen-tial recognition of letters and words. I wanted them to understand that, in order to make sense (construct meaning), readers:
>
> - make continuous use of minimal information selected from a complex but incomplete and ambiguous text;
> - draw on their knowledge of language and the world;
> - use strategies of predicting and inferring where the text is going.
>
> (Goodman, 1996, p. 115)

This is the perspective which underlies the teaching methods that empha-sise 'top-down' skills, stressing the use of semantic and syntactic cues:

> reading is a constructive process and . . . *I want to undermine any tendency . . . to think of reading as the 'simple' act of recognizing letters and/or words* . . . the sense you make of a text depends on the sense you bring to it . . . much misunderstanding still exists about reading and written language in general. I believe that this confusion exists largely because people have started in the wrong place, with letters, letter–sound rela-tionships and words. We must begin instead by looking at reading in the real world, at how readers and writers try to make sense with each other.
>
> (Goodman, 1996, pp. 2–3)

Goodman's psycholinguistic approach sees readers as attempting to understand what the author is trying to say, but actively constructing their own meaning. He describes the process of reading as comprising four cycles between the visual input supplied by the eyes to the brain, and the meaning constructed by the brain. These cycles are visual, perceptual, syntactic and semantic. Goodman summarises the key concepts in this approach:

> A few key ideas can serve as schemas to guide us as we probe the subtleties of this constructive reading process:
>
> • Reading is an active process in which readers use powerful strategies in their pursuit of meaning.
> • Everything readers do is part of their attempt to make sense.
> • Readers become highly efficient in using just enough of the available information to accomplish their purpose of making sense.
> • What readers bring to any act of reading is as important for successful reading as anything they use from the published text.
>
> (Goodman, 1996, p. 91)

Goodman is highly critical of phonic instruction for children with difficulties in the area of literacy development:

> For less sophisticated readers, the reading process is sometimes short-circuited by instruction. Instruction that strongly focusses on letter/sound matching or word identification can teach developing readers that the goal of reading is to decode print as sound, or to recognize a succession of words. Isolated phonics produces what some British folks have called 'barking at print.' Short-circuiting at the word level produces the monotone reading of a text as nothing more than a list of words. Only when the focus of the reader, at whatever level of proficiency, is on meaning is the whole process at work and short-circuiting minimized.
>
> (Goodman, 1996, p. 115)

Instead, in keeping with his view of reading as a guessing game, Goodman feels that those in the early stages of literacy development should be encouraged to decide for themselves whether they have read text correctly by continually monitoring for meaning. Only miscues that cause a loss of meaning need correction:

> Readers who correct miscues that don't need to be corrected are inefficient: they distract themselves from the central task of making sense by their preoccupation with accuracy. Readers who persistently fail to correct when they need to do so are likely to be ineffective: they lose a lot of the meaning.
>
> (Goodman, 1996, p. 114)

It is only when readers decide for themselves when they do or do not need to correct their reading that they are developing useful strategies for self-correction.

There are many examples across the world of reading programmes based on the whole-book/whole-language approach. In the UK, for example, Waterland (1985), an infant teacher, operating from an assumption that reading may be learned by an 'apprentice' working alongside skilled practitioners, developed and made popular the 'Apprenticeship Approach'. This approach has been linked with the whole-book/whole-language approach and combines emphasis on meaning and interest in text with awareness of the part that significant others, including parents, can play. A number of other versions of this approach exist, for example Paired Reading (see above), where a more experienced reader reads the text with the learner until s/he indicates that s/he wishes to read alone (Topping, 1995).

The tension between the two perspectives, phonic and whole-language/whole-book, can be illustrated by the difference in views expressed by Adams, the author of the US report commissioned to review all aspects of phonics and early reading instruction (see above, Adams, 1994) and two of her academic colleagues (Strickland and Cullinan, 1994) who published comments on Adams' final report. From the research studies reviewed in the report Adams argues that:

> the single immutable and non-optional fact about skilful reading is that it involves relatively complete processing of the individual letters of print.
>
> (Adams, 1994, p. 105)

Adams warns against encouraging beginning readers to rely too much on contextual cues to read text:

> overreliance on contextual cues should be a source of concern rather than pride for the educator for it is a strong sign that the reader's orthographic knowledge and skills have not been properly developed.
>
> (Adams, p. 140)

Adams' academic colleagues, Strickland and Cullinan, in an 'Afterword' to her report, feel that Adams' view of competence in phonics as prerequisite to reading development is mistaken and leads to an overly narrow view of reading instruction:

> We do not believe ... that phonics should be taught in isolation from other aspects of a child's literacy development or that it is a precursor to reading development. The necessarily narrow focus of Adams' book puts its readers at risk of ignoring the way phonics instruction fits into a broader framework of language learning.
>
> (Strickland and Cullinan, 1994)

They criticise the use of the terms 'prereaders', 'reading readiness' and 'prerequisite skills' as implying that children acquire literacy skills suddenly and as a result of formal instruction. They prefer the term 'emergent literacy' which implies that there is no one point when literacy development begins. They agree with Pearson (1989) that children's literacy emerges out of their interaction with language and their experience of the world of print around them. They argue that studies which show a strong relationship between linguistic awareness and literacy development do not provide any rationale for concluding that competence in phonics should be acquired before children are taught to read. It may be the case that competence in phonics develops as a result of access to stories and print rather than the other way round. Rather than direct instruction in phonics as a precursor to reading, Strickland and Cullinan feel that the emphasis should be on literacy-rich environments:

> Current naturalistic research strongly suggests that phonics is best learned in the context of reading and writing. If learning is to occur, we must give children good stories that intrigue and engage them; we must give them poetry that sings with the poetry of language; we must enchant them with language play; and we must give them opportunities to write. In short, we must surround them with literature that helps them understand their world and their ability to create meaning. We must read to children from the very beginning and read to them every day. . . . In print-rich early learning environments, reading and writing are incorporated into every aspect of the day. Children are encouraged to explore print materials in the same enthusiastic manner that they approach sand, blocks and outdoor games. They attempt to use literacy for their own purposes just as they see it being used by the adults around them. Because the learning is so joyful and natural, the development of specific skills may not be in evidence. Nevertheless, the skills, including phonics, are there.
>
> (Strickland and Cullinan, 1994, p. 428)

They conclude that instruction in reading should begin from an emphasis on meaning and should include phonics, rather than beginning with phonics:

> We believe the evidence supports a whole language and integrated language arts approach with some direct instruction, in context, on spelling-to-sound correspondences.
>
> (Strickland and Cullinan, 1994, p. 433)

Stanovich (2000) suggests that both top-down and bottom-up methods have limitations because readers draw on both processes when reading. He suggests that readers use information simultaneously from different levels and do not necessarily begin at the graphic (bottom-up) or the context (top-down). During the development of reading skills some readers may rely more heavily on some levels than others. Those children who are not proficient in the sub-skills of reading will not have the opportunity to acquire these skills because they do not have easy access to reading, the so-called 'Matthew effect'. Additionally he argues that the reader's weaknesses are compensated by her/his strengths. Stanovich called this process the Interactive Compensatory model because the various processes interact and also because the reader can compensate for weaknesses in one area by relying on strengths in the other aspects. Therefore the argument is that poor readers rely on context to compensate for their difficulties in processing the individual sounds of words.

In their study into the practices of effective teachers of literacy in UK primary schools, Wragg et al. (1998) found that few teachers seemed to subscribe exclusively either to a phonics or whole-book approach, and, in the classroom, were commonly using a mixture of different teaching methods. They conclude that reading is 'a complex, multifaceted activity' which requires 'broad-based instruction':

> Children need to learn processing skills, using context and knowledge of syntax to focus on the general meaning of the whole, and also decoding skills focusing on individual letters and words. They need specific teaching of both 'top-down' and 'bottom-up' skills; a certain amount of phonic instruction; careful monitoring in order to give early help to those who make a slow start; interesting meaningful texts; teachers who are enthusiastic about literacy throughout the whole primary range; encouragement from home; and lots of practice.
>
> (Wragg et al., 1998, pp. 32–3)

The balance to be achieved in this 'broad-based instruction' for students who experience difficulty might well be considered a matter for the professional judgement of teachers in discussion with colleagues and parents or carers, taking into account the learning needs of individual pupils. Pragmatically, however, as noted above, the degree to which real choice is open to teachers and others is variable.

Summary

Even in those countries which have a prescriptive National Curriculum, it is impossible for central government to prescribe every detail of a school's curriculum. Teachers and others often still have the opportunity to make decisions which may have a profound effect over the quality of pupil learning (Wragg et al., 1998, p. 23). However, choice of programme is not straightforward. There is no one programme or strategy that will work for every student with difficulties (Chall, 1967). As a result of the multiplicity of conflicting values and goals and the degree of uncertainty in both the area of difficulties in literacy and the rationale underpinning programmes designed to address these difficulties and their application there is a considerable dilemma in choosing between multiple possible approaches to practice. Choice of programme and, within that, choice of level at which it is appropriate to initiate an intervention to support a student's literacy acquisition cannot, therefore, simply be viewed as a question of solving a technical problem through instrumental means. It requires much more reflection on, and re-framing of, problematic issues faced by students with literacy difficulties and, sometimes, their families, in order to gain new understandings of uncertainties, complexities and conflicting viewpoints inherent in the current situation and to make informed decisions.

References

Adams, M. J. (1994) *Beginning to Read: Thinking and learning about print*, London: MIT Press.

Bronfenbrenner, U. (1974) *Is Early Intervention Effective? A report on longitudinal evaluations of pre-school programs: Vol 2*, Washington, DC: Department of Health, Education and Welfare, Office of Child Development.

Chall, J. (1967) *Learning to Read: The Great Debate*, New York: McGraw-Hill.

Chilman, C. S. (1976) 'Programs for Disadvantaged Parents: Some major trends and related research', in H. Leitenberg (ed.) *Handbook of Behavior Modification and Behavior Therapy*, Englewood Cliffs, NJ: Prentice Hall.

Cline, T. (1992) *The Assessment of Special Educational Needs*, London: Routledge.

Dale, N. (1996) *Working with Families of Children with Special Needs: Partnership and practice*, London: Routledge.

Davie, C. E., Butler, N. and Goldstein, H. (1972) *From Birth to Seven: A report of the National Child Development Study*, London: Longman/National Children's Bureau.

Donachy, W. (1979) 'Parent Participation in Pre-School Education', in M. M. Clark and W. M. Cheyne (eds) *Studies in Pre-School Education*, London: Hodder and Stoughton.

Glynn, T., Berryman, M. and Glynn, V. (2000) 'Reading and Writing Gains for Maori Students in Mainstream Schools: Effective partnerships in the Rotorua Home and School Literacy Project', paper presented at the 18th World Congress on Reading, Auckland, New Zealand.

Goodman, K. (1967) 'Reading: A psycholinguistic guessing game'. *Journal of the Reading Specialist*, 6(4), pp. 126–35.

Goodman, K. (1996) *On Reading*, Portsmouth, NJ: Heinemann.

Habermas, J. (1974) *Theory and Practice*, London: Heinemann.

Hannon, P. (1999) 'Rhetoric and Research in Family Literacy', *British Educational Research Journal*, 26(1), pp. 122–137.

Hewison, J. (1988) 'Parental Involvement and Reading Attainment: Implications of research in Dagenham and Haringey', in M. Woodhead and A. McGrath (eds) *Family, School and Society*, London: Hodder and Stoughton.

Hewison, J. and Tizard, J. (1980) 'Parental Involvement and Reading Attainment', *British Journal of Educational Psychology*, 50, pp. 209–215.

Martin, D. (1999) 'Bilingualism and Literacies in Primary School: Implications for professional development', *Educational Review*, 51(1), pp. 67–79.

McNaughton, S., Glynn, T. and Robinson, V. (1981) *Pause, Prompt and Praise: Effective remedial reading tutoring*, Birmingham: Positive Products.

Newson, J. and Newson, E. (1977) *Perspectives on School at Seven Years Old*, London: Allen and Unwin.

Pearson, P. D. (1989) 'Reading the Whole Language Movement', unpublished manuscript cited by Strickland and Cullinan (1994).

Schön, D. (1983) *The Reflective Practitioner*, New York: Basic.

Stanovich, K. E. (1986) 'Matthew Effects in Reading: Some consequences of individual differences in the acquisition of reading', *Reading Research Quarterly*, 21, pp. 360–406.

Stanovich, K. E. (2000) *Progress in Understanding Reading: Scientific foundations and new frontiers*, London: The Guilford Press.

Strickland, D. and Cullinan, B. (1994) 'Afterword', in M. J. Adams, *Beginning to Read: Thinking and learning about print*, London: MIT Press, pp. 425–33.

Topping, K. (1992) 'Short and Long Term Follow-up of Parental Involvement in Reading Projects', *British Educational Research Journal*, 18(4), pp. 369–79.

Topping, K. (1995) *Paired Reading, Spelling and Writing: The handbook for teachers*, London: Cassell.

Topping, K. (1996) 'Tutoring Systems for Family Literacy', in S. Wolfendale and K. Topping (eds) *Family Involvement in Literacy*, London: Cassell.

Waterland, L. (1985) *Read with Me*, Stroud: Thimble Press.

Wragg, E. C., Wragg, C. M., Haynes, G. S. and Chamberlin, R. P. (1998) *Improving Literacy in the Primary School*, London: Routledge.

Source

This chapter was written especially for this volume.

Part 1

Family and community

Chapter 2

Parents and teachers

Peter Mittler

> The closer the parent is to the education of the child, the greater the impact on child development and educational achievement.
>
> (Fullan, 1991: 227)

> It is the parents' unreasonable commitment to their child that makes them good parents.
>
> (Anon., quoted by Gascoigne, 1995: vi)

Reaching all parents

Home–school links: a fresh start?

In this chapter I want to suggest that we need to rethink the whole basis of home–school relationships for all children. Devising new ways of bringing teachers and parents into a better working relationship is worthwhile for its own sake and would benefit all children, parents and teachers. It could also make an impact on children's learning and promote social as well as school inclusion, especially for those parents who are experiencing social exclusion themselves. Children with exceptional needs and their families would automatically benefit without the need for special principles and procedures.

Despite all the fine words about working with parents, there is still a velvet curtain between home and school. Teachers and parents may be friendly, helpful and polite to one another but there is an unavoidable underlying tension that arises from the imbalance of power between them. Many parents are apprehensive and anxious about going to schools because they are still carrying the history of their own experiences of teachers and schooling. Schools have changed out of all recognition in a single generation but many parents have had little direct experience of such changes and obtain much of their information from the media and from casual encounters with neighbours. Parents of children with exceptional needs have a particularly great need for working relationships with teachers based on understanding and trust.

The whirlwind of change that has been sweeping through schools in the 1990s has been focused on raising standards. This has left little time to develop new ways of bringing local parents into partnership with schools. 'Links with the community' are often equated with business and industry rather than with partnership with parents. Rooms earmarked for parents' use in the past have had to be brought into service as classrooms in response to the open enrolment legislation.

Every school has a 'reputation' in its neighbourhood that is based less on league tables and SAT results than on local perceptions about the quality of the relationships between staff and children and how approachable and welcoming the school is to parents and to the local community. These intangibles cannot be measured by inspectors but they lie at the heart of any attempt to develop better collaborative relationships.

Some schools have travelled further along this road than others but many parents are still unreached and at risk of being labelled as 'unreachable'. Some parents do not necessarily want to attend school meetings or may be alienated by some of the language and documentation that they encounter. They should not be written off as 'uninterested in their children's education'.

It seems ironic that, at the very time when social inclusion and poverty are at the top of the government's agenda, many parents feel excluded from decisions being made or proposed in the schools that their children are attending, as well as those being taken at local or central government level. Information about good practice or new ideas is not widely known or disseminated and home–school links are not high on the priority list at any level.

Governments of both persuasions have sent out conflicting messages to parents. On the one hand, they have promoted the rights and interests of parents through, for example, the Parents' Charter (DfEE, 1995), which gives parents the right to information about their child's progress and achievements and about the work of the school as a whole. All parents (except, as we shall see, parents of children with exceptional needs) have the right to express a choice of school, to change the status of a school, to appeal against the decisions of schools and LEAs, to become school governors and to ensure that governors report to parents regularly. By these means, schools and LEAs are made accountable to parents. But governments have also encouraged parents to act as teacher watchdogs and to vote with their feet if schools do not match up to their expectations. This is not a good foundation for a climate of trust and partnership.

At the same time, parents are frequently blamed both by politicians and teachers' organisations for failing to ensure that children do their homework and do not roam the streets. Home–school agreements are being introduced to formalise relationships and ministers threaten children's curfews and fining parents whose children truant. Most recently, the DfEE guidelines on EAZs (DfEE, 1999) have highlighted the importance of support for families but the examples of desirable activities that they list seem to be concerned with compensating parents' weaknesses in language and literacy, rather then helping parents and schools to work together as partners, each with distinctive contributions to make.

Lack of professional preparation

How many teachers can remember any attention being given to working with parents in their initial training? How many have had opportunities to attend training days or courses on the needs of parents and families and how they might work together? How many have had the opportunity to listen to parents speaking about their needs and perceptions?

Most teachers insist that there was no reference to parents and families in their initial training and that there have been few opportunities to attend courses or training days since then. It is depressing, therefore, to find that the most recent TTA national standards for qualified teacher status also have almost nothing to say on parents (TTA, 1998). Only in the additional standards for teachers working in nursery and reception classes do we find a reference to 'having a knowledge of effective ways of working with parents and other carers' and a further standard on 'managing the work of parents and other adults in the classroom'. Parents are not mentioned in the main standards for primary or secondary teachers and receive only a passing reference in standards for head teachers. They fare a little better in the SENCO and national SEN specialist standards.

It is not just a matter of training in the conventional sense, but of teachers having opportunities to heighten their self-awareness and to think about their attitudes to families, how they perceive them and relate to them and to consider whether there may be alternative approaches for them as individuals and for the schools and services in which they work. The use of role play and simulation, with or without videorecording, has been used in race awareness sessions and can provide insight into one's own styles of interaction with parents, but some may find such approaches too intrusive or too disturbing.

Home–school policies

Every school needs its own home–school policy to go beyond fine words and include concrete proposals for achieving better working relationships with its parents and with the local community. Despite much rhetoric about the importance of working with parents, there is no legal requirement for schools or LEAs to have a detailed written policy on working with parents and therefore no guidelines about the headings under which such a policy might be developed. However, the OFSTED frameworks for inspection say that inspectors must evaluate and report on:

the effectiveness of the school's partnership with parents, highlighting strengths and weaknesses, in terms of:

- the information provided about the school and about pupils' work and progress through annual and other reports and parents' meetings;
- parents' involvement with the school and with their children's work at home;

- the contribution which the school's link with the community makes to pupils' attainment and personal development.

(OFSTED, 1995: 96)

There is a statutory requirement to obtain the views of parents on a school being inspected by means of a meeting between the registered inspector and parents and also through a questionnaire sent to all parents. Parents' views are sought under eight headings: pupils' attainment and progress; attitudes and values that the school promotes; information that the school provides to parents, including reports; help and guidance available to pupils; homework; behaviour and attendance; the part played by parents in the life of the school; and the school's response to their suggestions and complaints.

The evaluation schedules for the new inspection framework (OFSTED, 2000) include a section on 'How well does the school work in partnership with parents?' in which inspectors must report on:

- parents' views of the school;
- the effectiveness of the school's links with parents; and
- the impact of the parents' involvement with the work of the school.

A study of OFSTED reports by Blamires *et al.* (1997) indicates that schools that receive praise from OFSTED for their partnership with parents are characterised by:

- parents receiving a rapid response to requests;
- regular newsletters with a diary of forthcoming events;
- a member of staff or a working party being given responsibility for home–school liaison;
- information on children's progress being clearly presented to parents with opportunities for follow-up discussion;
- good use of home–school contact methods such as diaries and logs; and
- development of parental involvement in teaching their child through lending libraries for books/games or toys.

Schools also have a number of statutory requirements to report pupils' achievements to parents. The school SEN policy statements required by the Code of Practice must also include information about 'arrangements for partnership with parents' (DfE, 1994: 8–9).

Over and above the legal requirements, it is difficult to find factual information on how mission statements and policies that look good on paper translate
into practice. For example, what specific examples follow the 'blue sky' statements: 'all parents are welcome in this school at any time; we value parents
as partners in their children's learning and development'? How do schools
reach 'hard to reach' families who do not attend meetings or answer notes?
How often do teachers and parents meet to share information and experiences? Is it possible for teachers to offer to visit parents in their own homes?
How do parents and children react to such visits and do they have useful
outcomes?

About ten years ago, the NFER carried out a national study of parental
involvement in schools (Jowett and Baginsky, 1991). Information was collected from 70–80 per cent of all LEAs in England and Wales, and from interviews
with many parents and teachers. Although some excellent initiatives were
found in some schools and LEAs, they were still few and far between across
the whole country. It was clear that parents from all backgrounds were keen
to be more involved by schools but that teachers tended to underestimate
parental interest, particularly from parents in economically deprived areas.

Schools that want to review their home–school policies will find a great
deal of valuable information and support in a series of publications arising
from a major national project on home–school links, directed by John Bastiani.
This project, which began at Nottingham University and was later brought
under the auspices of the Royal Society of Arts, has resulted in a large number
of practical publications and newsletters and has been an invaluable resource
to schools that have wanted to use it. For example, the project has produced
an audit questionnaire to enable parents and schools to identify strengths
and needs and to improve the quality of communication between parents and
teachers (Bastiani and Beresford, 1995). A recent publication reviews the
contribution of parents in the context of school effectiveness (Wolfendale and
Bastiani, 2000); others include a guide to home–school agreement (Bastiani
and Wyse, 1999) and reports of links with parents in multicultural settings
(Bastiani, 1997). An interesting comparative study of home–school links in
nine countries, including England and Wales, has been published by the
OECD (1997).

The publication *Early Learning Goals* (QCA and DfEE, 1999) includes some
useful indicators for 'parents as partners', most of which seem relevant to the
whole age range.

> Parents are children's first and most enduring educators. When parents
> and practitioners work together in early years settings, the results have a
> positive impact on the child's development and learning. Therefore, each
> setting should seek to develop an effective partnership with parents.
>
>   A successful partnership needs a two way flow of information, know-
> ledge and expertise. There are many ways of achieving partnership with
> parents but the following are common features of effective practice:

- practitioners show respect and understanding for the role of the parent in their child's education;
- the past and future part played by parents in the education of their children is recognised and explicitly encouraged;
- arrangements for settling in are flexible enough to give time for children to become secure and for practitioners and parents to discuss each child's circumstances, interests, competencies and needs;
- all parents are made to feel welcome, valued and necessary, through a range of different opportunities for collaboration between children, parents and practitioners;
- the knowledge and expertise of parents and other family adults are used to support the learning opportunities provided by the setting;
- practitioners use a variety of ways to keep parents fully informed about the curriculum, such as brochures, displays and videos which are available in the home languages of the parents and through informal discussion;
- parents and practitioners talk about and record information about the child's progress and achievements, for example through meetings or making a book about the child;
- relevant learning activities and play activities, such as sharing and reading books, are continued at home. Similarly, experiences at home are used to develop learning in the setting, for example, visits and celebrations.

(QCA and DfEE, 1999)

Reaching the unreached

It is sometimes said that attempts to bring parents and teachers together using principles and practices such as those quoted above will not work for the poorest families, those who have literacy difficulties themselves or those whose first language is not English. Interviews with teachers taking part in the NFER study reflected pessimism and despair about the impossibility of reaching parents who never respond to notes or letters inviting them to attend parents' meetings. 'Good idea but it wouldn't work here' was a frequent response.

This pessimism is not borne out by the available research. The NFER survey (Jowett and Baginsky, 1991) and Topping's review (1986) showed that parents living in areas of poverty and disadvantage were just as interested in helping their children to learn as other families. A number of community education projects have enlisted the support of parents living in areas of poverty and disadvantage, including many from ethnic minorities (Widlake, 1985). Parents cooperate readily and reliably once they are convinced that a school or a particular project is genuinely committed to help their children to learn and, through education, to escape from poverty into a better life.

Similar findings were reported from other countries, including the US Head Start programmes (Sylva, 1999). In many of these projects, parents who were living in very poor conditions went daily to nursery centres to work as volunteers with groups of children. They also worked in one-to-one play sessions with their own child, in partnership with a practitioner, making up games and activities that seemed likely to help the child learn a skill or enjoy an activity. The same parents were glad to receive teachers into their own homes once a week.

Parents reading with children

We have known for many years that children learn to read better and with greater enjoyment if their parents listen to them read even for only a few minutes a day and are greatly helped by parents reading to them. An early book edited by Topping and Wolfendale (1985) brought together many successful examples of collaboration. Later publications have added further evidence (Hannon, 1995; Wolfendale and Topping, 1996). It is difficult to know what impact these studies have had nationally. Although many schools have successfully involved parents in shared reading, the positive lessons that have come from the research have not been widely adopted across the country.

Knowing what we know about the importance of parents listening to and reading with their children does not justify putting pressure on parents to sign a home–school agreement in which they commit themselves to spending set periods on such activities. Where there is already confidence and trust between home and school and between individual teachers and families, such schemes will already be in place, although lack of time on both sides may mean that opportunities for sharing of ideas are just not available. Where such trust is lacking or where parents and teachers do not value one another, contractual agreements are worthless.

Gregory (2000) argues that many of our assumptions about parental involvement in reading do not reflect or respect the cultural diversity of our society. Parents are asked to read with their children using strategies suggested by the school on the assumption that the same reading practices are suitable in all linguistic and cultural contexts when this may not be the case. For example, there is no tradition of one-to-one bedtime stories in some cultures and reading is a formal group activity that may take up a great deal of time and is taken very seriously.

Teachers visiting families

Teachers do not generally visit families at home for what appear at first to be very sound reasons. They are not professionally trained or psychologically prepared to do so and many would feel uncomfortable in straying from their own territory. Similarly, parents might well be surprised and suspicious if teachers tried to arrange such visits and the child may not be too happy either. Such a practice clearly has huge resource implications and would require earmarked funding. And yet teachers working in community schools have been visiting families for decades and so have their colleagues working in special schools.

Following the publication of the Plowden report, a number of LEAs funded schools to appoint home–school liaison teachers. These teachers were generally already on the staff of the school but were allocated up to 50 per cent of their time to make contact with parents in whatever ways were agreed to be convenient. Although these initiatives did not last long, the NFER survey did provide evidence of a small number of LEAs who continued to fund home–school liaison teachers up to the end of the 1980s. Examples were given of two large urban authorities who funded 60 and 127 teachers each.

Similar appointments could be revived today within some of the new programmes launched by the government, particularly EAZs and Excellence in Cities. Evidence available so far does not suggest that visits to families are a high priority among those bidding for funds under these initiatives.

Partnership or collaboration?

Many writers now agree that we need to make a distinction between partnership and collaboration. True partnership is a process rather than a destination. Like inclusion, it is a journey undertaken as an expression of certain values and principles. True partnership, as in any close relationship, implies mutual respect based on a willingness to learn from one another, a sense of common purpose, a sharing of information and decision making and, some would add, a sharing of feelings (Mittler, 1995).

These principles and values are relevant to work with all parents but they represent only the fundamental building blocks of a working relationship with families who are all different and who have unique needs. Getting to know the individuality of families is one of the most difficult tasks for any teacher because there are so few opportunities for them to get to know parents as people. This is why it is so important to meet parents on neutral territory.

Fundamental changes have taken place in the structure of families and in family life. Many children are experiencing the separation and divorce of their parents, are living in lone parent households or with one or more step-parents. They may suddenly find themselves with several new half brothers and sisters and rather more than four grandparents. The concept of the extended family has become much more complex, especially when we include members of a household who are not related. This means that many people will be involved in the life of a child with special needs, as with all children, and not just the parents.

Teachers in some schools have let it be known that, in addition to the 'normal' parent evenings, they were willing to meet parents living nearby in certain local pubs, with never more than one or two teachers in the same pub. Some parents who had never attended parents' meetings or any school functions were happy to talk informally on this basis, with not a register in sight.

Similarly, school playgrounds and football pitches have been used for car boot and 'bring and buy' or 'good as new' sales just to enable parents to meet teachers socially without necessarily settling down for an earnest conversation about their child.

Not all parents will welcome such creative and original ways of reaching them and will take evasive action accordingly. Even when there is an atmosphere of mutual trust and confidence, the relationship is not between equals because power and authority are vested not just in the teachers as individuals but in the school as a publicly funded institution. However hard teachers try to break down barriers, some parents will feel that the power relationship is loaded against them.

Teachers in their turn can feel threatened by parents who imply that the child's difficulties are at least in part related to the learning opportunities and the quality of teaching provided by the school, such as access to the curriculum, the school's discipline policy or the way it is enforced. These issues may remain below the surface partly because they are so sensitive but mainly because there is not enough time and psychological space for them to be discussed.

Implications for services

Professionals therefore need to learn to look beyond the child to the family setting in which the child is living. If families agree, they should visit the child at home and learn to see the child in the normal family environment. They may also need to adapt their own working practices by getting to know fathers, sisters and brothers and other members of the household such as grandparents. It is only on this basis that they can begin to explore the various possible options for the nature and extent of collaboration and learn to negotiate with families what kinds of demands and routines are and are not realistic in the context of the individual family.

Parents' rights, the Education Act 1981 and its successors

The Warnock report had made a strong case for the involvement of parents in decision making: 'The successful education of children with special educational needs is dependent on the full involvement of their parents; indeed, unless the parents are seen as equal partners in the educational process, the purpose of our report will be frustrated' (DES, 1978: para 9.1). This quote is typical of much of the rhetoric about the importance of partnership with parents. But, despite major improvements in many schools and services, the reality for parents is often very different from the official rhetoric.

Although many would argue that we are still in the consumer phase, some parents still feel that they are not given all the information to which they are entitled. A series of studies during the 1980s showed that half the LEAs omitted to include important information about parents' rights and entitlements under the Education Act 1981 (CSIE, 1986; Armstrong, 1995). Parents do not always feel welcome in schools and complain that they are sometimes ignored or patronised by teachers and other professionals. The notices saying 'No parents beyond this point' may have gone, but the attitudes remain.

The 1981 Act was a major landmark and has laid the foundations for all later legislation, particularly the Education Acts 1993 and 1996 and the Code of Practice. However, consultation is under way on a new Special Needs Bill, which will further strengthen parents' rights and bring education into the Disability Discrimination Act 1995.

The Education Act 1981 and the explanatory circulars and regulations that followed represented a radical departure from previous practice by putting a duty on LEAs to consult and work with parents.

Briefly, the Act gave parents the right to:

- request the LEA to conduct a formal assessment of their child;
- be involved in the process of assessment and in annual reviews;
- appeal against an LEA decision; and
- have their views taken into account in decisions concerning place-ment in special or ordinary schools.

The Act also gave parents the right to appeal to a local appeals committee and, under certain circumstances, to the Secretary of State for Education. The Education Act 1993 replaced this with an SEN Tribunal to deal with all appeals.

The Education Act 1981 stipulated that children with special educa-tional needs should be educated in mainstream schools, where parents request this, provided that:

- the child can receive appropriate provision;
- it is compatible with the efficient education of other children; and
- it is compatible with the efficient use of resources.

Named persons and named officers

The Warnock Committee had emphasised the importance of parents being given access to a 'named person' who would support them in stating their needs to decision makers and generally act as a single point of contact.

However, they also suggested that the named person might be a health visitor for under-fives, a head teacher for children of school age and a careers officer for school leavers. While these individuals might be very helpful and supportive, they are all part of the decision-making process and therefore anything but independent. An obvious example would be the head teacher of a special school when a parent is fighting for a mainstream placement.

The notion of the named person was not accepted by the government in the sense proposed by Warnock and was changed in the progress of the 1981 legislation through parliament into the proposal for a named officer of the LEA who would be responsible for ensuring that parents whose child had a statement were given information from that point on, for example about annual reviews. It has, however, worked well in Scotland (Russell, 1997).

The Code of Practice recommended a return to the proposal for a named person for children who already had or were about to receive a statement but stressed that it would be helpful for that person to be independent of the LEA and someone who would be trusted by the parent. The role of the named person was to give advice and information to parents about their child's special needs.

Parent partnership schemes

Since 1993, LEAs have been able to bid for 60 per cent of the cost of parent partnership schemes within the DfEE GEST, now replaced by an enlarged Standards Fund. Although most LEAs applied for and received funding, the new SEN Bill will place a statutory obligation on all LEAs in England to provide a parent partnership service. Guidelines for the new schemes are being drawn up in the light of the national evaluation, which has been carried out by the National Children's Bureau (Furze and Conrad, 1997; Russell, 1997; Wolfendale and Cook, 1997). In the light of some major problems that have emerged from these evaluations, the DfEE has commissioned a new study with the aim of highlighting good practice (Vernon, 1999).

One of the main functions of the new parent partnership service will be to recruit suitable local volunteers as 'independent parental supporters', the new name chosen in place of 'named person'. These can be members of a volun-tary organisation or just friends who are prepared to support parents engaged in the process of securing appropriate provision for their children at any stage of the Code of Practice, not just those who have received a statement. So far, most named persons have been recruited from parents and carers, voluntary workers, preschool playgroup workers, school governors, retired teachers and LEA personnel. Nearly all are women.

According to Simmons (1997) very few of the pilot schemes were managed by the voluntary sector, many of whom were apprehensive about giving wrong advice to parents involved in legal disputes or preparing for a tribunal hearing without training and support. Although LEAs generally ran the schemes, a few 'kept their distance' and limited their role to 'pay and rations'. Even so, the parent partnership officer (now to be known as a coordinator) is an LEA appointment.

Reviewing the first years of the Code of Practice and the partnership with parents scheme, Russell (1997) summarises its lessons as follows:

- The Code of Practice is very time-consuming for everyone working with parents.
- Many parents find partnership onerous.
- The role of the named person requires training, support and a clear skill base that empowers but does not dominate.
- The named person is accessible and enabling and sees the eventual autonomy of the parent (i.e. facilitating help) as a key objective.
- Partnership often starts too late.
- The requirement for a school SEN policy has been a positive vehicle for change; the debate has moved from statutory assessment to the school-based stages of assessment.
- Partnership with the voluntary sector has not been easy.

An early OFSTED report on the operation of the Code of Practice and the SEN Tribunal includes some disquieting findings about parental involvement (OFSTED, 1997). For example, few schools were aware of the parent partnership scheme and were therefore not in a position to inform parents about how they worked. Many parents whose children had a statement did not appear to have a named person; this is problematic, since only a third of parents of disabled children belong to a voluntary organisation who could alert them to their rights.

The evaluation carried out by Wolfendale and Cook (1997) produced some disquieting findings that will need to be addressed now that the scheme is being extended nationally and made available to parents whose children are at any stage of the Code of Practice.

- The majority view of parent partnership officers (PPOs), LEAs, professionals and parents is that partnership goals in the spirit of the Code of Practice have not been achieved.
- PPOs view their role as primarily providers of information and advisory services but only at around Stage 4 of the Code of Practice, although parents are approaching PPOs at Stage 3. PPOs seem to follow the LEA brief of reducing appeals to tribunal.

- Many schools do not make parents aware of the parent partnership service.
- SENCOs are beginning to take the initiative in making contact with PPOs and asking for in-service training.

SEN Tribunal

The SEN Tribunal was created by the Education Act 1993 to replace both the LEA appeal committees and the possibility of appeal to the Secretary of State for Education. In setting up the SEN Tribunal, the then government hoped that the Code of Practice would improve relationships between parents and LEAs and that the tribunal would be a last resort. This has not proved to be the case. The tribunal has not only been overwhelmed with appeals but its work has revealed major structural weaknesses in the system as a whole, with the result that it is now under review as part of the government's Programme of Action. The DfEE is consulting on new draft regulations and has also commissioned some examples of good practice in conciliation arrangements.

The main changes proposed are:

- changing the regulations to strengthen the rights of children;
- a change in requirements for lay panels;
- changing the time scales for LEAs to implement tribunal orders; and
- improved pre-tribunal conciliation procedures at LEA level.

The SEN Tribunal has published annual reports detailing the number, nature and outcomes of the appeals. The most recent records an increase of registrations from 1,161 in 1994–95 to 2,412 in 1988–99 and the rate is increasing by about 10 per cent year (SEN Tribunal, 1999). The work of the tribunal has also been scrutinised by the House of Commons Select Committee on Education (1996) and reviewed by OFSTED (1997), and a critical review has been published by Simmons (1997) based on a survey carried out by the Independent Panel Supporting Special Education Advice (IPSEA).

These and other reports highlight the main problems that have arisen, as follows.

- A disproportionate number of parents who have used the SEN Tribunal have been well educated, articulate people, particularly parents of children with dyslexia, autism and speech and language difficulties. This has created a two-tier system at LEA level, as was made clear to the House of Commons Select Committee on Education (1996) by LEAs themselves. Relatively few parents from poor backgrounds or from ethnic minorities have used the tribunal. This is not the fault of the tribunal but reflects unequal opportunities for parents in the system as a whole.

- LEA employees, particularly teachers and educational psychologists, have been reluctant to appear as witnesses if their professional opinion differs from that of their employers. There have been reports of pressure on LEA staff not to appear, unless a formal summons was issued. Parents have hesitated to call professionals because they did not want to put them in a difficult position. This has weakened their case.

- Despite all efforts, hearings have become more formal and therefore more confusing and intimidating to parents. Although LEAs are able to call on legal advice, only parents with a very low income can receive legal aid in preparing their case but not in presenting it. The presence of a solicitor at a tribunal hearing costs at least £1,000. The original intention that tribunal hearings should be parent-friendly does not seem to have been fulfilled. Indeed, Simmons (1997) concludes that the present impasse makes for confrontation rather than partnership.

- There is a major problem for parents in receiving support in preparing their case and in being represented at the hearing because there are simply not enough volunteers who are willing and able to help. The major voluntary organisations are reluctant to become too involved and are understandably fearful about the vulnerability of their volunteers on legal grounds. Finding volunteers and independent parental supporters is the responsibility of the parent partnership coordinators, who, in the last analysis, are also employees of the LEA, whatever safeguards are put in place to secure their independence.

- Although LEAs are legally bound to implement tribunal decisions, there is evidence that some are taking too long to do so when the decision has gone against them.

Despite these problems, the work of the SEN Tribunal has provided an essential safeguard for those parents who cannot resolve their differences with the LEA and has enabled many parents to ensure that their child's education is in accordance with their wishes and priorities. Some LEAs are proud of their record in never having to defend their actions at a tribunal, while others appear several times in the same year. These range from none in Middlesbrough and one in Barnsley to 81 in Manchester and 89 in Kent.

What is particularly disquieting is the evidence that reflects a conflict of interest between the LEA and its employees before there is any question of an appeal to the tribunal. Some years ago an educational psychologist was dismissed by his LEA for giving advice to parents that was not acceptable to the LEA, although the decision was subsequently overruled by an employment tribunal. LEAs take the view that it is the job of their employees, such as educational psychologists and SENCOs, to give advice on the needs of the child and not on where those needs should be met; this, they argue, is a matter for the LEA, using its knowledge of available resources and provision in the area.

Conclusions

Evaluations of the operation of the parent partnership service and the SEN Tribunal have highlighted deep-seated and endemic tensions between parents and professionals. The tribunal is merely the tip of the iceberg for parents who have the tenacity and the support to use its services. Despite the rhetoric that surrounds parent–professional partnership, we have very little information on day-to-day practice on the ground or about how parents feel about decisions made on their children's education, far less their progress within the system or the quality of their working relationships with teachers. As far as children with exceptional needs are concerned, we have little information at national level about how satisfied parents are with their children being put on a register in the first place, whether they feel they are getting enough information from the school about the progress their child is making or what they make of IEPs.

The debates about parent–professional relationships within the field of exceptional needs education are merely one facet of the universal question about home–school relationships for all children and all parents. The gulf between home and school is not the fault of either and cannot easily be bridged. Over many decades, the education system as a whole has somehow distanced itself from the communities it serves. Although many individual schools have not only retained but developed and enriched their links with their local community, as well as with their own parents, many others have just been too overwhelmed with meeting government targets and responding to constant exhortation to change.

A government committed to inclusion has to tackle the exclusion of so many parents from participation in discussion and decision making about the education of their children. A useful start has been made: for example, the Sure Start projects seem to have been based on genuine community involvement within a very small area in which attempts were made to visit all families with children in the appropriate age range of the scheme. Are there ways in which parents and communities could be approached to give their views on how they would like to be involved in discussion and decision making about the work of schools? Schools in their turn could try to find new ways of asking parents for their views about how home–school links could be strengthened. Closer links between parents and teachers cannot be prescribed from on high; they have to be founded on the wishes and priorities of those who are at the grass roots.

The last word goes to a group of parents of children with special needs and disabilities (quoted by Russell, 1997: 79):

- Please accept and value our children (and ourselves as families) as we are.
- Please celebrate difference.
- Please try and accept our children as children first. Don't attach labels to them unless you mean to *do* something.
- Please recognise your power over our lives. We live with the consequences of your opinions and decisions.
- Please understand the stress many families are under. The cancelled appointment, the waiting list no one gets to the top of, all the discussions about resources – it's *our* lives you're talking about.
- Don't put fashionable fads and treatments on to us unless you are going to be around to see them through. And don't forget families have many members, many responsibilities. Sometimes, we can't please everyone.
- Do recognise that sometimes we are right! Please believe us and listen to what we know we and our child need.
- Sometimes we are sad, tired and depressed. Please value us as caring and committed families and try to go on working with us.

References

Armstrong, D. (1995) *Power and Partnership in Education: Parents, Children and Special Educational Needs*. London: Routledge.

Bastiani, J. (ed.) (1997) *Home–School Work in Multi-cultural Settings*. London: David Fulton Publishers.

Bastiani, J. and Beresford, E. (1995) *Home–School Policies: A Practical Guide*. London: JET Publications.

Bastiani, J. and Wyse, B. (1999) *Introducing Your Home–School Agreement*. London: Royal Society of Arts.

Blamires, M. *et al.* (1997) *Parent–Teacher Partnership: Practical Approaches to Meet Special Educational Needs*. London: David Fulton Publishers.

Centre for Studies in Integrated Education (1986) *Caught in the Act?* Bristol: CSIE.

Department for Education (1994) *Code of Practice on the Identification and Assessment of Special Educational Needs*. London: DfE.

Department for Education (1995) *Our Children's Education: The Updated Parents' Charter*. London: HMSO.

Department for Education and Employment (1999) *Social Inclusion: Pupil Support*. Circular 10/99. London: DfEE.

Department of Education and Science (1978) *Special Educational Needs: Report of the Enquiry into the Education of Handicapped Children and Young People*. London: HMSO.

Fullan, M. (1991) *The Meaning of Educational Change*, 2nd edn. London: Cassell.

Furze, T. and Conrad, A. (1997) 'A review of parent partnership schemes', in Wolfendale, S. (ed.) *Working with Parents of SEN Children after the Code of Practice*, 82–97. London: David Fulton Publishers.

Gascoigne, E. (1995) *Working with Parents as Partners in SEN*. London: David Fulton Publishers.

Gregory, E. (2000) 'Recognising differences: reinterpreting family involvement in literacy', in Cox, T. (ed.) *Combating Educational Disadvantage: Meeting the Needs of Vulnerable Children*, 103–20. London: Falmer Press.

Hannon, P. (1995) *Literacy, Home and School: Research and Practice in Teaching Literacy Skills with Parents*. London: Falmer Press.

House of Commons Select Committee on Education (1996) *Special Educational Needs: The Working of the Code of Practice and the Tribunal*. London: HMSO.

Jowett, S. and Baginsky, M. (1991) *Building Bridges: Parental Involvement in Schools*. Slough: NFER-Nelson.

Mittler, P. (1995) 'Rethinking partnerships between parents and professionals', *Children and Society* 9(3), 22–40.

Office for Standards in Education (1995) *Guidance on the Inspection of Nursery and Primary Schools*. London: HMSO.

Office for Standards in Education (1997) *The SEN Code of Practice Two Years On*. London: OFSTED.

Office for Standards in Education (2000) *Inspecting Schools: The Framework*. London: OFSTED.

Organisation for Economic Cooperation and Development (1997) *Parents as Partners in Schooling*. Paris: OECD.

Qualifications and Curriculum Authority and DfEE (1999) *Early Learning Goals*. London: QCA.

Russell, P. (1997) 'Parents as partners: some early impressions of the impact of the Code of Practice', in Wolfendale, S. (ed.) *Working with Parents of SEN Children after the Code of Practice*. London: David Fulton Publishers.

Simmons, K. (1997) 'Supporting parents at the special educational needs tribunal', in Wolfendale, S. (ed.) *Working with Parents of SEN Children after the Code of Practice*, 114–26. London: David Fulton Publishers.

Special Educational Needs Tribunal (1999) *Annual Report 1988–1999*. London: DfEE.

Sylva, K. (1999) 'The role of research in explaining the past and shaping the future', in Abbott, L. and Moylett, H. (eds) *Early Education Transformed*, 164–79. London: Falmer Press.

Teacher Training Agency (1998) *National Standards for Qualified Teacher Status*. London: TTA.

Topping, K. (1986) *Parents as Educators: Training Parents to Teach their Children*. London: Croom Helm and Cambridge, MA: Brookline Books.

Topping, K. and Wolfendale, S. (eds) (1985) *Parental Involvement in Children's Reading*. London: Croom Helm.

Vernon, J. (1999) *Parent Partnership and Special Educational Needs: Perspectives on Good Practice*, Research Report 162. London: DfEE.

Widlake, P. (1985) *Reducing Educational Disadvantage*. London: Routledge and Kegan Paul.

Wolfendale, S. and Bastiani, J. (eds) (2000) *The Contribution of Parents to School Effectiveness*. London: David Fulton Publishers.

Wolfendale, S. and Cook, G. (1997) *Evaluation of Special Educational Needs Parent Partnership Schemes*. Research Report 34. London: DfEE.

Wolfendale, S. and Topping, K. (eds) (1996) *Family Involvement in Literacy*. London: Cassell.

Source

This is an edited version of a chapter previously published in *Working Towards Inclusive Education: Social Contexts*. 2000. Reproduced by permission of David Fulton Publishers.

Chapter 3

Collaboration between teachers and parents in assisting children's reading

J. Tizard, W. N. Schofield and Jenny Hewison

A collaboration between teachers and parents was organised so that every child in two randomly chosen top infant classes at two schools (one class at each school), randomly allocated from six multiracial inner-city schools, was regularly heard reading at home from books sent by the class teacher. The intervention was continued for two years, i.e., until the end of the first year in the junior school. Comparison was made with the parallel classes at the same schools, and with randomly chosen classes at two schools, again randomly allocated, where children were given extra reading tuition in school. This report presents cross-sectional analyses which show a highly significant improvement by children who received extra practice at home in comparison with control groups, but no comparable improvement by children who received extra help at school. The gains were made consistently by children of all ability levels.

Introduction

This chapter reports the main findings of an experiment designed to assess the effects of parental involvement in the teaching of reading. The study was based on an earlier survey finding that, in working-class families, children whose parents said they heard them read at home had markedly higher reading attainments at age 7 and 8 than children who did not receive this kind of help from their parents (Hewison and Tizard, 1980). This finding could not be accounted for in terms of differences in IQ, maternal language behaviour, or any of the aspects of upbringing style which were investigated. The study left a number of questions unanswered. Parents who listened to their children read were a self-selected group, and possibly the improvement was mainly due to the interest which they took in their children's schooling, of which help at home was only one powerful indicator, rather than to the help itself. Attitudinal data collected at the time went against this hypothesis; but questioning by parental interview may not be a very effective method of finding out about differences in parental 'style' of upbringing. Further, it might have been the case that only the best readers at school were allowed, or wanted, to take their reading books home.

More importantly, survey findings obtained from self-selected groups throw no light on the question of how far parental attitudes and practice are subject to change: can one, in other words, persuade all, or nearly all, parents to help their children at home – in this case, by hearing them read? Is it feasible for class teachers to try to ensure that *all* children will take their books home? Will they return books if they do? How many books will get lost or destroyed? How many parents will argue that it is the school's job not theirs to teach the three Rs? How many parents will 'help' in such a punitive or unsatisfactory way that children will be put off, rather than turned on, by reading practice at home? Can non-English speaking or illiterate parents be involved? And finally, will active parental help of the kind suggested actually lead to a measurable improvement in children's reading performance?

Questions such as these can only be answered by experiment, and we were fortunate in being able to carry out such an experiment, in partnership with the primary advisers and heads and class teachers in six infant and junior schools in the London borough of Haringey.

The overall purpose of the project was to find out if there was a causal relationship between active parental help and reading performance. To this end the main task of the project team was to establish an arrangement whereby all children in certain experimental classes were heard to read at home. The effectiveness of this treatment was to be measured against control children both within the schools where the intervention was to take place and in different schools, and also against a separate control in which children were given extra reading tuition by a qualified teacher in school, rather than by parents at home. The purpose of this control procedure was to gain some understanding of process factors: parental help, it was argued, might aid reading performance simply because it represented extra time spent on the learning task; alternatively, the improvement might follow primarily from the increased motivation of children whose parents became involved in their learning. By providing some children with extra practice given in school, it was planned to obtain some idea of the relative importance of these two factors as mediators of any established causal relationship between parental help and reading performance. As the schools sampled were multiracial, problems of organising extra reading practice in homes where English was not spoken and in homes where neither parent could read English were also to be examined.

Method

The main sampling frame was an opportunity sample and included all children in the middle infant, top infant, first-year junior and second-year junior classes at six schools in a disadvantaged working-class area of the London borough of Haringey present when tests were given at the end of 1975/76, 1976/77, 1977/78 and 1978/79 school years. For 1975/76 this totalled 1,867 children, and each subsequent year 400 to 500 children joined the sample on becoming middle infants and a similar number moved out on leaving the second year of the junior school. The schools were of similar multiracial character and occupations of fathers almost without exception were in the Registrar General's manual working-class categories.

Procedure

The field work for the interventions took place over a two-year period (1976–78) with a cohort of children studied first in the final year of their infant schooling (i.e., when the children were 6 to 7 years old), then in the first year of their junior schooling (7 to 8 years old). At the end of the 1975/76 school year baseline reading tests were given to all children in the four year-bands at the six project schools. The schools were assigned at random to three groups: parent involvement, extra teacher help and control. They were visited early in the 1976/77 school year and told into which category they had been drawn, and support was confirmed. One top infant class at each of the two parent involvement schools (schools 1 and 2) was chosen at random to receive the research intervention, and the remaining classes at each school formed the within-school control group for that school. Similarly intervention and control groups were randomly chosen at the two schools (schools 3 and 4) where the extra teacher help was to be given at school. It had been established previously from the summer reading data that the year group concerned had not been streamed, and that there were no significant differences in reading performance between those classes which would be receiving the interventions and those which would not. There were no interventions at schools 5 and 6 other than annual testing of reading attainment.

An experienced and qualified teacher was appointed (from more than 30 applicants) to implement the intervention at schools 3 and 4. She worked four half days each week at each school for the two years of the intervention. Her work was planned, in consultation with the class teacher, and involved not only hearing the children read but all aspects of the teaching of reading, since it was felt by the LEA advisers and the staff concerned that a teacher could not merely hear the children read as was intended for the parents. A second difference from the parent intervention was that the children were seen in small groups rather than individually, although of course reading was heard individually within those groups, each child reading to the teacher on average once or twice a week. These were professional decisions made by the staff concerned who felt that they were an advantage for the children receiving the extra practice in a school context.

The intervention began at schools 1 and 2 with a visit by a member of the project team to the home collaboration class assigned to his or her care: this division of responsibility was maintained for the two years of the intervention, and although the two researchers were in frequent contact with each other they advised and monitored exclusively in one school and with one home collaboration class. Thus an element of replication was built into the design.

Since both head teachers and class teachers actively, and with both good-will and effect, contributed to the implementation of the experimental intervention the organisation differed slightly between the two schools. At both schools an introductory letter from the Chief Education Officer was sent to each home. At school 2 the researcher concerned followed this letter by meeting the parents individually at a school open evening, and then by making a personal visit to each child's home to discuss the project in more detail. At school 1 the first step was fully school based: parents were invited to individual meetings with the class teacher and the researcher at individual interviews to discuss the project. There was a very high initial attendance, possibly because by that time the researcher was well known to the children. The few parents who did not attend were offered further opportunities, always by the head teacher, and were seen later. At both schools several parents were difficult to contact, but all were seen before half-term, either at school or at home.

Parents, almost without exception, said that they welcomed the project and agreed to hear their child read at home as requested and to complete a record card showing what had been read. All parents also agreed to allow the researcher to visit them at home two or three times each term to hear the child reading to them; the first of these visits was made to each home immediately after half-term and the intended monitoring was maintained for the two years of the intervention. During the home visits it was the practice of the researchers to observe the children reading to their parents. At school 1 for the first, and in some cases for the second visit, this was followed by the parent observing as the child read to the researcher, and specific advice was given to all parents on 'good practice'. Further, at school 1, during the final two terms of the project, children were also observed taking part with their parents in other literacy related activities sent from school, and parents were given advice by the researcher on how to deal with these. Parents were not given any special training in how to hear their children read beyond this specific advice from either class teacher or researcher. At both schools advice and demonstrations were given to the very small minority of parents – no more than one or two in each group – who adopted strategies which the researcher judged to be potentially counter-productive. It was noted that parents responded to these demonstrations, and were in general eager for advice and suggestions. This level of interest and co-operation was maintained, with only two or three exceptions, over the full two years of the project. Occasional difficulties arose as a result of housing or family problems, but again these affected only a small number of families, and in no case was contact completely lost.

Care was taken to ensure that visits were at times suitable for reading by the child and convenient to the family concerned. Mostly visits took place in the evening. They were always arranged in advance. For example, at one school times and days suitable for each family were known and the day before one such suitable occasion the researcher would send a note from school to say that a visit was intended. Parents were asked to send a message to school if the proposed visit was not convenient. Letters were individually written and sealed in an envelope, but the date and time were also written on the outside of the envelope where they could be seen by the child who took the letter home. The children seemed highly motivated by their involvement in the letter delivery. Non-English reading parents were also met at the school gate and told what was in the letter, or the letter was read carefully with an older sibling, or with the project child, before sealing. It was notable that the children did not lose the letters or forget to give them to their parents.

The school side of the home reading was organised at each school by the head teacher, the class teacher and the researcher. Teachers kept their usual records and in addition special records for the project including a reading card for parents to complete at home. The nature and frequency of reading material sent home varied between the two schools and between the infant and junior years of the intervention, in accordance with the wishes and customary practice of the teacher involved, but the common objective of reading practice at home was maintained. Mostly books were sent home on a minimum of three or four nights per week at school 1 and two or three nights per week at school 2. For the infant year at school 1 the book taken home was always the child's current class reader, but in the junior year at this school the reader was sent home once a week and a supplementary book from the reading scheme, or an appropriately selected library book, on the other nights. Also at school 1 in the final two terms of the project other literacy related work was sent home, including written work based on the material read, and parents were given advice on their handling of this. At school 2, a number of commercially produced schemes had been banded together, and each child was expected to read a variety of books at each level: at this school the book taken home was always the book the child was currently reading at school both during the infant and junior years of the project. At first children were told by their class teachers not to read ahead of material already covered in class, and teachers checked progress by hearing the child re-read whatever had been read at home. By the second term the children were reading so much more than had been anticipated that complete re-reading at school was no longer either desirable or necessary; however, limits continued to be placed by the teachers on the amount to be read at home. Accelerated progress led to a need for additional reading books and these were made equally available to experimental and control classes at the two home collaboration schools. Very few books were lost or damaged, and it was noted that new and attractive books were particularly cared for.

At the conclusion of the 1976/77 school year children in the intervention classes moved from the infant to the junior sections of their schools. For the parents involvement groups this involved establishing links between teachers and parents similar to those established in the infant year. This was facilitated by the contact the researchers already had with the parents, by the reading competence of the children (by then there were almost no non-readers in the home collaboration classes), and by the positive attitude to school which the teachers said they observed in the children.

As has been mentioned reading tests were given to all middle infant and top infants, and to all first and second year juniors at the conclusion of the 1975/76 school year immediately before the interventions began. This pattern of testing all four school year groups was repeated in July, 1977, on conclusion of the infant year of the intervention; again in July, 1978, on conclusion of the junior year; and finally, once again, in July, 1979, twelve months after the researchers had left the schools.

It had been intended that the cohorts following the intervention cohort through the schools would provide control information on attainment standards in the wake of the research project. In the event at schools 1 and 2, at both infant and junior levels, the head teachers and staff introduced their own parent collaboration schemes drawing on their experiences during the research years and extending what had been done to the lower classes in the schools. Thus although subsequent data for these cohorts lost their control value, they did provide a method of assessing the effectiveness of this follow-on work.

Throughout the project all testing was done by retired teachers or teachers on leave who were instructed on procedure and who had no information on which schools or classes were taking part in the interventions or what the interventions were.

Instruments

The disparity between the reading skills of 6-year-old middle infants at one end of the sample and 9-year-old second-year juniors at the other made selection of suitable tests difficult. The tests used were: middle infants, Southgate Group Reading Test 1; top infants, Southgate Group Reading Test 1, NFER test A, Carver Word Recognition Test (data available from LEA); first-year juniors, NFER Test A, Spooncer Group Reading Assessment; second-year juniors, NFER Test BD. Southgate and Carver are word recognition tests; both NFER tests are of reading comprehension; Spooncer contains word recognition, reading comprehension, and phonic sections. Southgate was given to groups of eight to ten children, and the other tests to complete classes, in suitably prepared accommodation.

Southgate (1958) reports a parallel form reliability of $r = 0.95$; Kuder-Richardson Formula 20 reliabilities for the other tests are all above $r = 0.95$ (NFER, 1973; Spooncer, 1977; NFER, 1974; Carver, 1970). The only test-retest reliabilities available were 0.96, reported for the Spooncer test, and 0.92 reported for NFER BD. The information available on validity was of variable quality, and mostly consisted of reported correlations of between 0.8 and 0.9 with well-known individually administered reading tests such as the Schonell or Neale.

Age and sex and number of half-days absent from school for each school year were obtained from school records for all children in the intervention cohort. To check comparability of control and experimental children, father's occupation, past attendance at nursery school or class, the language spoken at home, and time resident in the UK for children born abroad were obtained from the LEA.

Results

The main findings of the project are presented here in as straightforward and direct a form as possible. Future analyses will take advantage of the longitudinal and multivariate aspects of the data, and will make more extensive use of information collected from cohorts other than the one which contained the intervention children.

(a) Comparison of mean scores for experimental and control groups at the beginning, middle and end of the intervention period

When the reading attainment of 5- to 6-year-old middle infants was compared across the six project schools for the 1976 data, i.e., for before the intervention period, highly significant between-school differences in performances were found (one-way ANOVA on Southgate raw scores: $F = 6.66$, $df = 5.429$, $P < 0.0001$). Differences amongst the six schools in reading performance were also observed for top infants and first year juniors in 1976 but the rank order of the schools was not consistent across the different school year groups. Complex patterns of between-school differences were also observed in the 1977, 1978 and 1979 data. For this reason, the main statistical comparisons to be reported here were carried out on experimental and control groups within the same schools.

In each of the four schools where an intervention was to take place the 1976 middle infants reading performance of children assigned to experimental and control groups was compared: no significant within-school differences were found. Twenty-four children joined the intervention cohort (and were given the Southgate test) at the beginning of the 1976 autumn term, and 101 children left it over the following two years of the intervention. These changes did not affect the within-school comparability of experimental and control children. Table 3.1 gives, for each school, the middle infant reading score of those children who were to remain in the sample for the full two-year period. No significant within-school differences were found. The pattern of between-school differences was found to be similarly unaffected by sample changes. Overall, the 101 children who left the intervention cohort had a mean Southgate score of 15.0, while the mean of the 358 who remained was 15.8. There were no significant differences between experimental and control groups within schools, either at the beginning or at the conclusion of the two-year

Table 3.1 Middle infant reading scores on Southgate test at beginning of intervention period (July, 1976) and first year junior scores on NFER Test A at the end of the two-year intervention period (July, 1978)

School	Group	Southgate Raw Score 1976		NFER A Standardised Score 1978		
		Mean	SD	Mean	SD	N
1	Home collaboration	16.7	6.34	107.0	8.35	23
	Control	16.1	6.90	95.6	10.94	49
2	Home collaboration	18.1	7.21	101.9	12.74	28
	Control	18.5	6.79	94.1	11.06	37
3	Extra teacher help	11.6	7.82	93.15	17.51	20
	Control	12.9	7.02	97.9	13.80	45
4	Extra teacher help	16.2	7.32	104.3	15.86	25
	Control	16.3	7.31	98.5	13.34	21

intervention, on the classification of father's occupation, language spoken at home, nursery school experience, length of residence in the UK, or school attendance variables.

At the conclusion of the first year of the project children in the experimental classes at both home collaboration schools had higher mean scores on NFER Test A than children in the parallel control classes. However this difference only reached statistical significance at School 1 ($F = 12.86$; $df = 1.70$; $P < 0.0006$). For the groups which received the extra teaching help at school there was no significant difference at school 4, but at school 3 the children who had received the extra help were significantly behind those who had not ($F = 7.56$; $df = 1.58$; $P < 0.008$). The results were similar for all the reading tests used, including the LEA's own independent testing. Testing for this year was not entirely satisfactory in that the word recognition tests were too easy for many children, whereas the reading comprehension test was too difficult, resulting in score distributions with marked ceiling and floor effects respectively. These distributions were not strictly appropriate for parametric analyses and in non-parametric analyses based on group medians the only statistically significant differences were at school 1. Further, the project interventions, particularly in the two parent involvement schools, did not become fully operational until the late autumn of 1976 and consequently the effect being measured was not for a full school year.

In summer, 1978, after the full two-year intervention period had elapsed, the children's reading performance was tested for the third time. Table 3.1 also gives, for each of the intervention schools, the mean NFER Test A standardised reading score obtained by the experimental and control children at this time.

In both home collaboration schools a clear divergence of reading performance between experimental and control groups can be observed. At both schools the differences were highly significant (for school 1, $F = 19.60$; $df = 1.70$; $P < 0.0001$: for school 2, $F = 7.02$; $df = 1.63$; $P < 0.01$). Again the pattern of results was less clear at the schools where the intervention had taken the form of extra teacher help. Although the mean score for children who received the extra teacher help at school 4 was higher than for the controls the difference was not significant ($F = 1.79$; $df = 1.44$). At school 3 the children who received the extra teacher help had a lower mean score than the control subjects, but again the difference was not significant ($F = 1.37$; $df = 1.63$). An analysis of mean scores for the Spooncer test produced exactly the same pattern of results. The overall correlation between the two tests was 0.85.

(b) Relationship between performance levels at the beginning and end of the intervention period

To examine this question, the middle infant Southgate scores were divided to give three groups overall of approximately equal size: children with scores of 12 or below, scores of 13–19 and score of 20–30. With 1978 NFER A standardised scores as the dependent variable a three-way analysis of variance (School × Experimental Group × Initial Reading Band) for the two parent involvement schools yielded no interaction terms and three highly significant main effects. (For the effect of School, $F = 7.48$; $df = 1.125$; $P < 0.007$: for the effect of Experimental Group, $F = 28.30$; $df = 1.125$; $P < 0.001$: for Initial Reading Band, $F = 30.48$; $df = 2.125$; $P < 0.001$.) In a comparable analysis for the two extra teacher help schools the only significant main effect was that of Initial Reading Band ($F = 38.69$; $df = 2.99$; $P < 0.001$), and there was a significant interaction between Experimental Group and School ($F = 4.56$; $df = 2.99$; $P < 0.001$).

Two tests were given to the intervention cohort at the end of the intervention period and these analyses were repeated using the 1978 Spooncer scores as dependent variable. All main effects were similar to those reported for NFER Test A except that in the analysis for the parent collaboration schools the interaction between School and Experimental Group was significant ($F = 4.68$; $df = 1.125$; $P < 0.032$).

Taken together these statistical analyses show, first, that in all four schools and in each experimental group within the schools, early reading performance was an extremely powerful predictor of subsequent attainment; second, that the effect of parental help could be observed in children of all initial performance levels, and in both schools for NFER Test A but that a significant difference in the extent of the effect is evident in the Spooncer test scores; third, that any suggestion of benefit from extra teacher help was confined to one school but that the significant interaction was due as much to poor performance of the children who received the extra teaching help at school 3 as to the slight improvement of the children who received similar help at school 4.

(c) Group reading performance at the end of the first junior school year, expressed in terms of the proportion of children falling into different score bands

As an alternative to the calculation of a mean score, the reading performance of a group can be described in terms of the proportion of children scoring above or below particular threshold values. For practical purposes proportions, although using less of the available information than means, may be more readily interpretable. Teachers, for example, tend to characterise the reading performance of their classes in terms of the number of children reading at certain levels, rather than by reference to a group average figure. Further a description in terms of proportions can show whether a mean score, in this case for reading attainment, has been raised by improving the performance of good readers, or by reducing the number of failing readers, or by improvements at all levels.

In rough reading age terms, a standardised score of 99 or less on a test such as NFER Test A represents performance 'below age level'. In a representative national sample just under 50 per cent of children would be expected to obtain scores in this range. Data from the 1976 and 1977 testings were used to estimate the proportion of first-year junior children performing below this level for the six project schools. The figures are given in Table 3.2. In 1976, the proportion of children in this age group scoring 99 or below on NFER A was found to range from 56 per cent at school 1 to more than 80 per cent at school 4. For the six schools combined, the figure was 65 per cent, a high proportion by national standards, but not unexpected in an inner-city area. In 1977 the overall figure was very similar with 61 per cent of that year's first-year juniors scoring 'below age level'; but again schools varied considerably, school 1 now exhibiting the worst performance with 72 per cent of children

Table 3.2 Proportion of children who scored 99 or less on the NFER A at first-year junior level

School	Group	1976 Percentage	(Ratio)	1977 Percentage	(Ratio)	1978 Percentage	(Ratio)
I	Home collaboration	–		–		21.7	(5:23)
	Control	55.7	(64:115)	72.0	(72:100)	73.5	(36:49)
2	Home collaboration	–		–		42.9	(12:28)
	Control	63.6	(49:77)	65.6	(42:64)	67.6	(25:37)
3	Extra teacher help	–		–		60.0	(12:20)
	Control	63.9	(53:83)	61.1	(44:72)	57.8	(26:45)
4	Extra teacher help	–		–		40.0	(10:25)
	Control	82.5	(47:57)	52.0	(26:50)	52.4	(11:21)
5	Control	69.6	(64:92)	47.7	(41:86)	54.5	(36:66)
6	Control	64.9	(50:77)	64.3	(45:70)	47.7	(21:44)

scoring 99 or less. The best performance was in school 5 where only about 48 per cent of children scored in this range. In 1978 the cohort containing the intervention children were first-year juniors and had received the complete two years of the intervention. Table 3.2 gives, for that year, the percentage of 'below age level' readers found in experimental and control groups at the six project schools. In both parent involvement groups the proportion of children performing 'below age level' was reduced relative to within-school controls, reduced relative to the school's figures for the previous years, and reduced also relative to the national standard. Some improvement can be seen at one extra teacher help school, but none at the other. Results for schools 5 and 6 are also included in Table 3.2 primarily for the sake of descriptive completeness, but also to illustrate the absence of any general trend in reading standards over time. The figures for 1978 in Table 3.2 are for children present for the full two-year intervention, but the results are unaltered if the 1978 control estimates are based on all children on the roll, including newcomers, as were the estimates for 1976 and 1977.

More extreme groups on the reading scale were examined, but since the number of children falling in the separate bands was small the data for schools 1 and 2 were pooled to give a combined parental help group and a combined control group. A similar pooling of groups was made for schools 3 and 4. Table 3.3 compares the proportions – expressed as percentages – of experimental and control children falling into four reading bands for the pooled data. Chi-squared tests revealed that the distribution of the children across categories was significantly different for the experimental and control children from the two parent involvement schools ($\chi^2 = 18.77$, $df = 3$, $P < 0.0003$), but not for the groups from the extra teacher help schools ($\chi^2 = 3.58$, $df = 3$). From Table 3.3 it can be seen that parental help both reduced the proportion of failing readers (scores of 84 or less) and increased the proportion of able readers (scores of 115 or above). The lack of significant effect for the extra teacher help children appears most evident in the lowest attainment band.

Table 3.3 Proportion of children falling into four reading bands for the 1978 results

| Schools | Group | NFER Test A score band | | | | |
		84 or less	85–99	100–114	115 plus	N
1 and 2	Home collaboration	5.9	27.5	49.0	17.6	51
	Control	17.4	53.5	22.1	7.0	86
		($\chi^2 = 18.77$, $df = 3$, $P < 0.0003$)				
3 and 4	Extra teacher help	26.7	22.2	33.3	17.8	45
	Control	18.2	37.9	31.8	12.1	66
		($\chi^2 = 3.58$, $df = 3$, not significant)				
(Standardisation sample		15.1	33.6	34.6	16.7	7249)*

*Source: National Foundation for Educational Research, 1973.

(d) Reading standards in the second-year juniors: mean scores 12 months after conclusion of the intervention

The interventions ended in July, 1978, and there was no research presence in the schools during the following year. In July, 1979, the children, by then second-year juniors, were tested again to see if any gains made during the project had been maintained. In both schools 1 and 2 the parent involvement group continued to perform at a higher level than the control children, even though no intervention had taken place in the preceding year. This difference was highly statistically significant at school 1 ($F = 20.17$; $df = 1.64$; $P < 0.0001$) but not at school 2 ($F = 1.18$; $df = 1.56$). The mean scores are given in Table 3.4. Differential sample loss affected these mean scores particularly at school 2 where between 1978 and 1979 the control group lost three poor readers with 1978 scores of 77, 77 and 89; whereas the leavers from the experimental group had scores of 122, 106, 101 and 84. Differential sample loss affected mean scores at school 1 in the same direction, but to lesser extent.

In neither school 3 nor school 4 where the children received extra help from a teacher was the performance of experimental children significantly better than that of controls. For these schools differential sample loss affected mean scores in the opposite direction from that at schools 1 and 2. At school 3 the seven children who left the experimental group had a mean score of 83.1, while the five control children who left had a mean of 96.2. At school 4 differential leaving also acted in the same direction of raising the reading level of the experimental group, and lowering that of the control group.

Table 3.4 Second-year junior reading scores on NFER Test BD (July, 1979)

| School | Group | NFER BD Standardised Score | | |
		Mean	SD	N
1	Home collaboration	101.7	7.73	22
	Control	90.5	10.33	44
2	Home collaboration	96.2	13.34	24
	Control	92.6	11.59	34
3	Extra teacher help	94.7	14.39	14
	Control	93.5	12.49	39
4	Extra teacher help	97.8	10.20	23
	Control	92.2	12.62	19

(e) Reading standards in the second-year juniors; proportions of scores below standardised average for age

The biasing effects of differential sample loss must also be borne in mind when comparing the percentage of children from the different experimental and control groups who, in 1979, obtained standardised scores on NFER Test BD

Table 3.5 Proportion of children who scored 99 or less on the NFER BD at second-year junior level

School	Group	1976 Percentage	1976 (Ratio)	1977 Percentage	1977 (Ratio)	1978 Percentage	1978 (Ratio)	1979 Percentage	1979 (Ratio)
1	Home collaboration	–	–	–	–	–	–	45.5	(10:22)
	Control	79.6	(82:103)	81.7	(85:104)	78.7	(74:94)	84.1	(37:44)
2	Home collaboration	–	–	–	–	–	–	54.2	(13:24)
	Control	79.2	(57:72)	81.9	(59:72)	81.4	(57:70)	79.4	(27:34)
3	Extra teacher help	–	–	–	–	–	–	71.4	(10:14)
	Control	66.3	(63:95)	77.1	(64:83)	78.7	(63:80)	66.7	(26:39)
4	Extra teacher help	–	–	–	–	–	–	47.8	(11:23)
	Control	76.9	(50:65)	82.0	(50:61)	73.7	(42:57)	73.7	(14:19)
5	Control	73.7	(55:75)	64.4	(58:90)	65.6	(59:90)	69.5	(41:59)
6	Control	80.8	(59:73)	75.0	(54:72)	83.0	(49:59)	76.9	(30:39)

of 99 or less (Table 3.5). In both parent involvement schools there were fewer 'below age level' readers among the experimental children than among the controls. This was also clearly the case at one of the extra teacher help schools, school 4, but not at the other.

Second-year performance figures from 1976, 1977 and 1978, also given in Table 3.5, permit these results to be placed in the context of the schools' reading standards in previous years. In schools 1 and 2 standards for the second-year age group were found to be constantly poor over the period 1976–78 with between 75 and 85 per cent of children obtaining standardised scores of 99 or below, as against just under 50 per cent in the national standardisation sample. From Table 3.5 it can be seen that when children in the intervention cohort were tested as second-year juniors in 1979 the percentage of 'below age level' readers in the control groups at schools 1 and 2 were much the same as for previous years (84.1 per cent and 79.4 per cent respectively, giving an overall figure of 82.1 per cent); but for the experimental groups the figures were similar to the national sample (45.5 per cent and 54.2 per cent, overall 50.0 per cent). At school 4 the group which received the extra teacher help also contained fewer below average readers than would have been expected on the basis of previous years' standards (experimental 47.8 per cent, control 73.7 per cent) but this was not the case at school 3 (experimental 71.4 per cent, control 66.7 per cent). At schools 5 and 6 no changes over time can be observed comparable to those observed at the schools where the home collaboration took place. School 5 consistently had a smaller proportion of 'below age level' readers in its second year than did school 6, the percentages being in the order of 65–75 and 75–85 respectively. Thus the figure of around 50 per cent observed in the two parent involvement groups represents an improvement in standards over that usually achieved by even the most successful school in the sample.

Discussion and implications

In the social science and educational literature it is often stressed that relationships uncovered in survey research need to be investigated experimentally before much credence can be given to them, or indeed before anything can be usefully said about causality (Pedhazur, 1976). However, it is also known that, even when experimentation is possible in natural settings, conditions cannot be controlled as in the laboratory, and validity is threatened in many ways. The present chapter reports the main findings of a natural settings experiment carried out to investigate a relationship found in survey research between parents saying that they heard their children read at home and the tested reading performance of the children. Before the findings are discussed a number of points need to be made about the limitations the adopted research design imposed on the inferences which can be drawn.

The research design was a compromise between the strict requirements of an experiment and judgements about real world feasibility. The most important departures from a true experimental model were:

(i) When subjects were assigned to experimental groups the unit of randomisation was the intact class, not the individual child. Allocation of children to classes for the 1976–77 top infant year was not under the control of the research team, nor was the allocation of teachers to classes. Cook and Campbell (1979) suggest that the problems of sampling intact groups rather than individual subjects can be reduced by matching the groups before randomisation, and indeed that such matching is always advisable given the high variability associated with field research. Fortunately in the present case head teachers agreed to assign an even mix of pupils in terms of ability level to each class; and the class teachers agreed that the 'class plus teacher' units which included themselves could be assigned at random to intervention and control groups. The analyses confirmed that before the intervention began the groups were comparable not only in terms of the main dependent variable but also a variety of other relevant variables.

(ii) It would have been impracticable, and doubtless unacceptable to both teachers and parents, to encourage parental involvement for some children in a class but not for others. Consequently the design contained no within-class comparisons and the teacher effect was confounded with that of experimental group. Although the teachers had been assigned to experimental or control conditions at random, and not on the basis of personal qualities or professional expertise, and although an element of replication was a part of each strand of the design, the design left open the possibility that the performance of the children in the intervention groups was in some measure the result of specific teacher effects not related to the intervention. Further replications, involving extensive sampling of teachers and classes, would be needed to completely reject this possibility. Using the data collected on equivalent age groups in previous years it was possible to show that the standards achieved by the parent involvement children was higher than those previously achieved in the relevant schools. Although comprehensive comparisons between intervention classes, and equivalent classes taught by the same teachers in previous years, were not possible because of changes in staffing and composition of classes, useful evidence was available from the school where the greatest effect of the collaboration was seen. At this school for the year groups concerned there was staffing consistency and consistency in the allocation of pupils to classes for the years preceding the intervention. Both the teacher of the top infant year, and the teacher for the first year of the junior school made highly significant improvements in the performance of their classes in comparison with the remainder of the relevant year groups for the year of the home collaboration, but did not do so for previous years. Both teachers attributed this improvement to the collaboration with parents, and this does seem the most likely explanation.

(iii) The experiment was not a full 'crossover' design, i.e., not all experimental groups were to be found in each school, and thus direct comparison of parent involvement and extra teacher help groups is confounded with possible between-school differences. This compromise in the design was partly dictated by school size; some schools did not have sufficient top infant classes for two interventions and a control condition. But in any case the problems of main-taining two separate interventions in one school would certainly have threatened validity; and also staff could have compared the progress of the different classes, with further unknown consequences for the interventions. The analyses in this chapter have compared intervention and control groups separately for the parent involvement and extra teacher help schools, and this would seem adequate for the present purpose.

Apart from these design considerations direct comparison of the parent involvement and extra teacher help groups would be justified. The provision of extra teacher help at school was originally planned as a control to match the home collaboration; in the field, for practical reasons already described, it grew to be a small-scale intervention in its own right, but was in no way comparable in scope to the home collaboration. At home the children were helped individually, at school in groups. The type of help given at home and at school differed. The amount of help given to children in the two situations could not be precisely controlled and hence matched. Furthermore, the help in school was supplied to all children by the same teacher, whereas on the home collaboration side each child received help from his own parent or parents. Further, nothing can be said about the possible value of different forms of extra teaching provision in schools; different methods or different forms of provision might have produced different results.

Research into the contribution of these different factors to the beneficial effect of parental help would need to examine them systematically in a full experimental design. In the circumstances of the present study, however, the precise experimental control required for research of this kind would only have been achieved at the expense of policy relevance. The latter was the study's first priority, and it is in policy terms that the two kinds of extra reading help given to children in the project can most usefully be compared. The extra reading tuition at school was provided by a specialist teacher who worked with the children on a small group basis, seeing each child several times a week, for a two-year period. This represents a level of teaching provision which no local education authority could expect to match in a service setting; yet, even under these conditions, only limited changes in reading standards were obtained, with benefits being least apparent for initially low achieving chil-dren. On the other hand, organisation of a collaboration between teachers and parents did lead to significant improvement by children of all ability levels; further, organisation of such a collaboration does seem feasible within terms of resources already available in schools. Design considerations, discussed in this and previous sections, do limit the conclusions which may be drawn from the findings, but at the very least the results suggest that the difficulty of raising reading standards through conventional school-based means should not be underestimated, and that the reading failure of a sizeable minority of children in primary schools cannot be attributed unquestioningly to either lack of potential on the part of the child or to a shortage of resources.

(iv) From previous work (Hewison and Tizard, 1980) it would be expected that up to a half of the children in the control classes at all six project schools would be given reading practice at home by their parents. No attempt was made to prevent this happening, for both practical and ethical reasons, and thus comparison of home collaboration groups with controls understates to an unknown extent the effect of the experimental variable. It follows that the study can only provide a conservative estimate of the importance of parental help as a determinant of reading performance, and this would seem to strengthen the significance of the findings.

The experimental findings reported here provide evidence for a causal relationship between parents hearing their children read and reading attainment. Although further research would be required if the variables underlying the relationship are to be understood, this lack of understanding may not be important for most practical purposes. Of much greater practical significance is the fact that teachers and parents working in collaboration did improve the academic performance of the children without the parents being given any special training in the techniques of tutoring, other than advice and brief demonstrations during the monitoring of home reading or at meetings with the class teacher. A number of studies have examined the effect of non-professional tuition on reading performance, but in all cases the parents or other helpers were first given detailed instructions in the techniques of prompting and reward-giving favoured by the researcher directing the project (Ellson et al., 1968; Ryback and Staats, 1970; Staats et al., 1970; Wallach and Wallach, 1976; Glynn et al., 1979; Morgan and Lyon, 1979). Adopting a very different approach to reading failure Lawrence (1972) concentrated on the motivational and emotional needs of poor readers; he reported performance gains by children who had received non-professional counselling to improve their self-esteem, but no direct help with reading. Since these projects looked at children of different ages, and with varying degrees of reading difficulty, it is unfortunately not possible to compare the gains made by children given different types of help, and so increase understanding of the relative contributions made by practice and motivational factors to the reading progress observed.

The project involved not only the organisation and monitoring of the intervention and the testing of attainment but also the collection of qualitative, descriptive information on what was happening in the homes and schools relevant to each child's progress. Drawing on both sources a number of general conclusions follow with implications for future research and practice in schools. Firstly, in inner-city, multiracial schools it is both feasible and practicable to involve nearly all parents in formal educational activities with infant and first-year junior school children, even if the parents are non-literate or largely non-English speaking. Secondly, children who receive parental help are significantly better in reading attainment than comparable children who do not. Thirdly, most parents express great satisfaction in being involved in this way by the schools and teachers report that the children show an increased keenness for learning at school and are better behaved. Fourthly, the teachers involved in the home collaboration also reported that they found the work with parents worthwhile and they continued to involve parents with subsequent classes after the experiment was concluded, as did teachers who had taught parallel control classes during the intervention years. Fifthly, small-group instruction in reading, given by a highly competent specialist teacher, did not produce improvements in attainment comparable in magnitude with those obtained from the collaboration with parents. Sixthly, the collaboration between teachers and parents was effective for children to all initial levels of performance, including those who at the beginning of the study were failing to learn to read. Finally, the fact that some children read to parents who could not themselves read English, or in a few cases cannot read at all, did not prevent improvement in the reading skills of those children, or detract from the willingness of the parent to collaborate with the school.

Current developments in educational thinking and practice underlie the potential importance of these findings. The Taylor Report (1977) and the ongoing discussion about parental involvement in education suggest a need for further studies of ways in which parents, and the wider community, can be brought into closer partnership with schools and teachers. The fluctuations in pupil numbers and in the supply of teachers that are a feature of industrial societies today, coupled with the need for economy in resource allocation, raise profound issues concerning the training of teachers and the ways in which they can use their time most effectively. From a different perspective, the Warnock Report (1978) laid emphasis on the special needs of the large minority of pupils in ordinary schools who continue to present chronic educational problems. The findings of the present study suggest that staffing resources at present allocated by LEAs for remedial work in primary schools might be better employed, at least in part, in organising contact and collaboration between class teachers and parents – all parents, before failing is manifest for some children – on specific, practical teaching matters, and that this might prevent many children from falling behind with their reading in the first place.

Acknowledgement

This work was supported by a grant from the Department of Education and Science to the late Professor Jack Tizard who directed the research. Sections of this chapter were prepared before Professor Tizard's sad death in August, 1979. Many individuals participated in the research reported, and many more gave advice or support. The research team, which included Mrs Ena Abrahams and Mr A. C. Everton of the Haringey Education Service, were grateful to the Director of Education, London Borough of Haringey and his staff, and to head teachers, teachers, ancillary staff, parents and children; and to many others who helped with organisation, testing, scoring, data management, computing, or other aspects of the project.

References

Carver, C. (1970). *Word Recognition Test and Manual*. London: University of London Press.

Cook, T.D. and Campbell, D.T. (1979). *Quasi-Experimentation Design and Analysis Issues for Field Settings*. Chicago: Rand McNally.

Ellson, D.G., Harris, P. and Barber, L. (1968). A field test of programmed and directed tutoring. *Reading Res. Q.*, 3, 307–367.

Glynn, E.L., McNaughton, S.S., Robinson, V.M.J. and Quinn, M. (1979). *Remedial Reading at Home: Helping You to Help Your Child*. Wellington: New Zealand Council for Educational Research.

Hewison, J. and Tizard, J. (1980). Parental involvement and reading attainment. *Br. J. Educ. Psychol.*, 50, 209–215.

Lawrence, D. (1972). Counselling of retarded readers by non-professionals. *Educ. Res.*, 15, 48–51.

Morgan, R. and Lyon, E. (1979). Paired reading – a preliminary report on a technique for parental tuition of reading-retarded children. *J. Child Psychol. Psychiat.*, 20, 151–160.

National Foundation for Education Research (1973). *Manual of Instructions for Reading Test A*. London: Ginn.

National Foundation for Educational Research (1974). *Manual of Instructions for Reading Test BD*. London: Ginn.

Pedhazur, E.J. (1976). Analytic methods in studies of educational effects. *Rev. Res. in Educ.*, 3, 243–285.

Ryback, D. and Staats, A.W. (1970). Parents as behavior therapy technicians in treating reading deficits (dyslexia). *J. Behav. Ther. Exper. Psychiat.*, 1, 109–119.

Southgate, V. (1958). *Southgate Group Reading Tests Manual of Instructions*. London: University of London Press.

Spooncer, F.A. (1977). *Group Reading Assessment Manual of Instructions*. London: Hodder and Stoughton Educational.

Staats, A.W., Brewer, B.A. and Gross, M.C. (1970). Learning and cognitive development: representative samples, cumulative-hierarchical learning, and experimental-longitudinal methods. *Monograph of the Society for Research in Child Development*, 35.

Staats, A.W., Minke, K.A., and Butts, P.A. (1970). A token-reinforcer remedial reading programme administered by black therapy-technicians to problem black children. *Behav. Ther.* 1, 331–353.

Taylor Report (1977). *Report of the Committee of Enquiry into Management and Government of Schools*. London: HMSO.

Wallach, N.A. and Wallach, L. (1976). *Teaching all Children to Read*. Chicago: University of Chicago Press.

Warnock Report (1978). *Report of the Committee of Enquiry into the Education of Handicapped Children and Young People*. London: HMSO.

Source

This is an edited version of an article previously published in the *British Journal of Educational Psychology*, 52. 1982. © The British Psychological Society.

Chapter 4

Pause Prompt Praise

Reading tutoring procedures for home and school partnership

Ted Glynn

Home and school partnership

Children spend the first five or six years of their lives living at home with parents or caregivers. In this powerful, yet responsive, social context (Glynn, 1985) children typically acquire their first language and learn to use that language to enhance social and cultural relationships with adults and peers, and to develop important academic skills. Parents have typically played a major role in providing learning opportunities, and in providing a structured but supportive environment for their children's learning. Most children are already competent learners by the time they enter pre-school or school contexts. Further, after children have entered preschool or school, they still participate concurrently in responsive, social learning contexts at home.

Educators have long argued for a closer involvement of parents in their children's education. Involvement, however, has been vaguely and inconsistently defined. It has been taken to mean anything from having parents raise funds for their local school, to becoming members of school Boards of Trustees, and participating in all decision-making, from school maintenance to staff appointments and appraisal of principals. Parent involvement in education has also been taken to mean anything, from passive reception of teacher comments on their children's progress at parent–teacher meetings or participation in Individual Educational Plans (IEPs) with a range of educational professionals, to active engagement in teaching activities in their children's classrooms or active engagement in teaching activities with their children at home.

This shared responsibility for the same children presents strong arguments for parents and teachers to share common academic learning objectives for the children with whom they each interact, for example in the learning of oral language, reading, and writing skills. Skills acquired in one context (home or school) may or may not generalize to the other. Facilitating learning in one context may depend on knowing what behaviours are being acquired and reinforced in the other. Successful performance in one context may be precluded by the performance of incompatible behaviours in the other. The regular and reliable exchange of information between home and school about children's learning and behaviour, and a co-operative partnership (or work relationship) between parents and teachers, appear essential. Only by working together and freely sharing information data can parents and teachers enhance the generalization of skills learned at school to the home setting, and the reverse.

Research on generalization of literacy skills across home and school contexts is relatively rare. However, studies involving parents implementing a set of reading tutoring procedures, now known as Pause Prompt Praise, have demonstrated clear gains in children's reading at school resulting from parental intervention at home. Pause Prompt and Praise comprises a set of behavioural tutoring procedures designed to provide additional support for older low-progress readers. Tutoring is carried out by parents, peers, or community members in the context of reading meaningful stories, rather than with words and sounds taken out of context.

What is Pause Prompt Praise?

The Pause Prompt Praise reading tutoring procedures were developed in South Auckland in 1977. A team of researchers worked intensively with parents of a group of 10- to 12-year-old low-progress readers to produce a training booklet and video: *Remedial Reading at Home: Helping You to Help Your Child*. The booklet and accompanying research monograph were first published by the New Zealand Council for Educational Research (Glynn *et al.*, 1979; McNaughton *et al.*, 1981).

The initial research work with Pause Prompt Praise involved intensive observation and training in home settings with a group of older (10- to 12-year-old) readers and their parents, and resulted in the production of a parent training package (booklet and video). The project required close involvement of the researcher in both home and school settings, allowing access to information not readily accessible to teachers. Teachers of children in the original South Auckland project (Glynn *et al.*, 1979) and in a subsequent parallel study in Birmingham, UK (McNaughton *et al.*, 1987) perceived parents as apathetic towards their children's learning at school. Yet there was little evidence that teachers had had contact with their children's homes. The researchers in these studies found otherwise – that parents cared deeply about their children's reading difficulties at school, and were highly motivated to do something about it, to the extent of learning to implement the Pause Prompt Praise procedures. The strength of parents' motivation to help their children learning to read at home is illustrated in a study by Glynn and Glynn (1986) who established that Khmer-speaking mothers of 6- to 7-year-old migrant children were able to improve their children's rate of reading progress at school over and above that of children's participation in the school programme alone. This was achieved despite the mothers having only a few words of English and having little or no schooling in Cambodia. In this study mothers and children were invited to work together, using either Khmer or English to 'work out' the meaning of the stories sent home from the school following usual classroom practice. Mothers appeared to use children's new knowledge and recall of

English words learnt at school, and children appeared to use the mother's first-language skills (Khmer) to discuss the pictures and events portrayed in the stories. Important additional outcomes from this study were clear gains in English reading skills for mothers as well as children.

Subsequent research with the Pause Prompt Praise procedures (Glynn and McNaughton, 1985; Wheldall and Glynn, 1989; Wheldall and Mettem, 1985) led to the Research Monograph being published in the UK under the title *Pause, Prompt and Praise* (McNaughton *et al.*, 1987). Widespread and continuing interest in these procedures has resulted in an updated version of Pause Prompt Praise (Glynn *et al.*, 1992; Dick *et al.*, 1992). A Maori language version, Tatari Tautoko Tauawhi, has been developed and trialled by Maori staff of the New Zealand Special Education Service, and teachers, students and family members in several different schools in which children are being taught in Maori language immersion classes (Atvars and Glynn, 1992; Harawira *et al.*, 1993; Glynn *et al.*, 1993).

The Pause Prompt Praise strategies are derived from the theoretical perspective on reading developed by Clay (1979, 1991) and McNaughton (1987). This perspective views proficient reading as learning to use all the sources of information within and around a text to understand the particular message being conveyed. Differences between high-progress and low-progress readers are thought to lie not so much in their success at identifying letters and letter–sound combinations, but in the flexibility and fluency with which they use this information together with contextual information.

High rates of self-correction are associated with high progress during early reading (Clay, 1969, 1979, 1991). However, the reading contexts available to low-progress readers may be unhelpful in two ways. First, low-progress readers may be given fewer opportunities to read meaningful text material of appropriate difficulty. Second, the type of instruction they receive may prevent them from learning to integrate contextual and letter–sound information and to self-correct. This may lead to a state of 'instructional dependence' on over-intrusive remedial help (McNaughton, 1981).

Pause Prompt Praise is designed for use in a one-to-one oral reading context so that low-progress readers can receive more opportunities to self-correct errors and to practise problem-solving strategies. Assisting readers to learn these strategies requires tutors to learn to implement a set of specific tutoring skills.

Tutoring involves first *pausing* when a reader makes an error (to allow opportunity for reader self-correction without tutor help). Where the error is not self-corrected, tutors offer different types of *prompt* to assist the reader with the meaning of the work or with the letter or sounds in the word *when* the error indicates the reader has already understood the meaning of the word. Tutors also employ specific *praise* to reinforce readers' use of independent strategies such as self-corrections and corrections following tutor prompts. Extensive descriptive data reported by Wheldall *et al.* (1992) demonstrate that even trained practising teachers do not 'naturally' implement these strategies when hearing children read.

The majority of readers who have access to competent reading programmes learn these independent strategies from their regular engagement with texts, as part of their classroom reading activities. Indeed, applying Pause Prompt Praise to readers who are not experiencing difficulties or who are making better than average progress may be superfluous (Wheldall and Glynn, 1989).

Pause Prompt Praise aims to break into the cycle of dependence, in which low-progress readers encountering an unknown word may 'cue' the teacher to tell them the correct word immediately. The Pause Prompt Praise tutor behaviours cue the readers instead to use all available information to solve unknown words. Such information includes background knowledge of the story topic, familiarity with the language structure of the text, the meaning contained within the context of each sentence or paragraph, and the letter–sound information within words. Tutors are trained to give priority to the reader's understanding of the meaning of words, before attempting to focus reader attention onto letter and sound information. Tutors tell the reader the correct word only as a last resort and after two prompts have been tried. Tutors are not required to respond to every error a reader makes. Given the priority on helping readers understand the meaning of words, tutors may ignore minor errors which do not greatly alter the meaning of the text.

Successful use of Pause Prompt Praise requires readers to practise the skills needed to correct their errors. Successful use of Pause Prompt Praise, therefore, requires regular monitoring of the reader's accuracy level. Levels of text difficulty need to be adjusted (upwards or downwards) to maintain an optimal difficulty level for reader and tutor to work together.

How do you use Pause Prompt Praise?

Figure 4.1 outlines the use of Pause Prompt Praise. This figure has been modified from the original tutoring chart (Glynn *et al.*, 1979), as experience over the years has suggested the present layout is more helpful. In Figure 4.1 *Correct Reading* is linked directly to *Praise*. When a reader correctly reads a phrase, a sentence, a whole page of a beginning text, or perhaps a paragraph from a more advanced text, the tutor should praise this specifically. Experienced tutors will praise frequently enough to let the reader know things are going well, but not so frequently as to interrupt the flow of reading. In the figure *Incorrect Reading* refers to errors of omission (no response) as well as to incorrect words substituted or extra words added, whether they 'make sense' or not. Errors which are corrected by the reader *without any help from the tutor* are classed as self-corrections.

When an error occurs, the tutor's first task is to *Pause*. The pause prevents the tutor from interrupting too soon. This may allow readers to notice for themselves that what they have read may not quite make sense, and, possibly, to correct themselves. The pause also allows the tutor time to decide what kind of error has occurred – whether it is a non-attempt or a substitution which does not make sense or one which does make sense. Tutors should pause

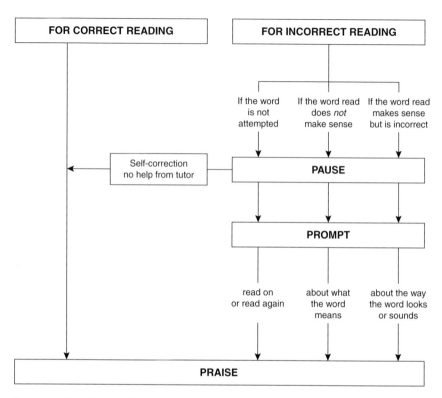

Figure 4.1 Pause Prompt Praise

Source: Adapted from Glynn *et al.* (1979).

for up to five seconds, during which a self-correction may occur, or, alternatively, pause until the reader has reached the end of the phrase or sentence containing the error.

After the tutor has paused, and if the reader has not self-corrected, the tutor offers a prompt to help the reader with the word (see *Prompt* in Figure 4.1). Here tutors learn to select one of three kinds of prompt, according to the type of error the reader has made. Moving from left to right in the Figure, these three kinds of prompt line up with the three types of error. Hence, for a 'non-attempt' error (which has not been self-corrected after a pause), the tutor prompts the reader either to 'read on' or 'read again'. 'Read on' prompts are used if the error is at the beginning or middle of a sentence or clause, and 'read again' prompts are used if the error is near the end. Sometimes this kind of prompt is sufficient for the reader to 'pick up' the meaning of the word from the context of the sentence or story. If this happens, the reader has made a 'prompted correction', and the tutor should provide specific praise. When the error is a word which does *not* make sense the tutor uses a 'meaning prompt' directing the reader's attention to what the word means (e.g. a question referring to the picture, the context of the sentence, the page, the whole story, or to the reader's prior knowledge and experience). When the error is a word which *does* make sense the tutor may then use a 'letter–sound prompt', directing the reader's attention to what the word looks or sounds like. Note that this kind of prompt is offered only when the error suggests that the reader has already understood something of the meaning of the word.

When readers read the correct word after a tutor prompt, these prompted corrections should be praised. Tutors should give no more than two prompts. After the second prompt, the tutor should tell the reader the correct word. This is the 'bottom line' which tutors try not to reach.

How effective is Pause Prompt Praise?

Effectiveness with low-progress readers

The majority of studies with Pause Prompt Praise have involved readers with considerable underachievement in reading. In five of the studies reviewed by Glynn and McNaughton (1985), the minimum underachievement was two years, and in one case this was three years. Readers in one study were all members of a special class for children with mild intellectual disability (Love and VanBiervliet, 1984), and in another, readers were all members of a semi-residential programme for children with behavioural and learning difficulties (O'Connor et al., 1987). Unfortunately, the generality of findings from small-scale intensive intra-subject research studies is often underestimated. However, a number of advocates for intra-subject research designs (Campbell and Stanley, 1966; Kratochwill, 1978; Robinson and Foster, 1979; Hersen and Barlow, 1977), following Sidman (1960), argue that detailed description and continuous measurement of changes in the behaviour of individuals under clearly specified conditions will lead to a greater confidence in the generality of findings than will merely employing large groups of subjects. Glynn and McNaughton (1985) reported that, following the original project, a further 11 studies had deployed the procedures involving 118 tutors, tutoring a total of 98 children aged between 7 and 12 years, all experiencing reading difficulties. Nine of those studies employed intra-subject research designs, and three employed group-comparison designs, one of these (O'Connor et al., 1987) employing both intra-subject and between-group comparisons.

Reading age gains across the 12 studies reviewed in 1985 ranged from between 1.5 and 2.0 months per month of trained tutoring, to between 10 and 11 months per month of trained tutoring. Particularly strong gains were reported for three of the studies in which Pause Prompt Praise was introduced concurrently at home and at school (McNaughton et al., 1981; Scott and Ballard, 1983) or concurrently in residential and school settings (O'Connor et al., 1987). Scott and Ballard (1983) implemented the Pause Prompt Praise remedial reading procedures concurrently with parents and teachers of children with severe reading difficulties. Parents and teachers learned the procedures together. Both parties were involved in the same intervention and monitoring of their own and children's behaviour – parents in the home setting, teachers in the school setting. Implementing this study itself increased the amount of parent–teacher contact and exchange of information about children's behaviour. Perhaps the shared control over the reading intervention contributed to the mutual respect parents and teachers had for each other's role. Data from the Scott and Ballard study showed a far higher rate of reading gain for these children than for children in similar studies where the same procedures were implemented by parents or teachers alone (Glynn and McNaughton, 1985).

Two later studies in the UK reported by Wheldall and Glynn (1989) investigated the effects of Pause Prompt Praise with children who were only slightly under-achieving, or who had advanced reading achievement. In the first of these studies, which involved 13-year-old peer tutors tutoring 9- to 10-year-old readers, there was only small advantage for readers tutored with Pause Prompt Praise over readers tutored by untrained tutors (12 months gain in reading comprehension compared with 9 months). The second study involved parent tutors tutoring readers whose achievement was up to 2.5 years in advance of their chronological age. Readers tutored with Pause Prompt Praise made no greater gains than readers given untrained tutoring. In these two studies readers of near average to above average achievement, in contrast with the low-progress readers in other studies, would likely have already learned strategies of self-correction and using contextual information from their school reading programmes and their experience with books. Additional input from Pause Prompt Praise tutoring would have been superfluous.

Range of successful tutors

Glynn and McNaughton (1985) reported successful implementation of Pause Prompt Praise procedures by the 118 tutors across the 12 studies reviewed. Successful implementation required major gains by tutors in their rate of pausing, in their rate of prompting (including their rate of successful prompts), and in their rate of praise. In the studies reviewed 62 tutors were parents tutoring their own children, 31 were teachers, parents of residential staff tutoring children other than their own, and 15 were older students tutoring younger students.

Subsequent to the Glynn and McNaughton review, Henderson and Glynn (1986) reported a study in which four parent tutors were trained by trainee teachers to implement Pause Prompt Praise successfully with their own children at home. Wheldall and Glynn (1989) summarized successful implementation of the Pause Prompt Praise procedures by the 26 junior high school and high school student tutors, who were tutoring younger, low-progress readers. Medcalf and Glynn (1987) carried out a study in which three 11- to 12-year-old, low-progress tutors successfully tutored three similar-age, low-progress readers, and Houghton and Glynn (1993) report successful tutoring by five low-progress, 13-year-old tutors tutoring similar-age, low-progress readers.

Reading benefits for tutors

One important trend emerging from research with Pause Prompt Praise is the finding of reading gains for tutors as well as readers. Peer tutoring of reading provides an important learning context for demonstrating reciprocal gains for tutors and tutees. By attending carefully to tutees' reading in order to implement Pause Prompt Praise correctly, tutors themselves stand to gain from the process. Hence it may be more appropriate to select, as tutors, readers who are themselves experiencing reading difficulties albeit [with texts] at higher levels than those read by tutees. In the study by Medcalf and Glynn (1987) an educational psychologist assisted three primary teachers to teach Pause Prompt Praise to three 11- to 12-year-old tutors who had reading deficits of between one and three years. These tutors in turn tutored three 11- to 12-year-old readers who were underachieving in reading by between four and six years. After eight weeks of tutoring, there were substantial gains for both tutors and tutees on an informal prose reading inventory, and on the number of successive book levels read to criterion.

Medcalf (1989) carried out another study with 10 9- to 11-year-old readers. Underachievement in reading ranged from between 0.7 and 1.7 years to between 4.3 and 4.9 years. Three readers who were slightly underachieving (between 0.7 and 2.5 years) were randomly assigned to tutor three other readers whose underachievement ranged from 2.0 to 6.3 years using Pause Prompt Praise. The four remaining readers were assigned to an individual tape-assisted reading programme. The mean gains from the six children in the Pause Prompt Praise programme (tutors and tutees) were 2.5 years on the informal prose inventory contrasted with gains of 1.4 years for children assigned to the tape-assisted programme. Among the children in the Pause Prompt Praise programme, tutors gained an average of 3.5 years, whereas tutees gained 1.6 years. Six months after the completion of the programme, the gains for children peer-tutored with Pause Prompt Praise and for children in the tape-assisted programme ranged from two to five years. The three children who had acted as Pause Prompt Praise tutors made the greatest reading gain (4.0 years). Houghton and Glynn (1993) also introduced Pause Prompt Praise tutoring to five pairs of 13-year-old readers. Both tutor and tutee children were below-average readers. Both groups made major gains in reading accuracy and comprehension.

It is interesting to speculate whether studies reporting gains for peer tutors employing Pause Prompt Praise might hold good also for parent tutors and sibling tutors. One study which offers some support for this claim is a study previously referred to (Glynn and Glynn, 1986). In this study, parallel reading gains were reported for Cambodian refugee mothers and their own children.

These mothers were invited to tutor their own children using reading books sent home from school, in the medium of their own Khmer language. However, because these Khmer-speaking women had minimal English at the time, only a modified version of Pause Prompt Praise could be attempted. Further, the then limited availability of Khmer translators precluded establishing how closely the procedures were implemented.

However, with the current revitalization of the Maori language in New Zealand, in which both Maori children and many of their parent generation concurrently are learning to read in Maori, an opportunity is available to assess the impact of Tatari Tautoko Tauawhi (Pause Prompt Praise) tutoring on the Maori language reading skills of the parent generation.

Tutor training

Given the growing evidence of the effectiveness of Pause Prompt Praise when implemented by both parent and peer tutors, attention has begun to focus on strategies for training tutors. Henderson and Glynn (1986) explored the effectiveness of feedback provided to parent tutors by trainers when the parents were learning the procedures. Four third-year College of Education students were observed as they provided feedback to parents who were tutoring their own children with Pause Prompt Praise. The study examined the type of feedback these students provided the parents, and then intervened to improve the effectiveness of that feedback. There were clear changes in trainee feedback behaviour from baseline (their 'natural' feedback style) to trained feedback conditions. In almost every instance, student trainees assumed a high level of control over the learning of parent tutors, allowing little opportunity for parents to recall or to self-correct their own tutoring behaviour. Following training, the student trainees showed a marked shift from their baseline feedback patterns. They allowed parents much more opportunity to recall and explain their own use of the procedures with individual errors. They provided parents with prompts or cues about tutoring procedures that were far less intrusive than those used as baseline. Concern over excessive dependence of some readers on over-intensive 'help' from tutors may be paralleled by concern over excessive dependence of some tutors on over-intrusive trainers.

From Pause Prompt Praise to Tatari Tautoko Tauawhi

Pause Prompt Praise has recently been reconstructed in the Maori language, and presented at a hui (formal gathering or meeting conducted according to Maori protocol) for Maori staff of the New Zealand Special Education Service. Together with people of the Ngai Te Rangi and Ngāti Ranginui groups in Tauranga, the author and Maori staff of the New Zealand Special Education Service introduced the procedures (known in Maori as Tatari Tautoko Tauawhi) to assist children who are learning to read in Maori. Tatari Tautoko Tauawhi was trialled within a tuakana–teina (peer tutoring) context. Glynn *et al.* (1993) report that tuakana (tutors) were quite successful in using the procedures in Maori. Following training with Tatari Tautoko Tauawhi they responded to four times more teina (tutee) errors, doubled their rate of pausing and doubled their use of 'read on' and 'read again' prompts. They also doubled their use of praise for prompted corrections. Although this initial study was brief, data indicated a lower error rate and a slightly higher correct rate for teina (tutee) children, in contrast with non-tutored children. The tuakana children also benefited from decreased error rates, consistent with gains reported from peer tutors using Pause Prompt Praise (Medcalf, 1989; Medcalf and Glynn, 1987; Houghton and Glynn, 1993).

Delivery of tutor training

Training in the delivery of the Pause Prompt Praise and the Tatari Tautoko Tauawhi version of the procedures is currently delivered through two separate workshop sessions. Full details of the content covered in each session are described in the bilingual *Resource Manual for Staff* (Atvars *et al.*, 1994).

The first workshop trains tutors to implement the procedures with tutees. It consists of six components:

1. A brief introduction, locating Pause Prompt Praise in the context of learning to read as a process of learning to 'make sense' of continuous text material, by drawing on whatever information is available (whether from the story context, the illustrations, the reader's prior experience, or from knowledge of letters and sounds).
2. A brief discussion of how to prepare for a successful tutoring session, including choosing a suitable time and place and selecting appropriate books (taking into account both reader interest and difficulty level).
3. A brief discussion of the different kinds of errors readers can make (omissions, insertions, substitutions which do not make sense, and substitutions which do make sense).
4. An examination of the process of reader self-correction of errors, and the importance of this as an indicator of the learning of independent reading skills.
5. An examination of all the specific tutoring behaviours involved in implementing Pause Prompt Praise.
6. Opportunities to role play both tutor and reader behaviour and to receive feedback on programme.

Throughout this training workshop, participants are shown the relevant sections of the training video, and the session ends with a series of role plays in which each participant experiences both the reader and the tutor role under supervision of a trainer.

The second workshop prepares trainers to train new Pause Prompt Praise tutors. Intending trainers must have participated in the first workshop session.

They then supply a brief audio tape of their own implementation of the procedures, which demonstrates their use of all tutoring behaviours in response to a range of reader errors. This tape is scored by a member of the National Delivery Team comprising Special Education Service staff, teachers skilled and experienced in delivering the procedures, and the present author. Following this, intending trainers are invited to plan and implement their own local tutor training workshop for a group of parents or community members. National Delivery Team members attend this workshop to assess trainers' knowledge and skill in implementing the procedures, and their conduct of the workshop from the point of view of coverage of items (1) to (6) above, and (in the case of the Maori language version of the processes), from the point of view of trainers' use of culturally appropriate activities and learning styles.

Blackstone (1979) advanced three types of argument in support of parental involvement in education. The first embodied the rights of citizenship and the rights of parents to have a say in controlling agencies and social services which affect their lives. This argument supports parent representation on school Boards of Trustees, and on ethical and research committees. Blackstone's second argument is based on the belief that parents (or their behaviour) 'must be changed so that their children's learning needs can be met more adequately'. Woods (1988) cautions of the dangers of such a pathological or deficit model. Professional input at home, following such a model, may lead to undue dependent behaviour on the part of parents. Parental roles in such a model, Woods claims, can be demeaning or insulting, and can even deskill rather then enskill parents. Furthermore, parental assertiveness in challenging professionals can be interpreted as an additional indication of pathology.

Blackstone also describes a third argument, a 'utility' argument, in which a greater extent of overlap between teacher and parent roles is desired for its own sake. The degree of overlap between parent and teacher roles in preschool education is seen as a positive model for parent–teacher partnership higher up in the education system. This model, Blackstone argues, is likely to result in increased parent–professional contact, exchange of information between settings, and an enhanced respect for the knowledge, status, and competence of each party with regard to facilitating children's learning.

There are clear arguments supporting the use of parent–teacher partnership programmes such as Pause Prompt Praise within the context of parental involvement in their children's learning. Further research studies need to be designed to capitalize on the strengths of parental input into children's literacy skills at home, and to combine those strengths with those of teacher input into children's literacy skills at school. A longer-term follow-up study of the effects of Pause Prompt Praise is currently in progress with 11- to 12-year-old Maori readers in several classrooms in an intermediate school in Mount Maunganui, NZ. Such studies need to be designed so that they can embody elements of parent–professional partnership and shared control. After seventeen years since the original study began, and more than fifteen years since the first training booklet and video, Pause Prompt Praise continues to be implemented successfully by both parent and peer tutors to assist readers who are experiencing difficulties.

References

Atvars, K. and Glynn, T. (1992) *Tatari Tautoko Tauawhi: Hei Awhina Tamariki ki te Pānui Pukapuka*. Videotape, produced by Audiovisual Section, Higher Education Development Centre, University of Otago.

Atvars, K., Berryman, M. and Glynn, T. (1994) *Tatari Tautoko Tauawhi: A Resource Manual for Staff*. Tauranga: Bay of Plenty East, Special Education Service.

Blackstone, T. (1979) Parental involvement in education. *Educational Policy Bulletin*, 7(1), 81–98.

Campbell, D.T. and Stanley, J.C. (1966) *Experimental and Quasi-experimental Designs for Research*. Chicago: Rand McNally.

Clay, M.M. (1969) Reading errors and self-correction behaviour. *British Journal of Educational Psychology*, 89, 47–56.

Clay, M.M. (1979) *Reading: The Patterning of Complex Behaviour*, 2nd edn. Auckland: Heinemann Educational Books.

Clay, M.M. (1991) *Becoming Literate: The Construction of Inner Control*. Auckland: Heinemann Educational Books.

Dick, M., Glynn, T. and Flower, D. (1992) *Pause, Prompt and Praise Reading Tutoring Procedures: Tutor Training Video*. Audiovisual Unit, Higher Education Development Centre, University of Otago.

Glynn, T. (1985) Contexts for independent learning. *Educational Psychology*, 5, 5–15.

Glynn, T. and Glynn, V. (1986) Shared reading by Cambodian mothers and children learning English as a second language: Reciprocal gains. *The Exceptional Child*, 33(3), 159–72.

Glynn, T. and McNaughton, S. (1985) The Mangere Home and School Remedial Reading Procedures: Continuing research on their effectiveness. *New Zealand Journal of Psychology*, 66–77.

Glynn, T., McNaughton, S., Robinson, V. and Quinn, M. (1979) *Remedial Reading at Home: Helping You to Help Your Child*. Wellington: New Zealand Council for Educational Research.

Glynn, T., Dick, M. and Flower, D. (1992) *Pause, Prompt and Praise Reading Tutoring Procedures: Tutor's Booklet*. Department of Education, University of Otago.

Glynn, T., Atvars, K., Fulong, M., Davies, M., Rogers, S. and Teddy, N. (1993) Tatari, Tautoko, Tauawhi: Hei Awhina Tamariki ki te Pānui Pukapuka. *Culural Justice and Ethics Symposium Report*. Wellington: New Zealand Psychological Society.

Harawira, W., Glynn, T. and Durning, C. (1993) *Tatari, Tautoko, Tauawhi: Hei Awhina Tamariki ki te Pānui Pukapuka*. Tauranga: Bay of Plenty East, Special Education Service.

Henderson, W. and Glynn, T. (1986) A feedback procedure for teacher trainees working with parent tutors of reading. *Educational Psychology*, 62, 159–77.

Hersen, M. and Barlow, D.H. (1977) *Single Case Experimental Designs: Strategies for Studying Behaviour Change*. New York: Pergamon Press.

Houghton, S. and Glynn, T. (1993) Peer tutoring of below-average secondary school readers with Pause, Prompt, Praise: Successive introduction of tutoring components. *Behaviour Change*, 10, 75–85.

Kratochwill, T.R. (ed.) (1978) *Single Subject Research: Strategies for Evaluating Change*. New York: Academic Press.

Love, J. and VanBiervliet, A. (1984) Training parents to be home reading tutors: Generalization of children's reading skills from home to school. *The Exceptional Child*, 31, 114–27.

McNaughton, S. (1981) Low-progress readers and teacher instructional behaviour during oral reading: The risk of maintaining instructional dependence. *The Exceptional Child*, 28, 167–76.

McNaughton, S. (1987) *Being Skilled: The Socializations of Learning to Read*. London: Methuen.

McNaughton, S., Glynn, T. and Robinson, V. (1981) *Parents as Remedial Reading Tutors: Issues for Home and School, Studies in Education No. 2*. Wellington: New Zealand Council for Educational Research.

McNaughton, S., Glynn, T. and Robinson, V. (1987) *Pause, Prompt and Praise: Effective Remedial Reading Tutoring*. Birmingham: Positive Products.

Medcalf, J. (1989) Comparison of peer tutored remedial reading using the Pause, Prompt and Praise procedures with an individualised tape-assisted reading programme. *Educational Psychology*, 9(3), 253–62.

Medcalf, J. and Glynn, T. (1987) Assisting teachers to implement peer-tutored remedial reading using pause, prompt and praise procedures. *Queensland Journal of Guidance and Counselling*, 1, 11–23.

O'Connor, G., Glynn, T. and Tuck, B. (1987) Contexts for remedial reading: Practice reading and pause, prompt and praise tutoring. *Educational Psychology*, 7, 207–23.

Robinson, P.W. and Foster, D.F. (1979) *Experimental Psychology: A Small-N Approach*. New York: Harper and Row.

Scott, J. and Ballard, K. (1983) Training parents and teachers in remedial reading procedures for children with learning difficulties. *Educational Psychology*, 3, 15–31.

Sidman, M. (1960) *Tactics for Scientific Research*. New York: Basic Books.

Wheldall, K. and Glynn, T. (1989) *Effective Classroom Learning*. Oxford: Basil Blackwell.

Wheldall, K. and Mettem, P. (1985) Behavioural peer tutoring: Training 16-year-old tutors to employ the 'pause, prompt and praise' method with 12-year-old remedial readers. *Educational Psychology*, 5, 27–44.

Wheldall, K., Wenban-Smith, J., Morgan, A. and Quance, B. (1992) Reading: How do teachers typically tutor? *Educational Psychology*, 12, 177–94.

Woods, S. (1988) Parents: Whose partners? In L. Barton (ed.) *The Politics of Special Education Needs*, 190–207. London: The Falmer Press.

Source

This is an edited version of a chapter previously published in S. Wolfendale and K. Topping (eds) *Family Involvement in Literacy*. 1992. Reproduced by permission of Continuum International Publishing Group Ltd.

Chapter 5

Dyslexia
Parents in need

Pat Heaton

Introduction

Public interest in dyslexia or specific learning difficulty has increased substantially over the last decade, media coverage and so forth leading to a more informed perception of the dyslexic's difficulties and needs. That children in need are a first consideration goes almost without saying, but it is important to remember that the dyslexic child does not live in a vacuum. His[1] parents and family also have needs and these needs are very real.

I believe that the needs of parents are often forgotten; the professionals involved (psychologists, teachers and so on) prioritise the child's problems and, naturally, a parent's first concern is the dyslexic himself.

Of course, dyslexia-related problems do vary tremendously, but it seems to me that the parents of language-disabled children have much in common. For example, they generally want to know how to discriminate between significant and irrelevant symptoms and also how to help with both the academic and emotional aspects of dyslexia. Very importantly – in this context – they usually want to know about the day-to-day, practical management of the syndrome. As one father put it, 'I don't doubt that the professionals know what they're doing but I want to know from someone who's lived with it. It's no joke. I need to know how to help and how to survive dyslexia.'

This chapter addresses a few children and others similarly placed. Parents' responses to a questionnaire inform the main text.

Feelings, families and dyslexia

How did you feel when you were told that your child was dyslexic?

To appreciate that relief is sometimes the first reaction to a diagnosis of dyslexia is to begin to understand the worries and fears experienced by many parents of dyslexic children. Diagnosis often comes after months or, in some cases, years of anxiety and frustration; it is therefore not so surprising that the identification or labelling of the problem sometimes comes as a relief. 'I was so relieved to know that it had a name', said one mother who recognised that she had been a victim of her own imagination.

Such responses are not uncommon. It seems that for many people not knowing is worse than knowing. Having said that, several fathers had apparently experienced very mixed feelings when investigations began – especially if they were themselves dyslexic. Similarly, every mother involved in the survey had been fearful, but determined.

> I was scared to death of what they might tell me but I knew we couldn't go on ignoring the fact that he couldn't read. Whatever they said though, *any* diagnosis had got to be better than this never-ending thinking about what had caused it.

That the pain and vulnerability of parents is very real is obvious:

> When he couldn't get going with reading I thought he had a brain tumour.

> I had been nagging for two years to try and find out what was wrong, but nobody would listen ... I was worried sick about how she'd survive in secondary ... they all promised but nobody *did* anything. The assessment was the best thing that had happened in months!

> When they told me he was clever but dyslexic, I could have cried. It was such a relief to know that it could be treated.

> My family had begun to hint that she might be mentally retarded because she was illiterate. I could never explain why I knew she wasn't so the diagnosis helped me a lot.

Many parents described early attempts to explain something they themselves didn't understand and residual bitterness is not unusual. One parent said she felt very angry when she was finally told that her son was dyslexic. 'The people who should have been helping me fobbed me off ... he should have been assessed and helped earlier ... they pretended they didn't know what I was talking about.'

Bitterness, anger and guilt were mentioned frequently when parents recalled what they felt when they discovered their child was dyslexic:

> All those years trying to bully and bribe him into reading ... I felt so guilty.

> It was a relief but I also felt very guilty as if I'd let her down. I knew she was intelligent, you see. When she forgot things I thought it was on purpose, for attention.

It's difficult enough being a parent these days but when you're told they're dyslexic, you wonder how you'll cope. You also wonder if it's your fault in some way.

I suspected that I might be dyslexic myself so I had very mixed feelings about it all, guilt I suppose. My wife's had a lot to put up with, with two of us . . . I knew what he was going through as well but, at that stage, I couldn't see how diagnosis and assessment could help. I know better now, of course. Diagnosis means he's getting the right treatment though I still feel it's my fault that we've had all these problems.

That difficulties with literacy and numeracy might also affect behaviour was a revelation to a number of parents:

What the psychologist said made a lot of sense to me. I suppose it's obvious but I didn't think of it. His ego's bound to be fragile and that's why he's so difficult to handle. When she explained all the other things about dyslexia, I began to understand what was going on better. I began to understand myself as well – from what she said, I think I'm dyslexic so I've had to do some rethinking on my own behalf . . . it's not been easy.

Post-mortems and analysis seem to be a common consequence of assessment and diagnosis:

We discussed it for hours, days, we couldn't leave it alone. It brought all sorts of things into the open, things we'd never talked about before.

Once we'd read the report, I couldn't stop thinking about it. It explained such a lot, not only about his problems with spelling but about his bad temper. And I have to admit – in the first instance – each of us blamed the other.

For some families, exchanges like this may be a necessary part of coming to terms with the disability. Having said that, many parents said that they regretted that stage, seeing it as damaging to family relationships and – most importantly – unhelpful to their child.

Then again, a positive aspect was identified:

At least the problem was well and truly aired and all the family knew about it.

We felt very much on our own at that stage but in a funny sort of way that was good . . . it made us closer . . . we both knew we had to pull together . . . nobody else was going to help . . . we had to share the responsibility.

The degree of familial support to be expected after diagnosis appears to vary considerably and the involvement of extended family and friends seems to be a mixed blessing. Apparently, a problem shared is not necessarily a problem halved!

> There are only two members of my family who know, I haven't told any of my husband's family because they would make a big issue of it.

> Family and friends tried to be helpful but they didn't really understand.

> Mixed reactions from my family, some still say she is a late developer.

> Friends tended to react as though it was some sort of contagious life-threatening disease.

Hurt feelings arising from lack of understanding are mentioned frequently though most parents seem to manage to forgive and forget the past, eventually.

By contrast, for some families the debate about 'labelling' never ends. Many parents perceived both advantages and disadvantages in labelling a child dyslexic: a number of parents pointed out that, although a particular teacher's (or in later years, employer's) response may be quite positive, this type of reaction cannot be generally assumed. (A prospective employer, for example, might well reject the dyslexic candidate in favour of what he sees as a better speculation.)

Generally speaking, parents disliked the idea of a permanent label but appreciated the advantages of assessment and diagnosis. 'Now I look back, I can see it was the beginning of the end although I don't like the labelling.' Responses like this were typical and certainly the majority of parents involved in this survey saw formal recognition as informing and precipitating the long looked-for specialist remediation.

Perhaps equally important, a positive diagnosis of dyslexia appears to promote confidence and assertiveness. Given a label, parents seemed more inclined to do their own research and to read up on the subject. 'I know what I'm talking about now. I don't much care what they call it so long as they get on and do something about it.'

Such robust attitudes are not unusual. A few parents believed that any negative consequences of labelling the child dyslexic were small compared with the advantages.

> As soon as I knew it had a name I felt better.

> We had a focus then, before that we'd wondered about everything and anything.

Generally speaking, parents felt that labelling was recognition and that one was a consequence of the other. Certainly, diagnosis and recognition had, in the first instance, been a tremendous relief to confused and worried parents.

Having said this, it is important to remember that recognition is only a step along the way, so to speak. The interactive and extensive nature of the innate disabilities causes many problems, some more obvious than others. Assessment and diagnosis merely identify the disability; they do not cure it.

How has dyslexia affected family life?

Replies to this enquiry will probably be of particular interest to parents of children very recently identified as dyslexic. Responses tended to revolve around three interrelated themes. Some parents compared attitudes and behaviour before and after diagnosis/tuition whereas others described some practical problems associated with dyslexia. All parents mentioned the cost and/or other consequences of specialist remediation.

> I know we're very lucky, we're not paying for the teaching but it still costs, in other ways. We have to remind her about doing her 'special homework' and I think sometimes that the other two must get fed up of all this fuss about dyslexia but I don't see how you can avoid it.

> Private tuition has put a strain on finances which would otherwise have been used for holidays/pleasure. Having said that, it's been worth every penny.

> We have to keep Saturday morning free for her to have private tuition; if there had been more real help in school and they recognised the problem, it would have saved our family budget about £14 per week.

> It's sometimes a strain to keep up with the extra tuition both from the financial and the supervisory point of view. Homework can be a real battle. My wife and I both work full-time and homework can be the last straw. Basically, the dyslexia takes time, energy and money we can't really afford. On the other hand, I can really see a difference in him.

Not surprisingly, most parents were unhappy about having to pay for private tuition; the majority of parents interviewed here were also unhappy with their particular local education authority.

> We are very disappointed in the local education system. If you want anything special, you have to fight very hard and wait a long time to get anything done. Fighting for recognition and tuition caused a lot of stress . . . I was forever having to take time off to go to school for meetings and one thing and another. The specialist tuition should be more freely available.

> I don't really believe in private education but what else can you do? We were getting desperate. He had absolutely no confidence in himself, he

was so desperate to please, it was pitiful. It got to the stage where his dyslexia was affecting everything. We were becoming an 'at risk' family.

That many dyslexics feel diminished by poor literacy skills is not surprising. Reading and spelling are usually central to success in the education system; if a pupil cannot keep up with his peers in this respect, he will probably have a poor self concept. That this is not unusual is shown by the following extracts from questionnaire responses:

Before diagnosis and/or tuition

Very quiet with all members of the family. When we used to visit my sister he would just sit there, quiet and nervous until we went home. I used to make excuses for him ... I feel awful now when I think what I put him through, but I didn't see a connection between his poor school work and his shyness.

He was shy even with relatives and close friends. He found conversation really difficult. I was forever trying to bring him into the conversation but when I managed it, half the time I'd wish I hadn't; he'd say something that made sense only to me.

She was so inhibited and seemed to cry at nothing: that's not a bit like our family. She seemed to get swamped by it all, she hated the Sunday tea-party at my mother's. I couldn't understand it.

After diagnosis and/or tuition

He's much friendlier when visiting. I suppose he's more confident, he's up and down playing with different things. He's more talkative, wants to know what's what. He actually sings to himself, I can't tell you how marvellous it is to hear it. I honestly think we're a happier family now that we know what it is we are dealing with.

He now enjoys the company of the family and close friends. He likes to show them the work he has done with his specialist tutor and the models he makes. It is obvious that he is much more confident.

I can't quite explain it. She's sort of much more light-hearted; before we knew what the problem was, life was so very serious. Now I think about it, it must have seemed very confusing. Now that she's happier we're all happier. If she's had a bad day – been put down a lot – we all have a 'scratchy' evening.

Most families have problems at one time or another and dyslexia is an added complication. On occasions, dealing with dyslexia seems to stretch resources (finances, energy and so on) to the limit. In this situation, even the most patient parent feels under pressure:

> It drives me crazy at times. I've got three dyslexics to deal with: my husband and both children are dyslexic ... I'm the only one with a memory ... well that's how it feels. Quite seriously, one way and another dyslexia has put our marriage and family life under a lot of stress. I know there are worse things and other mothers tell me it'll all be worth it but can you imagine how shattered I am when they've all gone out in the morning? They all have to be reminded about what they need that day ... and then I've to go to work.

That occasional irritation is an inevitable consequence of daily dealings with dyslexia was confirmed by every participating parent:

> Getting organised in a morning can be a nightmare. I know all about colour-coding the calendar so that a green Tuesday means he has to take his green swimming trunks but there's a lot more to it than that. I think that he honestly does try but he forgets where things are and sometimes the patience just runs out.

> If we're running late it's a disaster ... everything goes from bad to worse. He always ties his shoelaces in a funny way but if we're late it gets even more convoluted. Even the language goes, under pressure ... I have to try to seem calm or he'll never be able to find the name of what it is he's to take ... I'll have to guess what 'a thingy' is!

> It was ages before I could delegate anything; I couldn't send him to the shop because he'd come back with the wrong things; I couldn't ask him to phone my mother for me because he'd ring the wrong number or give her the wrong message. Of course, when he began to take some responsibility it seemed marvellous ... I never take it for granted.

> Dyslexia's limited her independence. At 14, she ought to be able to go into town on her own but she's nervous about it. I understand it but I sometimes run out of patience ... it doesn't help that we live between B— and D— and that the numbers on the front of the buses are very similar. She once got on the wrong bus and had to walk home ... you can imagine the effect of that!

Responses like this give some idea of the ways in which family life is affected by what has been called 'a hidden handicap'. The description appears to be very appropriate; the problems are real but they are not always tangible and this can be frustrating. As one father said:

If you could see something everybody would be more helpful. He *is* profoundly disabled but it isn't obvious. Having a poor memory, for example, *is* disabling in all sorts of different ways – practical and educational. I get sick and tired of trying to explain, of having to fight every step of the way. And I have to admit, I forget myself. I think I'd have more patience if I could *see* something. It would be a reminder of what it's like for him.

The whole that is dyslexia is clearly far more than the sum of its parts. Although parents recognised the positive side of diagnosis and tuition, they also felt that dealing with dyslexia had not improved the quality of family life; many potentially irritating aspects of the disability were believed to be exacerbated by the stresses and strains of modern living. A number of parents felt that their tolerance, energy and drive fell short of what was required and all said that they had felt guilty about this at one time or another.

Two fathers who are themselves dyslexic expressed a very particular sort of guilt:

On top of our son's problems, my wife has to help me. I'm self-employed *and* dyslexic. My wife has to help me with the books, with letters and quotes, with spelling . . . with almost everything except the practical side of the business. I don't know that dyslexia's done either of us any good. If I'm honest, I think we've both resented my dependence at times but without her the family just wouldn't function – at any level.

I know my wife takes more responsibility than she should have to. She sorts out all the family's organisational problems. When it comes down to it, I'm not much better than my son . . . I do try to teach him the few strategies I've learnt myself, but there never seems to be enough time.

Perhaps every parent of a disabled/handicapped child experiences this at some time; to balance professional, domestic and other commitments is in itself no small task and any complication increases the pressure on both the individual and the family. Any 'handicap' in a member of the family creates additional problems.

Furthermore, expectations affect behaviour; the expectations of parents, siblings and so on tend to be based on norms and some families find accommodating abnormal behaviour harder than others. Coping with dyslexia is – in this respect – little different from dealing with other handicaps and each handicap has its own characteristics. However, these characteristics are often fairly obvious and that is perhaps a key issue here. The dyslexic's weaknesses are *not* immediately obvious or classifiable. Furthermore, his way of dealing with the demands of home and school may be particularly idiosyncratic and/or irritating; he is coping with many interacting disabilities That dyslexia substantially affects family life in many different ways is obvious. Maybe the dyslexic's family too should be recognised as disabled and disadvantaged.

Help and advice: method and management

What advice would you give to the parents of a child whose dyslexic condition has only recently been identified?

Clearly, it is impossible to offer advice to suit every age, stage and circumstance but many parents drew general conclusions from their personal experiences. Both awareness and organisation were seen as central to the successful management of dyslexia. Managing paperwork and procedures, awareness and development, dealing with teaching and emotions were the main themes here.

First then, regarding the paperwork involved in making the case for recognition, assessment and (perhaps) statementing,[2] all parents were unprepared for its volume and complexity.

> What I would say is, create a system or it'll drive you crazy. I was always losing things and that just adds to the pressure. It caused rows in our house.

> Make a filing system: photocopy everything and keep a diary. Don't rely on your memory; this is probably going to go on a long time and you're bound to forget the one thing you need. Remember, you're dealing with professionals and they probably have their own filing clerk – and filing system – for a very good reason!

> Be prepared to spend time and energy on letter writing, filling in forms and that sort of thing. You'll be amazed by how much there is and you'll not see the point of a lot of it. That's one of the reasons I got so frustrated but I do know now that I'd have coped better if I'd allowed more time . . . it's a job in itself . . . you can't just tuck it in somewhere between washing up and cleaning up. Sometimes it took me a whole morning to get a set of papers together.

The advantages of being proactive were mentioned by several parents, many of whom had made contacts at both local and national level:

> Join the local dyslexia organisation or mothers' support group. That way you'll get both support and information . . . my local group helped and encouraged me such a lot . . . the thing is, you're benefiting from the experience of those who've been there. Without help, I'd never have got to grips with the statementing procedure. [See note 2.]

> Getting myself on the governors really paid off and getting elected is not as hard as you might think. Once you're on you're right at the centre of it. You know what they're supposed to be doing.

Find out about training courses. Some institutions will take you on even if you're not a teacher. It really is worth the effort and the money. I did an awareness course at my local college. If yours doesn't have one, ask if they'll consider it. I learned such a lot in a short time . . . about the teaching, about why he acts as he does . . . it was really helpful.

Start networking. Write off to any organisation that has any connection with dyslexia. Once you're on their mailing list you'll get all the latest information. You don't have to buy services and products but you can pick up a lot of incidental and free information from advertising packs.

I did the Open University unit on Specific Learning Difficulty/Dyslexia and I've never looked back. It's given me so much confidence in so many different ways. I know I'm much better informed than I was . . . I suppose that's why I'm so assertive about his and my rights these days.

Advice about teaching, homework and education in general also featured prominently in parents' replies:

Get some teaching organised. Go privately if you have to – talk to your local association – we had a private tutor at first because the LEA took so long. It was money well spent. She made terrific progress. Also, it meant we knew what we were looking for when we were offered help in school.

Many parents had learned that the appropriateness of methods and remediation should not be assumed. 'Find out about the first principles of teaching dyslexics. I took everything for granted and, of course, he didn't make much progress; we had spent six months doing more of the same – but slower!'

That multisensory methods and structured phonic language programmes are best for dyslexics is well established, but the terminology had initially defeated at least two of the mothers involved in this survey:

Find out what it means. It's not that difficult once you get down to it. Basically, it's lots of repetition and lots of different ways of doing the same thing. Ask the teacher if you can sit in; I found that really helpful and it means I'm better at helping with the homework.

If you find out what it's all about you'll know what to look for. You want a fully qualified specialist who really understands everything about dyslexia. He had a 'baby sitter' until I realised what was going on . . . Keep an eye on the homework, you'll learn a lot about all sorts of things.

A number of parents had an eye to the future:

Make sure that every teacher knows he's dyslexic. It can make all the difference when it comes to streaming and setting. If you're like me you'll find that you have to go into school several times before you're satisfied. I don't know how it happens but at every parents' evening I used to find at least one teacher who was totally unaware of his problems. (See Dealing with the practicalities, pp. 82–7.)

As soon as he's in secondary, start thinking about exams, what concessions might be available, what resources he might need. You need to know what the options are, whether it's to do with exams, training courses or further and higher education. You might even think he should be registered as disabled. The point is, you'd be well advised to start thinking early because everything takes so long. It can be very frustrating.

That the dyslexic himself is often frustrated and emotional is hardly surprising given the largely literacy-based school environment. Strenuous effort may not be rewarded and emotional outbursts are common. Families recognised this and suggested different ways of coping with the many causes and effects of frustration.

Try not to take over-reactions to heart. The frustration has to come out somewhere and home's the best place. If he's going to stab the paper with his pen, he's better doing it at the kitchen table.

Try and get him to talk about it; bottling it up is not a good idea. I can remember J— getting beside himself about really trivial things and finding out later that something had happened at school.

I've always encouraged other kids in the class to come round. It's good for all sorts of reasons, not least because you get a better idea of what's going on, a better perspective. Don't *ever* spring into action on the strength of your child's report of an incident/grievance. Talk first and always remember that there are children with worse – but – different problems.

Compensating for language-based failures was a priority for several parents:

You must re-build their confidence. We had to find something that she did really well and even better than other children her age. It wasn't easy but we encouraged her to try anything she fancied and eventually we found that she excelled in things like art. We bought her books, took her to some exhibitions, even arranged for a few lessons on perspective. We never thought she was going to be another Picasso but it helped boost her ego.

Make a positive effort to find time to listen, even if it means a bit of reorganisation. Listening's a priority and you shouldn't insult him by half-listening while you're doing something else. He gets enough insults – one way and another – at school.

Even when you're tired yourself you *must* support and encourage. You might have had a bad day but think what they've had to put up with. If you think about it, while they're in school they're failing almost all the time and there's no prospect of escape from either the failure or the environment. Imagine how desperate you'd feel if your job were like that.

Managing the emotional turmoils of a dyslexic and a family as well is not easy and an ongoing battle about provision does not help matters. It is easy to see why dyslexia could become a full-time preoccupation. Two parents had learned from bitter experience:

Don't get obsessive about it – I did and it's a mistake. It's better for all concerned if you don't get too emotional about it. If you're really desperate about some hurt or injustice, write it down and look at it again after a week!

The best advice I ever had was to forget about revenge. For some reason I felt a need to get my own back and I've realised that's not uncommon. Don't waste your own or the family's time and energy. Just get on with it. Coping with it is the best revenge.

Advice on coping with, organising and managing different aspects of dyslexia has been the focus of this chapter which collates parents' responses to the question at the beginning of this section. It is hoped that parents newly coming to terms with their child's innate difficulties will benefit from the experiences of those involved in the initiative.

Dealing with the practicalities: strategies/resources/ tactics

Thinking of the practical, day-to-day management of dyslexia, which strategies/resources/tactics have proved useful and why

This section describes various tried, tested and practical ways of dealing with dyslexia and its associated manifestations: poor organisation, limited recall, difficulties with time/space and so forth. Parents' ingenuity and initiatives were impressive but one of the simplest strategies is possibly amongst the most important:

Immediately after she'd seen the psychologist, I drafted a brief letter which began, 'Dear Teacher'. I then photocopied it many times and every September I send a personally addressed copy to all the teachers involved in her education. I also send one to any new member of the school staff or if subject tutors change.

I did this because other parents had told me about break-downs in communication. Apparently it's not unusual for parents to go to Open Evening and discover that some staff are unaware of the problem. If you do it my way it puts people in the picture. It also makes everyone concerned accountable.

Draft letter

Dear Teacher,

You may have been told that my son P__ is disabled by specific learning difficulties/dyslexia and I am now writing to confirm this.

Kindly contact either my husband or myself if there are any problems arising.

Yours sincerely,

That liaising with school is usually worthwhile goes almost without saying; parents have to sort out many school-related practicalities. Several useful ideas emerged:

Schools tend to use a standard book for written work and he was forever getting them and his papers mixed up. In desperation, I bought a different coloured file for each subject. I cut a tiny strip off each one and then stuck strips on the appropriate books and folders.

It saves time when he's packing his bag and he no longer turns up to, say, geography with a writing book full of history homework.

The contentiousness of homework was mentioned frequently and several parents said that compromise had proved the most successful strategy:

Agree on the time to be spent and set an alarm. Don't cheat by trying to coax him to do more. When the alarm goes off he should be allowed to stop immediately.

I've found that this works reasonably well and we're not always at each other's throat. In any case, I'm not sure about the value of work done under threat of punishment.

One mother reported a more positive attitude to homework when it was done first thing in the morning:

It's a pain but we both get up 45 minutes early. I can always find something to do and I'm on hand if he needs help . . . The house is quiet, we're both fresh and – if it's for a test that day – he's more likely to remember.

A poor memory is typical of the dyslexic and most parents had found that easily available aids helped with maths and number work:

Buy a pencil box with the times tables printed on the lid. It might seem like cheating but I don't think so. He can't help forgetting which number he's just said . . . I know he's good at maths and he estimates well so why shouldn't he take the drudgery out of calculation?

Get him a calculator and show him how to get the best out of it. It's a useful thing to know in any case and it will save a lot of grief.

One parent, on the other hand, had persevered with a times table tape[3] and found it useful. 'I kept it in the car so it was no trouble really. I just switched it on automatically . . . I suppose it was the constant repetition that did it.'

Tape-recorders can also be used for reminders/reinforcement and were recommended by a number of parents:

Get into the habit of leaving his messages on tape; he can play it back as many times as he needs to. You need to think about what you're going to say, of course. Organise instructions according to an 'Order of mention'.

I tape any comprehension passages he has to read. He finds the playback and repetition helpful. He can read at that level but it's slow and painful and we think there are better uses for his energies.

Post-it notes were also recommended, a particularly strategy being explained by a foster parent who participated in the survey:

We bought lots of pads of different coloured Post-it notes and each child picked a colour. We stick them on the inside of the front door. It's become a routine: first job every morning is to check if there's a message for you – it can be a reminder about taking something to school or just anything. It's obviously better if the child's a reasonable reader but it's amazing what can be done with pictures and diagrams once you get the hang of it.

Another small aid which features in almost every answer was the Franklin Spellmaster. In addition to the fun of playing its word games, it is said to be useful for – amongst other things – spelling and dictionary work.

More expensive items were also said to have been a good investment:

The computer is the best thing we ever bought but you need to make sure you get the right one. We were interested in the word-processing facility and spellchecker but nearly got talked into a much fancier package. The first chap we saw tried to sell us something that had all sorts of options but we were never going to use them. I believe that the visual/spatial dimension of the keyboard and screen helps dyslexics.

What we've got works for us because his handwriting and spelling are poor and the word-processing package has improved presentation. It's also given him a lot more confidence and – because it slows him down – we feel the spelling has got better.

Lap-top computers also featured in more than half the answers to this question, the following response being fairly representative:

> We bought an Amstrad Notepad Computer and it's just about right for us. We bought it mainly for the spellchecker but the whole family gets some use out of the Address Book and Alarm. You do need access to a printer but school's been very good about that.

That dyslexics generally have difficulty with time/space/direction is well known and several practical tips were forthcoming:

> We bought him a Timex watch. The 'past' half's in red and the 'to' half in blue; that was a real help when he was learning to tell the time.

> A watch with Arabic (rather than Roman) numbers, clear dates and an alarm has been worth its weight in gold. Apart from the obvious practical aspects, the alarm has 'saved his bacon' and preserved our sanity on numerous occasions; if he has to be in by a certain time I make sure he sets the alarm and then we all know what time he's expected home. It works well.

> Get him a year planner and help him mark off important dates, birthdays, that sort of thing. We talked about the seasons and the weather as we did it the first time and I believe that was the beginning of understanding so far as time was concerned.

This mother also described how she had started to teach orientation:

> I gave him a strategy for left and right and kept checking that he remembered. I told him that his watch would *always, always* go on his left hand and I still check regularly, even when he's not wearing it.
> I suppose that's the best strategy I've found. Once he's learned something, KEEP CHECKING AND REMINDING. They forget so easily and if they don't remember it, you may as well not have bothered in the first place. They do remember if you practise enough. I know that's how it works for spelling and it seems to work for practical things as well.

Given the dyslexic's inherent difficulties, poor practical organisation skills are almost inevitable. All families said that domestic organisation was a problem but, again, some initiatives were reported to work well. Two mothers mentioned clothes and dressing:

When it comes to footwear I avoid anything with laces; those high modern boots with lots of laceholes are a disaster waiting to happen. If he had those, he'd either get the laces in the wrong holes (and we'd have tears) or he'd just give up and trip up. He's learned to like anything that fastens with Velcro and whenever possible, flip-flops. I also avoid anything double-breasted and try to buy sweaters which have a very obvious front and back – a patterned front and plain back is good.

Don't just tell him how to organise his clothes, show him. Help him set them out, in the same order, five or six times at least. If there are variations for Winter/Summer, talk about the changes and decide what the new order should be. Then rehearse it so that he puts everything on as it should be. Before I'd come to this strategy, we'd had vests on top of pullovers and all sorts of strange combinations.

Untidiness is a mundane – but important – fact of the dyslexic's domestic life. It appears to be a general and on-going problem, though a few successes were reported:

My best tactic has been to insist that everything belonging to him goes home to his bedroom every night. It was hard to insist on that at first but I persisted and it's been worth it. I'm happy with the rest of the house and his room is his responsibility. If he wants it cleaned and dusted *he* has to clear all surfaces. Agreeing to this has meant a lot less rows in our house.

Get hold of a few big jars, the largest size pickled onion jars are best. Use them to store those bits and pieces you find all over the house. It works because you can see what's in and no one can be accused of disposing of vital treasure!

Not least mentioned were the resources provided and/or recommended by the British Dyslexia Association. The following replies were typical:

The BDA's got a leaflet for everything, young children through to adult dyslexics. We found the one advising about examination concessions really useful.

The 20p I spent on the one called *Dyslexia and the Young Child* was one of the best investments I ever made. Apart from anything else, it gave me the confidence to go into school. I had something, written by an expert, which described the signs no one else had noticed. Something in writing made all the difference to my confidence and determination.

I like the *Guidelines for Parents* best. I don't get involved with the teaching but we do play the recommended games, often in the car. It's surprising how much you can do to help once someone's given you the ideas and the reason for doing something. I've sent for a few leaflets over the years.

A relatively new resource was mentioned by a number of parents. The coloured filters discussed in the *Optometric Quarterly*[4] apparently help some children. 'He definitely reads better when he uses it. He's more fluent and *he* says it stops the print wobbling. I was sceptical myself at first but it does seem to help.'

That there exists some overlap between dyslexia and what is called Scotopic Sensitivity Syndrome appears to be agreed. Even more firmly established though is the popularity of *Alpha to Omega*[5] Hornsby and Shear, a language programme designed specifically for dyslexics. Almost every parent in this survey was familiar with Hornsby's phonetic, linguistic approach to the teaching of reading, writing, speech and spelling.

When the teacher first sent it home I couldn't make head nor tail of it; it just didn't make any sense but I kept looking at it and reading bits and eventually I saw what it was driving at. Once you get the basic idea, you realise how sensible – and simple – it is.

It's changed the way I think about spelling and I know I'm more help to her now. I don't do the teaching, as such, but I support more effectively. I know to group words in families and I invent things for different words. We all use the 'Alpha' trick for spelling NECESSARY.

Finally, and on a rather lighter note, one father said that the Roald Dahl books had been – and were – his favourite resource. He explained his choice:

He actually laughed out loud when I read them to him and because he enjoyed them he was determined to learn to read. I don't know whether that's what you'd call useful but that's what it's all about as far as I can see.

It would be difficult to quarrel with either these sentiments or any of the many recommendations reported earlier in this section. That the parents involved in the survey have probably spent a more than average amount of time, energy and capital on resources and initiatives is clear. Equally obvious – but rarely expressed – was their satisfaction in having found ways of managing this complex and frustrating syndrome.

Questions and responses: conclusions

That families involved in both the survey and its piloting were generous with their time, energy and interest must be plain. Hopefully, their experiences will help other parents, especially those newly coming to terms with the syndrome commonly known as dyslexia.

Presumably, at the very least, some parents will begin to realise that their situation is not unique and also that their perceptions and intuitions are probably sound. They will almost certainly recognise not only the signs and symptoms described but also many of the fears and frustrations.

It appears that dyslexia can cause both stress and distress for all concerned. Nevertheless, it seems that the syndrome can be managed reasonably well and that there are tried and tested solutions to many of the associated problems. Indeed, most of the participating families appeared to have come to terms with this relatively rare and often misunderstood disability.

Moving on to the mechanics of the enterprise – the questions and commentary – it is impossible to say whether the questions were the right ones or whether the best use was made of responses. All I can say is that I have tried to exclude irrelevancies and to intrude on parents' responses only where appropriate. Finally, and as mentioned earlier, although this was never intended to be a reference or research text it is an honest attempt to describe and explain the reality of dealing with dyslexia.

Notes

1   For he/his, read she/her if appropriate.
2   Statementing procedures deal with formal recognition/provision by the Local Education Authority.
3   *Tables. Disco.* Webucational, Wimborne, Dorset. *Multiplication Tables.* Cadence Cassettes, Totton, Southampton.
4   *Optometric Quarterly*, XIII, 95, British College of Optometrists.
5   Hornsby, B. and Shear, F., *Alpha to Omega*, Heinemann.

Source

This is an edited version of a chapter previously published in *Dyslexia: Parents in Need.* 1996. Reproduced by permission of Whurr Publishers Ltd.

Chapter 6

Rhetoric and research in family literacy

Peter Hannon

The term 'family literacy' now figures prominently in the discourses of early childhood education, literacy and adult education in several English-speaking countries. It can refer to a focus for research or to a kind of educational programme. This article distinguishes family literacy programmes which combine adult basic education for parents with early literacy education and parental involvement from other kinds of family literacy programmes and terms the former 'restricted' programmes. The rhetoric concerning restricted programmes, and relevant research, is examined in relation to five issues: the usage of the term 'family literacy'; the targeting of restricted programmes for selected families; the accessibility and take-up of such programmes; their educational effects; and their socio-economic effects. Drawing on evidence from Britain and the USA, it is argued that, although rhetoric has sometimes been informed by research, it has also obscured, misinterpreted, ignored and exaggerated research findings. Some implications for policy, practice and research are identified.

In this article I wish to draw attention to some strands of the rhetoric of family literacy. By 'rhetoric' is meant discourse largely 'calculated to persuade or influence others' (the 'others' here being policy-makers, educators, and citizens with some interest in education). Examining the rhetoric of family literacy means examining explicit and implicit claims for certain programmes. I also wish to explore how those claims relate to educational research and hope to show that, although rhetoric has sometimes been informed by research, it has also obscured, misinterpreted, ignored and exaggerated research findings. Although many studies will be described or quoted, the purpose of this article is not to provide a review of the field but to show through examples that there is a rhetoric and to seek research evidence for claims made within that rhetoric.

The focus is on what will be termed 'restricted' programmes in family literacy. To explain what is meant by this it is necessary to review the use of the term 'family literacy'. Ten years ago it was not much used or known in education. It had some currency within a relatively small circle of literacy researchers who were interested in young children's literacy development before school and out of school. Taylor (1983) in the USA had coined the term to refer to the interplay of literacy activities of children, parents and others which she found in six families studied over periods ranging from months to years. She concluded that 'literacy is a part of the very fabric of family life' (p. 87). There were other studies around the same time (e.g. Heath, 1983; Teale, 1986) which took a similar sociocultural approach to understanding literacy development in communities and families, although they did not use the term 'family literacy'.

Later in the 1980s in the USA, 'family literacy' acquired a different meaning, referring not to a *research focus* but instead to *educational programmes*. This meaning subsequently reached Britain and other English-speaking countries. Two main concepts of family literacy programmes can be distinguished from that period.

The first, broad concept of family literacy programmes included any approach which explicitly addressed the family dimension in literacy learning, e.g. parental involvement in schools, pre-school interventions, parenting education, family use of libraries, community development, and extensions of adult literacy education to include children (McIvor, 1990; Nickse, 1990b). In terms suggested by Nickse (1990b), some of these programmes focused directly on children and only indirectly, if at all, on parents as literacy learners. Others focused on parents and only indirectly on children. What they all had in common, however, was a recognition that individual literacy learners were members of families, and that families affected, and were affected by, the individuals' learning. When the focus was on children this usually meant parental involvement in children's learning.

This broad concept has been reflected in publications from the International Reading Association, detailing schemes across the USA in the early 1990s (Morrow, 1995; Morrow et al., 1995). Wolfendale and Topping (1996) adopted a similar perspective in their compilation and review of developments in Britain, Australia and New Zealand. In this sense family literacy programmes have been around for two or more decades but the new descriptor 'family literacy' is more inclusive and useful than, say, 'parental involvement', which tends to convey the idea that parents are the only members of a family worth involving in children's literacy development. 'Family literacy' can also convey the idea that there is pre-existing literacy activity in families, that older family members may be engaging children in those activities (and vice versa), and that in practice most programmes often do not deal with isolated individuals but with members of a family.

The second concept of family literacy programmes referred to programmes which combined direct adult basic education for parents with direct early childhood education for children, i.e. where there was a dual, simultaneous focus on two generations. Often these programmes also sought to change how parents interacted with their children and supported their literacy development. A prime example was the 'Kenan model', promoted with great vigour by the National Center for Family Literacy (NCFL), established for that purpose in Louisville, Kentucky (Perkins and Mendel, 1989). Thus, Sharon Darling, president and founder of the NCFL, defined family literacy in these terms:

> At NCFL we prefer to define family literacy as a holistic, family-focused approach, targeting at-risk parents and children with intensive, frequent, and long-term educational and other services. Total family literacy programs include four components which are integrated to form a unique, comprehensive approach to serving families: (1) basic skill instruction for parents or caregivers, (2) preschool or literacy education for young children, (3) regular parent and child interaction, and (4) parent education/ support activities.
>
> (Darling, 1993a, p. 3)

This concept of a 'family literacy' programme (developed by others as well as the NCFL) was basically new. Several years later there is still no commonly accepted term by which it can be distinguished from the 'broad' concept of family literacy programme described earlier. Not being able to draw this distinction makes for difficulties in discussing family literacy programmes because it may not be clear which kind of programme is being referred to, and what is said about one kind may not apply to the other. It is at this point that issues of rhetoric arise, for the choice of term can itself be an act of persuasion. Darling, in the quotation cited earlier, used the word 'total', which implies that other kinds of programme are 'partial' – something less than the real thing. It is not easy to find a term which is neutral and accurate ('combined', for example, will not do because most family literacy programmes combine different components). For the purposes of this article I choose to use the term 'restricted'. This might be regarded as having somewhat negative connotations but that may be no bad thing if it offers an alternative rhetoric to that to be described later. 'Restricted' is an accurate term because the programmes concerned are restricted to families who participate in *all* components and because the programmes constitute a restricted subset of family literacy programmes in general. It is not suggested here that the family literacy addressed in such programmes is restricted (it may or may not be) but that the programmes are restricted in the sense of setting very specific entry requirements for families. The rhetoric to be discussed in this article relates mainly to restricted programmes.

Most of the rhetoric associated with restricted programmes is found in the USA but echoes of it can be detected in other countries, including Britain where, in 1993, the government-funded Adult Literacy and Basic Skills Unit (ALBSU, since renamed the Basic Skills Agency, BSA) launched a family literacy initiative which promoted restricted programmes. Demonstration programmes funded in this initiative had to provide '1. accredited basic skills instruction for parents; 2. early literacy development for young children; 3. joint parent/child sessions on supporting pre-reading, early reading and reading skills' (ALBSU, 1993a, p. 4). The similarity of the ALBSU concept to that of the NCFL, quoted earlier, was later acknowledged.

> In developing this model we looked at the development of family literacy in the United States and tried to learn from the best of what was going on in the US as well as avoid less effective practices.
>
> (BSA, 1996, p. 3)

From the start, family literacy programmes, particularly restricted ones, had an uneasy relationship with family literacy research. Programmes and research studies both acknowledged the importance of the family as a site for literacy activities and literacy learning but, as Auerbach (1989) pointed out, the assumptions underpinning programmes were often at odds with research findings. For example, according to family literacy research, very few, if any, families could be said totally to lack literacy or concern for children's development and education yet some programmes appeared to be premised on such beliefs. Auerbach noted 'a gap between research and implementation: existing models for family literacy programs seemed not to be informed by ethnographic research' (Auerbach, 1989, p. 167).

Throughout the 1990s, the term 'family literacy' became steadily more familiar to policy-makers and practitioners on both sides of the Atlantic in discourse about literacy education, standards of literacy, and teaching methods. In part this was due to government funding of restricted programmes (in the USA, the Federal 'Even Start' programme; in England and Wales, the ALBSU/BSA Family Literacy Initiative). In part it reflected the development of broader forms of practice at local level (Hannon, 1995; Morrow, 1995; Wolfendale and Topping, 1996). There may also have been deeper cultural currents in this period – relating to anxieties about national literacy levels and the position of families in society – which made programmes labelled 'family literacy' particularly attractive to policy-makers and funders. Whatever the reasons, the result is that 'family literacy' has figured prominently in educational discourse, for example, in special issues of journals (*Language Arts*, 1993; *Journal of Reading*, 1995; *RaPAL Bulletin*, 1994; *Reading*, 1995; *Reading and Writing Quarterly*, 1995; *Australian Journal of Language and Literacy*, 1994; *The Reading Teacher*, 1995; *Viewpoints*, 1993), in special conferences, in numerous references in broadcast and print media, and in government documents such as the National Literacy Act (PL 102–73) 1991 in the USA or the Education White Paper for England, *Excellence in Schools* (Department for Education and Employment [DfEE], 1997).

There have been many criticisms concerning the alleged 'deficit view' of families implicit in some family literacy rhetoric (a collection of such criticisms, and alternative conceptions of families' literacies, has been assembled by Taylor [1997]). In this regard Auerbach (1997) and Grant (1997) have examined specific claims and myths in family literacy in the USA and Australia. There is no need to go over the same ground in this article. Instead, other features of family literacy rhetoric which are no less important but which have not received equal attention will be examined. The examination relates to two countries, the USA and Britain, and focuses on five areas: (1) usage of the term 'family literacy'; (2) targeting of programmes for selected families; (3) accessibility and take-up of programmes; (4) educational effects; and (5) socio-economic effects. In respect of rhetoric in each area, one can ask, 'How does this relate to research?' The article concludes with a discussion of what research is needed to develop practice and policy in this field.

Usage of the term 'family literacy'

Earlier, a distinction was made between 'family literacy' as a term which referred to a research focus and as a term which referred to certain forms of educational programmes. The former meaning came first historically but has now been almost entirely obliterated by the latter. For example, notice in the earlier quotation, from Darling, that she says, 'we prefer to define family literacy as a holistic, family focused approach, targeting at-risk parents and children'. 'Family literacy' is now commonly used to refer only to programmes – as shorthand for 'family literacy programme'. Sometimes it is only restricted programmes that are referred to as if there were no other kind. Such are the resonances of the words 'family' and 'literacy' at the present time that it is a great rhetorical advantage for politicians and advocates of certain kinds of programmes to be able to refer to them simply as 'family literacy'. The rightness and merit of such programmes for funding seems irresistible.

This has two consequences. First, the vocabulary of educational research is weakened by the loss of a term which defined a valuable line of research thus rendered less visible. It should be noted, however, that such research has continued. In the USA, following the work by Taylor, Heath and Teale mentioned earlier, there have, for example, been studies of families' literacies by Taylor and Dorsey-Gaines (1988), Baker et al. (1994), Purcell-Gates (1995) and Voss (1996). In Britain, Weinberger (1996), Gregory (1996), and Barton and Hamilton (1998) have illuminated aspects of family literacy in different communities. This line of research has become obscured by discourse in which family literacy research means research into family literacy programmes.

A second consequence is that, as this line of family literacy research is obscured, it becomes more difficult for practitioners and policy-makers to draw on it to develop family literacy programmes. If 'family literacy' always refers to programmes it is harder to conceive of it as something which could occur independently of programmes. The situation lamented by Auerbach (1989) is in danger of getting worse. Auerbach (1995) has gone on to suggest that there is a continuum of programmes from those which ignore pre-existing family literacy to those which see the social context as a rich resource that can inform rather than impede learning. The former, she argues, are inevitably prescriptive and interventionist; the latter can be participatory and empowering. It does seem likely that programme developers who remain ignorant of existing patterns of family literacy will work at one end of the continuum without being fully aware of possibilities at the other end. The rhetorical restriction of the term 'family literacy' just to programmes devalues research which could inform those programmes.

Targeting of programmes for selected families

Crucial to the rhetoric of restricted programmes is the claim that there is a significant number of families in which parents have literacy difficulties and in which children also have (or will later have) low literacy achievement. That is the justification for restricting programmes to families willing to address both parental and child literacy simultaneously. Although it is undoubtedly the case that there are families in which parents have literacy difficulties and that there are families in which children have low literacy achievement, it is necessary to ask how many of each kind there are, and to what extent they are the *same* families. There is likely to be some overlap between the two kinds of family but it is often implied that they coincide completely and constitute a large number which ought to be selected as the target of family literacy programmes.

The rhetoric asserts (a) that parents with literacy difficulties will have low achieving children, and (b) that low achieving children have parents with literacy difficulties. Obviously, (a) and (b) are logically distinct propositions but they are often taken together as if each entailed the other. It is claimed that children can be identified as at risk of literacy underachievement on the basis of parental literacy difficulties. The parents' literacy, or lack of it, is put forward as a *cause* of the children's difficulties. The literature on family literacy abounds with references to a 'cycle of underachievement' which can be broken by targeting parents' and children's literacy at the same time in the same programme.

Examples of this rhetoric from the USA are provided by Darling (1993b) and Nickse (1990a).

> Family literacy programs recognise that these two groups – undereducated adults and educationally 'at risk children' interlock; they are bound so tightly together that excellence in public school education is an empty dream for youths who go home each afternoon to families where literacy is neither practised or valued.
>
> (Darling, 1993b, p. 2)

> The goal of family literacy programs is to enhance the lives of both parent and child: to improve skills, attitudes, values, and behaviors linked to reading.

Table 6.1 Relation between children's reading
achievement and parents' reported reading
difficulties as presented by ALBSU (1993)

	Parent reading difficulty?	
	Yes	No
Child's reading test score	%	%
1. Low	48	24
2.	22	25
3.	17	25
4. High	13	26
n (100%)	107	2500

Source: ALBSU (1993c), Table 1, p. 10.

These programs try to break the cycle of low literacy, a cycle which
limits lives.

(Nickse, 1990a, p. 4)

This powerful intervention holds great promise for breaking the intergenerational cycle of undereducation and fulfilling America's broadest
educational aims.

(Darling, 1993b, p. 5)

In Britain ALBSU echoed these claims.

Programmes which offer a combination of teaching for parents and children can prevent failure, break the cycle of under attainment and raise
confidence and achievement across the generations.

(ALBSU, 1993b, p. 1)

Gillian Shephard, a former Secretary of State for Education in England, has
stated:

Family literacy schemes break the vicious circle where parents pass on
poor literacy and numeracy to their children.

(Department for Education, 1995)

There is a surface plausibility about the assumptions underlying these statements but how well do they relate to research evidence? Do children who
achieve poorly in school in fact have parents with literacy difficulties? Can
parental literacy difficulties be used to identify children likely to fail and for
whom a family literacy programme would be appropriate?

To answer these questions one needs to survey a representative sample of
families and examine the association between parents' and children's literacy.

Such a study has been carried out in Britain. It has been cited in support of the earlier claims but when examined closely it can be seen that it actually contradicts them.

The research in question was carried out in 1991 for ALBSU by a team from the City University, London. Using a subsample of 1,761 families with 2,617 children drawn from the fifth sweep of the British National Child Development Study, children's reading was tested on the Peabody Individual Achievement Test Reading Recognition Assessment and parents were asked as part of a longer interview whether they had problems with reading, writing or spelling (ALBSU, 1993c). Data were also collected on other family characteristics and children's attainment in mathematics.

Children's reading achievement was categorised in four levels, 1–4, according to quartiles of age-standardised scores. Table 6.1 shows some of the findings as presented by ALBSU (1993c). It can be seen from Table 6.1 that there was a clear association between children's reading test scores and parents' reported reading difficulty. It is particularly interesting that 48 per cent of the children whose parents had reading difficulties were in the 'low' reading group (compared to 24 per cent from other families). One can agree with the Director of ALBSU, Alan Wells, who claimed that the study provided 'the first objective evidence of the link between a parent's competence in basic skills and the competence of their children' and that it indicated 'a very strong correlation between low basic skills of parents and low attainment of children' (Wells, 1993, p.3). Correlation, however, is one thing, identification quite another.

Further analyses in the ALBSU study showed that in low income families and in families where parents had no educational qualifications as well as reading difficulties the proportion of low reading children rose to 72 per cent. The proportion of children who were low in either mathematics or reading in such families was 76 per cent. The study concluded:

> The combination of parental literacy and numeracy problems, with a low level of parental education of low family income, *can be used to identify the children who were most likely to perform badly* in the maths and reading tests.
>
> (ALBSU, 1993c, p.19, emphasis added)

This statement is highly misleading. The fact that certain parental characteristics are associated with children's low reading achievement does not mean that they can be used to identify those children. To understand why, return to Table 6.1. Data were presented there by ALBSU (1993c) in a manner likely to persuade – perhaps even calculated to persuade – that parental literacy difficulties account for much of children's poor literacy achievement, but if the data are recast in the form of Table 6.2 it can be seen that this is not so. In Table 6.2 children in the higher three quartiles on reading test scores have been grouped together as 'other' to clarify comparisons with the 'low' group

Table 6.2 Data from Table 6.1 expressed in terms of inferred numbers of children

| Child's reading test score | Parent reading difficulty? | | |
	Yes	No	Totals
Low	51	600	651
Other	56	1900	1956
Totals	107	2500	2607

Source: Derived from ALBSU (1993c), Table 1, p. 10.

and instead of percentages there are the inferred numbers of children in each cell (calculated by reference to the cell percentages and column totals given in Table 6.2). The figures in Table 6.2 were directly inferred from the Table 6.1 although they were never presented in this form by ALBSU.

It can be seen from Table 6.2 that 51 out of the 107 children whose parents had reading difficulties were in the low reading group (this is the 48 per cent referred to earlier) but the table also enables a judgement to be made of the value of parental reading difficulty as a method for identifying children with low reading. It shows that it is very insensitive for it only identifies 8 per cent (51 out of 651) of the low reading group. Any programme targeted on this basis would miss 92 per cent of the lowest achieving children. Almost as bad is the fact that 52 per cent (56 out of 107) of the children identified would be in the higher reading achievement groups and would be targeted for a programme they might not need with a consequent waste of educational resources and the families' time.

It might be argued that the method of identification could be improved by adding identifiers of low family income and parents' lack of qualifications and combining them to identify children whose achievement was low in either mathematics or reading (as described by ALBSU, 1993c, in the quotation given earlier). Table 6.3 shows the relevant figures, derived from another table in the ALBSU report (as before, the cell figures were calculated by reference to the percentages and column totals given in the report). Data were not presented in this from by ALBSU but it can be seen that 76 per cent of children mentioned earlier (as having parents with reading difficulties, low income and no qualifications who were in the low reading group) comprised 22 out of 29 children.

Table 6.3 reveals that the sensitivity of this method is now absurdly low in that it identifies only 2 per cent of all the children in the low reading group. It should also be noted that the target group, comprising 29 out of the 2,619 children, is only 1 per cent of the population. The best that can be said for this as a method of identification is that it does not falsely identify as low achievers quite so many of the children in the higher groups as did the previous

Table 6.3 Inferred numbers of children with low scores in reading or mathematics according to parental characteristics

Child's test score in reading or mathematics	Parent reading difficulty, low income and no qualifications?		Totals
	Yes	No	
Low in either	22	921	943
Other	7	1669	1676
Totals	29	2590	2619

Source: Derived from ALBSU (1993c), Table 8, p. 18.

method (24 per cent of those identified being false positives compared to 52 per cent previously).

The rhetoric that family factors identify poor readers is therefore not borne out by this research. There is an overlap between families where parents have literacy difficulties and families where children have low literacy achievement but it is an extremely small overlap. Targeting just those families will not meet the needs of many others.

Might other studies, using different measures and different populations, find better methods of identification? Possibly, but the examination of this particular study highlights pitfalls likely to be encountered by research in any country which seeks to identify children with low literacy achievement on the basis of family characteristics. One is the tendency to believe that a significant correlation implies an acceptable method of identification. It has been shown that this does not necessarily follow. Another is that the prevalence of reported literacy difficulties in families is relatively low in countries such as the USA or Britain. If one devised a broader concept of parental literacy difficulty with higher prevalence one could expect to identify a greater proportion of children who were poor readers but the proportion of better readers falsely identified could also rise.

The search for methods of identification is often driven by policy-makers' wish for the 'magic bullet' which, targeted selectively at a few families, eliminates social problems. There is no evidence that targeting restricted programmes on the basis of parental literacy difficulty can be sufficiently accurate. One policy alternative to restricted programmes is universal, literacy-oriented early childhood education (including pre-school education). This could include ongoing assessment of children's literacy learning, accompanied by appropriate intervention as and when needed. Such early literacy education could seek to include parental involvement and provide opportunities for adults to develop their literacy too if they wanted to. There would in effect be a broad range of family literacy programmes within which restricted programmes would be just one variety. This would be a larger scale, more expensive option than a policy of providing restricted programmes, which claims to achieve the same with fewer resources.

Accessibility and take-up of programmes

Even if there was an accurate method of selecting families for programmes the rhetoric glosses over some potentially fatal difficulties in practice. It cannot be taken for granted that parents will take up the programmes offered. There are several factors which might prevent this happening. First, parents may not accept that they have the educational needs which professionals ascribe to them (whether for basic literacy or other adult education). Second, even if they agree they have needs, they may not wish to do anything about them. Third, they may not wish to get involved in promoting their children's literacy. Fourth, even if none of these factors apply and parents are willing to join family literacy programmes, practical problems of programme organisation may reduce take-up. Is there research which can help assess the seriousness of these factors?

Regarding the readiness of parents to accept professionals' definitions of their educational needs, it is hard to identify directly relevant research but professional educators experienced in working with adults outside institutional settings will surely recognise that many poorly educated adults simply do not feel the needs which well-educated professionals expect them to feel. They may judge that their literacy competence is not a significant problem compared to others they face. In the US context, for example, Gadsden (1994) has suggested how this can be so.

> In low-income communities where many family literacy programs are targeted for African-American and other families of color, the programs address only a small, and, for some participants, relatively unimportant part of the problems facing them, problems that they see as centered in the ability to obtain employment. The appearance, if not reality, of a declining economy and labor force have been evidenced in low-income communities through increases in lay-offs, the reminders of 'last hired–first fired' for many people of color, a growing crisis of labor force partici-pation among African-American males, and crime and hopelessness that occur in tandem or shortly after economic hardship and crisis.
>
> (pp. 18–19)

Suppose, in such circumstances, that parents nevertheless accept that they have literacy needs, how many are prepared to do anything about them? Research suggests that it might be only a small minority. A British study by Bynner and Fogelman (1993), using the National Child Development Study sample when adults were aged 33, found that less than one-fifth of those who reported literacy problems had ever attended an adult literacy class.

One can be more optimistic about parents' willingness to be involved in their children's literacy. Many parental involvement programmes have secured near 100 per cent take-up and continuing high levels of participation even in neighbourhoods considered disadvantaged (Hannon, 1995). Much depends upon how parents are invited to take part, what they are asked to do, and the programme's responsiveness to different families' circumstances. The research evidence suggest that this factor does not present insuperable difficulties.

Regarding the fourth factor, whether programmes can be organised so as to be accessible in practical terms to all parents wanting to participate, there must be doubts. It is known, for example, that centre-based parent involvement programmes typically achieve lower take-up and participation rates than home-based ones. Parents' circumstances vary so much (in terms of domestic commitments, ages of children, housing, travel, and work hours if employed) that programmes which rely on only one format (e.g. a weekly daytime class) are bound to be inaccessible for some families. If the parent and child components take place simultaneously, in parallel groups, the flexibility of programmes is further reduced.

Doubts relating to these factors could be allayed if there was evidence that take-up of restricted programmes was in fact satisfactorily high. That would mean that in practice none of the factors had a seriously adverse effect. Since take-up is crucial to programme success (where it is low the programme fails even in reaching, never mind benefiting, its target group), one might expect it to have been researched across a range of programmes. This had not happened. Sometimes the issue is treated in terms of whether or not places are filled on a programme or whether families in programmes are from the target population (e.g. St Pierre et al., 1995; Brooks et al., 1996) but this provides no information about what proportion of the target group takes up the programme. Research into take-up can be difficult in that it requires a target group to be defined and its size measured or estimated, as well as some agreement about what counts as an invitation to participate, but in principle it is a perfectly researchable issue.

Meanwhile, it is interesting that the most common barriers identified by Even Start programmes in the USA, according to St Pierre et al. were 'difficulties in the recruitment, retention, attendance and motivation of families' (p. 86). In Britain, a later phase of the ALBSU initiative funded over 400 small-scale restricted programmes but an evaluation by Poulson et al. (1997) implied, even if it did not explicitly so state, that recruitment difficulties may have led some programmes to be less than frank initially with parents about their aim to help them with basic skills or to recruit parents without such needs. The rhetoric will carry more conviction when it can cite evidence that a high proportion of families judged to need restricted programmes in family literacy do take them up.

Educational effects

The rhetoric of restricted programmes is quite emphatic about their effectiveness. For example, in the USA, Darling (1992) claimed that 'A recent study of Kenan Model programs has shown lasting educational benefits for both parents and children' (p. 23). Padak and Rasinski (1997) have stated, 'Family literacy programs do work, and their benefits are widespread and significant' (p. 2). In Britain, ALBSU claimed that family literacy 'shows greater gains, for adults and children, than in separate programmes, and better retention rates' (ALBSU, 1993b, p. 3).

Before turning to available research to see whether it can support such claims, it is worth pausing to ask what would count as 'success' for restricted programmes, and how rigorously it should be demonstrated. 'Success' requires, first, that children and parents derive clearly identifiable benefits from participating in programmes. However, that is not enough, for the rhetoric makes a further claim that because restricted programmes focus simultaneously on both parents and children they are more effective than programmes that focus on either parents or children separately. Thus, Darling (1992) claimed:

> Family literacy programs place equal emphasis on two generations and two goals, maximising the effects of early education for children and literacy instruction for adults. The synergy of reciprocal learning and teaching among family members creates a home environment that both supports and enhances learning.
>
> (p. 23)

Brooks and Hayes (1998) have described what is expected thus:

> high-quality, comprehensive family literacy programs should be *designed* to encourage maximum positive interaction among the parts to produce a result that is much more than the sum of the results of the separate parts. That interaction is intended to result in an added value of comprehensive family literacy programs over single-service programs, even if a family is provided all the services of family literacy program but as separate services.
>
> (Brooks and Hayes, 1998, p. 3)

In Britain, Wells (1995) explained, 'Family literacy programmes offer what the Americans describe as "double duty dollars" because they target both parents and their children' (pp. 1–2).

The suggestion here is that something extra can be expected from restricted programmes, that parents will gain more than they would from conventional adult education programmes and also that children will gain more than they would from early childhood education parental involvement programmes. If this were not so, the basic case for restricted programmes would collapse.

Research, therefore, has to compare not just 'restricted programmes versus no programme' but, more importantly, 'restricted programmes versus other programmes'. Hence, it is not enough to say of restricted programmes simply that 'they work'. Rhetoric using the word 'work' implies that criteria for success are as unproblematic as those for telling whether a washing machine works. It may 'work' in the sense of meeting a narrow functional criterion but may fail in relation to other criteria or in comparison to other methods. A key question is whether restricted programmes work better than the obvious policy alternatives, which in this case is not 'no programme at all' but separate adult education and early childhood literacy parent involvement programmes or flexible family literacy programmes. A further issue is whether, as Wells (1995) has implied, restricted programmes are more cost-effective than other provision.

The most convincing way to demonstrate that any educational programme is more effective than another is through a true experimental design in which there is random allocation – in this case of families – to each programme (and to a control no-programme condition) followed by a comparison of educational outcomes across groups. It is not easy to conduct such a study in field conditions but given the resource implications of national family literacy policies one would expect it to be done. If a true experimental design cannot be followed, then a good quasi-experimental design is the next best thing. It is important to evaluate outcomes for all those invited to participate in programmes, not just those who take up an invitation and continue to participate. Evaluation should be open to the possibility (hinted at by family literacy advocates) that restricted programmes might be more effective because they have higher retention.

The quality and extent of research into restricted programme effects falls well short of what is required. Take, for example, the claim by Darling (1992) quoted earlier that there are 'lasting educational benefits for both parents and children'. No reference is given to the 'recent study' mentioned but it is presumably one reported by Seaman et al. (1991) and Seaman (1992) of 14 programmes which had concluded that the Kenan model was 'a successful intervention strategy for breaking the cycle of illiteracy which plagues millions of families in the United States' (Seaman, 1992, p. 80). Yet this 'finding' was reached without representative sampling of participants in programmes, without considering families who dropped out, without any comparison of programme participants to a control group (or even to a quasi-experimental comparison group) and without independent measures of educational outcomes. Making totally unsupported claims for the success of an educational programme without citing evidence is bad enough but to imply that there is research evidence when that evidence is seriously inadequate is perhaps worse.

Several commentators have noted the lack of research. Nickse (1993) observed that 'there is but modest evidence to date that family and inter-generational literacy programs work' (p. 34). Gadsden (1994) has commented, 'Studies that explore the parameters of literacy programs are limited, and the potential impact of the activities in them on the families that they are intended to serve is relatively unknown' (p. 2). Topping and Wolfendale (1995) commented, 'It seems that, although the evaluation research on parental involvement in reading is generally positive, the picture for family literacy is still incomplete. Evaluative evidence to date is very varied in quality and quantity' (p. 31). However, since these rather bleak comments were made, findings from two well-designed evaluations of restricted programmes – one in the USA (St Pierre et al., 1995) and one in England (Brooks et al., 1996) – have become available.

St Pierre et al. (1995) reported the final evaluation of the Even Start family literacy programme. This included an experimental study in which 200 families were allocated at random to programme or control conditions. Programme effects in the experimental group were rather disappointing. There were no significant gains for parents' literacy in terms of an adult reading achievement test. Children in the programme, despite doing well in the early stages, were eventually no better than the control group on measures of emergent literacy, vocabulary and school readiness. The researchers suggest that this may be 'because control children enrolled in preschool or kindergarten, and because some Even Start children no longer participated in an Even Start early childhood program' (p. 246). Another way to interpret the findings is to see the experiment as actually a comparison between restricted programmes (prone to drop-out) and more conventional early childhood education programmes (which might well have included some parental involvement), which shows that both produce gains for children but neither is any more effective than the other. The experimental study was only one part of a larger evaluation which used data from 270 projects nation-wide in 1992–93 involving over 16,000 families. This was inevitably less rigorous than the experimental study but it did find evidence of benefits for parents and children, although none to support the claim that restricted programmes are superior to others.

Brooks et al. (1996) reported an evaluation of four demonstration programmes, involving over 300 families, established as part of the ALBSU initiative. The study found benefits, including gains on literacy measures, for both parents and children and a follow-up study was able to demonstrate that these were maintained 20–34 months later (Brooks et al., 1997). Children's gains were shown by comparing their progress in reading test scores to that of a national sample of children tested in an earlier survey but, unlike the Even Start study, there was no direct comparison of the restricted programme with any other kinds of programme. Neither was programme take-up directly investigated. This study is in many ways a model evaluation – evidence-based, well designed, efficient in use of resources, technically highly competent and clearly reported – but its weakness is that it leaves unanswered the central question about the effectiveness of restricted programmes, namely whether or not they are any better for children or parents than stand-alone programmes or flexible family literacy programmes. It did not answer this question because it did not address it. It did not address it because ALBSU, which commissioned the research, did not ask for it to be addressed.

In summary, there is now evidence from evaluations in Britain and the USA to support claims that restricted programmes have positive educational effects for parents and children but there is none to show that they have greater effects, or are more cost-effective, than separate child-focused or adult-focused programmes. To that extent rhetoric about restricted programmes lacks research support.

Socio-economic effects

Finally, one strand of family literacy rhetoric which cannot go unremarked is the extravagance of claims made for the socio-economic benefits of restricted programmes. Examples are confined to the USA and – perhaps exclusively – to the National Center for Family Literacy.

> At its most basic level, the power of family literacy is the power of change. It is enabling at-risk families with little hope to reverse the cycle of under-education and poverty in their own lives. The empowerment they attain through the education and knowledge they acquire in a family literacy program allows them to take control of their lives, and consequently, to change the destiny of their families for generations to come.
>
> (National Center for Family Literacy, 1994, p. 1)

> Family literacy can help break the intergenerational cycle of poverty and dependency. Family literacy improves the educational opportunities for children and parents by providing both learning experiences and group support. In the process, family literacy provides parents with skills that will improve their incomes. It provides disadvantaged children with educational opportunities that can enable them to lift themselves out of poverty and dependency.
>
> (Brizius and Foster, 1993, p. 11)

> A child's first classroom, the home, can be changed from a hopeless environment to one in which an attitude of appreciation and respect for education are modelled for the children. These changes pave the way for school successes, and thereafter life successes. The message to policy makers and legislators, then, is that family literacy can reduce the number of people on government assistance and increase the number of productive citizens.
>
> (National Center for Family Literacy, 1994, p. 1)

In Britain, the claims have been more modest. Writing of the ALBSU initiative, Hempstedt (1995) has stated, 'We have tried to avoid some of the more inflated claims, found in some American programmes, which suggest that family literacy has the capacity to effect wider social and economic change' (p. 10).

There are several reasons to treat the US claims with caution. The long-term effects of well-designed pre-school programmes reported by Lazar *et al.* (1982) show that, although they can bring welcome socio-economic benefits for children later in life, these are not nearly as dramatic as those promised in the earlier cited quotations. Research in Britain using the National Child Development Study sample suggests that thus far education has had limited success in changing the socio-economic circumstances of families (Feinstein, 1998). Bernstein's (1970) dictum, 'Education cannot compensate for society' would be one way to summarise the position. Graff (1991) has shown that claims that literacy produces economic benefits (rather than vice versa) cannot easily be substantiated. It is likely that Freire (1972) was nearer the mark when he pointed out:

> Merely teaching men [sic] to read and write does not work miracles; if there are not enough jobs for men able to work, teaching more men to read and write will not create them.
>
> (Freire, 1972, p. 25)

Against this background it would be surprising if restricted programmes in family literacy were more effective than others in overcoming the effects of poverty, bearing in mind that there are unanswered questions about the take-up of programmes and that they have not been shown to be any more effective in educational terms than other programmes. One must wonder, then, about the rhetoric which is being employed. It may be motivated by the need to secure funding from employers, business and government for specific pro-grammes. However, as Auerbach (1995) points out, the consequences of such rhetoric could be unfortunate:

> Suggesting that enhanced family literacy interactions will break the cycle of poverty or compensate for problems facing the educational system only reinforces the ideology that blames poor people for their own problems and leaves social inequities intact.
>
> (p. 23)

Apart from the rhetoric, what?

One has to conclude that rhetoric about restricted programmes in family literacy is poorly linked to available research evidence. The rhetoric obscures research findings about family literacy as something which occurs in most families, quite independently of any programmes, and which is worth understanding better. It misleadingly suggests stronger links between parental and child literacy than actually exist. It fails to appreciate the paucity of research on take-up and participation levels and ignores that which suggests there could be serious problems. Its claims for educational effects are not supported by available evidence and its claims for socio-economic effects are implausible.

It might be objected that this verdict fails to give due recognition to the positive findings of St Pierre *et al.* (1995) and Brooks *et al.* (1996) – two well-designed studies which found benefits for children and parents in restricted programmes. However, these studies do not indicate the proportion of families willing to participate in such programmes and therefore what proportion of children and parents stand to gain – other evidence discussed suggests that it could be a rather small minority. Neither, of course, do these studies indicate that there is only one kind of family literacy programme.

This critique is not meant to deny the many positive achievements of family literacy programmes in general. The rhetoric which causes so many difficulties mainly concerns restricted programmes. Most of the problems with restricted programmes would disappear if the *insistence* on combining adult basic education with other components was dropped. This would of course make them like other forms of flexible family literacy programmes. One can imagine a range of literacy programmes for adults, including parents, in which parent involvement in children's literacy could be an *option* but not a prerequisite for entry to the programme. Ideally, it ought to be possible for all adults, including parents, to access basic education in different ways according to their interests and circumstances (Bird and Pahl, 1994). Similarly, one can imagine a range of programmes mainly concerned with children's literacy education and parental involvement in which adult basic education for parents would be an *option* for those who want it. There is every reason to incorporate adult basic education in family literacy programmes *as a response to the adults' interests*, just as it is desirable to have it as an adjunct to many forms of community education or workplace training. Parental involvement (a form of adult education in itself) is not the same as basic literacy or numeracy education and should not have to be combined with it unless it clearly meets parents' interest to do so. Within the range of family literacy programmes there could be some in which, where it suited families, all components were combined in the manner of restricted programmes but this would only be one choice among many.

Relieved of the necessity to include all components in a programme there would be less need for the questionable ideology of a cycle of low literacy. Problems of recruitment and take-up could be eased and programme advocates might be under less pressure to make extravagant claims about effectiveness. There would still be problems and dilemmas common to all such programmes (e.g. relating to conceptions of literacy, avoidance of deficit characterisations of families, programme delivery, and effectiveness) but most of these have to be faced in any form of education.

There are alternatives to restricted programmes. Several models have been documented by McIvor (1990), Morrow (1995), Morrow *et al.* (1995), Wolfendale and Topping (1996), and Hannon (1998b). They need to be systematised and evaluated more stringently by programme developers and researchers. The family literacy policy options are certainly wider than 'restricted programmes or nothing'. The policy difficulty posed by reliance on restricted programmes is that parents' readiness to undertake a certain form of adult basic education, at a certain time and place, becomes the price of children's admission to a programme. If the parent's interest in adult basic education coincides with their interest in getting involved in their children's education then there is evidence that restricted programmes can be valuable but there is as yet no research evidence to justify such programmes being the paradigm into which all families must be squeezed.

Practice and policy needs to be informed by research into the broad category of family literacy programmes. Where possible, practitioners in the field should be supported in doing research themselves so that they can act on what they find and be better prepared to make use of other researchers' findings (Hannon, 1998a). Alternatives to restricted programmes needs to be identified, documented and evaluated in terms of feasibility and outcomes and, if possible, compared to restricted programmes. The theoretical base for programme design, and particularly the vexed question of linking home and school literacies without denying the existence of either, could be helped by more research, in more communities, into existing patterns of family literacy. The issues of recruitment, take-up, participation and drop-out need to be investigated directly rather than regarded as inconvenient complications in evaluation studies. More needs to be known about programme effects, what can be expected from specific approaches used singly and in combination. The meaning of programmes to participants needs to be explicated in order to understand the effectiveness or ineffectiveness of programmes.

It is frustrating for educational researchers to see developments in their field driven by rhetoric rather than research but family literacy is not the first case of this happening and it will not be the last. Researchers are not – and, it is to be hoped, never will be – solely responsible for developments in policy and practice. However, they are responsible for the quality of their work and for showing its relation to policy and practice. It is in that spirit that this critique is offered.

Acknowledgements

I am grateful to many practitioners and researchers for discussing with me the issues addressed in this article and also to Valerie Hannon, Angela Jackson, Elaine Millard, Cathy Nutbrown and Jo Weinberger, who commented on an earlier version of the chapter. Responsibility for the views expressed about research studies and for the arguments presented in the article remain with me.

References

Adult Literacy and Basic Skills Unit (ALBSU) (1993a) *Framework for Family Literacy Demonstration Programmes* (London, Adult Literacy and Basic Skills Unit).
Adult Literacy and Basic Skills Unit (ALBSU) (1993b) *Family Literacy News*, *No. 1* (London, Adult Literacy and Basic Skills Unit).

Adult Literacy and Basic Skills Unit (ALBSU) (1993c) *Parents and Their Children: the intergenerational effect of poor basic skills* (London, Adult Literacy and Basic Skills Unit).

Auerbach, E.R. (1989) Toward a social-contextual approach to family literacy, *Harvard Educational Review*, 59, pp. 165–181.

Auerbach, E.R. (1995) Which way for family literacy: intervention or empowerment? in: L.M. Morrow (ed.) *Family Literacy: connections in schools and communities*, pp. 11–27 (Newark, DE, International Reading Association).

Auerbach, E.R. (1997) Reading between the lines, in: D. Taylor (ed.) *Many Families, Many Literacies: an international declaration of principles*, pp. 71–82 (Portsmouth, NH, Heinemann).

Baker, L., Sonnenschein, S., Serpell, R., Fernandez-Fein, S. and Scher, D. (1994) *Contexts of Emergent Literacy: everyday home experiences of urban pre-kindergarten children*, Reading Research Report No. 24 (Athens, GA/College Park, MD, National Reading Research Center).

Barton, D. and Hamilton, M. (1998) *Local Literacies: reading and writing in one community* (London, Routledge).

Basic Skills Agency (1996) *Update*, No. 13 (London, Basic Skills Agency).

Bernstein, B. (1970) Education cannot compensate for society, *New Society*, 26 February, pp. 344–347.

Bird, V. and Pahl, K. (1994) Parent literacy in a community setting, *RaPAL Bulletin*, No. 24, pp. 6–15.

Brizius, J.A. and Foster, S.A. (1993) *Generation to Generation: realizing the promise of family literacy* (Ypsilanti, MI, High/Scope Press).

Brooks, G. and Hayes, A. (1998) Issues in Evaluating Family Literacy programs in Britain and the United States, paper presented to the *Reading Research Conference, International Reading Association Annual Convention*, Orlando, FL, 2 May.

Brooks, G., Gorman, T., Harman, D. and Wilkin, A. (1996) *Family Literacy Works* (London, Basic Skills Agency).

Brooks, G., Gorman, T., Harman, J., Hutchison, D., Kinder, K., Moor, H. and Wilkin, A. (1997) *Family Literacy Lasts* (London, Basic Skills Agency).

Bynner, J. and Fogelman, K. (1993) Making the grade: education and training experiences, in: E. Eerri (ed.) *Life at 33: the fifth follow-up of the National Child Development Study* (London, National Children's Bureau).

Darling, S. (1992) Toward a unified vision of US education, *Reading Today*, June/July, p. 23.

Darling, S. (1993a) Focus on family literacy: the national perspective, NCFL Newsletter, 5, p. 3.

Darling, S. (1993b) Family literacy: an intergenerational approach to education, *Viewpoints*, 15, pp. 2–5.

Department for Education (1995) Break the vicious circle – Shephard, *News 36/95* (Press Release) (London, Department for Education).

Department for Education and Employment (1997) *Excellence in Schools* (White Paper, Cm 3681) (London, The Stationery Office).

Feinstein, L. (1998) Which children succeed and why, *New Economy*, June, pp. 99–104.

Freire, P. (1972) *Cultural Action for Freedom* (Harmondsworth, Penguin).

Gadsden, V. (1994) *Understanding Family Literacy: conceptual issues facing the field*, NCAL Technical Report TR94–02 (Philadelphia, PA, National Center on Adult Literacy, University of Pennsylvania).

Graff, H. (1991) *The Literacy Myth: cultural integration and social structure in the nineteenth century*, 2nd edn (New Brunswick, NJ, Transaction Publishers).

Grant, A. (1997) Debating intergenerational family literacy: myths, critiques, and counterperspectives, in: D. Taylor (ed.) *Many Families, Many Literacies: an international declaration of principles*, pp. 216–225 (Portsmouth, NH, Heinemann).

Gregory, E. (1996) *Making Sense of a New World: learning to read in a second language* (London, Paul Chapman).

Hannon, P. (1995) *Literacy, Home and School: research and practice in teaching literacy with parents* (London, Falmer Press).

Hannon, P. (1998a) An ecological perspective on educational research, in: J. Rudduck and D. McIntyre (eds) *Challenges for Educational Research* (London, Paul Chapman Publishing/Sage).

Hannon, P. (1998b) How can we foster children's early literacy development through parent involvement? in: S.B. Neuman and K.A. Roskos (eds) *Children Achieving: best practices in early literacy* (Newark, DE, International Reading Association).

Heath, S.B. (1983) *Ways with Words: language life and work in communities and classrooms* (Cambridge, Cambridge University Press).

Hempstedt, A. (1995) 'A good start for learning': family literacy work by the Basic Skills Agency, *Reading*, 29, pp. 10–14.

Lazar, I., Darlington, R., Murray, H., Royce, J. and Snipper, A. (1982) Lasting effects of early education, *Monographs of the Society for Research in Child Development*, 47, (2–3, Serial No. 195).

McIvor, M.C. (1990) *Family Literacy in Action: a survey of successful programs* (Syracuse, NY, New Readers Press).

Morrow, L.M. (ed.) (1995) *Family Literacy: connections in schools and communities.* (Newark, DE, International Reading Association).

Morrow, L.M., Tracey, D.H. and Maxwell, C.M. (eds) (1995) *A Survey of Family Literacy in the United States* (Newark, DE, International Reading Association).

National Center for Family Literacy (1994) Communicating the power of family literacy, *NCFL Newsletter*, 6, p. 1.

Nickse, R.S. (1990a) Foreword, in: M.C. McIvor (ed.) *Family Literacy in Action: a survey of successful programs*, pp. 4–5 (Syracuse, NY, New Readers Press).

Nickse, R.S. (1990b) *Family and Intergenerational Literacy Programs: an update of 'Noises of Literacy'* (Columbus, OH, ERIC Clearinghouse on Adult, Career and Vocational Education, Ohio State University).

Nickse, R.S. (1993) A typology of family and intergenerational literacy programs: implications for evaluation, *Viewpoints*, 15, pp. 34–40.

Padak, N. and Rasinski, T. (1997) *Family Literacy Programs: who benefits?* (Kent, OH, Ohio Literacy Resource Center (EDRS No. ED 407 568)).

Perkins, D. and Mendel, D. (1989) *A Place to Start: the Kenan Trust family literacy project* (Louisville, KY, National Center for Family Literacy).

Poulson, L., Macleod, F., Bennett, N. and Wray, D. (1997) *Family Literacy: practice in local programmes* (London, The Basic Skills Agency).

Purcell-Gates, V. (1995) *Other People's Words: the cycle of low literacy* (Cambridge, MA, Harvard University Press).

Seaman, D. (1992) Follow-up study of the impact of the Kenan Trust model of family literacy, *Adult Basic Education*, 2, pp. 71–83.

Seaman, D., Popp, B. and Darling, S. (1991) *Follow-up Study of the Impact of the Kenan Trust Model for Family Literacy* (Louisville, KY, National Center for Family Literacy).

St Pierre, R., Swartz, J., Gamse, B., Murray, S., Deck, D. and Nickel, P. (1995) *National Evaluation of the Even Start Family Literacy Program* (Washington, DC, US Department of Education, Office of Policy and Planning).

Taylor, D. (1983) *Family Literacy: young children learning to read and write* (Exeter, NH, Heinemann).

Taylor, D. (ed.) (1997) *Many Families, Many Literacies: an international declaration of principles* (Portsmouth, NH, Heinemann).

Taylor, D. and Dorsey-Gaines, C. (1988) *Growing Up Literate: learning from inner-city families* (Portsmouth, NH, Heinemann).

Teale, W.H. (1986) Home background and young children's literacy development, in: W.H. Teale and E. Sulzby (eds) *Emergent Literacy: writing and reading*, pp. 173–206 (Norwood, NJ, Ablex).

Topping, K. and Wolfendale, S. (1995) The effectiveness of family literacy programmes, *Reading*, 29, pp. 26–33.

Voss, M. (1996) *Hidden Literacies: children learning at home and at school* (Portsmouth, NH, Heinemann).

Wells, A. (1993) Foreword, in: ALBSU, *Parents and Their Children: the intergenerational effect of poor basic skills* (London, Adult Literacy and Basic Skills Unit).

Wells, A. (1995) Foreword, in: Basic Skills Agency, *Family Literacy Works: key findings from the NFER evaluation of the Basic Skills Agency's demonstration programmes* (London, Basic Skills Agency).

Weinberger, J. (1996) *Literacy Goes to School: the parents' role in young children's literacy learning* (London, Paul Chapman).

Wolfendale, S. and Topping, K. (eds) (1996) *Family Involvement in Literacy: effective partnerships in education* (London, Cassell).

Source

This is an edited version of an article previously published in *British Educational Research Journal*. 1999. Reproduced by permission of Taylor & Francis Ltd.

Chapter 7

Developing literacy in families with histories of reading problems*

Bente E. Hagtvet, Erna Horn, Liv M. Lassen, Kirsti Lauvås, Sol Lyster and Sidsel Misund

This chapter reports on an ongoing longitudinal study, including 149 children in families with a family history of dyslexia and 300 control children from unaffected families, who were studied cross-sectionally. The aim of the study is to explore the developmental links between early linguistics, cognitive and emotional factors and later problems with written language. Preliminary findings on prevalence, early precursors of reading problems and the potential influence of parental attitudes on the literacy development of the children are discussed.

It is frequently observed that a number of children have problems in learning to read and write despite normal cognitive skills and sensory functions, and assumed satisfactory educational stimulation. Such cases, also referred to as dyslexic, are observed even in egalitarian societies like the Scandinavian, with equality in school opportunities and generally good educational systems. Ever since the beginning of this century, it has been reported that reading problems in a number of cases run in families (Fisher, 1905; Thomas, 1905). Support for an inheritary component in certain reading disorders is found in church examination books from the last century in Sweden (Lundberg and Nilsson, 1986), in longitudinal studies of identical and fraternal twins (e.g. Olson *et al.*, 1989) and in genetic linkage studies aiming at location of a gene for dyslexia on one or more chromosomes (e.g. Lubs *et al.*, 1991; Grigorenko *et al.*, 1997).

Reading is a complex linguistic and cognitive task that can be negatively affected by a great number of biological and environmental factors. The primary cause of specific reading difficulties (dyslexia) is unknown, but low sensitivity to the phoneme structure in oral language has been nominated a core problem (Lundberg and Høien, 1989; Perfetti, 1985; Snowling, 1987; Stanovich, 1988). Whether the ultimate cause may be located in even more basic skills (e.g. auditory perception) is a matter of disagreement. Tallal and co-workers associated the primary cause with a non-verbal auditory

---

* [*Original subtitle*] Preliminary results from a longitudinal study of young children of dyslexic parents.

perceptual deficit, which during early development interferes with the acquisition of language (Tallal, Miller and Fitch, 1993).

Most efforts at identifying the cause(s) of specific reading disorders have focused on weaknesses in the individual. However, whatever the individual qualifications are, environmental influences will always play an important role. One might even argue that, at the end of the day, everything is a matter of adequate stimulation. The more limited the individual qualifications are, the greater is the need for qualified stimulation adapted to the needs of the individual. Different aspects of reading may be more susceptible to influence from genetic than environmental factors. Twin studies indicate, for example, that the ability to manipulate phonological segments in language is generally genetically transmitted, while the ability to read orthographic entities like meaningful words is more influenced by environmental factors (Olson *et al.*, 1989). Even though the ultimate cause appears to be genetically determined, symptoms are thus modifiable by learning. The course of inheritance in dyslexia is therefore complex and still unclear, and the determinants of reading disabilities constitute a complex interacting net of biological and social factors.

Written language is parasitic on oral language, and in more recent attempts at clarifying the roots of reading problems the identification of their oral language precursors has been the focus. Scarborough's (1989, 1990, 1991) seminal study of 34 children in families where one or both parents suffer from dyslexia focused on the relations between early spoken language and later written language. Sixty-five per cent of these children developed reading problems, compared with 5 per cent from families unaffected by dyslexia. The reading disabled children could be distinguished from groups of control children who did not develop reading problems as early as at 30 months of age on the basis of their oral language abilities. The children at risk used a simpler syntax and exhibited more phonological errors in production. At later ages deviancies in all aspects of language were reported (i.e. in phonology, syntax and semantics). Scarborough's study included a limited number of children, and also a limited number of variables. It does, however, strongly corroborate results suggesting that children from families where one of the parents is dyslexic have an increased risk for developing a reading problem.

In 1993, and influenced by Scarborough's research, a longitudinal study of the development of Norwegian children of dyslexic parents was initiated at the Institute of Special Needs Education, University of Oslo, Norway. A total of 149 families in which either mother or father or both parents considered themselves dyslexic were included in the study.[1] The purpose of the study was to investigate the extent to which Scarborough's findings would replicate in a different culture and language and with a broader set of variables. We focused on linguistic, cognitive, emotional and motor skills in the children and also on variables that were potentially ingredient parts in the 'social inheritance' associated with these families. Information was therefore collected on questions like the school experience of the affected parents, how the reading problems had affected these parents' lives and how the parents stimulated the children's literacy development, and the expectations, fears and worries of the parents regarding their own children.

[. . .]

Methodological issues: design, sample and procedures

The sample consists of children from families where at least one of the parents has/has had reading problems, totalling 149 families, in addition to controls from unaffected families (approx. 300 children). About half of the affected families were given a counselling programme for parents when their child turned 5 years. Thus, three groups were included in the study:

1. *Group 1 (N = 74): Children from affected families, with intervention when the child is 5 years old.*
    Followed longitudinally from age 2 to 9 years, and assessed yearly.
2. *Group 2 (N = 75): Children from affected families without intervention.*
    Followed longitudinally from age 5 to 9, and assessed yearly.
3. *Group 3 (N = 300): Controls from unaffected families.*
    Followed cross-sectionally, and assessed at each of the same age levels as Groups 1 and 2 (approx. 40 in each group).

Preliminary analyses indicate that the affected parents in all but a few cases fall within the category of 'dyslexic', but that their difficulties today vary depending on the degree and quality of the original problem and on the education they have received.

The fathers were affected in 51 per cent of the cases and the mothers in 45 per cent, and in 4 per cent of the cases both parents considered themselves dyslexic. When taking into consideration that men are over-represented in the dyslexic population, this distribution of women and men presumably reflects a particularly great interest in the project in the female subgroup. Most typically, it was the mothers who registered their child for participation.

Socio-economically the families cut across the whole span of educational levels and occupations. Most – including the dyslexic parents – had finished nine years of compulsory education and also had some occupational training. However, only a few of the affected parents had a college degree at BA level. On the other hand, only two of the affected parents (out of 149) were without employment for long periods of time; and in both cases, this was due to physical illness and not directly or indirectly to reading problems. Generally, the subjects showed a degree of knowledge, awareness and concern about their children which is typically associated with middle-class and upper-middle-class values. This must be seen in connection with the way the families were recruited for project participation. The project was advertised via the Norwegian Dyslexia Association, and members were invited to participate. Participants were also recruited via local newspapers and community health clinics in the Oslo and Akershus county. While subjects by this procedure were randomly selected, it favoured parents who were orientated in the media, able to take initiative to participate and who were conscious and concerned with regard to their own disability.

The children were assessed at least once a year – at the point in time when they had their birthday (plus/minus one month). They were assessed at the Institute of Special Needs Education, and one or both parents accompanied their children. A battery of tests and observational procedures were designed for assessments. The sessions were video taped and later transcribed. Variables focused on were story-book reading (adult and child), language comprehension, language awareness (phonemic, morphemic, syntactic), expressive language (labelling objects, defining words, retelling of stories), mathematical thinking, verbal and non-verbal intelligence (Wechsler, 1967), motor milestones, concentration and focused attention, stress/anxiety and self-concept.

The parents were regularly interviewed about their child's development. At ages 2 years (Group 1) and 5 years (Group 2) anamnestic data were collected; and in the year their child turned 7, and was formally introduced to reading and writing in school, an in-depth interview with the affected parent was carried out. The interview covered a whole range of topics – e.g. the life history of the parent, worries and concerns about the future education of their child, views on what might be the best strategy, etc. Also, to get an impression of the severity of the reading problem of the affected parent(s), his/her present skills in reading and spelling were assessed, as was their non-verbal problem-solving ability.

Parents of Group 1 additionally participated in the counselling programme when their child was 5 years old using an educational video as a trigger for discussing crucial literacy-engendering situations – e.g. book reading, writing notes and memos together, playing with rhymes and letters, telling jokes and stories, reading logos, etc. An experienced clinician watched the video with the parent, stopping it regularly to discuss various essential aspects. At the same age, Group 2 received general tips and advice, while Group 3 received no parent counselling.

Preliminary results

Prevalence of reading problems

Norwegian children have traditionally been formally introduced to the written language at school, starting in August during the year they turn 7. Since the time it takes to acquire reading and writing fluency varies considerably even within the normal variation, it is difficult to make valid assessments about prevalence of reading disabilities before age 9 – i.e. after two years of formal education. Only 38 of the children in Group 2 (and none in Group 1) have, at the time of writing, reached this age. About 50 per cent of these children show problems in learning to read. This percentage is somewhat lower than the 65 per cent in Scarborough's (1989, 1990, 1991) study in the USA, but considerably higher than in the population in general. More precise prevalence measures in the Norwegian sample, as well as qualitative descriptions of reading and spelling problems, will be presented in forthcoming articles when we have relevant information on the whole sample.

Furthermore, unexpectedly many children who mastered the technical aspects of reading at age 8, and who were therefore considered 'not at risk', at age 9 had great problems in coordinating the technique they mastered with meaning, indicated by slow and laborious reading and by little comprehension of what they read. Thus, many Norwegian children appeared to have fewer problems in breaking the alphabetic code and reading alphabetically correctly than is typically described with reference to English-speaking samples (Hagtvet and Lyster, 1999). This may be related to a fairly high degree of sound–letter regularity in the Norwegian orthographic system and corroborates findings in German-speaking populations, where the problems of poor readers have been associated with speed of reading rather than with reading accuracy (Wimmer and Frith, 1994). The automation of the technique and the coordination of technical reading with meaning and understanding did, however, cause problems for a great number of children, underscoring needs these children have for continued help in school, even after they have learned to read technically.

Early precursors of reading problems

Previous research findings of pre-school, at-risk factors have focused upon a range of linguistic variables (Scarborough, 1989, 1990, 1991). It is essential to emphasize that, at this point in time, our groups of children from affected families are only *genetically* at risk of developing a reading problem. Only when we retrospectively can compare the developmental characteristics of those who develop reading problems with those who develop normal abilities can we talk about true at-risk signs. This can only be done in three years when all the participating children have reached age 9 years. We must keep in mind that approximately 50 per cent of the children in the affected families (Groups 1 and 2) are expected to develop normal reading abilities. The language problems of children with specific reading difficulties are, furthermore, typically subtle and difficult to detect in everyday communication, but evident once we challenge the developing language system of the child (Hagtvet, 1996). For these reasons, delays or deviancies in the groups of children who are genetically at risk (Groups 1 and 2) are expected to be small and detectable only in relation to tasks that the children at each point in time experience as challenging.

Preliminary results confirm this expectation. The groups from affected families showed a minor weakness in verbal compared to non-verbal areas. The average verbal intelligence score for both Groups 1 and 2 at age 5 as assessed by the children's version of the *Wechsler Scale* (WPPSI: Wechsler,

1967) was, for example, considerably lower for verbal than for non-verbal intelligence (Hagtvet and Lyster, in preparation; Horn and Lauvås, 1998). Also, differences between affected children (Group 2) and the control group (Group 3) were at ages 5 and 6 larger for metalinguistic tasks and in relation to comprehension of complex syntax than for verbal comprehension in contextualized settings (Hagtvet and Lyster, 1999). Thus, there were variations across language tasks in accordance with expectations, and the extent to which the oral language correlates of reading difficulties are narrowly localized in phonological skills or in broader language skills including syntax and semantics will be discussed in future publications.

Prevention of reading problems

In the discussion of the causes(s) of reading problems the relative importance of biological and social factors is, as mentioned above, crucial (e.g. Elley, 1992; Swedish Official Report on Reading, 1997). Reading disabled adults are reported to have a lower educational level than normally reading adults, and they are more often found to be on welfare (Elbro, 1994). One might assume that a low literacy level and a negative life situation directly or indirectly would be transmitted to their children. A child growing up in this environment might presumably experience few literacy-stimulating role models, little direct relevant teaching or reading and spelling and negative expectations about school failure. Through the law of the self-fulfilling prophecy, or 'the Pygmalion effect', negative expectations about an unsuccessful literacy development might be fulfilled (Rosenthal and Jacobson, 1968). Negative expectations might also mediate a negative self-concept, which might further contribute to a negative reading and writing development (Skaalvik, 1994).

However, after having interviewed more than half of the parents in the study, it is our impression that negatively operating social inheritance is not the most probable causal pattern when trying to understand the reading development of these children. We did, on the other hand, register a high degree of concern about their child's future. This was the very reason why the parents volunteered to participate in the project in the first place: 'If Thomas gets the same problems as me, it might be useful to be backed by a university institute, because then parents are not enough.' As early as the first assessment at age 2 (Group 1), the parents manifested great concern for their children's upbringing. Seventy-six per cent of the children went to some kind of day care, and more than 90 per cent of the parents reported that they read to their child daily. In many families the non-dyslexic parent read to their child, and he or she expressed a special responsibility to do so if the affected parent had negative feelings about reading aloud to their child. This basic concern about the future of their children characterizing these parents, in most cases, appeared to operate more like a resilience factor than a negative factor contributing to the creation of the problem.

Even though all parents by the very act of participating indicated some worries about their child's school career, only five parents in Group 1, at the time when their child was 2 years old, explicitly said that they were worried the child would develop a reading problem. When the parents' degree of concern was compared with the clinician's judgement based on test results and clinical observations, there was an agreement of worry in 75 per cent of the cases. This suggests that the parents were, on the whole, not overly or irrationally anxious about the future of their child. Neither did they just passively wait and see. Rather, most parents appeared to be 'on the alert' and prepared to act if need be, with the conviction that the child would need support if problems arose – as expressed by a single mother coming from a family where many members were reading disabled (grandmother, sister, uncle, cousins and nephews):

> I am not really worried about John. He appears so happy and healthy and enjoys himself in nursery school every day. Even if he develops problems, I know because of my family that he will manage and do OK. One of my uncles is a lawyer. The other is an able carpenter. So, I'm not worried about John.

There are, however, tendencies in the data which indicate that parents became more worried as the children became older and approached school age.

Supportive parental care is the most important variable in the development of a positive self-concept. It is also a critical component in the resilience towards negative development that is sometimes seen in children who suffer from serious and chronic disabilities (Garmezy, 1993; Rutter, 1985). In such a perspective, the special experience, insight and knowledge possessed by this group of parents may play a crucial role in the *prevention* of reading problems in their children. In the case that their child develops problems, it may also turn out to be the most important resilience factor acting like a 'buffer', in addition to being a source for specific remedial strategies adapted to the problems experienced by their child (Lassen, 1998).

The extent to which this coping behaviour expressed by the parents turns out to become a resilience factor or a negative factor contributing to the fulfilment of the reading problems will be an important issue in future reports. Preliminary analyses underscore the positive support associated with the special background of these parents. This corroborates Scarborough's analyses of the development of children from dyslexic families in the USA. Scarborough's original working hypothesis was that reading difficulties were, to a large extent, created by the environment and inadequate educational stimulation (Scarborough, personal communication, 1991). After having worked with the families and assessed the children regularly for seven years, the conclusion was drawn, however, that the problems appeared mainly child driven.

The American parents engaged in literacy activities like story-book reading regularly. The problem was that those children who later developed reading difficulties did not *want* to engage in such activities as often as did their sisters and brothers who developed normal written language skills. As early as at age 2 to 3 years natural observations, as well as parents' reports, indicated that children who later developed a reading problem took fewer initiatives to engage in story-book reading. This limited interest, in combination with their documented – and presumably related – linguistic weaknesses, thus appeared to contribute doubly to their negative literacy development. One cannot, of course, on this basis draw the conclusion that the child alone determined the development. On the contrary, recent research suggests that reading problems may, to a large extent, be prevented by educational efforts – e.g. by play-oriented language games before children start formal reading instruction (Bradley and Bryant, 1983; Lundberg *et al.*, 1991; Lyster, 1996). For this reason, the families in Group 2 in the present study received the parent counsel-ling programme, mentioned above, when their child turned 5 years. The hypothesis was that the play-oriented activities suggested by the programme would develop a positive interest in sounds, letters and written text, in addi-tion to a positive self-concept, and thus make the child better prepared for formal instruction in school. It is, of course, too early to evaluate the effect of this programme. At a minimal level, we expect that the intervention will shed light on some of the mechanisms which are at work in the parent–child interactions in these families, and also on the strategies that counsellors and educators have to go by in working with families which either at a conscious or repressed level may be concerned about the future school career of their child.

Concluding remarks

With reference to a large-scale longitudinal study including 149 children in families with a family history of dyslexia, we are tracing the developmental links between early linguistic, cognitive and emotional factors and later problems with written language. Preliminary findings suggest that the heredity component is considerable, and that the problems in many cases are associ-ated with a subtle language problem that typically is difficult to detect in everyday verbal interactions. These linguistic components presumably interact with the child's cognitive and emotional systems and with environmental variables, and if the worst comes to the worst, may develop into a serious learning problem in school if not met with appropriate educational means. It is the main purpose of this study to shed light on this dynamic net of inter-acting variables by assessing and observing the children, by interviewing the parents and by carrying out a programme of parent counselling. Future reports will focus on variables that may act as resilience factors, as well as on those that appear to reinforce the development of reading problems.

Note

1 Many research groups are presently studying the developmental paths of reading disabilities in children with dyslexic parents. Such studies are now being conducted at the University of Colorado at Denver, USA (by Bruce Pennington); at the University of York and University of London, UK (by Maggie Snowling and Uta Frith); at the University of Copenhagen, Denmark (by Carsten Elbro); at the University of Jyväskylä, Finland (by Heikki Lyytinene); and at the University of New England, Armidale, Australia (by Brian Byrne).

References

Bradley, L. and Bryant, P.E. (1983). 'Categorising sounds and learning to read – a causal connection', *Nature*, 301, 5899, 419–421.

Elbro, C. (1994). 'Funktionelle læseferdigheder' ['Functional reading skills']. In: Hagtvet, B.E., Hertzberg, F. and Vannebo, K.I. (eds) *Ferdigheter I fare? [Skills in Danger?]*. Oslo: Ad Notam Gyldendal, pp. 47–65.

Elley, W.B. (1992). *How in the World Do Students Read? IEA Study of Reading Literacy.* The Hague: International Association for the Evaluation of Educational Achievement.

Fisher, J. (1905). 'Case of congenital word-blindness (inability to learn to read)', *Ophthalmic Review*, 24, 315–318.

Garmezy, N. (1993). 'Vulnerability and resilience'. In: Funder, D., Parke, R., Tomlinson-Keasey, C. and Widman, K. (eds) *Studying Lives through Time*. Washington, DC: American Psychological Association.

Grigorenko, E.L., Wood, F.B., Meyer, M.S., Hart, L.A., Speed, W.C., Shuster, A. and Pauls, D.L. (1997). 'Susceptibility loci for distinct components of developmental dyslexia on chromosomes 6 and 15', *American Journal of Human Genetics*, 60, 27–39.

Hagtvet, B.E. (1996). *Fra tale til skrift. Om prediksjon og utvikling av leseferdighet i fire-til åtteårsalderen [From Oral to Written Language. On the Prediction and Development of Reading Abilities during the Age Period 4 through 8]*. Oslo: Cappelen.

Hagtvet, B.E. and Lyster, S.A.H. (1999). 'Spelling errors of good and poor decoders'. In Goulandries, N. (ed.) *Dyslexia: A Cross-linguistic Perspective*. London: Whurr.

Hagtvet, B.E. and Lyster, S.A.H. (in preparation). Early precursors of reading difficulties. Ms. Institute of Special Needs Education, University of Oslo; mimeo.

Horn, E. and Lauvås, K. (1998). On the relation between language and attention. Unpublished ms., Institute of Special Needs Education, University of Oslo.

Lassen, L. (1998). Parenting children 'at risk' for developing dyslexia: dyslexic parents' concerns and worries with regard to 2-year-olds. Unpublished ms., Institute of Special Needs Education, University of Oslo.

Lubs, H.A., Duara, R., Levin, B., Jallad, B., Lubs, M.L., Rabin, M., Kushch, A. and Gross-Glenn, K. (1991). 'Dyslexia subtypes: genetics, behavior, and brain imaging'. In: Duane, D. and Gray, D. (eds) *The Reading Brain: The Biological Basis of Dyslexia*. Parkton, MD: York, pp. 89–118.

Lundberg, I. and Høien, T. (1989). 'Phonemic deficits: a core symptom of developmental dyslexia?', *Irish Journal of Psychology*, 10, 4, 579–592.

Lundberg, I. and Nilsson, L. (1986). 'What church examination records can tell us about the inheritance of reading disability', *Annals of Dyslexia*, 36, 217–236.

Lundberg, I., Frost, J., Petersen, O.P. and Olofsson, Å. (1991). Long-term effects of a preschool programme for stimulating phonological awareness: the effect on low achieving children. Paper presented at the Fourth European Conference for Research on Learning and Instruction, Turku, Finland, 24–26 August.

Lyster, S.A.H. (1996). Preventing reading and spelling failure. Doctoral dissertation, University of Oslo, Department of Special Needs Education.

Olson, R.K., Wise, B., Conners, F., Rack, J. and Fulker, D. (1989). 'Specific deficits in component reading and language skills: genetic and environmental influences', *Journal of Learning Disabilities*, 22, 339–348.

Perfetti, C.A. (1985). *Reading Ability*. New York: Oxford University Press.

Rosenthal, R. and Jacobson, L. (1968). *Pygmalion in the Classroom*. New York: Rinehart and Winston.

Rutter, M. (1985). 'Resilience in the face of adversity: protective factors and resistance to psychiatric disorder', *British Journal of Psychiatry*, 147, 598–611.

Scarborough, H. (1989). 'Prediction of reading disability from familial and individual differences', *Journal of Educational Psychology*, 81, 1, 101–108.

Scarborough, H. (1990). 'Very early language deficits in dyslexic children', *Child Development*, 61, 1728–1741.

Scarborough, H. (1991). 'Antecedents to reading disability: preschool language development and literacy experiences of children from dyslexic families', *Reading and Writing: An Interdisciplinary Journal*, 3, 219–233.

Skaalvik, S. (1994). Voksne med lese- og skrivevansker [Adults with reading and writing difficulties]. Doctoral dissertation, University of Trondheim.

Snowling, M.J. (1987). *Dyslexia*. Oxford: Basil Blackwell.

Stanovich, K.E. (1988). 'Explaining the differences between the dyslexic and the garden-variety poor reader: the phonological-core variable-difference model', *Journal of Learning Disabilities*, 21, 560–612.

Swedish Official Report on Reading (1997). *Att lämna skolan med rak rygg. Om rätten till skriftspråket och om förskolans och skolans möjligheter att förebygga och möta läs- och skrivsvårigheter*. SOU 1997. Stockholm: Department of Education, p. 108.

Tallal, P., Miller, S. and Fitch, R.H. (1993). 'Neurobiological basis of speech: a case for the pre-eminence of temporal processing', *Annals of New York Academy of Sciences*, 682, 14, 27–47.

Thomas, C.J. (1905). 'Congenital "word blindness" and its treatment', *Ophthalmoscope*, 3, 380–385.

Wechsler, D. (1967). *Wechsler Pre-school and Primary Scale of Intelligence: WPPSI Manual*. New York: The Psychological Corporation; Norwegian standardization by Marit Langset, 1976.

Wimmer, H. and Frith, U. (1994). 'Reading difficulties among English and German children: same cause – different manifestation'. In: Frith, U., Ludi, G., Egli, M. and Zuber, C. (eds) *Proceedings of the Workshop on Contexts of Literacy. Vol. III, Nice, 21–24 September 1994*, pp. 257–274.

Source

This is an edited version of an article previously published in *European Journal of Special Educational Needs Education*, 14 (2). 1999. Reproduced by permission of Taylor & Francis Ltd.

Chapter 8

Partnership approaches
New futures for Travellers

Elizabeth Jordan

Introduction

Travellers in the UK are not a homogeneous group but are several, disparate and uniquely individual in their cultures and life-styles. A common experience shared by all of them is a difficulty in accessing and maintaining contact with one school throughout the compulsory school years. High levels of illiteracy and lack of formal qualifications signal the failure of state education to overcome the barriers associated with mobility in life-style, racism and institutional discrimination.

Gypsy Traveller groups engage in resistance and rarely continue with formal schooling into the secondary stages. Showground families usually rely on school-based learning packs to support them during the travelling season (March–October). The lack of continuity and coherence, particularly at the early stage of literacy acquisition, affects pupils' attitudes to school work and has evident consequences for their attainment.

Relevance in the curriculum, teacher–pupil relationships, expectations and aspirations all play a strong part in the progress of any child, but for Travellers these are key issues. For groups whose cultural and business lives are strongly centred within the extended family, home-learning is highly valued. The role of schools is critical in supporting and enabling this approach with school learning. Schools and Traveller teachers have developed a range of approaches (peer and paired support, taped and audio books, writing into reading, desktop publishing, etc.) and resources (Traveller-related content, role models, videos, photographs and ICT) which are proving to be motivating and help to overcome some of the barriers.

For those Traveller pupils whose literacy difficulties are persistent and more long term, innate or specific difficulties must be considered. There is already some evidence of familial patterns of dyslexic type difficulties emerging within some closely related groups. Providing appropriate and adequate teaching support for such pupils is challenging, for both teachers and the families.

Traveller communities

Travellers are groups with a long history as distinctive communities found in most countries in Europe (Fraser, 1992) and latterly in the USA, Canada and Australia. The name Traveller indicates a close connection with a history of mobility and in some respects is misleading and even unhelpful today. Many Traveller groups never travel and most are mobile only as and when it is an appropriate mechanism for earning or avoiding dispute. At European Union level, a decision was taken to identify two discrete groupings whose lifestyles and cultural traditions were 'different' to the dominant settled communities (EC, 1987) and who were largely marginalised from mainstream education provision as a result of racism. The Gypsy and traditional Travellers are generally signalled in written documents as Gypsy/Travellers for brevity, but without any intention of disrespect for the diversity within this generic term, while the term Occupational Travellers is used to denote Circus, Fairground and Bargee groups (Kiddle, 1998). Migrant workers are not included within either definition, but in the UK some street market traders are increasingly viewed as Occupational Travellers. A newer group of Travellers has emerged within the UK since the late 1950s, the New Travellers, or New Age Travellers, some of whose families are now into the third generation.

Historically Travellers have undertaken occupations associated with buying and selling, artistic and artefact productions (including entertainment and light metalworking) and various roles within the agricultural domain. In all cases the driving force has been to achieve financial security and independence while also maintaining their distinctive cultural mores and identities. This continues today with families diversifying their skills to occupy niche markets which support their traditional lifestyles. Thus, for many Travellers, mobility is still a strong feature, with most using housed accommodation, as and when appropriate to their needs.

Since the inception of public schools Travellers have experienced difficulties in securing access, continuity and coherence in formal education. Today Travellers continue to suffer such discrimination with the result that levels of illiteracy are high and lack of formal qualifications adds to their exclusion from the waged job markets. However, Travellers themselves also exert agency (Danaher, 2000) and many prefer to continue their traditions of education being undertaken within the family and community: education to be a Traveller is equally, or even more, important than education for employability (Liegeois, 1998). For Gypsy/Travellers, in particular, this is a significant feature in maintaining and strengthening ethnic role boundaries (Acton and Mundy, 1997).

It is against this richly diverse and complex background that this chapter attempts to signal the specific issues that have to be addressed in order that schools ensure that Travellers achieve the levels of formal education necessary for independence and empowerment within our society.

Racism and bullying

Travellers experience racism in their daily lives and mobile families are easy targets. Within schools they are faced with daunting institutional racism, where access to a place on the school roll, appropriate curriculum subjects, learning support and other services can be almost impossible to obtain when only temporarily in an area. All Traveller children are subject to name-calling and other forms of bullying, particularly in the playground and on the journey to and from school. Such regular attacks on the group identity, added to a lack of confidence related to lack of experience or bad experiences in schools in the past, contributes to low self-esteem, depressed expectations and, ultimately, few educational aspirations. The relationship between esteem and the ability to capitalise on learning experiences is well documented, so, for this reason alone, Travellers must be considered an 'at risk' group of learners. This is not to problematise Travellers and their cultural life-styles, but rather to expose the critical role of education providers in establishing the necessary conditions for successful learning.

Racism and bullying are endemic in schools and are reflective of the attitudes within the school community. While schools work at eliminating such negative attitudes, unless the school involves its wider community in the developments there will be no significant change in behaviours. All Travellers recount incidences of name-calling and many experience more serious forms of racism, some of it from staff (Lloyd, Stead, Jordan and Norris, 1999). Travellers regularly report that they have to sit at the back (or at the side) of the class and are often left to do some colouring-in or to work on their own with the few books and papers which they have brought with them. Being thus regularly marginalised further contributes to their rejection of schooling and causes them to fall back instead on their own resources in home-learning (McKinney, 2001).

Many teachers do resent the interruption to their class plans when a new pupil arrives and leaves during term time, often after only a short stay. There is a danger that regular such occurrences will be allowed to justify a lack of drive towards developing inclusive approaches for Travellers unless the school management gives a strong lead in ensuring a genuine welcome and providing appropriate levels of support while the children are enrolled. Good practice involves placing the Traveller pupil with a supportive buddy and within peer groups for as many activities as possible. By demonstrating that s/he is part of the class the other children are given a positive role model of inclusive behaviour. Research shows that there has been an improvement in the primary sector in recent years (HMI, 2001) but as yet less success at post-primary stages.

Parents and home-learning

Traditionally the family has been the main source of education and training for Traveller youngsters. Cultural traditions, family histories, knowledge of the country and ways of dealing with society, day-to-day living, skills in self-representation, selling, finding work opportunities, health care and child rearing are all considered to be integral to the role of the family; not just the nuclear, but extended family kinship grouping, is traditionally involved in this process. Family-centred approaches are, therefore, very important resources for schools to use in enhancing Traveller children's learning. Parents, or older siblings, can act as home tutors, supporting formal learning through dialogue with the school and home tutor. Such tutors benefit from training, that is, being given the skills and knowledge which allow them to undertake the role of listener and advocate and where possible to model reading and writing. Home-tutors have to be aware that they have an important role in supporting the teacher by setting aside time at home for school work, ensuring some space, and in the care and management of learning resources. Where there is limited space, as in a caravan on the move, these issues take on an enormous organisational significance, especially where the home-tutor is also involved in the family's earning enterprises.

Traveller parents may rely heavily on oral communication with the school, often through their children. Youngsters' misunderstandings of teachers' words have long been a source of mirth for adults, but when there is no way of checking out their version with the written form parents can be left feeling confused, embarrassed and even slighted. Schools must review their communication approaches to prevent any parent being misinformed or lacking full information. Most schools are already adopting inclusive approaches for other minority ethnic groups' language needs, but often forget Travellers' needs in this respect. Face-to-face and telephone communication provide appropriate channels for building rapport and securing co-operation. Travellers value highly teachers who take the trouble to get to know them and their children and usually improved attendance is seen in such schools.

For a non-literate family there are enormous challenges presented today by the expectation in schools that parents will take a significant role in supporting their children's formal learning. This of course includes the acquisition of literacy skills, particularly at the early stages. Many Travellers need the support of verbal and practical instructions, modelled by teachers at school meetings, in the home and on video clips. Such approaches are working, with more and more Travellers engaging successfully with primary schools.

Parents need instructions on how actively to listen to children's reading and writing. Parent prompts in video format are especially easy to use as many Travellers have video recorders. Giving stickers for them to attach to the work supervised also allows them to demonstrate the success or otherwise of the child's efforts. Regular, warmly supportive check-up phone calls by the school are also motivating and help ensure trusting, collaborative relationships. This works too with older pupils who are learning at a distance while they travel. Keeping in touch with their 'own' teacher(s) plays a significant part in keeping pupils on track with their studies (Carroll and Jordan, 1994).

Oracy

As with most sectors of British society up to the nineteenth century, the opportunity to acquire literacy and formal book-based learning was unavailable to Travellers, so oral transmission remained the dominant form of communication. The languages and dialects which they spoke thus remained unrecorded and largely unknown to outsiders (Bakker and Kyuchikov, 2000). With the advent of compulsory schooling for all, many Travellers did attempt to attend school, usually during the winter period (Whyte, 1979). However, bullying and other discriminatory treatment, both personally racist and institutionalised, helped to marginalise Travellers further within the dominant society and thus confirmed them in their belief in relying on their own resources (Kiddle, 1998). Skills, knowledge and cultural codes continue to be transmitted orally from generation to generation.

Oral skills are thus valued and the development of high levels of listening and talking skills are essential characteristics of successful Travellers. There are today significant differences between the languages of Gypsy/Travellers and those of Fairground families. With the schism between the two broad groups in the UK in 1886 these differences have become more pronounced and the different patterns of travelling and school attendance have also contributed to the changes. At present there are four main Gypsy/Traveller languages or dialects within Great Britain, Romani, largely spoken in England, Gammon or Kalo in Wales, Shelta in Ireland and Cant in Scotland. As yet, these are under-researched and only now are some being recorded in written form, with Romani being the dominant and, to some extent, international language. Many Gypsy/Travellers express reservations about the publication of their 'secret' languages and some even resent this imposition by a dominant, international group of Romani and Gypsy academics. Few Travellers in Britain are aware of this development, and even fewer have access to the texts now becoming available, often through small and relatively obscure publishers. There is then an added complexity for young Travellers entering school, where not only the language of school is not always explicitly taught, but teachers are also unaware of the complexity of the languages used by Travellers. Traveller parents who have had little, if any, formal schooling do not have the necessary common understandings adequately to prepare their young for school entrance, nor to argue for appropriate provision. At the same time it is important not to underestimate the very real knowledge and skills in oracy which they have and which can be developed further within the school curriculum.

Traditional modes of working and earning a living have ensured that all Travellers have become orally adept at establishing a quick rapport with possible clients; negotiating deals and persuading 'punters' to part with their money. Being able to convince and maintain a line of argument, demonstrating awareness of social signals and appropriate knowledge, being alive to subtle nuances of reaction in clients and overcoming reticence, all allow them to operate successfully without recourse to any written materials. Children can be encouraged to discuss their perspectives on aspects of conflict and racism within Language, Moral and Religious Education and Personal and Social Development. Drama and storytelling offer opportunities for Traveller children to work collaboratively with others in exploring stereotyping, bias, pejorative use of words and the use of genre to convey message to different audiences. Tape recording of agreed outcomes can support oral productions into text, particularly group writing.

Within their family and community lives aural memory is highly valued and building significant memory banks of facts, such as telephone numbers, geographical, technical and scientific information, is an essential prerequisite for survival. Such skills can be exploited in the development of storytelling, reciting rhymes and poems, singing and abstracting facts from TV and audio programmes in a variety of subjects. Traveller-specific rhymes and stories are no longer abundant within the community so schools should check the young child's level of awareness of rhymes and rhythm. Most are likely to be more familiar with TV jingles and pop music than with the stereotyped socialising of storytelling round the campfire.

Relevance of literacy

Practical reading and writing skills, reading with a purpose, recognised and valued within the family, are necessary approaches to engage the reluctant Traveller. This is helped by the requirement for a written exam as part of achieving a driver's licence. For all Traveller males (and increasingly females) a licence is a prerequisite for self-employment, yet fewer males attend even primary schools on a regular basis so are less likely to be competent readers. One young Gypsy/Traveller girl (a good reader) has successfully coached her older non-literate brothers to pass the test orally. The relevance of reading is further reinforced by the need to cohere with safety regulations on the collection and disposal of different types of scrap materials, long a source of income for some. Traveller teachers use these practical needs as a basis for setting up family literacy schemes.

Schools which capitalise on family interests, such as certain TV programmes, the close-knit relationships and celebration of community events not only show respect for that family's life-style, acknowledging the diversity and drawing out the similarities in behaviours in the class membership, but also promote the significance of the affirmation of family life to children's learning. Rather than the school arranging to have a project on the Fairground or the Circus when one visits the town it is better to draw on the Fairground or Circus child's talk and writings to act as a catalyst for the class to engage in further study later. As one Show parent so graphically described it, 'My child knows all about the Shows; she teaches it in every school she ever attends! She already knows all that, but I want her to learn something new, something we can't give her.'

It is generally thought that the lack of culturally relevant reading materials is a contributing factor in academic under-achievement in Traveller communities. There are several Traveller writers publishing widely today whose stories can be used to raise awareness of the contribution to storytelling made by Gypsy/Travellers. Books by Duncan Williamson can be read by older children themselves, as can those by Stanley Robertson. Both authors, and other Travellers, are available as storytellers to schools through the Scottish Arts Council schemes.

Several Traveller Education Services (TES) have developed a range of culturally orientated resources with some being of a very high quality. Materials, such as *Just Like You, A Horse For Joe, The Smiths, Shaun's Wellies*, are attractive for any child at the early stages of literacy, while *The Life and Story of May Orchard* and *Moving with the Times* provide a sound basis for raising awareness (within the whole class) of Gypsy/Traveller cultural mores. A range of low cost alphabet booklets and early readers, based on Traveller life, are produced by several TES but some Travellers express resentment when their children are given books which are different to the others in the class. Such materials are best kept in the library corner and for home reading.

Some other approaches which have been shown to be relevant have included letter writing, desktop publishing, motor mechanics, hair-dressing and clothes magazines, baby care, Health and First Aid certificates.

Letter writing, particularly to family members who are away for significant periods, is seen to be especially valuable when it includes personal photographs. This allows families to keep in touch and is motivating for youngsters who can demonstrate newly learned practical skills. Birthday, wedding and anniversary cards are particularly popular, as is the advent of any new baby. Using desktop publishing software, pupils can create their own message and incorporate quality photographs relevant to the sender and receiver. Spell check and grammar correction software aids the writing process and removes much of the frustration, as do content-free programmes where teachers can enter essential words appropriate for the pupil's task.

The use of technology, which includes giving pupils cheap cameras to take photographs in their home settings, acts as a spur for the development of talking skills and ultimately underpins the need for writing skills. Scanning in Traveller images to computers allows the construction of personalised and culturally correct productions such as jigsaws, posters and postcards to send back to school in order to keep in touch with the class when travelling.

Supported family learning sessions, where several members are included in activities within Community Learning Plans, can also help to support the development of literacy competence within a less formal setting than that of the school.

Learning difficulties

The variations in teaching styles which mobile pupils meet can add to difficulties in literacy if staff are not sufficiently sensitive to the need for some continuity and coherence. Supporting the Traveller pupil's use of the learning pack they bring, or using it as a basis for some integrated work with the class or group, can provide such a bridge.

Given the lack of coherence and continuity in some Traveller pupils' experience of the school curriculum it is perhaps not surprising (though not necessarily to be expected) that some may take longer to acquire competency in literacy than their settled peers. The research on whether mobility *per se* affects performance is not conclusive, although most schools would support such a notion, as indeed they do for other interrupted learners, such as Forces' children (Dobson and Henthorne, 2000).

Children who experience literacy difficulties still require direct teacher intervention on occasions, but most often this is not available outside of schools. Rapid access to learning support staff and reading specialists can be arranged in schools which have seasonal influxes of Travellers, for example Eastbank Academy in Glasgow (*Interrupted Learners*, 1998).

Such cases of reading retardation are best reviewed as individuals, with an assessment of the whole learning context, including the pupil's individual strengths and weaknesses. Arranging such a comprehensive review can be problematic where the pupil not only is an infrequent attender, but also changes schools and even crosses local authority boundaries. Missing out on standardised and national testing is common, so learning difficulties often go undetected and unrecorded.

Recording and record keeping play a critical part in contributing to the process. Travellers themselves sometimes do not aid this process as they may move on, either temporarily or for longer periods, without informing the school. It is all the more important then that schools keep the records and contact their local TES or TENET (Traveller Education Network in Scotland) to alert them to the existence of the records should they be required elsewhere.

There is some unpublished evidence of a familial incidence of specific literacy difficulties within some Traveller extended families. Schools should be prepared to explore this possibility when the child is still struggling after a period of good teaching input. Families (when approached in a supportive manner) are usually forthcoming with details of literacy difficulties. The picture can be compounded, of course, by many difficulties being attributable to poor attendance rates in past generations and the perceived lack of relevance in school curricula.

Whatever the underlying or contributing causes may be, the actual follow-up process can be even more problematic. A mobile family may not be in a position to remain in school for a significant period and may even not know where their next stay will be. Hand-held records become a necessity for ease of transfer. Glasgow City Council has developed just such records covering the full 5–14 curriculum for their winter resident community of Fairground families. These go with them in the spring to keep updated as and when the children complete units of work or go into other schools. Several TES in England and Wales have developed their own versions, particularly covering the Key Stages in literacy and numeracy.

Distance learning

Mobile Travellers are increasingly demanding and making use of distance education packs. Unlike Australia, where there is an educationally sound viable alternative to school-based learning (Danaher, 1998), there is no bank of published distance learning resources in the UK to cover the full school curriculum. Usually a base school, or TES where there is one, selects appropriate texts and resources to segment into chunks of work for use by the learner when out of school for a significant period. While this can be beneficial for practice, rehearsal and revision of work already learned, it is not, as yet, sufficiently funded to allow the full-scale development of a quality distance education approach. The need for a teacher, an adult who interacts with and gets to know the learner as an individual and who takes cognisance of his/her preferred learning style, remains critical in the formal learning process (Carroll and Jordan, 1994).

In Australia, the development of national policies and statewide provision to support these has led to families, at all levels of competence, being able to access quality distance education, where both published resources and human teaching support services are provided, irrespective of place or style of residence. There a learner can succeed and achieve at levels commensurate with their peers, through the use of distance education from early years' groups to senior secondary, FE and, ultimately, University levels. Some TES and schools in the UK, in collaboration within EFECOT EU projects (EFECOT, 1999), have developed appropriate resources and modes of delivery for Occupational Traveller pupils. These have demonstrated the viability of distance education approaches for Travellers.

However, constructing learning materials for a pupil with real literacy difficulties whose family may not have adequate levels of literacy or experience of schools themselves, is not easy and is as yet taxing all who work with Travellers. Most cases require input from teaching staff, sometimes achieved through supported study programmes. Some families have altered their work patterns to include more regular visits back to the base school for direct tuition from familiar teachers, with promising results to date (Jordan, 2001).

Maintaining personal contact plays a significant part in supporting learners at a distance: telephone, fax and e-mail all provide forms of contact for schools. However, e-mail and interactive computer-based learning can be problematic when the Traveller family has difficulty in accessing suitable electricity and internet connections. Access and costs are critical considerations in ensuring equality through the use of ICT. Drop-in facilities in learning centres where they can get ready access is one way of ensuring equality of opportunity but setting up such facilities in each area generally has not been a priority within the local authority Traveller education budgets.

Many of the problems experienced by Travellers are similar to those of other interrupted learners. Governmental directives, both national and local, have rarely made the necessary connections but instead try to address each individual group's needs on an ad hoc basis. The skills and knowledge derived from each such project are rarely used to inform other projects so that scarce resources are dissipated and effort duplicated: best value approaches are evidently not being applied at the highest levels to providing services for pupils at the margins. The Notschool.net project is currently developing approaches to help engage learners in a variety of out-of-school settings, all supported by tutors (Heppell, 2000). Until such time as there is a national commitment to supporting formal learning in a range of settings for the variety of circumstances that families experience, then Travellers will remain at the margins in state education.

References

Acton, T. and Mundy, G. (eds) (1997) *Romany Culture and Gypsy Identity*. University of Hertfordshire.

Bakker, O. and Kyuchikov, H (eds) (2000) *What is the Romani Language?* University of Hertfordshire.

Carroll, L. and Jordan, E. (1994) *Attendance Patterns of Showground Pupils in Secondary Schools in Glasgow*. STEP, Moray House Institute of Education.

Conlon-McKenna, Marta (1992) *The Blue Horse* (Irish Children's Book of the Year Award). The O'Brien Press.

Danaher, P. (1998) *Beyond the Ferris Wheel*. Central Queensland University.

Danaher, P. (ed.) (2000) Mapping International Diversity in Researching Traveller and Nomadic Education. *International Journal of Educational Research* 33 (3): 221–230.

Dobson, J. and Henthorne, K. (2000) *Pupil Mobility in Schools*. London University College.

EC (1987) *School Provision for Gypsy and Traveller Children. A synthesis report*. Office for Official Publications of the European Communities.

EFECOT (1999) *TOPILOT: To Optimise Independent Learning in Occupational Travellers. A report*. EFECOT Bureau.

Fraser, A. (1992) *The Gypsies*. Blackwell.

Haringey Traveller Education Service (1998) *Just Like You*.

Heppell, S. (2000) *eLearning Ultralab/paper* http://www.ultralab.ac.uk/papers/

HMI (2001) *Managing Support for the Attainment of Pupils from Minority Ethnic Groups*. HMI 326 OFSTED.

Interrupted Learners (1998) Scottish Traveller Education Programme, video. Edinburgh University.

Jordan, E. (2001) Interrupted Learning: the Traveller Paradigm. *Support for Learning. The British Journal of Learning Support* 16 (3): 128–134.

Kiddle, C. (1998) *Traveller Children. A Voice for Themselves*. Jessica Kingsley.

Liegeois, J.-P. (ed.) (1998) *School Provision for Ethnic Minorities: the Gypsy Paradigm*. University of Hertfordshire.

Lloyd, G., Stead, J., Jordan, E. and Norris, C. (1999) Teachers and Gypsy Travellers. *Scottish Educational Review*, 31 (1), 48–65.

McKinney, R. (2001) *Different Lessons. Scottish Gypsy/Travellers and the Future of Education*. Scottish Traveller Consortium.

Norfolk Traveller Education Service (1995) *Shaun's Wellies*.

Orchard, Dorothy. *The Life & Story of May Orchard*. Devon Traveller Education Service.

Reilly, Goodily. *Moving With the Times*. Devon Learning Resources.

Smith, E.D. *The Smiths: The Secondary Literacy Programme*. National Association of Teachers of Travellers.

Whyte, B. (1979) *Yellow On The Broom. The Early Days of a Traveller Woman*. Chambers.

Wiltshire Traveller Education Service. *A Horse for Joe*. Reader & Pupils' Activity Sheets.

Source

This chapter was written especially for this volume.

Part 2

School and classroom

Chapter 9

Using Soft Systems Methodology to re-think special needs

Norah Frederickson

Many researchers suggest that there is a need to re-think special educational needs. This chapter addresses the practical issue of *how* we should go about this rethink. It is first of all argued that, however we go about it, our approach should be systematic and explicit. The second part of the chapter introduces one approach – Soft Systems Methodology (SSM) – which appears particularly suited to conducting an action-orientated rethink of special needs in mainstream schools. The final section outlines ways in which SSM has been used by groups and individuals in schools and Local Education Authorities to reflect on practice and effect improvement.

Special needs: a complex mess?

It may appear unnecessary to dwell on the assertion that any rethink of special needs should be conducted in a systematic and explicit manner. It might be accepted as obvious and uncontroversial in this era of accountability. However, it is not the way in which change has typically been designed and managed in educational contexts. Indeed words such as 'designed' and 'managed' are part of a new vocabulary which appears to fit uneasily with talk of 'philosophy' and 'good primary practice'. Dyson's (1990) comments about the 'whole school approach' to special educational needs could as easily have been directed at any number of educational practices brought to the fore by the pendular swings of fashion, 'the approach as a whole seems to have found its way into educational practice without any sort of rigorous evaluation and there is little or nothing in the literature about how it has been or might be evaluated.'

There are, of course, well developed and highly respected methods for conducting rigorous evaluation, within the scientific tradition, and it is perhaps not surprising that authors engaged in debate on special needs have urged the use of empirical data and experimental trials, 'from which one could make generalizations according to the canons of scientific research' (Kauffman, 1989). However, schools have little in common with well controlled laboratories and repeatable experiments, in human science contexts, are difficult to achieve as Checkland and Scholes (1990) point out. Nonetheless, there has been extensive application of scientifically based ideas to the field of special needs by the various professionals involved whose activities are well described by Schön (1983) in his critique of the 'technical rationality' view of professional activity: 'professional activity consists in instrumental problem solving made rigorous by the application of scientific theory and technique'. This is well illustrated by the prominence of scientifically based problem solving approaches in educational psychology over the past decade (Cameron and Stratford, 1987; Frederickson, Webster and Wright, 1991). While acknowledging the existence of 'high, hard ground where practitioners can make effective use of research-based theory and technique', he argues that practitioners may more often find themselves in a swamp where many of the problems of greatest human concern exist as, 'confusing "messes" incapable of technical solution'. Soft Systems Methodology has been developed as an organized way of tackling messy situations in the real world. It provides an intellectual framework based on systems thinking which allows a practitioner, operating in an action research mode, to make sense both of the situation and of their involvement in it. In education and social science generally the label 'action research' is applied to much wallowing around in real world messes. Checkland and Scholes (1990) lament that discussions of action research, 'on the whole unfortunately neglect the crucial importance of declaring the intellectual framework' as 'it is with reference to the declared framework that "lessons" can be defined' (p. 16).

A major contributing factor to the 'messiness' of many problematic situations and issues in education is substantive differences in the perceptions and intentions of those involved. In these cases it is not possible to embark on a classical problem solving approach because it is not possible to agree on a definition of *the* problem or achieve consensus on the objectives of any change. In these situations there is a need for an explicit approach which can represent the range of views held without requiring that they be reconciled in order for progress to be made. This is likely to be particularly important in the field of special needs as the current US debate over the Regular Education Initiative (REI) illustrates. There is a number of illuminating parallels between the REI debate and the 'Dyson Debate' (Dyson, 1990; Butt, 1991) on the future role of the special needs co-ordinator in UK schools, however, the following brief discussion will focus on those aspects which illustrate the need for an approach which can accommodate a range of conflicting views.

The Regular Education Initiative is an umbrella term for a set of proposals for radical restructuring of special and general education in the US. At its core is the, not unfamiliar, view that education for pupils with special needs will be best served by the improvement of education for all pupils. It is further elaborated by Kauffman (1989), one of its main opponents, as requiring that:

> Students of every description are fully integrated into regular classes, no student is given a special designation (label), costs are lowered by the elimination of special budget and administrative categories, the focus

becomes excellence for all, and federal regulations are withdrawn in favour of local control.

(p. 256)

Proponents of the Regular Education Initiative (McLeskey, Skiba and Wilcox, 1990) are critical of the current fragmented approach to pupils with special needs and are concerned about the stigmatization of pupils on 'pull out' (withdrawal) programmes. They argue, along similar lines to Booth (1986), that values rather than data should determine social policy. 'Data can be used to evaluate progress towards the goals established by values, but data cannot alter the value itself' (McLeskey, Skiba and Wilcox, 1990, p. 322). They therefore point to the right of all children, under Public Law 94–142, to a free appropriate education in the least restrictive environment as central.

Opponents of the Regular Education Initiative (Kauffman, 1989) criticize its proponents for naivety on two accounts. They first of all argue that a mainstream classroom may not be the least restrictive environment for all children, and indeed that the objective of providing appropriate education should take precedence over that relating to the setting in which it is provided. Secondly they demonstrate that the Regular Education Initiative can be perceived as being underpinned by a quite different set of values from those espoused by its proponents. Hence Kauffman (1989) argues:

> The belief systems represented by the REI are a peculiar case in which conservative ideology (focus on excellence, federal disengagement) and liberal rhetoric (non-labelling, integration) are combined to support the diminution or dissolution of a support system for handicapped students.

The critique of Kauffman's paper by Goetz and Sailor (1990) in which they paraphrase him thus, 'REI is a Reagan–Bush plot to cut the costs of special education' (p. 335) will sound familiar in the context of UK debates on integration and in-class support strategies.

Kauffman characterizes proponents and opponents of the Regular Education Initiative as espousing an opposing set of assumptions or beliefs:

Proponents hold that:	*While opponents believe that:*
Pupils are more alike than different. The same basic principles apply to learning of all, so no *special* teaching is needed by any.	Some pupils are very different from most and special educational approaches are required to meet their needs.
Good teachers can teach all pupils, using the same basic techniques but making some adjustments for individual differences.	Not all teachers are equipped to teach all pupils; special expertise is required to teach pupils with special needs who are particularly difficult to teach.

All pupils can be provided with a high quality education without identifying some as different and targeting funding separately.	Pupils with special needs must be clearly identified to ensure that they receive appropriate services.
All pupils can be taught and managed effectively in the mainstream classroom; segregation of pupils with special needs in any way is ethically unacceptable.	Education outside the mainstream classroom is sometimes required for part of the school day to: (a) provide more intensive individualized instruction, (b) provide instruction in skills already mastered or not needed by most pupils, (c) ensure the appropriate education of the other pupils.

Attention has also been drawn to the impact of these different sets of beliefs on the UK debate on the future role of special needs co-ordinators. Dyson (1990) argues that the 'whole school approach' is founded on assumptions, 'that special needs children learn in much the same way as all other children, and that the so-called expertise of special needs teachers can in fact be spread amongst subject and class teachers' (p. 118).

The above discussion demonstrates that the field of special educational needs is characterized by a diversity of approaches, underpinned by conflicting beliefs and riven by disagreement about fundamental issues – such as how special educational needs should be defined. It would appear to be well characterized as one of Schön's (1983) 'confusing messes' and, in its rethinking, to require an approach which can bring systematic, logical analysis to bear without oversimplifying the real complexities of the situations studied or underestimating the impact of human perceptions and interests in effecting or resisting change.

Soft Systems Methodology

Soft Systems Methodology (SSM) is an approached which can be used to guide intervention in the kinds of ill-structured, real world problem situations common in the field of special needs. Checkland, who is Professor of Systems and Information at the University of Lancaster, developed the methodology through a programme of over 100 action research consultancies in commercial and service environments, including health and social service contexts (Checkland, 1981; Checkland and Scholes, 1990). Soft Sytems Methodology adopts a positive approach which is sensitive to context. It does not focus on the problem but on the situation in which there is perceived to be a problem, or an opportunity for impovement. The initial task is not to converge on a definition of a problem to solve, but to build up the richest possible picture of the situation in question, drawing on the disparate perceptions of those involved.

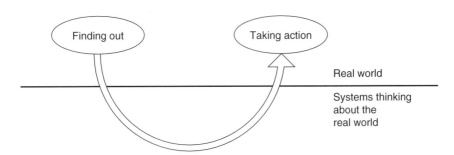

Figure 9.1 The essential nature of SSM (from Checkland, 1986)

The essential nature of SSM is summarized in Figure 9.1. In overview, it consists of some stages where you engage in findings out about and developing a representation of reality, some stages where you develop a model of a system which might be relevant to changing/improving reality and, finally, some stages where you draw comparisons between your model and your representation of reality in order to generate improvement suggestions/recommendations for action.

For descriptive purposes SSM consists of the seven stages which are represented diagrammatically in Figure 9.2.

In Stages 1 and 2 you would be involved in finding out about a particular problem situation, collecting information and identifying important themes and issues. You may collect information by a number of different means, for example, interviewing, observation. These are practical activities where you will need to do something in the real world.

In Stages 3 and 4 you would use aspects of systems theory to analyse the problem situation to build models of systems which may be relevant to improving it. Notice the words used. A model relevant to improving a problem situation does not purport to be a model of a problem/or a problem situation. These activities are purely logical/theoretical. A more detailed discussion of different strands of systems theory and their application in schools can be found in Frederickson (1990a).

In Stages 5 to 7 you would be involved in suggesting possible changes to the real world situation whose desirability and feasibility those directly involved could debate and, if appropriate, implement. (The last three stages again involve practical activities, such as meetings and feasibility studies which would need to be carried out in the real world.)

You will notice the distinction which is drawn between Stages 3 and 4, the below line stages, and the other five stages, the above line stages. Stages 3 and 4 are theoretical in that they involve formal systems thinking whereas the other five stages are practical in that they involve activities which are carried out in the real world.

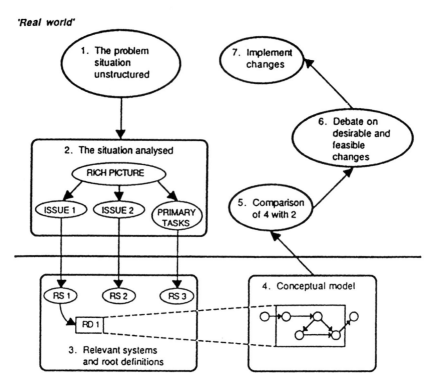

Figure 9.2 The essential nature of SSM (from Checkland, 1986)

The seven stages of Soft Systems Methodology are now described in more detail.

Stage 1. The problem situation: unstructured

The task in Stage 1 is to find out about the problem situation while trying not to impose a particular structure on it. Checkland suggests a number of things which it might be useful to find out about the problem situation. He suggests that you attempt to identify elements of structure in the situation (relatively static aspects such as physical layout, departmental structure, staff hierarchy, patterns of communications) and elements of process (relatively dynamic aspects which operate within the framework of the structure, for example planning, decision making, monitoring). The relationship between the elements of structure and process which you have identified will give an indication of the 'climate' existing in the problem situation.

Checkland provides the following additional specific guidelines to assist you in the initial stages of finding out:

1. *Find out about the context of the analysis itself*
   This will involve asking three questions about roles which exist in the problem situation as a corollary of the analysis:

   - Who is the client? (The client is the term used to describe the person who has caused the analysis to occur.)
   - Who are the problem solvers? (The persons trying to make the analysis.)
   - Who could be regarded as the problem owners? (The problem solvers can decide who to include in the list of possible problem owners, whether or not those persons would necessarily see themselves in that role. It is recommended that they include themselves and the client among others.) Answering this question helps the problem solvers appreciate the problem situation from a variety of different perspectives.

2. *Find out about the social aspects of the situation*
   Find out about the norms, roles and values which exist in the situation. What roles (formal or informal social positions) are accepted, what behaviour is expected in them and how is performance judged? Why is Sue Brown regarded as a good class teacher or a weak headteacher or a supportive colleague? What do you have to do to get on in All Souls High School?

3. *Find out about the political aspects of the situation*
   What are the sources or commodities of power in this situation? (They may have to do with access to or control of certain information or people, the ability to set up structures, long involvement with the organization, role in the organization and external recognition.) How are such commodities obtained, preserved, passed on, for example?

Stage 2. The problem situation: expressed

The information obtained is used in Stage 2 to express, represent or describe the problem situation – to build up the richest possible picture of the situation. This may be a pen picture but it is often found to be more useful to express the information diagrammatically or indeed pictorially.

A rich picture is defined as an evolving diagram which collects together and portrays key information and impressions about a complex situation in a loosely structured and evocative way. Such a picture is likely to contain patterns or aspects which the problem solvers regard as significant in some way or encapsulate particular features of the situation – these can be selected as problem themes. Such a picture is also usually capable of being viewed from a variety of different perspectives. At Stage 3 consideration of these different viewpoints and problem themes will allow the problem solvers to select a number of particular systems which they hypothesize to be relevant to debate about the problem situation with a view to bringing about improvement. Figure 9.3 contains an example of a rich picture (of the operation of a Local Authority secondary support base for 'vulnerable' pupils) where the emphasis is on the structural and procedural aspects of the problem situation. Figure 9.4, on the other hand, contains an example of a rich picture (of the problem situation faced by a group of staff charged with the production of a curriculum five year plan for their school) where the social and political aspects of the situation are evocatively expressed.

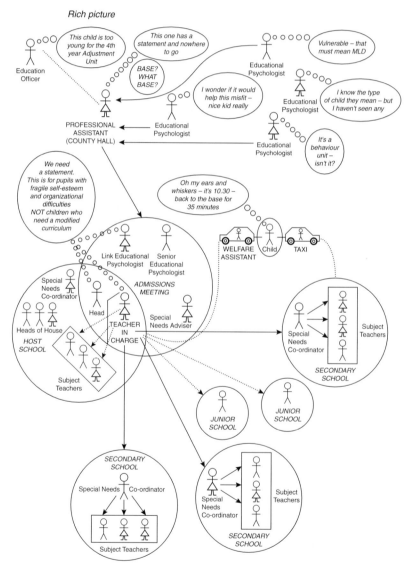

Rich picture

Figure 9.3

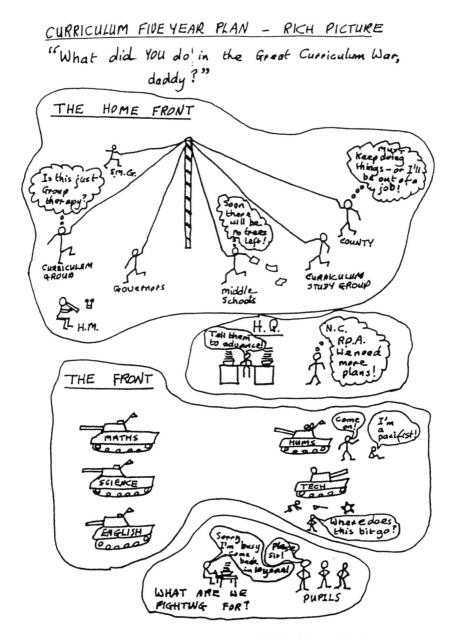

Figure 9.4 Curriculum five year plan – rich picture 'What did you do in the Great Curriculum War, daddy?'

Stage 3. Relevant systems and root definitions

At Stage 3 then the problem solvers attempt to analyse the situation system-atically by taking the viewpoints/issues identified at Stage 2 and naming a number of notional systems which may be of relevance (Relevant Systems). For example, Naughton (1984) suggests that either of the following systems might be considered relevant if the problem situation were an English pub:

> an alcohol retailing system;
> a system for initiating adolescents into the adult culture.

He identifies the first as a fairly obvious example of a primary-task system whereas the latter is a rather unexpected example of an issue-based system. The usefulness of each of these two perspectives is likely to differ depending on the particular problem situation.

As a further example consider the following notional systems which proved relevant to the resolution of a particular parent–school conflict over the school's homework requirements. The viewpoint which suggested each of these systems as potentially relevant is noted in brackets:

> a system to consolidate pupil learning (teachers);
> a system to enhance the school's academic reputation (head);
> a system to cover exam course work which isn't covered in class because
>   the teachers can't keep order (pupil);
> a parent undermining system (objecting parent).

In naming possible relevant systems there is no attempt to imply that any of these different perspectives is right or more accurate. In Soft Systems Methodology a system is a hypothetical construct which is used to think about some real world activity from a particular perspective (such as the four perspec-tives listed above). Care has been taken not to describe the school's homework programme as 'the homework system' since this everyday use of the word 'system' would be incorrect and confusing. Soft Systems Methodology makes a clear distinction between formal systems thinking and the real world. The purpose in naming relevant systems is not to claim that is how it really is. Rather the purpose is to attempt to find some potentially useful or insightful ways of viewing the problem situation.

Having identified a number of relevant systems, the problem solvers then have to select some to develop further. This selection is made on the basis of subjective judgement and experience. Naughton points out:

> Many other systems might also be relevant to any particular case. The criteria of relevance are, of course, ultimately subjective and the skill of choosing systems which yield fruitful analyses is an important element in the craft knowledge of the business.

For the novice in Soft Systems Methodology there is at least the possibility of cycling again through Stages 3, 4 and 5 should the first attempt at analysis fail to yield a useful outcome.

Checkland and Scholes (1990) state that an important aim of Soft Systems Methodology is, 'to take seriously the subjectivity which is then the crucial characteristic of human affairs and to treat this subjectivity, if not exactly scientifically, at least in a way characterized by intellectual rigour' (p. 30). The rest of Stage 3 and Stage 4 therefore involve the logical development of the Relevant Systems which have been selected. The relevant systems are first defined more clearly. This is done through producing a root definition of each, which describes its basic nature in a way designed to be revealing to those in the situation. The value of root definitions is not judged in terms of their correctness, but in terms of their usefulness in illuminating ways in which aspects of the problem situation can be helpfully changed.

To provide a clear definition of the system under consideration, the root definition should contain the following six elements:

C – Customers (victims or beneficiaries of the system).
A – Actors (who carry out the activities of the system).
T – Transformation process (what the system does to its inputs to turn them into outputs).
W – *Weltanschauung* (the view of the world that makes this system meaningful).
O – Owner (who could abolish this system).
E – Environmental constraints (what in the environment this system takes as given).

Here is an illustration which is taken from a worked example on in-service training provision for special needs which was generated by Peter Checkland during an advanced professional training course for educational psychologists and senior secondary teachers held at University College London in July 1988. One of the Relevant Systems selected was: a system to provide special needs in-service training for mainstream teachers. The following CATWOE analysis was produced:

C – mainstream teachers.
A – those who do in-service training.
T – need to cope with Special Needs in mainstream >T> need met by in-service training.
W – desirable/possible to educate special needs pupils in mainstream.
O – headteacher.
E – 1981 Education Act, resources available, school culture and structure.

The associated Root Definition was: A headteacher-owned system, staffed by INSET trainers which, given the constraints of the 1981 Education Act, available resources and the school structure and culture, provides to selected teachers that INSET which is deemed necessary to enable them to cope with pupils having special educational needs in mainstream lessons.

The transformation process is at the heart of the root definition. It should be noted that the input to the transformation process must be present in the output although in a changed form; in the example given the input is a need and the output is that need met.

Stage 4. Building conceptual models

The root definition describes what the system *is*. In order to describe what it *does* it is necessary to build an activity model of the system. This model will be conceptual in that the problem solvers must strive to make it a purely logical representation of the activities which would necessarily have to happen in the system described by the root definition. No attempt should be made either to model what really happens or what might ideally happen. Your model is only a relevant intellectual construct to be used to help structure debate. At this stage comments are often made about the advantages of having included among the problem solvers an 'outsider' whose greater distance from the real world situation helps to retain an appropriate focus on the logical and conceptual nature of the model building.

The crucial components of the model will be activities, represented on paper as verbs. The task is to assemble in correct order the minimum number of activities required in the operation of the human activity system described by the root definition. The aim is to have between six and twelve main activities. These may subsequently be broken into sets of subsidiary activities as necessary. Conceptual models may be constructed as follows:

- write down verbs associated with obtaining input;
- write down verbs associated with the transformation;
- write down verbs associated with dealing with output;
- arrange the list of verbs into a logical sequence, connect verbs with arrows which indicate logical dependencies;
- to the structured set of verbs comprising the operations of the system add a control system of the general form:

   (i)   define criteria for measure of performance;
   (ii) monitor operations;
   (iii) take control action.

In considering the issue of evaluation Checkland argues that five different aspects need to be considered: efficacy, efficiency, effectiveness, ethicality and elegance (the last two of these having recently been added to the first three, Checkland and Scholes, 1990). In evaluating efficacy one needs to ask whether the system is in fact functioning, whether the transformation is being carried out, whether the means selected works. In evaluating efficiency one needs to ask whether the system is operating with minimum resources, including time. The evaluation of effectiveness involves asking whether the transformation at the heart of the system is the right activity to be doing in the first place. You should notice that questions about effectiveness can only be answered from outside the system in question, by reference to larger systems of which it is a part. Considerations of ethicality require us to consider whether the trans- formation is a moral thing to do, while the evaluation of elegance would focus on the extent to which the transformation is aesthetically pleasing.

The conceptual model shown in Figure 9.5 was developed from the root definition in Checkland's worked example which was described above.

It is important to note that conceptual models describe *what* must be done rather than *how* it is to be done. The example in Figure 9.5 includes 'decide who shall provide INSET' as a stage in the model. There is no indication how

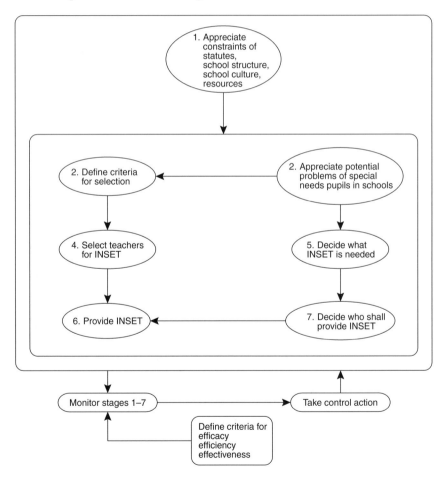

Figure 9.5 Conceptual model of a system to provide special needs INSET

this decision should be made, but a clear indication of what should precede it (a decision about what INSET is needed).

Stage 5. Comparison

At Stage 5 the conceptual models which have been produced during Stage 4 are compared with the real world (the problem situations expressed in Stage 2). This comparison may reveal mismatches:

- Are some logically necessary stages simply left out of the process which operates in real life?
- Is operational effectiveness being reduced by the inclusion of unnecessary stages?
- Are activities happening in an illogical order?
- Are the activities being performed well?

Stage 6. Debate on feasible and desirable changes

The identification of mismatches at Stage 5 is used at Stage 6 to structure a debate among those who inhabit the problem situation about possible changes which could improve the situation. Checkland and Scholes (1990) emphasize that consensus is only occasionally likely to be achievable. In general the aim will be to achieve an accommodation between different interests, 'in which the conflicts endemic in human affairs are still there, but are subsumed in an accommodation which different parties are prepared to go along with'. The debate aims at identifying changes which meet two criteria; the changes must be systemically desirable, as indicated by the conceptual modelling activity and they must be culturally feasible, given the characteristics of the situation and the people in it. Note that in the real world it may be desirable to move the real situation further away from that expressed in the model. For example, a model of a prison as a system to train criminals might well be relevant, but the Home Office would hardly wish to make it more so!

Stage 7. Action to improve the situation

Stage 7 involves the implementation of the changes which have been agreed. This may be straightforward or it may generate other difficulties which can in turn be tackled using the methodology in further cycles.

Although the methodology has been described in stage by stage sequence, in the interest of clarity of exposition, Checkland emphasizes that much iteration between stages is expected and indeed desirable. For example, in selecting relevant systems at Stage 3 it may well be useful to test out various possibilities by quickly looking ahead to Stages 4, 5 and 6 and seeing what kind of models might follow from the root definitions considered and what kinds of changes are likely to generated in the comparison stage. Also, Stage 5 almost always leads to more finding out being thought necessary.

Checkland points out that the methodology should not be regarded as a once-and-for-all approach to something sharply defined as a problem but as a general way of carrying out purposeful activity which gains from the power of some formal systems thinking but at the same time does not require individual human beings to behave as if they were rational automata. Hence the methodology deals with fuzzy real world messes, whereas many alternative approaches require clearly defined problems/objectives. Such 'hard' approaches also typically produce ideal systems, modelled by experts, which are imposed on the situation and the people within it as solutions. Soft Systems Methodology, by contrast, produces systemically desirable and culturally feasible changes to the existing situation, these changes having been selected by those who live in the situation.

However democratic this sounds it must be acknowledged that inequalities of power in the existing social order can be expected to influence the debate. (It would be a brave probationary teacher who persisted in arguing against the headteacher's point of view.) In criticism, therefore, it could be argued that SSM merely facilities a social process in which essential elements of *status quo* are reproduced. This will depend on the way in which it is used. As a cyclic learning process the methodology as described is essentially neutral. Any use of it will not be. It will be radical or reactionary depending on the user and the situational constraints. In this respect the explicitness built into SSM is particularly valuable. Anyone nominating a potentially relevant system must be prepared to state the *Weltanschauung* underlying it.

Dyson (1990), for example, speculates that special needs co-ordinators may only continue to be employed with the advent of financial delegation if they can demonstrate their cost-effectiveness. It is perfectly possible, using Soft Systems Methodology, to work through, 'a system to maximise the cost-effectiveness of special needs co-ordinators to their schools'; but not without explicitly stating the *Weltanschauung* underlying it – which may be something like 'a school's most important task is to balance its budget'. Following this scenario through to its logical conclusion would result in a very different vision of the future for special needs co-ordinators than that portrayed by Dyson (1990) or Butt (1991) – a group of legal eagles, totally *au fait* with all the legislation circulars of guidance and case law relating to pupils with special needs. Through producing exquisitely documented cases they will seek to attract to their school the maximum possible allocation of Local Management of Schools (LMS) special factor funding and maximize the numbers of pupils receiving additional funding through statements. (Advice and assistance to parents on requesting an assessment under the Education Act 1981, and on formulating an appeal to the Secretary of State should their request be refused, may be a related activity.) Another strand of work might entail setting up and managing the paperwork associated with the alternative educational programmes to run from March to August in Years 9 and 11 to accommodate those pupils for whom General Directions under Section 19 of the Education Reform Act provide a convenient means by which the school's published assessment results can present the best possible picture in the open enrolment market place.

This example is intended to illustrate graphically the way in which Soft Systems Methodology can assist in suspending preconceptions and allowing a range of possible purposes to be logically worked through, future scenarios constructed, their implications systematically identified and their cultural feasibility openly debated. Although it is more common to model relevant systems which most participants regard positively, much can also be learned from exploring familiar issues from an unfamiliar perspective – one school quickly instituted new procedures after discovering how closely a model of 'a system to discourage poor attenders from coming into school' matched their present approach! Modelling scenarios which are regarded as potentially threatening and undesirable may help to identify ways in which they can be averted just as modelling culturally feasible scenarios should help to identify positive action which will effect improvement.

Applications of Soft Systems Methodology in schools

Prior to the 1988 course in Soft Systems Methodology at University College London taught by Peter Checkland only one unpublished master's dissertation recorded an attempt to apply SSM in a school. Following the course a booklet of the resulting studies with a foreword by Checkland was published (Frederickson, 1990b). The studies differ considerably in terms of the amount of time devoted to them and the level within the organization at which issues were addressed: individual pupil, classroom, department, heads of faculty, senior management team, whole school, cross school project team, local education authority working group. The studies also differed greatly in terms of the problem situations on which they focused, although the predominance of educational psychologists and special needs staff involved resulted in a high representation of special needs issues:

- the operation of support teaching in a secondary school containing integrated provision for physically handicapped pupils;
- the provision of whole school in-service training in behaviour management at primary level;
- facilitating the operation of local education authority working group on 'disaffected pupils' and quickly pulling together a coherent set of recommendations;
- providing a framework to guide the work of a secondary school's behaviour project team in helping four recently amalgamated schools review their rules and routines;
- assisting heads of learning in a secondary school to review their work, identifying and implementing desired changes;

- offering an approach to school self-review in a secondary school concerned to address the question, 'the average child, the silent majority, could we be doing more for them?'.

The booklet also contains a number of accounts where the methodology is used by individual practitioners to think through some aspect of their work in a coherent way; a teacher describes an analysis of a successful change in classroom layout while an educational psychologist describes an application in a school-based consultation about an individual child.

Finally the booklet contains one account of the kind of consultancy work using Soft Systems Methodology which is now offered by the Educational Psychology Group at University College London. It describes an application of SSM as a framework for evaluating a new local authority provision – a secondary support base for 'vulnerable' pupils. Anyone who is planning to become involved in school inspections would be well advised to give thought to the desirability of basing their work on a systematic and explicit approach, just as schools will be well advised to hold such teams to account in providing justification for the questions asked, the evidence collected and the conclusions drawn.

The authors of the accounts in the booklet record difficulties encountered as well as successes achieved, problems experienced with aspects of the methodology as well as positive aspects of its use. Overall there emerges a view that SSM is a useful approach in tackling constrictively the fuzziness and complexity of many problems currently facing schools. It is to be hoped that it will prove of value to practitioners engaged in the task of rethinking special needs.

References

Booth, T. (1986) 'Is integrating the handicapped psychologically defensible?' *Bulletin of The British Psychological Society* 39, 141.

Butt, N. (1991) 'A role for the SEN co-ordinator in the 1990s: a reply to Dyson', *Support for Learning*, 6(1), 9–14.

Cameron, R.J. and Stratford, R.J. (1987) 'A problem-centred approach to the delivery of applied psychological services', *Educational Psychology in Practice* 2(4), 10–20.

Checkland, P.B. (1981) *Systems Thinking, Systems Practice*. London: Wiley.

Checkland, P.B. (1986) *A Basic Introduction to Systems Thinking*. Unpublished paper, University of Lancaster.

Checkland, P.B. and Scholes, J. (1990) *Soft Systems Methodology in Action*. London: Wiley.

Dyson, A. (1990), 'Effective learning consultancy: a future role for special needs co-ordinators?' *Support for Learning* 5(3), 16–127.

Frederickson, N. (1990a) 'Systems working EP practice: a re-evaluation', in N. Jones and N. Frederickson (eds) *Refocusing Educational Psychology*. London: Falmer Press.

Frederickson, N. (ed.) (1990b) *Soft Systems Methodology: Practical Applications in Work with Schools*. University College London: Educational Psychology Publishing.

Frederickson, N., Webster, A. and Wright, A. (1991) 'Psychological assessment: a change of emphasis', *Educational Psychology in Practice* 7(1), 20–29.

Goetz, L. and Sailor, W. (1990) 'Much ado about babies, murky bathwater and trickle-down politics: a reply to Kauffman', *The Journal of Special Education* 24(3), 334–339.

Kauffman, J.M. (1989) 'The Regular Education Initiative as Reagan–Bush education policy: a trickle-down theory of education of the hard to teach', *The Journal of Special Education* 23(3), 256–278.

McLeskey, J., Skiba, R. and Wilcox, B. (1990) 'Reform and special education: a mainstream perspective', *The Journal of Special Education* 24(3), 319–325.

Naughton, J. (1984) 'Soft Systems Analysis: an introductory guide', in *Complexity, Management and Change: Applying a Systems Approach. Open University Course T301, Block IV*. Milton Keynes: Open University Press.

Schön, D.A. (1983) *The Reflective Practitioner: How Professionals Think in Action*. London: Temple Smith.

Source

This is an edited version of a chapter previously published in A. Dyson and C. Gains (eds) *Rethinking Special Needs in Mainstream Schools*. 1993. Reproduced by permission of David Fulton Publishers.

Chapter 10

Case studies of individual classrooms

E. C. Wragg, C. M. Wragg, G. S. Haynes and R. P. Chamberlin

In this chapter we focus on six teachers in order to explore what factors appeared to be influential in improving levels of literacy. Teachers have been selected from across the primary age range. Inevitably there are differences in context and observed behaviour, but this does not mean that there are no common characteristics, even if these are varied in their interpretation. What these might be will be discussed at the end of the chapter.

The six case studies in this chapter will be described in ascending order of age group taught, starting with a Reception class of 4- and 5-year-olds. Two of the teachers were members of staff at the same school, while the others came from different schools. Three of the teachers held the post of language co-ordinator in their school. Three of the four LEA areas studied in this research are represented by these six histories. Inevitably, of course, the teachers manifest features which are indicative of their effectiveness as teachers not just in the field of literacy, but more generally as well.

Miss Dobson – Reception teacher

Miss Dobson had been teaching for eight years at Beverley Road Community School. It was her first teaching post and she had gained experience of teaching each of the infant-age groups, from 4- or 5- up to 7-year-olds. Her Reception class had thirty-two children, all of whom started in the September after their fourth birthday, in keeping with that LEA's policy. Her classroom was full of colourful displays of children's work on walls, doors, windows and hangings from the ceiling (at children's height), plus alphabets, questions and challenges, and signs written in different languages. The corridor was used as an extension of the classroom, housing a workbench, sand tray, work table and book corner with seats and carefully laid-out displays of fiction and non-fiction books.

Only one pupil had English as his first language, the others speaking Punjabi, Bengali, Urdu or Gujerati as their mother tongue. Miss Dobson worked closely with her multi-lingual classroom assistant, who translated when necessary, but English was used as much as possible in the classroom, the classroom assistant adding just a few words of explanation in Urdu, Gujerati or Punjabi when needed, or making reference to cultural differences, as this incident shows:

Miss Dobson is reading a story about a family with a new baby. She reads slowly and shows the pictures to the children as she does so. The classroom assistant looks around the class, seeking out those whose attention seems to be wandering, or assessing who may need help. From time to time she asks a question in the child's home language, or gives a word of explanation. When a 'tea cosy' is mentioned, she laughs and tells Miss Dobson, 'They aren't all that common in Gujerat'.

Miss Dobson was able to describe clearly the many different activities and strategies she used to teach reading, but had not been on any courses since leaving college, and did not display knowledge of what she called 'literacy jargon', or the latest theories. The children first learned the letters of their names, then other letters, and worked on initial sounds. Beverley Road School used the Oxford Reading Tree scheme and this was introduced gradually as the children were considered ready. Before starting them on the scheme Miss Dobson familiarised the children with the characters by reading the stories and by calling the children's work groups after the characters – 'Floppy', 'Kipper', 'Biff', etc.

The very first reading book each new pupil had was a personalised book dictated by the child and written by Miss Dobson, about the child's family and the things they liked doing. Making these individual books for thirty-two children consumed a great deal of time, but Miss Dobson believed it was worth it. For their second book she made a story about the child, which also included a character from the reading scheme. After that she decided if the pupil was ready for the first scheme books, or needed another one specially made.

Each personalised book had a 'word wall' on the back cover, with all the vocabulary listed, so pupils could read the words out of context as well as in. The children did a lot of sentence work using these words from their personalised books and in other contexts, with Miss Dobson writing down the children's own words, cutting the sentences up into individual words, getting the children to replace them in the right order, and finally to stick them in a book kept for that purpose. Each pupil built up a personal sight vocabulary of words to do with themselves and their families, plus high-frequency words which they used in and out of context. When their sight vocabulary had reached a certain standard she allowed them to take words home in a tin to build sentences at home. The word 'allowed' is her choice of vocabulary when presenting the idea to the class. She regarded it as a privilege, and consequently that was how the children saw it.

Once children had started the reading scheme they became involved in a group reading method, taking turns to read and also being involved in discussions about the story, vocabulary, characters and illustrations. In one observed session the children all read several times. The story prompted discussion about: whether fathers should help with the washing; 'feeling poorly'; a child whose father had diabetes and what this meant; what a cheque was. Miss Dobson was able to concentrate on one group at a time because of the way she organised the session and the help she received from the classroom assistant who dealt adeptly with other children.

Miss Dobson combined energy and enthusiasm with meticulous organisation. The reading work was structured and monitored closely, so that, without looking at her records, she could tell the interviewer about each child's progress: that Bilal now knew fourteen sight words, for example. When the researcher visited the school to hear the six selected children read for the first time, she was presented with a folder by Miss Dobson. This included a timetable for when the child should be heard, a copy of each child's 'word wall', the school's policy on reading records, the Assessment Statement Bank, a Phonic Assessment sheet and the Oxford Reading Tree book list.

In reply to the interview question about differences between Key Stage 1 and Key Stage 2, Miss Dobson referred to the teacher's attitude, saying that with younger children the teacher could go 'a bit over the top' with enthusiasm and praise. When asked what she would do if a child miscued and read 'boot', instead of 'book', her first comment was: 'Give praise for a good try and point out what was right', before saying: 'Point to the end and ask if it made sense.'

Certainly there was considerable and regular public recognition of approved work and behaviour, as she frequently told children how clever they were, commented that she could see a group 'working so hard over there', or that she had noticed 'some brilliant readers in the corner'. The children appeared to respond favourably and seemed to make more progress than the norm in classrooms in similar circumstances. They themselves believed they had made a good start at reading, as Reception class children often do, and ''cos Miss Dobson says' was sufficient answer to the interviewer's questions about why they thought they were good at reading, why they should learn to read, or, indeed, why they should do anything.

It may appear that Miss Dobson made her pupils too dependent, but their citing her as an authority was largely out of respect, rather than subjugation. In the classroom it was their *independence* that was noticeable, as they were usually engrossed in their work, without the need for constant supervision. Although they covered the usual range of Reception class curricular activities, there was little or no wasted or 'waiting' time. By 9.05 a.m. all the groups were busily engaged in their first activity. Observation data show that Miss Dobson's on-task involvement level averaged at 81, high for a Reception class. The work appeared to be pitched appropriately, so no individual was inactive for long. Miss Dobson's assurance that they were a truly marvellous class seemed to have a positive effect on children's self-esteem.

We were not able to use the NFER Reading Test at the beginning and end of the year, since they were only 4–5 years old, but children's work was monitored on each visit and all six target pupils made good progress, though at different speeds and from different starting points. This may be explained by a powerful combination of positive expectations, skilful class management, well-organised and varied classroom activities, pupil independence, an intimate familiarity with each individual child's progress, harmonious personal relationships and considerable help from a classroom assistant who understood the language and cultural background of Asian children.

Miss Brown – Year 1

Miss Brown, a Year 1 teacher, was in her third year of teaching at Charldeen School when she took part in our research. As a newly qualified teacher joining the staff she had found the school's reading policy an invaluable tool, helping her to structure the children's reading and to plan for their development:

> It's been really useful ... I've used it to structure what the children are doing and I've been able to take the ones who are doing well a little bit further. It's very easy to know what you're doing in your own year group but you do get children who are sort of bright and are rushing ahead – so it's useful from a progression point of view, to know where to take them.

The reading policy was the result of extensive consultation by the language co-ordinator and the head teacher with staff at curriculum meetings. One of its central tenets was that every child should read to an adult every day. Miss Brown confessed that sometimes this target was not always realised, but she supported the objective without reserve and often used her lunch-time to catch up on readers:

> Hearing children every day is absolutely crucial and I do like to hear readers myself, not just delegate it all to mums and the classroom assistant, because reading's so important. It underpins everything else you do.

Children's reading within the classroom was structured through the use of a colour-coded collection of various reading schemes. Most children had free choice within a colour band. With the less able, Miss Brown herself chose the child's next book, usually working through one reading scheme's books before starting another. Miss Brown carefully assessed each child's stage of development, matching reading tasks to their ability. She explained how this worked:

> It depends on the child ... With James, these books are very simple and they've only got one or two words on each page and there's a lot to talk about in the pictures, so, for him, I would keep him on this particular set until he's been through all the very basic ones of those, and then I'll perhaps move him on to a different set. Once they're actually beginning to read, or beginning to recognise some of the words, then I let them have free choice within a colour band ... If I have a child who's on yellow books, say, and has been through the majority of what's in my box and isn't ready to move on, I can send them to another classroom and there's different books in there, in the same colour band.

Phonics work was a strong feature of the classroom and was structured by the school's phonics policy which detailed the stages. Miss Brown's timetabled weekly phonics lesson was consistently reinforced by language games during 'on the carpet' sessions, and by discussing the sounds of letters with children while they were writing or reading. At the back of each child's reading record was written the alphabet, and whenever an adult read with a child, the adult was expected to check the child's competency at letter sounds. Miss Brown had also modified a published 'word list' scheme, which contained lists of words for the children to learn and which they took home at weekends. She explained that, with these, the emphasis was on 'sounding them out' with the intention of developing the child's word-building skills. She felt they were a particularly successful tool:

> I've found that, as soon as the children start on the word lists, I can see an improvement in the way they start to approach their reading. It gives them confidence with their reading, that they know how to try and work out a word they don't know. And, of course, it links with their writing and spelling.

At the back of each child's reading record, in addition to the alphabet, there was also an initial list of twelve key words, which was gradually extended until 100 key words were known. Even with these, Miss Brown asked the children to learn them first by sounding them out, although she admitted that some parents seemed to test the children 'as if the words are sight vocabulary'. She regretted that a reduction in her classroom assistant's hours in the summer term had made it impossible to give as much attention to the pupils' learning of the key words:

> I don't practise those with them when they read to me. At the beginning of the year Lyn [the classroom assistant] used to do that. She'd have the less able children every day and she'd practise their words with them. Now I only have Lyn for 0.5 of a week so there's just not time to do the words every day. That's a real pity, because they came on so much better when they did that on a daily basis.

Accurate spelling and punctuation were valued highly. The researcher's observation notes contained many examples of the teacher highlighting these aspects of a child's writing, as she walked round the room discussing their work with them. Children in the class made extensive use of their own personal word books and commercial dictionaries. Spelling tests took place once a week. The same early morning routine applied every day: on entering the classroom children were to learn and check spellings, and then read further in their book before the register was taken.

Underpinning Miss Brown's very structured approach to the teaching of reading was a hugh personal enthusiasm for books. This manifested itself in her classroom and in her teaching in a number of ways. Over the years she had built up a large personal collection of children's literature, which she used to supplement the school's own reading materials. These books were kept in a cupboard in the classroom but children were allowed to borrow them to read in school.

In interview, Miss Brown claimed 'I find every opportunity to talk about books'. Observation of her lessons showed that one of the main ways in which she did this was by having 'our author of the week'. She collected as many books as possible by one author and tried to read one each day to the class with time for discussion afterwards. During the week the books were attractively displayed in a specially designated 'Author's Corner' to encourage the children to read these books themselves at other times, something children were frequently observed doing. Questions about the current books were included in the display, designed to set children thinking about the stories. Miss Brown was one of the few teachers observed in this study whose 'Author's Corner' books were changed on a regular basis. In some classrooms observed the same author's works were often displayed all term, or even all year, from September through to July.

Miss Brown used the organisation of her classroom to capture children's attention and maintain their interest in books and reading throughout the year. Her 'home corner' was a dynamic part of the classroom, changing each term from a home, to a shop, to a travel agent. Reading materials appropriate to its current use were available to the children including newspapers, comics, magazines, brochures, catalogues and timetables. During the February half term she also moved her book and reading corner to another part of the classroom. Her reasons were twofold: she felt that, if the books were in the same place all year, the children were not constantly motivated to read them, and it allowed her to monitor more closely the children's reading during the period before registration, as it now contained her 'teacher's chair'.

A constantly reflective teacher, Miss Brown, critical of the way in which she had used the school's library in the previous year, changed her approach and felt she had improved the use of her library period to induct children into better understanding of libraries:

> Last year, I sort of just took them down and showed them how to find books and that was about it. This year, I've really focused in closely on how to use the library system – showing them the simple Dewey system and how to use books.

Miss Brown placed a great deal of emphasis on building children's confidence in their reading, as her comments about her least able pupil reveal, when asked what she would do if he could not read a particular word:

> With somebody like Paul, I would probably mouth the first sound of the word to see if he can get it right. Because that way he feels he's got it right – I haven't told him.

Her use of praise was noted regularly during classroom observation and seemed to be appreciated by the children. This was backed up by the systematic use of rewards, an approach highly developed throughout the school. Miss Brown believed that stickers and stars were good motivators, but she also demonstrated how she valued the children's writing through carefully assembled wall displays of the pupils' work. A highly structured monitoring and assessment system was in place throughout the school. Each teacher kept a record card for each child which, for reading, incorporated details such as the child's phonological awareness, knowledge of key words, reading strategies and behaviour. This was then passed on to the next teacher so that a detailed account of progress was available throughout a child's time at the school.

A key feature of Miss Brown's approach to the teaching of reading was the way in which she differentiated tasks and reading materials to accommodate the wide range of reading ability within her Year 1 class, whether of high, medium or low ability. Oliver, a very able boy with a voracious appetite for reading, was allowed to take nine books home to read during the February half term. By this stage of the school year he had read 115 books from school since the previous September.

Oliver was a pupil of high ability who was making rapid progress. Miss Brown nonetheless provided him with individualised tasks to develop his reading skills even further. These included: giving him more detailed research tasks than were assigned to other pupils, where he had to write up what he had learned from a particular non-fiction book; talking about particular authors and why he liked them; and writing more book reviews, something more commonly observed with older children. He was given numerous opportunities to use the Dewey system in the school's library and was often observed using the contents and index sections of non-fiction books to find information quickly.

Miss Brown emphasised the importance of establishing a good relationship with parents, stating, when interviewed, that she saw them as 'partners in their children's education'. All teachers tend to say this, but our interviews with parents of pupils in her class confirmed the quality of the relationship. They described her as keen to listen to their concerns and ideas about their own children's reading, and willing to try to pay heed and act on what they said.

Miss Brown's class made considerable progress during the year. Her ability to match tasks and books to individuals, her undoubted industry and the careful structuring of her lessons and the children's programme may well have been instrumental in this, though they were not the only likely causes. Underpinning Miss Brown's effective teaching of reading were considerable class management skills. Her on-task involvement levels were consistently high, averaging 83. Lessons were carefully prepared and, if appropriate, materials were set out on tables before the children arrived in the morning, reducing the amount of time taken to settle children to tasks. Relevant development activities were in place so that children who finished their work early could extend it to a higher level. Children were well aware of the classroom routines and made efficient use of resources. Her relationship with the children was firm, but warm. Her overwhelmingly positive attitude towards reading and books was apparent to anyone entering the classroom and seemed infectious and hard to resist. As she herself put it:

> I love books, I really, really do. I'm so enthusiastic about reading and stories that my children just can't not be, really!

Miss Stinton – Year 2

Miss Stinton was in her first year at Hilton Primary School and had not been qualified as a teacher for very long. When she was initially asked to define the term literacy she was eager to penetrate beneath the surface of the concept:

> [It's] enabling people to communicate through speech, writing and reading. Not just having the basics of that, but being questioned enough to understand what you're reading and what you're writing. It's not just getting by in the world of language, but having a bit more depth than that.

If Miss Stinton had only been interviewed and not observed, it would have been difficult to ascertain whether this statement was merely a pious ideology or reflected what actually happened in her classroom. As the school year progressed, however, observation of lessons and interviews with her pupils increasingly confirmed that Miss Stinton put a great deal of time and energy into ensuring that her philosophy became reality for the children in her class and was not mere rhetoric. Over the year all the children were regularly heard reading, irrespective of ability, and each kept a clear reading record.

When the researcher heard the six target pupils reading and interviewed them, it was notable that a premium had been put on understanding, and indeed on autonomy. All six, irrespective of ability, used a range of strategies to help them understand the text. They talked freely about the pictures in their books, self-corrected words when they realised they had made a mistake, tried sounding out words when they encountered difficult ones, or split the words up and looked to the pictures and the context of the story for clues. There was very high congruence between what Miss Stinton said she did and what was observed in the classroom. She had explained in interview what she would do if a child got stuck on a word:

> I'd encourage them to read the sentence again and see if that helped, so they're reading it for meaning. I might read the sentence to them and stop at the word, give it the sort of intonation, so it could help to give them a clue; encourage them to look at the picture ... it depends what stage they're at. If they were quite good readers already, I would encourage them to read on a little bit further. That sometimes gives them a hint as well. And look at the initial sound, maybe the initial two sounds, depending on the word. And if they really couldn't get it, I'd tell them because otherwise

they're reading just for words rather than for whole meaning. If they're spending too much time on decoding one word then they've lost the thread of the story, which is what it should all be about really.

One of the two improvers identified by Miss Stinton was a girl called Marti. Her reading age improved from 6.9 at the beginning of the year to 9.3 at the end of the year, and she exemplified how this philosophy had been translated into practice. Marti told the researcher that she loved reading in Miss Stinton's class, something she reiterated at the end of the school year. She was reading a play from a reading scheme and she had been encouraged to go through all the characters first, before starting on the text. She discussed the pictures and referred back to the character list to help her understanding of the story. As her confidence and understanding of text increased, Miss Stinton helped her gradually introduce more intonation into her reading and discussed what was happening with her. Marti was effusive about all aspects of reading and explained that it made you use your imagination more. She read a lot and liked silent reading and shared reading, time in the classroom which she used assiduously.

Silent reading and shared reading were not the only means by which Miss Stinton encouraged improvement in her pupils' reading. She tried to work explicitly on particular skills and combined this analytical approach with comprehension and enjoyment:

> I read individually with them and they do with other adults. I share lots of books and show them what I am reading, so I'm showing them the print as well. I teach them phonics too and blends, so they can decode the beginning of a word, but mainly encourage them to read for enjoyment and for meaning. Many of them are starting to use books for other purposes like information, finding out things.

This emphasis on understanding and using books for a purpose was neatly illustrated when the class was observed during a 'sharing time' period. One pupil, John wished to show the rest of the class an encyclopaedia:

Teacher: (*To the rest of the class*) Can you remember what it is called?
Pupil 1: Is it like a dictionary?
Teacher: That's a good idea, can you remember what it is called at the back?
Pupil 2: Information.
Pupil 3: Introduction.
Teacher: Yes, it does start with 'In'.
Pupil 4: Index.

John turns to the back of the book, looks something up in the index and then flicks through the encyclopaedia to the relevant page. As the discussion continues, Miss Stinton used different opportunities both to expand the pupils' knowledge base and to learn more about how reference books can be used.

This was a good example of her making the acquisition of literacy something that penetrated beneath the surface.

Miss Stinton is another teacher in this study with good class management skills. Her on-task involvement levels were high and averaged out at 83, which meant that effective use of time was a significant element in her teaching. She also created a rich literacy environment. Her classroom had over 600 books in it and the pupils also had access to a new infant library that had just been restocked. Miss Stinton always had a display of books supporting the current topic and linked this to other features of whatever was the theme of the moment. When the topic was 'Communication', there was a 'hands-on' post office display in the classroom, which included envelopes, cards, forms and a post box. All areas were clearly labelled with information prompts such as: 'Use the index to research' and displays were regularly changed and updated.

Although Miss Stinton took great pains to structure activities and ensure that pupils were clear about what it was that they were expected to do, she also exhibited considerable patience when expanding the pupils' own attempts to comprehend the task in hand. She provided explanation, but also evoked interest by trying to fire the pupils' own imagination, often capitalising on curiosity. In one lesson she started to describe someone from a story, in an intriguing voice, while holding a little box in her hand:

> *Teacher*: This person walks very slowly into an enchanted forest. She's got a big black bag, and inside her big black bag there is . . . what do *you* think?
> *Pupil 1*: A magic wand.
> *Pupil 2*: Toys.

The teacher continues to tell the story, asking for ideas as to which story she is telling; after a few guesses each time, she tells them a bit more of the story. When the children have guessed the story correctly she tells them that she is putting her box back into her cupboard now, because it is a magic box. The children all say 'Ahhh' in disappointment that it is over. The teacher then explains what she wants them to do and says when they have written their story it will go into a big self-made book.

She explained why she had done that type of lesson:

> It's just to inspire them really . . . I introduced [a] magic shell earlier with them. It's really just to get their imagination going . . . they put it in the middle and touch it if they need an idea. It's just getting ideas flowing, rather than just saying, 'Go and write a story'. And the other thing I might

do . . . I want to get hold of a cloak that's got pockets in it and pull objects out of that – as a story aid.

Miss Stinton's lessons were a combination of well-organised and stimulating activities and discussions, often involving plays, poems, games, sharing ideas. She translated her aspiration to help children understand what they were reading into action, reflecting a great deal on different ways of stimulating their imagination. She often explained something in detail to them when she thought it necessary, but at the same time encouraging them to be independent thinkers, so they became autonomous. During 'sharing books' time the pupils' discussions were very animated and observations of individual children showed that all appeared to be discussing their books and genuinely enjoying what they were doing.

Mrs Hutchings – Year 2/3

Mrs Hutchings, a very experienced teacher, had recently joined the staff of Suttwell School as a member of the senior management team and as language co-ordinator for Key Stage 1. Suttwell School gave language a high priority and had been placed highly in the local authority's league tables showing the results of national tests on pupils aged 11. She regarded the Schools Library Service as an excellent resource for topic packs and her own professional literature, so it was used extensively, as was the resources centre at the local university. The school was keen to bring in outsiders, such as story-tellers, poets and drama specialists, to provide the pupils with a rich variety of language experiences.

Although the approach to the teaching of reading within the school when Mrs Hutchings arrived had been closely structured around two core reading schemes, she explained that her own philosophy was firmly grounded in 'real books', and she had removed the existing scheme books from the shelves in her classroom by the end of the first term. She said she found the parents' expectations that their children would follow a reading scheme to be an unwelcome pressure, 'because I'm not used to teaching like that'. She particularly objected to the competitive element which she believed a scheme encouraged. Mrs Hutchings acknowledged, however, that some children needed a more structured approach to reading and was a keen advocate of the 'Longman Book Project', which the school subsequently acquired during the period of the research project for the Reception/Year 1 class and the less able Year 2 readers. She favoured this scheme because she felt 'it contains real books by real authors, offering the children the chance to experience a variety of styles, combined with a graded vocabulary'.

Mrs Hutchings considered most of the children in her class to be 'fluent readers', but she had some children who undertook extra literacy activities to raise their standard of reading:

> They're doing structured reading books with a lot of phonic input as well, plus whole word skills from when I work on the easel and also we do spelling and reading of key words. I use a phonic work-shop on the computer; usually they do that with the classroom assistant.

The more able children were guided towards 'appropriate reading materials'. Mrs Hutchings said she had 'roughly organised the class books according to their difficulty', although they were not in any way colour coded. She supplemented the school's resources with books from her own children's library at home, finding that she needed to provide more early 'chapter books', such as Young Puffins, for the developing readers.

Uniquely amongst the teachers interviewed in this LEA, Mrs Hutchings indicated that if a child did not know a word when sharing a book with her, she would stress the context cue first of all:

> The first thing I usually do is read the rest of the sentence and get the cue from that, then [I] suggest phonics, if it worked for that word, or stress the picture.

This emphasis on meaning underpinned Mrs Hutchings' approach to the teaching of reading, along with her conviction that books must always be for pleasure. If children chose a book and then found they did not like it, she insisted they change it:

> I say to them 'If you don't like it, just go on to something else. Don't continue with a book that you don't like. Don't read it!'

When asked what strategies were particularly important in improving children's readings, Mrs Hutchings highlighted both sharing books with children and matching reading materials, not only to children's stage of reading development, but also to their interests:

> We do take time trying to fit books to children quite a bit – that we think they would really like. If they seem to be getting a bit fed up, we try and branch off a bit and do other things.

Classroom observation of her lessons revealed that a key feature of Mrs Hutchings' approach to reading was that, when she was reading a book with a child, she allowed no interruptions from other children.

Many teachers in the study talked about the importance of engendering in their pupils 'a love of books and reading'. In Mrs Hutchings' class children clearly seemed to enjoy their quiet reading time after lunch, when they could share books with each other, or read individually. This was evidenced by an extraordinarily high average on-task involvement score during these sessions of 98, meaning that only one child was slightly off-task, and also by the consistency with which the children brought their favourite books from home to share with the teacher and the class. Time was made available for this at the end of each quiet reading session.

Writing pupils' own books was a regular activity. It was also notable that there was a high degree of individual initiative in this class. Not only was writing a self-made book a task set by the teacher, it was also initiated by pupils themselves and undertaken in their own time or at home. They produced both fiction and non-fiction books themselves, including atlases, and these were displayed alongside the commercially published reading materials for other children to read. Time was regularly set aside for children to share their own writing with the rest of the class. The account below is typical of what took place in these sessions. Mrs Hutchings used them in a number of ways: to develop the children's speaking and listening skills, to explore with them their thoughts about their writing, to talk about words, to show they are valued as writers. She was also sensitive to the fact that some children might feel shy reading publicly in front of the whole class:

> As the children arrive in class, some tell the teacher that they have written stories at home. After the register has been taken the teacher invites these children to come to the front of the class with their stories.
>
> *Teacher*: This is a listening time. One person will be speaking, so the rest of you have to listen. (*Reading out the title of Claire's story*) 'The Party' by Claire, aged 6. Do you want to read it yourself to the class, Claire?
> *Claire*: (*Nods. She reads out her story, standing beside the teacher*)
> *Teacher*: That was lovely, Claire. Did anything give you the idea for that story?
> *Claire*: I asked my mum to give me a title so that I could then write a story.
> *Teacher*: What a good idea, Claire! Would anyone like to ask Claire anything about her story?
>
> Some children put their hands up. Claire answers the questions confidently. The teacher praises Claire again and then asks Charles to come to the front.
>
> *Teacher*: Charles has written a story, too. Are you reading it, Charles?
> *Charles*: No, you read it.
>
> The teacher reads it for him, using a great deal of voice expression. When she has finished she comments: 'I liked some of the words you used in your story, Charles, like "investigate".'

When the researcher interviewed the pupils in this class, nearly all of them responded to the question 'Who reads to you in class?' by saying 'the children at book time'. It was spoken with approval and was clearly a routine which the pupils valued and enjoyed.

Mrs Hutchings had generated in her class not only an enormous enthusiasm for books but also an awareness of style and words. The children often identified different authors' styles of writing and then tried them out for themselves in their stories. In one book read to the class by Mrs Hutchings, the story had appeared to come to an end, but then the next page had said, 'But that wasn't quite the end of the story . . .' and had continued. The children had been attracted to this strategy and in the ensuing two weeks many of them adopted variations of this piece of teasing intrigue in their own story writing. Mrs Hutchings regularly talked about particular words, exploring their meanings with pupils, whereupon these words would often appear in the children's writing. It was another feature of her teaching that was commented on with approval by pupils. When interviewed, one child explained how she had deliberately helped to build his vocabulary, saying that he liked reading 'because I can use good words like "exaggerate" when I'm writing'.

Lesson observations regularly identified incidents in Mrs Hutchings' classroom showing that each individual child was valued. Her interactions with the children were full of positive reinforcement: praise for good work, good effort and good behaviour. Every child's work was displayed on the walls. Humour was also a notable feature of her lessons and she frequently shared gales of laughter with the children. They responded by producing work of a high quality. Of the ten 7-year-old children in the class who took national tests, nine scored above the national average in a not especially privileged area. Central to Mrs Hutchings' successful teaching of reading was the extremely high degree of involvement in the task, which ensured consistent concentration on their work by her pupils. The quality of these skills was brought into sharp focus when a student teacher took some of her lessons during a final teaching practice in the summer term of the observation period. In lessons observed given by the student, on-task involvement levels fell to 72. Mrs Hutchings' score over the year averaged 93.

Miss Lansbury – Year 3

Miss Lansbury had taught for twenty-five years, the first eighteen of them in secondary schools, and she was now the language co-ordinator at Broadlands Primary School, teaching a Year 3 class. She had attended a variety of LEA courses relating to literacy, which she described as 'very helpful and full of good concrete ideas as well as theory', and she seemed knowledgeable about teaching English, with a clear idea of what she was doing and why.

A noticeable feature of Miss Lansbury's teaching was the use of information technology. She was very enthusiastic about using interactive technology for improving literacy, and Broadlands Primary was exceptionally well equipped with computers, so the pupils were very computer literate. They had individual floppy disks so that they could undertake extended writing and graphics projects, and they were used to demonstrating the various programs to the many visitors the school attracted. The computers were always in use, with children either writing their own work or using CD-ROMs to find out about Ancient Rome, or to work on their spelling, vocabulary and comprehension, as well as to record their own progress.

There was more evidence of the pupils' extensive use of computers in Miss Lansbury's classroom wall displays. These showed computer designs of bridges, word-processed factual information about how they had designed them, alongside poems about bridges. Books were also given a high profile, with table displays of books about the class's current topic and a book corner set in an alcove, attractively set out like a bower. The importance of reading was signalled in many ways to pupils. Both intrinsic and extrinsic rewards and recognition were common. The school had a 'Good Readers' board displaying names of pupils who had been doing well, and bookmarks were presented in assembly for progress.

Miss Lansbury was flexible and adapted her teaching to individuals. If a particular approach or book appeared not to be working very well for one child, she used her extensive knowledge of resources and individual children's interests to find something more suitable. The main reading scheme was *Story Chest*, which she liked because of its breadth and the inclusion of non-fiction poetry and plays as well as stories. She identified 'group reading' as her main approach to the teaching of reading, with the children arranged in ability groups. This, she said, was particularly appropriate for teaching a wide variety of reading skills, from inference and deduction to reading with expression:

> I think group reading is the single, most fundamental thing that has affected the teaching of reading in this school. I would always do it now because I think it works better than any other method. I think it's non-threatening because the children are in a group. They feel less threatened than in a 'one-to-one'. I think you can give them more attention than if it's one-to-one and, because you've got a group of four of five, you can actually teach them for 10 to 15 minutes, whereas if you're just hearing a child read, that's not really teaching reading at all.

Some children still needed phonics work and, for a few, she arranged paired reading sessions, with children of average ability helping poorer readers, which, she believed, helped them both. The children had a session with everyone reading each day, and there was what she called 'guided choice' of books from the class library. Miss Lansbury stressed the importance of reading in other curriculum areas as well, mentioning reading for meaning, following instructions in maths, and using research skills for topic work.

Miss Lansbury had a very pleasant, easy manner with her children, and personal relationships seemed extremely positive. Her response to noisy chatter was to signal disapproval not by reprimand but by using the word 'excited'. It was a code that the pupils understood, and the mention of it quelled any noise. She could modify their behaviour when necessary by making comments such as, 'Goodness, you are excited this morning!' When asked to find words to describe a castle in one lesson, the noise level from a particular group was getting higher, so she asked, 'Are you all right? I can hear you're getting excited!' They told her they were on their third page of words. She replied, 'Third page! My goodness. Three pages of ideas!' and the pupils continued with the work, pleased with themselves, but also modifying their voices in discussion.

In interview she stressed that her aim was to make the children independent, and this was reflected in her comments about their work, which she discussed with them in a noticeably egalitarian manner, talking to them as sensible people who just happened to be younger than she was. She gave explicit advice on the process of improving a piece of work, but left it to individuals to decide how to use it on any particular piece of work, which she said was theirs, so they must make the decision. 'Did you mean to leave us not quite sure about what he knew? Is that what you wanted?' she commented on one occasion, when children were redrafting a story, 'OK. That's fine. You're the author.'

This manner of talking to pupils did not appear to give *carte blanche* to the lazy or easily satisfied, as Miss Lansbury's praise for what they had already done was mixed with encouragement to do even better. She taught skills such as redrafting in a systematic and cumulative way, providing prompt sheets with questions for children to ask themselves. There were notices and charts on the walls giving guidelines about making notes, writing a draft, or finding more interesting words for a particular context, and these contributed to what seemed an unoppressive drive for improvement. On numerous occasions she would publicly urge the class to ask themselves the question: 'Is this the best, the very best, that I can do at eight years old?'

In one lesson observed, on the subject of 'punctuation and how to use question marks', she started by getting children to ask each other questions. After a number of expected ones, such as, 'Do you like cabbage?' and 'Have you got any brothers and sisters?', one girl asked Miss Lansbury, 'Is there some job you would have liked, if you weren't a teacher?' Miss Lansbury thought for a moment and then replied, 'Not really. Perhaps something to do with publishing books, but, no. On a good day, teaching is the best job in the world.' She said it with conviction.

Mrs Turner – Year 5

Mrs Turner, a Year 5 teacher, had taught at Hilton Primary School for many years and was one of their more established members of staff. She had seen many changes, including a new head in the previous year, but although maintaining what she regarded as her 'traditional' teaching style, she was always very interested in new initiatives and anything that might help her pedagogy. She was the school's language co-ordinator and therefore had a personal and formal interest in disseminating good practice in the teaching of literacy to the rest of the teaching staff.

For her work as language co-ordinator she was given a 'quite generous half day per week non-contact time', during which she had the opportunity to visit other year groups. Although she ran staff meetings for other teachers and disseminated information to teachers after attending courses herself, she recognised the professional knowledge of the other staff: 'I need to involve the expertise of those with experience of younger children', and she was prepared to 'bow to the superior knowledge of the Key Stage 1 co-ordinator'. Her approach to literacy was that of a team player, working to create a policy that involved the knowledge and input of all the school's staff.

Within her own classroom her approach to reading was enthusiastic and she adopted a varied approach that was designed to provide a high degree of structure in the first instance, but progression towards a more individual and independent approach for those who were able to cope with it:

> It depends on the ability of the child. The children who have specific problems with reading are still being given phonic work and we use the Oxford Reading Tree and ask the Special Needs Co-ordinator for appropriate worksheets and so on for them. We use ancillary work to do it. The more able readers are being weaned off the reading scheme and have a free choice of books at certain times of day, but other parts of the day they have guided choice and the same goes for the most able readers.

Her emphasis in teaching was on building confidence and matching the reading material to the individual ability of the child, to try to ensure that every pupil might experience success. She combined reading for pleasure with reading for a purpose, so that pupils could see why it was that they needed to be able to read. She offered them a wide range of materials, including reading schemes, plays, fiction and non-fiction, puzzle books, joke books and poetry. She also had a regular time in class where pupils were timetabled to listen to story tapes and, in response to the lack of short commercially produced ones, she had taped most of the selection herself. Such sessions were carefully structured, with pupils asked to follow the text closely as they listened to the tapes. All her teaching materials were clearly labelled and well organised in a designated area of the classroom.

In Mrs Turner's class there was never any ambiguity about what pupils were expected to do. They had regular pre-programmed slots in the day for particular activities, which included story tapes, ERIC time when all pupils read, held at exactly the same time every morning and offering 'guided choice'. In the afternoon she also had a reading time which was 'free choice' and once a week there was a timetabled visit to the library. Mrs Turner always had a class reader, from which she read to the class at the end of every day and the pupils were expected to follow the text. She also made sure that she differentiated according to individual ability when helping children read their books, choose new books, or when she discussed the class reader with them. Differentiation was a particular issue in this class. When tested at the beginning of the year, the reading ability of these 9 and 10 year old pupils ranged from a reading age of below 6 to above 13:

> We have a class reader . . . for some stories, like the Victorian one I am doing at the moment . . . We've all got a book and I read it for them to follow a text and hear it read with expression. I read it to them for 15 minutes at the end of the day, more or less every day. And then I also use it when we are talking about and discussing the story, to talk about characterisation, or plot, or language, so that they can then use the text to substantiate what they are saying. And in that way I have to differentiate by the sort of questions I will pose to the sort of people. I'll know that the least able are just staring at the book but they've got the feeling that they're doing the same as everyone else, so it's quite a useful, efficient way of quite a lot of people being able to discuss a piece of literature and presumably sharing in the enjoyment of sharing.

Mrs Turner's organisation, planning and class management skills were conspicuously well developed, and her class's on-task involvement averaged over 82 during the researcher's visits. Any instructions she gave were clearly expressed with attention to detail. She tried regularly to involve pupils in discussion to enhance their comprehension of the task. She talked with enthusiasm of the English language and took as many opportunities as she could to discuss different words and meanings with the class. On one occasion the children came back from an assembly and she immediately held an impromptu discussion with them about the story they had been reading:

> Mrs Turner starts by asking those who had been in assembly to talk to those who had not been there about the Greek myth they had heard, reminding them beforehand that there are 'lots of lovely long words to remember'.
>
> *Teacher*: What was the story about?
>
> One child starts the story off.
>
> *Teacher*: Who did she marry?
> *Pupil*:   An old King.
> *Teacher*: Can anyone remember his name?
>
> A pupil answers correctly.
>
> *Teacher*: Oh, well done. What nation did he come from?
> *Pupil*:   Troy.
> *Teacher*: Yes, he was from Troy, he was a Trojan.

Mrs Turner continues the discussion, using questions and answers to recapitulate on the story, taking the answers one at a time and suggesting that pupils do not take the story forwards too quickly. The discussion ends with the teacher commenting on how many of the words and sayings from the Greek myth are now used in the English language.

This event, like many others, exemplified her style of teaching. It was structured, carefully pre-planned, but also flexible, related to individuals of widely varying ability, involved a high degree of social control, but stressed the pleasure and interest that children could find from the exploration of language.

Common features and differences

In this chapter we have described six teachers, selected from the thirty-five studied in this research. These six teaches ranged in experience from two years to over twenty years and were working in a range of schools, from a small village primary through to a large inner city school in Birmingham. Each teacher was unique, bringing her own individual personality and her own personal experience of what worked well to her teaching of reading. Some were highly organised in advance, others more opportunistic. Their approaches to teaching, the materials they used, the authors they favoured, the structure of their day, the context in which they taught, their views of pedagogy and of their pupils, were different. Some made skilful use of a classroom assistant, but others did not have one available.

Despite this uniqueness, a number of common characteristics can be identified from these six and the other highly competent teachers not described here. While the ten characteristics listed below may show a certain amount in common, however, the individual expression and manifestation of them was often different.

1. *Teachers had a high level of personal enthusiasm for literature and reading* which was translated into attractive well-stocked class libraries and book corners. In many classrooms the teachers supplemented the school's reading resources with their own personal collection of books, as in the cases of Miss Brown and Mrs Hutchings.
2. *Teachers had good professional knowledge,* not only of children's authors, but also of teaching strategies and pedagogy generally. In the case of teaching strategies, this was especially noteworthy with those who were language co-ordinators. All teachers knew of and used a variety of strategies, even though each had particular favourites, such as group reading, or vocabulary building.
3. *Literacy was made very important.* The classrooms themselves were rich literacy environments. Attractive and high-quality displays of all the children's writing, not just the best, dominated the walls in the upper Key Stage 1 and Key Stage 2 classrooms. Interactive displays which asked the children questions about items on show were common. Where lack of wall space limited the amount of displays, teachers produced class books of children's work. These covered all areas of the curriculum. In

Miss Brown's class, the children's science work on 'Hot and Cold' was collated in an attractively made book and placed in the book corner for children to read. The importance of literacy was further emphasised by the recognition and celebration of it when it occurred, as described in the next point below.

4. *Teachers celebrated progress and increased children's confidence.* This was often done through drawing attention to someone who had made progress and using focused praise. In all classes there was emphasis on the satisfaction children could obtain from a job well done, while in some classes recognition was more formalised through the use of ex-trinsic rewards, such as stickers, stars, or certificates presented in school assemblies.

5. *Teachers were able to differentiate and match effectively teaching to pupils* because of their intimate knowledge of available reading materials and individual children themselves, taking account not only of varying levels of ability, but also of individual personal interests. This seemed particularly important with less able and more reluctant readers, where considerable expertise was required to engage and sustain the children's interest. Miss Dobson made skilful use of a bilingual classroom assistant, so that, by better understanding their language and culture, she could match the work closely to individual Asian children whose mother tongue was not English. By successfully differentiating tasks according to ability, these teachers ensured the children's confidence in their own reading.

6. *Systematic monitoring and assessment was notable,* though the form of it varied. Usually there was comprehensive written recording of children's reading strategies and behaviour, in addition to the books being read, but some teachers, like Miss Dobson, were also able to keep their records in their head and knew, without checking, what each child was achieving. The most comprehensive assessments included monitoring children's levels of phonic awareness and sight vocabulary. Some systems had been developed at school level but in most cases there had been some LEA input.

7. *Regular and varied reading activities were seen as crucial to improving the children's reading standards.* Some phonics work was undertaken in all the Key Stage 1 classes observed, although different teachers placed varying degrees of emphasis on this particular aspect. Language games were used to reinforce formal lessons. All teachers made strong links between reading and writing. Of particular note was the way in which these teachers made use of opportunities to highlight and discuss publicly many different aspects of literacy with their class, whether it concerned the meaning and use of words, what a writer of a book is called, or aspects of spelling and punctuation. The example described in the account of Miss Turner was typical of the way in which most of these teachers could capitalise on unplanned opportunities. The children in these classes were

developing a rich vocabulary and confidence with which to discuss language and literature.

8.   *Pupils were encouraged to develop independence and autonomy.* In different ways, even in classes where activities were highly structured, or where the teacher had a dominant personality, pupils were encouraged to develop ways of attacking unfamiliar words, taking their own reading forward, or backing their own judgement as authors when writing. Books written by pupils themselves were as highly valued as other books in the classroom and were displayed prominently for others to borrow and read, thereby giving the children's writing a genuine purpose and audience.

9.   *Underpinning effective teachers' strategies for the teaching of reading were a high degree of classroom management skill and good-quality personal relationships with pupils.* These classrooms were orderly environments where the children understood the set tasks, knew where and how to access resources, and were able to concentrate on their work. The pupil on-task levels recorded during classroom observation were universally high, some being amongst the highest we have recorded in research projects in primary schools. This is not to say that teachers were dour and puritanical, lacking warmth or humour. Quite the reverse. Most of these teachers had a good rapport with their pupils, were able to joke with them when appropriate and could defuse the occasional potentially disruptive incident with a light-hearted remark, rather than enter into a confrontation.

10. *Teachers had positive expectations.* All the teachers in this group emphasised that children should strive to reach a high standard, whatever their circumstances. Miss Lansbury publicly stressed the need for her class to do the very best they could for an 8-year-old. All wanted children to redraft their writing to improve it. Miss Dobson regularly told the whole class how marvellous she thought they were. Even more importantly, perhaps, the teachers made the children feel that they were interesting young people and valued, so pupils knew their teacher had very high expectations of them all, not just a few.

Source

This is an edited version of a chapter previously published in *Improving Literacy in the Primary School*. 1998. Reproduced by permission of Taylor & Francis Ltd.

Chapter 11

Contradictory models

The dilemma of specific learning difficulties

Alan Dyson and David Skidmore

Models and change in special needs education

It is tempting to regard the history of special needs provision in mainstream schools as one of unequivocal and unidirectional progress towards more effec-tive teaching and more enlightened attitudes. As schools and teachers become more sophisticated, we suppose, so outdated segregatory approaches are replaced by powerful integrationist techniques which enable pupils with special needs to learn effectively within a common curriculum and alongside their peers in ordinary classrooms.

There may be, however, an alternative interpretation of history which is less committed to explanations in terms of 'progress'. Such an interpretation would see change in special needs provision as the successive hegemony of a series of *models* of provision. These models can be understood as having a *tech-nological* aspect; that is, they take the form of strategies and techniques for intervening in children's leaning and organising educational provision. However, they also have an *assumptional* aspect: that is, they are structured around sets of assumptions about the nature of learning, the nature of children's difficulties in learning, the aims of intervention and so on. To this extent, models of special needs provision can be seen as analogous to (though clearly on a smaller historical scale than) the paradigms which Kuhn (1970) suggests dominate the practice of nature science.

Changes in special needs provision, therefore, can be understood as changes in the models of provision. In other words, they are not simply changes in technology (brought about, perhaps, by increasing sophistication), but changes in both technology and assumptions. As models succeed each other, they do not so much achieve similar aims in increasingly more effective ways, as set about addressing very different aims based on different assumptions with different technologies. Whether one model constitutes 'progress' *vis à vis* its predecessors, therefore, depends on some assessment of its foundational assumptions. It is a question, ultimately, of values.

Looking at the development of special needs education in ordinary schools from this perspective, the seminal 1978 HMI progress report (SED, 1978) marks a transition in the Scottish education system from one such model of special needs provision to another. In the 1970s, provision in mainstream schools was, as the report makes clear, dominated by a remedial model. Based on a predominantly psychological perspective (Tomlinson, 1982), this model saw children who were experiencing difficulties at school as suffering from particular weaknesses in cognitive functioning. However, although these weaknesses might form part of an overall intellectual limitation, they could nonetheless be diagnosed and, to a greater or lesser extent, remedied. In particular, a good deal of work went into the diagnosis and remediation of difficulties in reading (e.g. Tansley, 1967), since there appears to have been an unspoken assumption that reading was the key both to the curriculum and also to later effective functioning in adulthood. Not surprisingly, therefore, HMI found special needs provision dominated by the 'remedial' teaching of reading in a situation which constituted both locational withdrawal from the classroom and educational withdrawal from the curriculum offered to the majority of children.

The alternative model which HMI proposed was to go on – in the form of 'Learning Support' or the 'whole-school approach' (Dessent, 1987) – to dominate special needs provision in mainstream schools for well over a decade and still forms the basis of much official guidance offered to schools (SOED, 1994). It is not enough, HMI argued, to address children's difficulties in reading through specialist interventions delivered by specialist teachers. Children who have such difficulties are likely to have difficulties right across the curriculum which may be related to their inability to manage the linguistic and conceptual content of the curriculum as much as to any particular problems with reading. What they need, therefore, are forms of teaching that respond to their needs right across the curriculum – 'appropriate, rather than remedial education' (p. 31) as HMI put it. 'Appropriate education' thus becomes 'a responsibility of the whole school, whether remedial staff are employed or not' (p. 22), and the proper role of special needs specialists includes supporting both children in the mainstream curriculum and their teachers in the development of appropriate styles of curriculum delivery.

Although space does not permit a fuller explication and critique of this 'new' model, it is important to note some of the assumptions which underpin the HMI progress report:

- Children who have learning difficulties are assumed to have difficulties right across the curriculum; HMI argue explicitly against a 'narrow' conception of remedial education as being solely about addressing difficulties that are *specific* to the area of reading.
- Access to a broad curriculum is assumed to be a major educational aim; schools are explicitly warned against withdrawing children from areas of the curriculum where they might experience success in order to 'remediate' their difficulties. This characteristic of learning support and the whole-school approach, of course, has latterly been much reinforced by the advent of a curriculum framework viewed as an entitlement for all pupils.

- 'Appropriate' teaching for children with learning difficulties is assumed to be something of which all teachers are and should capable, albeit with advice and support from specialists. It is, therefore, implicitly (though this has subsequently often been made explicit) assumed to be a subset of 'good' teaching for all children.

It is these assumptions and the hegemony which the HMI model has exercised over special needs provision in mainstream schools which forms the context for the emergence in recent years of specific learning difficulties as a rapidly expanding form of special need. It is salutary, therefore, to set alongside the HMI progress report this definition of dyslexia:

> Dyslexia can be defined as a specific difficulty in learning, constitutional in origin, in one or more areas of reading, spelling and written language, which may be accompanied by difficulty in number work. It is particularly related to mastering and using written language (alphabetic, numerical and musical notation) although often affecting oral language to some degree.
>
> (Crisfield and Smythe, 1993, p. 8)

or this definition of specific learning difficulties:

> Specific Learning Difficulties can be identified as distinctive patterns of difficulties relating to the processing of information, within a continuum from very mild to severe, which result in restrictions in literacy development and discrepancies in performances within the curriculum.
>
> (Reid, 1994, p. 3)

It is immediately apparent that we are dealing here with a set of assumptions which are significantly different from those which informed the HMI progress report. Specific leaning difficulties are assumed to be just that – specific to certain areas of functioning, and most definitely not generalised across the whole curriculum. In particular, problems in reading are assumed to constitute the most significant of these difficulties rather than being one set of difficulties amongst many. 'Appropriate' teaching, therefore – at least if that means adapting the *conceptual* content of the curriculum – is unlikely to be quite so appropriate for children whose difficulties lie not in handling conceptual complexity but in information and language processing.

Given these assumptions, it is scarcely surprising that the forms of provision which are frequently advocated for children with specific learning difficulties sit somewhat uneasily with the orthodoxies of learning support and the whole-school approach. The literature on specific learning difficulties is full of recommendations for teaching programmes and approaches. However, these programmes frequently take the form of individualised interventions which are aimed at children's supposed 'underlying' difficulties, and which, therefore, as Reid puts it, 'cannot naturally and easily be accommodated within the school curriculum and the mainstream class' (Reid, 1994, p. 91). Indeed, some of these interventions are not, strictly speaking, educational at all, but more properly belong to the world of paramedical therapies (e.g. Dennison and Hargrove, 1985; Stone and Harris, 1991). Not surprisingly, many programmes, therefore, cannot be delivered by class and subject teachers with only minimal levels of support. Instead, they demand specialist teachers who are trained not merely in special needs generally, but in specific learning difficulties as such – which is why, of course, some specific learning difficulties organisations feel it is essential to deliver or accredit their own training courses for teachers.

In other words, what we are faced with is a 'model' of specific learning difficulties provision which differs in terms both of its assumptions and its technology from the 'model' of learning support and the whole-school approach. This inevitably faces schools with a dilemma: on the one hand, they are, by and large, committed to an approach to learning support which has been powerfully advocated at national level, and which appears to have important benefits for children with 'general' learning difficulties. On the other hand, there is growing pressure to them to adopt a somewhat different approach which is claimed to be more effective for children with specific learning difficulties, but which does not sit easily with their established learning support provision. This dilemma, we suggest, gives rise to three specific issues with which schools are faced:

- How should they reconcile their existing commitment to curriculum access and development as a major strategy for meeting special needs with the requirement for extra-curricular interventions which specific learning difficulties seem to carry?
- How should learning support teachers reconcile their existing commitment to collaborative teaching and consultation with mainstream colleagues with the 'new' demand that they become trained specific learning difficulties specialists working directly with individual pupils?
- How should schools manage their limited resources equitably so that they are able to meet the needs of both an established population of pupils with 'general' learning difficulties and an apparently growing population of pupils with 'specific' learning difficulties for whom individualised, extra-curricular and specialist provision may prove relatively costly in resource terms?

These issues are made more complex for schools by the nature of the existing literature and guidance on specific learning difficulties. The emphasis within learning support on issues of mainstream pedagogy and curriculum development and on questions of school organisation has produced for schools a substantial literature which is of immediate use to head and principle teachers in the management of provision. However, the model underpinning specific learning difficulties provision focuses much more on questions of assessment, diagnosis and individual intervention. It has, therefore, relatively little to say on how provision within mainstream schools might be organised and managed. Pumfrey and Reason's (1991) comprehensive review of research, for instance, contains only one brief chapter on the management of provision, and that confines itself to a rehearsal of standard learning support strategies. Although, therefore, a few accounts are now beginning to appear of how schools are organising themselves to respond to specific learning difficulties (Brown, 1993; Lewis, 1995), there is a substantial gap in the literature which leaves schools somewhat bereft of guidance.

A model for specific learning difficulties provision

It is in the light of this perceived gap that the Special Needs Research Group in the Department of Education, University of Newcastle upon Tyne, has been undertaking a series of linked studies of emerging forms of provision in secondary schools. Principal amongst these has been a study, sponsored by the Scottish Office Education Department, of provision in 27 schools across 5 Regions in Scotland (Dyson and Skidmore, 1994). In parallel with this was a smaller study of 14 schools in England. Finally, there have been two studies sponsored by English LEAs: in a study sponsored by Cleveland LEA, four schools took part in a cost-benefit analysis of their specific learning difficulties provision (Dyson, 1995); and a survey of provision in all the middle and high schools in a further English LEA (Dyson and Wood, 1994). The schools included in these studies do not constitute a nationally representative sample (in either Scotland or England); indeed, in all but the LEA-wide survey, schools were selected precisely because of their unusually well-developed approaches to specific learning difficulties. Nonetheless, we believe that these studies together allow us to describe secondary schools' emerging responses to specific learning difficulties with far greater confidence than has hitherto been possible. They also, we suggest, usefully complement the important study undertaken by Sheila Riddell and colleagues at the University of Stirling (Riddell, Duffield, Brown and Ogilvy, 1992).

Rather than setting out the findings of each study in detail, what we propose to do is to describe a common model which we believe underpins provision across many of the schools we investigated. This model is like other models of special needs provision outlined in the preceding section in that it comprises both technological and assumptional components. Like those models too, its implementation in detail varies considerably from school to school and the assumptions upon which it is based are not necessarily made explicit by the schools. In other words, it is a model which can be *inferred* from schools' practice and teachers' accounts of that practice, rather than an explicit blueprint upon which those schools have deliberately sought to build their provision. Nonetheless, it does offer a means of accounting for the forms of provision we found as rational responses to specific learning difficulties and

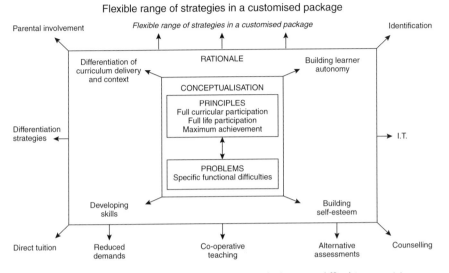

Figure 11.1 A possible model of an approach to specific learning difficulties provision

© Alan Dyson and David Skidmore, 1994.

it therefore offers other schools a means of reviewing and developing their own provision in some rational manner. The model is represented diagrammatically in Figure 11.1.

The model comprises three levels which link its assumptional and technological components. It is founded upon distinctive *conceptualisation* of specific learning difficulties which is somewhat different from that frequently found in the literature. This gives rise to a *rationale* for the school's response to specific learning difficulties, and it is around this that the detailed features of *provision* are organised.

Conceptualisation

Within the current literature, as we have seen, specific learning difficulties tend to be conceptualised from a psychological or psycho-medical perspective, in terms of information-processing deficits or phonological or other linguistic weaknesses. Within this model, however, specific learning difficulties are conceptualised much more as a series of *functional* problems which prevent the realisation of certain educational and social entitlements. Children are seen as entitled to participate in a common curriculum, to experience educational achievement and ultimately to enjoy a fulfilling adult life. Some of them have weaknesses in specific areas of functioning which threaten their social and educational entitlements. 'In other words,' as one school put it, 'there is a discrepancy between what a pupil can do and understand and what he/she can show he/she can do and understand.' In such a situation, the aetiology and diagnosis of those weaknesses are seen as less important than their impact on participation and achievement.

Rationale

This conceptualisation leads directly to the rationale upon which provision is based. So long as the focus is on the aetiology of children's weaknesses, then provision is likely to be concerned with the remediation or amelioration of those weaknesses – as is the case with many of the programmes advocated in the specific learning difficulties literature. However, if specific learning difficulties are conceptualised in terms of threats to educational and social entitlements, then the rationale for provision is likely to be the *delivery* of those entitlements.

The following are typical of the sorts of rationales which the schools we studied were able to provide for their provision:

> Our rationale is: to provide access to the mainstream curriculum; improvement in basic skills; appropriate means of circumventing specific learning difficulties in order to enable pupils to achieve their maximum potential and, where appropriate, access to further and higher education; and to raise self-esteem and confidence.

Or again:

> We hope that pupils are able to show what they are capable of, despite their specific difficulties. We hope to give them a range of coping strategies and a sense that they are valued as individuals, and can achieve without undue frustration. We want them to take full part in the life and work of the class and the school.

These rationales, in common with many others, de-emphasise the notions of diagnosis, intervention and remediation in favour of notions of circumvention, coping, participation and achievement. In particular, they indicate four broad aims which provision should fulfil:

- *Differentiation.* If pupils are to participate in a common curriculum despite their functional difficulties, then that curriculum has to be delivered in ways which are differentiated to take account of those difficulties.
- *Building self-esteem.* If pupils are to achieve their potential in education and beyond, they need to see and value themselves as potential learners and potential achievers. They should be helped, therefore, to move beyond the negative views of themselves which an exclusive focus on their difficulties might create.

- *Building learner autonomy.* If pupils are to participate in a common curriculum without massive (and ultimately disabling) levels of support, then they need to learn how to function autonomously, drawing on their strengths and circumventing their weaknesses.
- *Developing skills.* If pupils are weak in certain skill areas, then some attempt might be made to address those weaknesses directly. However, such attempts have to take place alongside the three other aims of provision, and therefore do not form the basis for a full-blown return to 'remedial' education.

These four aims constitute a synthesis of 'established' and 'novel' approaches characteristic of the schools in our studies. The notion of differentiation (as opposed, perhaps, to its practice) is 'established' in that it has been at the centre of the whole-school approach. Similarly, the aim of skills-development has an even longer history in remedial education, and appears to be enjoying something of a revival within schools' approaches to specific learning difficulties. Building autonomy and building self-esteem, on the other hand, mark crucial boundary between rationales for specific learning difficulties provision and those for learning support. The latter has historically been concerned with generalised difficulties and has often tended to focus on devising and delivering what our respondents called a 'restricted' or 'reduced and/or adapted' curriculum. This is probably still the case, even where the notion of 'curriculum adaptation' has been replaced by the rhetoric of 'differentiation' (Hart, 1992; Thompson and Barton, 1992). However, such restriction is now viewed as necessary for children who have significant strengths to offset their weaknesses, and therefore, in the words of one learning support teacher:

> Children with specific learning difficulties are given access to the full curriculum.

Given this approach, it is essential that such children are able to capitalise on their strengths and circumvent their weaknesses. It follows that the building of autonomy and self-esteem are not the desirable – but optional – extras they may perhaps have been in Learning Support, but are absolutely central to effective responses to specific learning difficulties.

Provision

This four-fold rationale directly informs provision in the schools in our samples. Given what we said in the preceding section about the synthesis of established and novel approaches within schools' rationales, it is significant that many of the forms of provision which schools are using are drawn from the repertoire of learning support. Many schools are happy to base their provision on the established role of the learning support teacher and to draw on standard techniques of assessment, co-operative teaching, the production of differentiated materials and so on. However, specific learning difficulties provision appears in our model as distinctive in three particular respects:

Eclecticism

Because the aim of provision is to enable the child to function effectively in the full curriculum, schools tend to draw on anything which might be helpful in this respect. As one teacher put it, 'We try anything!' Standard learning support techniques are, as we have indicated, prominent; however, other, more distinctive forms of provision are also in evidence: some of the psycho-medical interventions advocated in the specific learning difficulties litera-ture; programmes of counselling as means of developing pupils' self-esteem; programmes of thinking skills and problem-solving, aimed at developing learner autonomy; the provision of lap top computers, spell-checkers and other IT aids for the same purpose; and so on.

Pragmatism

Significantly, in a field which is frequently characterised by ideological conflict, learning support teachers in our studies tend to select the particular techniques and forms of provision they wish to use on a pragmatic basis. They are, in the words of one Learning Support teacher, 'Not greatly impressed by theories.' The criterion for using a particular technique, therefore, is not whether it conforms to some theory about the aetiology and treatment of specific learning difficulties as such, but whether it is of immediate use in enabling a particular child to function effectively in the curriculum.

An example of this fundamental pragmatism can be seen in the attitude which many teachers take towards the issue of withdrawing pupils from ordi-nary lessons. Withdrawal is, in many ways, the battle ground between the older remedial approach to special needs provision, with its emphasis on tack-ling pupils' areas of weakness directly, and the newer Learning Support approach, with its emphasis on access to a differentiated curriculum. By and large, the teachers who responded to us subscribe to neither of these positions, seeing withdrawal as simply one more technique which might – or might not, depending on individual circumstances – be helpful in furthering the aim of effective functioning in the full curriculum. One respondent summarised the paradox in this way:

> Pupils have an entitlement to access the curriculum but they do not have to by physically in the classroom at all times.

Or, as another teacher put it:

> It all depends on the balance of advantage for the child.

Customisation

This pragmatic tendency directly informs a highly individualised approach to the structuring of provision for particular pupils. Learning support has, of course, traditionally stressed individualisation at the level of access to the curriculum. However, the strategies it has relied upon to achieve this (differentiation, co-operative teaching, curriculum adaptation and so on) have – by dint of the numbers of pupils involved – tended to be applied in much the same way to all. However, the strategies for specific learning difficulties provision tend much more to be assembled into customised packages for particular pupils. 'We wouldn't,' one teacher explained, 'do the same thing with two pupils'.

Moreover, a significant consideration in assembling these packages is the child's own wishes; if a pupil is happy to use a lap-top, for instance, s/he is given one, but if s/he feels out of place using one in class, then the lap-top is withdrawn. In other words, provision is determined not simply by what the child is believed to 'need' but also by what s/he wants.

A model for reconciliation?

We suggested earlier that the dominant model of specific learning difficulties stands in contradiction to the model which informs learning support and the whole school approach. Moreover, the emergence of specific learning difficulties as an issue faces schools with three crucial dilemmas: how to reconcile the aim of curriculum access with the need for extra-curricular interventions; how to reconcile a collaborative teaching role with a more specialist role; and how to manage limited resources equitably across different groups of children with special needs. It is important to determine, therefore, the extent to which the model we have described as emerging in schools actually resolves these issues.

We believe there is an important sense in which this model does offer some way out of the dilemmas which schools face. By reconceptualising specific learning difficulties in terms of curriculum access rather than psycho-medical deficits, it offers a way to connect schools' approaches to specific learning difficulties with their wider educational concerns, particularly in respect of pupils with other forms of special need. Hence, strategies drawn from the specific learning difficulties literature – individual extra-curricular programmes, intervention by specialist teachers, and so on – find a place as part of a wide range of strategies whose ultimate aim is to enable pupils to function within the curriculum. The *ideological* conflict which has beset specific learning difficulties provision is thus resolved at the level of *pragmatic* decisions about means of ensuring access and achievement for particular children.

The model also goes some way towards resolving resourcing dilemmas. In the first place, it draws heavily upon other sorts of learning support resources and expertise which are already well-established in schools. By and large it does not require a massive re-skilling of learning support teachers not an investment in new materials and equipment. Moreover, the emphasis on curriculum access and effective functioning rather than on curative interventions gives a defined focus to provision. There is no open-ended commitment to working with a child until s/he is 'cured' of specific learning difficulties; neither is there any suggestion that such children will need highly specialised teaching right across the curriculum. Rather, the aim of curriculum access offers a criterion for determining how much special provision is necessary and what form that provision should take. As one teacher put it:

> There's no reason to interfere with a child's learning if they're coping.

In other words, intervention is only necessary when and insofar as a particular pupil is not functioning effectively within the curriculum, and its aim is limited to restoring such effective functioning.

This, coupled with the customising approach described above, allows schools to structure a staged response to specific learning difficulties rather than relying on a high level of 'blanket' provision. For some children, very little more will be necessary than a sympathetic response from class teachers and the offer of specific support as and when needed; indeed, schools reported a number of pupils who very much preferred this 'hands-off' style of provision. For other children, much more intensive forms of intervention and support will be necessary – though even in these cases, the focus on curriculum access and the use of standard techniques drawn from learning support means that much of this provision will be made by subject and class teachers working within ordinary classrooms.

There are, however, some slightly more problematic aspects of this proposed model. Although schools are currently finding its resource demands more or less manageable, the customising of provision does nonetheless make such demands. On the whole, these are probably higher than the demands made by established forms of learning support and, moreover, relate to groups of pupils who are only just beginning to attain prominence within schools. As one teacher somewhat wryly commented:

> The more you look, the more you find.

In consequence, some schools in our samples are finding that the demands made by this emerging group are beginning to divert resources away from other pupils with special needs, and that the school's capacity to sustain both high quality learning support provision and specific learning difficulties provision based on the model we have outlined is becoming increasingly stretched. In some cases, this diversion of resources is exacerbated by the success of parents and lobby groups in the area in persuading or compelling local authorities and schools to place particular emphasis on provision for pupils with specific learning difficulties.

What is evident is that the viability of the model depends either on a balance being maintained between the level of demand and the level of available resources, or on a significant increase in resources to match the growing level of demand. We shall return to this point in our concluding section.

Specific learning difficulties: a way forward?

We suggest that there are some important points which emerge from the foregoing discussion, and which may offer a way forward in respect of specific learning difficulties:

Models and debate in special needs education

We wish to begin with what may appear to be a theoretical issue, but which nonetheless, we suggest, has major practical implications. We regard much of the debate which takes place within the field of special needs education as impoverished by its uni-dimensionality. A whole series of debates – withdrawal *versus* in-class support, integration *versus* segregation, common curriculum *versus* alternative curricula, and, of course, specific learning difficulties *versus* the whole-school approach – have been conducted as though a resolution of the issues they raised was possible at the purely *technological* level. In other words, it has been assumed that evidence could be found to show that one form of provision was unequivocally 'better' than the other. The concept of 'special need' as something which is self-evident in any assessment of a particular child serves, of course, to rationalise this style of debate by implying that the 'meeting of needs' is an unproblematic touchstone which can be used to evaluate competing approaches.

Our contention, on the other hand, is that such debates have a significant *assumptional* component. The different positions which engage with each other rest on often unspoken assumptions about the nature of special needs and the purposes of education. It is the incompatibility of competing assumptions, we believe, which often makes such debates somewhat fruitless. The notion of 'models' of provision seems to us much more productive. By focusing on the conjunction of particular technologies with particular assumptions, it makes it possible for the full implications of a proposed form of provision to be explicated with an open acknowledgement that values and beliefs are inextricably bound up in the positions adopted by parties to the debate.

In the field of specific learning difficulties in particular, we suggest that some of the impasses between the 'dyslexia lobby' and its 'opponents' (Riddell, Brown and Duffield, 1994) could be opened up if there was an acknowledgement that each was operating on the basis of a different *model* of provision. The debate is often conducted as though determining whether or not dyslexia 'exists' and whether or not it has a distinctive symptomatology and aetiology would *ipso facto* reveal what an appropriate educational response should be. In fact, as we have seen, much of the psychological literature on dyslexia and specific learning difficulties makes an unspoken assumption, about the centrality of curative intervention as an aim of provision, which ought itself to be the subject of debate. An alternative model along the lines that we have described is, however, at least equally defensible. Such a model has little to say on the 'existence' or otherwise of dyslexia because it is founded on assumptions about the centrality of curriculum access and maximal achievement as educational goals. It is not that these assumptions are necessarily more valid than any others, but that opening them up to debate and acknowledging the way they inform the conceptualisation of specific learning difficulties and the preferred form of intervention may offer a more fruitful way forward than the conflicts which currently characterise this field.

The model and school self-review

One of the investigations which contributed to the development of the model was a survey of specific learning difficulties in all the middle and high schools of one English LEA (Dyson and Wood, 1994). The results were extremely worrying: many schools had no clear conceptualisation of specific learning difficulties, had little or no idea of how many of their pupils had such difficulties, and could point to no differentiation between the provision for general and for specific difficulties. In such a situation, it is scarcely surprising if concerned parents come to distrust schools and to press for alternative forms of provision.

We believe, therefore, that there is much to be gained if schools use our model as the basis for a review of their current provision. This is particularly the case in view of the flexibility inherent in the model, which avoids committing schools in very different contexts to a uniform response. What matters is that each school develops, in a way which matches its available resources and preferred styles of working, means of realising the four aims of the rationale. This ought to be a realistic possibility for all schools which have an established approach to learning support since the model draws heavily on such approaches.

Moreover, the increasing emphasis in government policy on parental rights, and the increasing activity of the 'dyslexia lobby', together with the educational justifications for parental involvement, mean that schools need to be in a position to justify publicly their approaches to specific learning difficulties. We suggest that the model provides a basis for such justifications, enabling schools to propose to parents and their associations an educationally-meaningful alternative to the highly individualised and remedially-oriented provision which they may (understandably) see as the only possible response to their child's needs.

The model and government policy

This leads us, inevitably, to the implications of our model for government policy. We regard a significant strength of the model we have described as being its incorporation into the concept of specific learning difficulties of some notion of educational aims and purposes. It is this notion – however ill-defined – which allows schools to consider rationally the point at which a relative weakness in some area of functioning becomes a 'learning difficulty', and to begin to determine the sort of intervention which might be necessary if educational aims are to be realised for this child.

We note that the concept of 'special educational needs' and the government policy which is based on that concept do not appear to contain any equivalent articulation of educational aims. It is not surprising, then, that, as the government's own agencies have pointed out (Audit Commission and HMI, 1992), there seems to be no rational way of determining what needs for what interventions arise from what learning characteristics. It is similarly unsurprising that, in the field of specific learning difficulties, there are problems in deciding who has what special needs as a result of such difficulties, and what resources they are entitled to on the basis of such needs. We anticipate similar problems occurring as other 'new' forms of special need – Attention Deficit Disorder (Reid, Maag and Vasa, 1993; Cooper and Ideus, 1995) seems to be the current leader – begin to emerge, and we predict that the necessary balance between demand and resources will become increasingly difficult to maintain.

Our view is that such issues are always problematic, that hard decisions about resource-deployment are inevitable, and that easy solutions are not available. Nonetheless, we also believe that rational debate on these issues and rational decision-making in particular cases will only be possible when some explicit notion of educational aims is set alongside the concept of educational needs. The introduction of national curricula of differing sorts in both Scotland and England has gone some way towards achieving this. It may well be, however, that if the demand from specific learning difficulties and other 'new' forms of need increases, such a move will be essential if the education system is not to collapse under the strain. In this case, the model we have described and similar models that emerge from the practical decision-making undertaken by schools, might prove a useful starting point for debate.

References

Audit Commission and Her Majesty's Inspectorate (1992). *Getting in on the Act: Provision for Pupils with Special Educational Needs: the National Picture.* (London, HMSO).

Brown, M. (1993). Supporting learning through a whole school approach, in: Reid, G. (ed.), *Specific Learning Difficulties (Dyslexia): Perspectives on Practice.* (Edinburgh, Moray House Publications).

Cooper, P. and Ideus, K. (1995). Is attention deficit disorder a Trojan Horse? *Support for Learning*, 10(1), 29–34.

Crisfield, J. and Smythe, I. (ed.) (1993). *The Dyslexia Handbook 1993/4.* (Reading, British Dyslexia Association).

Dennison, P.E. and Hargrove, G. (1985). *Personalised Whole Brain Integration.* (California, Educational Kinaesthetic).

Dessent, T. (1987). *Making the Ordinary School Special.* (London, Falmer).

Dyson, A. (1995). *Provision for Pupils with Specific Learning Difficulties in Cleveland Secondary School: A Cost Benefit Analysis.* (Special Needs Research Group, University of Newcastle upon Tyne for Cleveland LEA).

Dyson, A. and Skidmore, D. (1994). *Provision for Pupils with Specific Learning Difficulties in Secondary Schools: A Report to SOED.* (Special Needs Research Group, Department of Education, University of Newcastle upon Tyne).

Dyson, A. and Wood, B. (1994). *A Survey of Provision for Pupils with Specific Learning Difficulties in Middle and High Schools Maintained by [One] LEA.* (Special Needs Research Group Department of Education, University of Newcastle upon Tyne).

Hart, S. (1992). Differentiation – way forward or retreat? *British Journal of Special Education*, 19(1), 10–12.

Kuhn, T.S. (1970). *The Structure of Scientific Revolutions* (2nd edn). (London, University of Chicago Press).

Lewis, J. (1995). The development of a unit for dyslexic children in a British comprehensive school, *Dyslexia*, 1(1), 12–18.

Pumfrey, P.D. and Reason, R. (1991). *Specific Learning Difficulties (Dyslexia): Challenges and Responses.* (Windsor, NFER-Nelson).

Reid, G. (1994). *Specific Learning Difficulties (Dyslexia): A Handbook for Study and Practice.* (Edinburgh, Moray House Publications).

Reid, R., Maag, J.W. and Vasa, S.F. (1993). Attention Deficit Hyperactivity Disorder as a disability category: A critique, *Exceptional Children*, 60(3), 198–214.

Riddell, S., Duffield, J., Brown, S. and Ogilvy, C. (1992). *Specific Learning Difficulties: Policy, Practice and Provision: A Report to SOED.* (Department of Education, University of Stirling.)

Riddell, S., Brown, S. and Duffield, J. (1994). Conflicts of policies and models: The case of specific learning difficulties, in: Riddell, S. and Brown, S. (eds), *Special Educational Needs Policy in the 1990s: Warnock in the Market Place.* (London, Routledge).

Scottish Education Department (SED) (1978). *The Education of Pupils with Learning Difficulties in Primary and Secondary Schools in Scotland: A Progress Report by HM Inspectors of Schools.* (Edinburgh, HMSO).

Scottish Office Education Department (SOED) (1994). *Effective Provision for Special Educational Needs: A Report by HM Inspectors of Schools.* (Edinburgh, SOED).

Stone, J. and Harris, K. (1991). These coloured spectacles: What are they for? *Support for Learning*, 6(3), 116–118.

Tansley, A.E. (1967). *Reading and Remedial Reading.* (London, Routledge and Kegan Paul).

Thompson, D. and Barton, L. (1992). The wider context: A free market, *British Journal of Special Education*, 19(1), 13–15.

Tomlinson, S. (1982). *A Sociology of Special Education.* (London, Routledge and Kegan Paul).

Source

This is an edited version of a chapter previously published in G. Reid (ed.) *Dimensions of Dyslexia*. 1996. Reproduced by permission of Moray House Publications.

Chapter 12

The National Literacy Strategy and dyslexia

A comparison of teaching methods and materials

Judith Piotrowski and Rea Reason

Combining expertise in primary and special education, the authors consider the potential of the NLS to prevent and alleviate learning difficulties of a dyslexic nature. They evaluate the usefulness of published teaching materials in terms of eight questions based on learning theory relevant to reading acquisition. They conclude that general schemes focusing on phonological development would provide an ideal basis for inclusive practices if they contained explicit guidance on 'assessing to teach' and the principles and practices of 'mastery learning', i.e. on planned repetition and revision that ensures retention of what has been learnt.

Introduction

Within the context of the National Literacy Strategy, dyslexia (or specific literacy difficulties) can be defined as marked and persistent problems at the word level of the NLS framework. The definition implies that accurate and fluent word reading and/or spelling is developing very incompletely or with great difficulty despite appropriate learning opportunities. It provides the basis for a staged process of assessment through teaching (Reason *et al.*, 1999).

Given this focus on teaching, research and practice in the area of literacy difficulties we need to consider ways of evaluating learning opportunities and teaching methods within a mainstream educational setting. Two interdependent questions now arise. First, to what extent is the NLS curriculum appropriate for struggling literacy learners, whether they are regarded as dyslexic or not? Second, in what ways are the instructional approaches introduced under the heading of dyslexia similar or different to those in general use with all children?

This article seeks to answer these two questions. It starts with an outline of word level learning within the NLS and then considers the teaching approaches in relation to those commonly recommended under the heading of dyslexia. We then compare three kinds of commercially published teaching materials: (a) those developed for all children as meeting the requirements of the NLS at the word level; (b) those intended for learners making slower progress in literacy; (c) those targeted at learners regarded as having difficulties of a dyslexic nature. What are the similarities and differences between these materials in terms of their rationales? What are the implications for practice?

The National Literacy Strategy

The influence that special education has had on the development of the NLS curricular framework has perhaps not been recognised enough. No more are there polarised debates about teaching methods that focus either on language experience or structured cumulative approaches. It is clear that children need both. Within the NLS, text level work ensures that children understand and enjoy the very purpose of reading and writing – communication – while sentence and word level work provide the more structured elements within the framework. In some ways general education can now be regarded as part of special education rather than vice versa.

There are of course areas of concern: first, to what extent can children with learning difficulties participate in and learn during the Literacy Hour and, second, how can they start to reach the very ambitious learning targets set out in the framework? The guidance on special educational needs within the NLS makes it very clear that, with rare exception, every child will participate in the 'hour' and that additional support should become an integral part of the NLS framework.

Whole class interactive teaching provides the rationale for the shared reading and writing activities of the NLS. All the children are exposed to these activities for a much longer time than they would be during individualised instruction. They listen to the teacher, they respond together to the teacher, they observe the models of the other children and they take turns to respond individually. If we learn to read through reading then, overall, the NLS whole class activities can provide many more planned opportunities to read.

But being exposed to reading does not necessarily mean that all children will learn to read. If those with learning difficulties are to benefit from the 'hour', then the starting point has to be that all teachers develop their skill of noticing individual differences and adjusting the level of questioning and the responses required. With guided group reading and writing there can of course be better opportunities for differentiation than with whole class teaching.

Perhaps most important is the common language of the NLS that enables class and support teachers to work together. Support teachers now have a central role in preparing children for classroom activities through their assessments, targets and additional teaching as necessary. The information provided by support teachers enables class teachers to adjust their teaching to individual needs.

This way of working assumes, of course, that we have the pre-requisite teacher time, expertise and resources. Far from doing away with special needs support, the NLS requires that all those involved, including classroom assistants and parents, have a good understanding of teaching and learning within the NLS. The NLS extends far beyond the 'hour' and children with special needs such as dyslexia can now be prepared for the whole class lessons during supported individual and group work. This can include the more deliberately planned and repetitive approaches outlined in this article.

Phonics within the NLS

In line with current research (for a review see Beard, 1998), word level targets contain a heavy emphasis on the development of children's phonological competencies and word recognition skills based on phonics. The Reception Year starts with activities to encourage and consolidate the development of the children's phonological awareness, i.e. the discrimination of sounds in words. Even at this stage, it is possible to notice those children needing more assistance and practice with these important skills. There is controversy, however, about the ambitious targets set from Year 1 onwards and the risks of some children being regarded as dyslexic simply because they cannot keep up with the pace.

The learning of lists of words that share particular letter patterns does not necessarily generalise to the reading and writing of continuous text (Reason, 1998). Children might be able to read and spell the words as lists while still not using this information for the purposes of written communication. In order to encourage the transfer of learning from lists, the NLS includes approaches such as the reading and construction of sentences containing the words and the linking of reading and writing activities in order to reinforce the learning.

Teachers following the NLS framework are expected to know what the particular phonics targets are for the class or the group so that familiar patterns can be pointed out and reinforced when reading continuous text together. In this way, words containing selected patterns are taken from the texts being read, practised in lists as necessary, and then re-read in the context of the text. This is illustrated in teaching examples contained in the NLS training video on phonics within word level work.

Cognitive research now also supports what many teachers have been doing for years. In terms of connectionist modelling (Snowling, 1998; Reason, 1998), readers need both phonological and semantic information to be able to cope with all types of printed word. We can read, for example, 'eat a mint' and 'drink a pint' without any confusion about the pronunciations of mint/pint because we have learnt to read these words in the context of meaningful text.

In terms of developmental longitudinal research (Rego and Bryant, 1995; Lazo, Pumfrey and Peers, 1997), children combine semantic, syntactic and phonological knowledge in a complex and interdependent way when learning to read. Continuous text with a rich and varied content plays a central role in furthering this development. The more children read the better they get at reading. Shared and guided reading of interesting material requires culturally relevant contents that are also appropriate for the purposes of learning phonics (Reason, 1998).

The NLS word level targets and in-service materials incorporate two ways of teaching phonics to young children. These two ways have been labelled respectively 'small unit' (synthetic) and 'large unit' (analytic) approaches in the research literature. The 'small unit' approach starts by showing children how words are built from single phonemes, e.g. c-a-t. The alternative 'large unit' approach draws on a developmental framework that introduces *onset/rime* combinations first (e.g. d-og, l-og, f-og, fr-og). Both are included in the targets of the NLS framework.

Some argue that it is more economical to teach in small single letter units (p-a-t, p-o-t, p-i-t, p-e-t, p-u-t) in that several words can be made up from a limited number of letters. Others, however, argue that this goes against the grain of what we now know about children's development in terms of learning to perceive and use phonological regularities. It is also argued that English is more regular at the rime level than at the individual sound level (e.g. b-all is not b-a-l-l). There is currently debate about the merits of these two approaches. The issue is no longer whether we should teach phonics carefully and deliberately but how it might best be done.

A steep learning curve

Overall, the NLS framework can provide a pathway for the cumulative, hierarchical and incremental presentation of word level targets. The Reception Year places emphasis on the securing of a confident knowledge of phoneme/grapheme correspondences in line with research regarding the importance of knowledge and experience at school entry of rhyme, alliteration and letter sounds (for a current review see Johnston, 1998). The Reception Year targets appear both informed and acceptable. Indeed, anecdotal evidence from many teachers suggests that the children are coping well and that skills in reading and spelling c-v-c words (e.g. hat, red, bin) are noticeably more advanced than with previous cohorts.

However, Year 1 Term 3 and Year 2 Term 1 require a pace and momentum that will present many teachers, children and their parents with considerable demands. For all but the fastest learners, the objectives seem very ambitious within the prescribed time-scale. The amount to be covered in one term by children aged around six years is shown in Table 12.1.

Although there is some overlap between these targets and those in the previous and subsequent terms, the danger is that the targets will not receive the careful and systematic coverage required to ensure that children have really learnt them. The lack of time may seriously compromise the development of word level knowledge and skills of some of the children. It is, for example, possible that summer term birth children, still five years old as they complete Term 3, will be considered to have special needs or dyslexic difficulties simply because the pace is too fast and the coverage too superficial.

In the light of experience, we may need to reconsider the detail and sequence of phonic knowledge covered in the transition from Year 1 to Year 2 and the

Table 12.1 Phonic targets in Year 1 Term 3

ee:	'ee'	(feet),	'ea'	(seat)				
ai:	'ai'	(train),	'a-e'	(name),	'ay'	(play)		
ie:	'ie'	(lie),	'i-e'	(bite),	'igh'	(high),	'y'	(fly)
oa:	'oa'	(boat),	'o-e'	(pole),	'ow'	(show)		
oo:	'oo'	(moon),	'u-e'	(tune),	'ew'	(flew),	'ue'	(blue)

possibility of an extension of this work into Year 3 to ensure thorough and confident learning of the targets. Such a move is unrelated to any lowering of expectations but would reflect an informed knowledge of the pace at which young children develop their competencies in these areas.

There is also debate as to the advisability of grouping together different spelling patterns that represent the same phoneme as shown in Table 12.1. If the pace is fast and the patterns are only partially learnt, then the spelling of words that sound the same but are written differently may become confused. This may be even more likely if the words are learnt in lists containing a mixture of confusing spelling patterns and not in the context of meaningful text.

Another issue that demands more careful consideration is the learning of lists of high frequency words in isolation from their semantic contexts. Traditionally such word lists have been associated with the content of reading schemes closely matched to the individual child's rate of development through the scheme. We have now observed instances where long lists, taken from the NLS framework, are being practised as flash cards. As high frequency words are the least easy to learn and remember in isolation, we wonder whether this was, in fact, the intention of those who developed the framework.

Teaching methods and dyslexia

Teaching methods in the field of dyslexia are documented in several sources such as Miles and Miles (1990) and Pumfrey and Reason (1991). The programmes, illustrated in the next section of this article, have been informed by the work of charismatic pioneers such as Orton (1937), Fernald (1943), Gillingham and Stillman (1946) and Norrie (1960) and are not, as such, based on a body of systematic research. The predominant and persistent features of these approaches can be summarised as follows:

- a hierarchical, structured study of language, in particular phonics;
- detailed, incremental coverage of phonics;
- 'multisensory' methods with emphasis on the links between seeing, hearing and tactile stimulation, kinaesthetic feedback and the development of motor memory;

- learning to the point of mastery/automaticity;
- acknowledgement of the learning bias of the child with regard to auditory or visual preference.

The content and structure of the NLS addresses several of the critical features listed above. Specifically, the NLS comprises:

- cumulative sequences of phonics targets;
- an emphasis on the hierarchical, structured study of language;
- implicit reference to mastery learning via the specified targets for R, Y1, 2, 3 and 4.

The NLS training materials (DfEE, 1998), distributed to all primary schools in the UK, provide suggestions and activity resource sheets to inform and support teaching in the classroom. The purpose of the word level activity resource sheets at KS1 is to develop 'accurate reading and spelling strategies by focusing on the common spelling patterns of most phonemes'. At KS2, the focus moves away from phonics to 'the rules which govern written language and the morphemic structure of words'. There are four elements to the word level work at KS1:

- phonological awareness, phonics and spelling;
- word recognition, graphic knowledge and spelling knowledge;
- vocabulary extension;
- handwriting.

The activity resource sheets promote both analytical (onset and rime) and synthetic (single phoneme) approaches. The strategies to be used are listed as: direction, demonstration, modelling, explanation, questioning, initiating and guiding exploration, investigating ideas, discussing and arguing, listening to and responding. Teaching methodology is not described in more detail and does not explicitly emphasise aspects such as mastery learning.

A comparison of teaching materials

We have argued in this article that the NLS word level work and the teaching approaches under the heading of 'dyslexia' both contain cumulative sequences of phonics targets. In order to discuss similarities and differences in emphasis and coverage between them, we examine below three kinds of commercially published teaching materials. First, those developed for all children as meeting the requirements of the NLS at the word level, second, those intended for learners making slower progress in literacy and, third, those targeted at learners regarded as having difficulties of a dyslexic nature. From the information available to us and the comprehensive lists and descriptions published by NASEN (Hinson and Gains, 1997; Hinson and Smith, 1997), we have selected four

Table 12.2 Phonics schemes/materials intended for all children

---

1   Oxford Reading Tree Rhyme and Analogy (Goswami, 1996)
The focus of this scheme is the use of onset, rhyme and rime analogy and comprises twelve story rhymes (big and small books), tapes, alphabet frieze, alphabet mats and activity materials. Significant features of this scheme are the emphasis on oral work, links between reading and writing and thorough learning at each stage. The approach to phonics is 'large unit' (analytical) and could be integrated to match NLS targets.

2   Rhyme World (Reason, Wilson and Huxford, 1998)
Rhyme Wolrd is a scheme of early phonics taught through big and small books of rhyming stories and accompanying activities. The books are presented in four stages: (i) phonological awareness – rhyme, alliteration and the alphabet; (ii) introducing onset and rime; (iii) developing onset and rime; (iv) from rime to phoneme. NLS phonics targets from Reception to the end of Year 2 are covered. The scheme is largely based on a 'large unit' (analytical) approach to phonics.

3   The Phonics Handbook: Jolly Phonics (Lloyd, 1992)
The manual introduces letter recognition, letter formation, blending and identifying sounds in words. It is intended for children in their first year of learning to read and write and the initial 8–9 weeks are spent learning the letter sounds, i.e. one letter a day. After that, alternative spellings of vowels are grouped together (e.g. ai, a-e, ay). The approach to phonics is 'small unit' (synthetic).

4   Ginn Spelling (Bell and Fidge, 1992)
The developmental structure comprises four stages linked to levels 1 to 4 of the National Curriculum. The first two stages include initial letter sounds, alphabetical order, common letter patterns and monosyllabic key words. For the next two stages the approach switches to analogy and morphology including word families and the roots of words. Ginn has augmented the classic 'look, cover, write and check' with 'look, *say*, cover, write and check'. The scheme moves from small units in the early stages to large units.

---

examples of each type as representative of current materials. All have in common a strong emphasis on the teaching of phonics. Short descriptions of the materials included in the comparison are provided in Tables 12.2, 12.3 and 12.4.

For the purpose of our comparison, we have drawn up a set of questions based on three areas of influence. The first is established learning theory that has emphasised the importance of repetitive and cumulative practice to the point of 'mastery' (Kulik, 1991; Linsley, 1992), the second is research that has demonstrated the effectiveness of teaching approaches that introduce code instruction in the context of reading and writing meaningful text (Adams, 1993; Hatcher, Hulme and Ellis, 1994; Wasik and Slavin, 1994), and the third is research that stresses the importance of a sense of competence and control as the basis for ensuring motivation to learn (Ames and Archer, 1988). The questions are listed under eight headings:

1. *A comprehensive model:* With their focus on phonics, do the materials reflect a comprehensive model of reading and/or spelling development, i.e. NLS searchlights that include comprehension of the text as a whole and the anticipation of words and letter sequences?
2. *Progression:* Do the materials show a clear progression of phonological targets, starting from phonological awareness and moving gradually to more advanced phonic structures?
3. *Speaking and listening:* Are children exploring and reinforcing the learning of phonogical regularities through both speaking and listening?
4. *Reading and writing:* Are children exploring and reinforcing the learning of phonological regularities through both reading and writing?

Table 12.3 Materials intended for learners making slower progress in literacy

---

5 Fuzzbuzz (Harris, 1986)

Developed specifically for the child who is 'still a non-reader at the age of seven or eight and upwards', the first six books develop a sight vocabulary of 100 words and the next twelve books take that up to approx. 250 words. The child does not read the book until the requisite words have been learned to mastery level. This is achieved through a range of activities including games. The scheme then introduces phonics in a cumulative sequence.

6 MIST: Middle Infant Screening Test and Forward Together Follow-Up Programme (Hannavy, 1995)

The MIST screening activities lead into the Forward Together follow-up programme. The latter involves parents in working through an activity book with their children over a period of eight to twelve weeks under the guidance of the teacher. Where it is not possible to involve the parents the programme can be carried out in school. There are three sections: (i) reading, (ii) handwriting, and (iii) letters, words and sentences. Individual letters, rhyme and analogy are taught through a series of activities. The scheme supports the NLS word level target for Year 1.

7 Skill Teach (Shelton, revised 1997)

Skill Teach is intended for individual teaching and consists of a manual and packs of material that adopt a three-stranded approach to the mechanics of reading: phonic skills, sight words and contextual skills. The materials are regarded as suitable for a wide age range and start with a detailed assessment of the learner's current skills. The phonic progression is presented in eight phases. While most materials are 'small unit', there is an alternative 'large unit' supplement.

8 Helping Children with Reading and Spelling (Reason and Boote, 1994)

The manual contains initial assessments of individual progress and suggested teaching sequences. The approach is based on a model of literacy learning that covers the areas of meaning, phonics and fluency. There are four broad stages of progression. The materials are intended for individual instruction but some examples are provided of their use with groups. The teaching of phonics is primarily 'small unit' and includes rhyming word families that reflect a 'large unit' approach.

Table 12.4 Materials targeted at learners with difficulties of a dyslexic nature

---

9   Alpha to Omega (Hornsby and Shear, 1993)
Alpha to Omega is highly repetitive and based on phonetics and linguistics.
There are diagnostic tests to ensure that the learner starts at the appropriate
point in the three stages. The materials are intended for older learners but
cover in the first stage NLS Reception to end of Year 2 targets. Each stage has
flash cards and activity packs.

10 Hickey Multisensory Language Course (Hickey, 1992)
This is a systematic and cumulative approach to remedying difficulties in
reading, writing and spelling. Intended for older learners, the course itself is
divided into six major sections covering all and more than the NLS word level
targets for Reception to end of Year 2. Letters are introduced individually in a
prescribed order. Long vowels are covered later in the programme due to
their complexity.

11 Teaching Reading and Spelling to Dyslexic Children (Walton, 1998)
The manual presents a sequence of phonics teaching under two charts. Chart 1
refers to earlier stages involving single letter sounds and simple blends and
Chart 2 is designed for the later stages that include vowel combinations and
letter groupings that occur relatively rarely. The charts are primarily used for
record keeping while the order for introducing particular letter combinations is
linked with suggestions for teaching. The approach is mainly 'small unit' and
based on individual instruction.

12 Overcoming Dyslexia (Broomfield and Combley, 1997)
The book starts by considering the research basis of literacy as a language
learning process. The importance of phonological awareness and the use of
analogy in reading is stressed. The subsequent programme offers a cumulative
sequence of phonics applicable to a broad age range of learners. The
development of automatic sound symbol links is developed through teaching
methods that use both small and large phonological units.

---

5. *Assessing to teach*: Do the materials provide guidance on 'assessing to teach',
    i.e. on assessing what the children know in order to plan, in appropriately
    small steps, what should be learnt next?
6. *Mastery learning*: Are the materials based on 'mastery learning', i.e. on
    planned repetition and revision that ensures the retention of what has
    been learnt?
7. *Role of the learner*: In terms of motivational influences, is there explicit
    guidance on the involvement of the children themselves in setting their
    own targets and monitoring progress?
8. *Home–school links*: Is there clear guidance on how parents and carers can
    help their children at home?

Our comparison of the materials is based on an examination of the teachers'
guides, books (when relevant), and learning content in each publication. We
have also drawn on our own experience of using the materials and/or observing

Table 12.5 A comparison of teaching materials

	1: Comprehensive model	2: Progression	3: Speaking and listening	4: Reading and writing	5: Assessing to teach	6: Mastery learning	7: Role of learner	8: Home–school links
Materials for all children								
Rhyme and Analogy	3	2	3	1	1	–	–	2
Rhyme World	3	3	3	1	2	–	–	2
The Phonics Handbook	1	2	3	2	1	–	–	–
Ginn Spelling	2	3	1	2	2	–	–	–
Materials for learners making slower progress								
Fuzzbuzz	1	2	1	2	2	3	–	–
MIST: Forward Together	1	2	1	2	3	2	2	3
Skill Teach	2	3	2	2	3	3	–	–
Helping Children with Reading and Spelling	3	3	2	2	3	3	2	2
Materials for learners with dyslexia								
Alpha to Omega	1	3	2	3	2	3	–	–
Hickey Multisensory Language Course	1	3	2	3	2	3	–	–
Teaching Reading and Spelling to Dyslexic Children	1	3	–	3	2	3	–	–
Overcoming Dyslexia	2	3	1	3	2	3	–	–

Key: 1 = implicit but not explained; 2 = included and expected; 3 = major emphasis their use in schools. As shown in Table 12.5, each of the 12 publications/ schemes is evaluated in terms of the eight questions, outlined above, on a rating scale consisting of the following three categories: 1 = implicit but not explained; 2 = included and expected; 3 = a major emphasis.

It can be seen in Table 12.5 that the materials developed for all children are more likely to have a comprehensive model of literacy as their major emphasis. Most of the special programmes in contrast, may contain an implicit assumption that the learning of phonics is but one element of literacy but explicit links between text, sentence and word levels are not made.

All the materials contain a progression of targets as a basis for phonics teaching. The learning is more likely to be through activities involving speaking and listening in the materials developed for all children and through repetitive reading and writing in the dyslexia oriented publications.

The headings 'assessing to teach' and 'mastery learning' bring out the differences between the publications. It would seem that those materials intended for learners making slower progress place an even greater emphasis on 'assessing to teach' than do the programmes developed under the heading of dyslexia. Both kinds of special programmes have, as their major emphasis, 'mastery learning', which remains implicit but not explained in the general programmes.

Motivational theories that emphasise the importance of the active involvement of learners in setting and monitoring their own targets appear to be implicit but not explained in most of the materials examined. It seems to us that the inclusion of explicit guidance would benefit all types of programmes. With regard to the heading 'home–school links' we gave a rating of 2 or 3 only to those materials that included written instructions for parents in their texts. We do not doubt that the developers of all materials are aware of the importance of this aspect.

Conclusion

In evaluating the suitability of the NLS framework for all children we need to consider how teachers are interpreting and adapting the NLS requirements and how schools are preparing children and their parents/carers for active participation in the teaching of reading. The assumption of the NLS is that teachers will have a clear idea of what their children have learnt, select achievable targets, teach phonological regularities in context of appropriate texts and pace the learning to ensure that targets have really been achieved. Many of these aspects are similar to the approaches followed under the heading of 'dyslexia' but, as shown in our comparisons, 'dyslexia' tends to imply a narrower focus, probably more suitable for older learners likely to benefit from repetitive and rule-based phonics programmes.

The eight questions we have drawn up for our comparisons of teaching materials can also provide a starting point for examining other schemes. For us, they highlight the similarities and differences between the approaches included here. Of particular note is the issue of reciprocal assessment and teaching (described as 'assessing to teach' in Table 12.5). If those following the materials developed under the heading of 'dyslexia' assume that the learner inevitably needs to start from the beginning of the programme and plough through every aspect of it, then this may result in frustration and boredom. Conversely, the general programmes, and the NLS itself, do not seem to provide enough guidance or detail on how to establish what each child has learnt and how to plan and teach following the principles of 'mastery learning'. If these aspects were addressed more explicitly, the teaching materials would be suitable for all children, including those with learning difficulties of a dyslexic nature, and would provide the basis for the kind of inclusive practices in schools advocated by Ainscow (1998).

In the context of the Literacy Hour, it can be argued that there is simply not enough time for such detailed observation and planning. There are examples, however, of practices where, in the course of the 'hour', teachers are noticing individual differences and adjusting their teaching to take account of different rates of progress (Hinson, 1999). Within the framework provided by the NLS, specialist and support teachers have a central role in providing the detail and in working together with class teachers. Even in those extreme cases, where the progress of the individual and the rest of the class has become too disparate, the NLS provides a common approach that enables decisions to be made as to which aspects of the 'hour' are beneficial and how additional provision can fit in with it.

In reviewing the research basis and educational precedents of the NLS, Beard (1998) refers to work in the USA and Australia involving additional resources that enable early intervention for pupils who have not made expected progress after one year at school. Similar developments are starting in this country through the deployment and training of staff to act as providers of Additional Learning Support (ALS). They will initially help children at the beginning of KS2 who have not made the progress expected by the NLS. At the time of writing, however, we are aware of the many areas that will need to be considered and developed. Central among these is the inter-relationship to be created between the teachers and assistants involved.

In terms of structure and content, the overall framework of the NLS is a positive development that may, in time, present and alleviate the difficulties of a dyslexic nature experienced by some learners. Residual issues of concern relate to aspects of methodology and the pace of learning required particularly in Year 1 Term 3 and Year 2 Term 1. In our view, the evaluation of the effectiveness of the NLS should not focus on those children who have always learnt quite well but on the progress of those who may need more time to learn. This would ensure that the NLS addresses the 'tail' of underachievement observed to be relatively greater in the UK than in other countries (Brooks, Pugh and Schagen, 1996).

References

Adams, M.J. (1993) Beginning to Read: An Overview. In R. Bread (ed.) *Teaching Literacy: Balancing Perspectives*. London: Hodder and Stoughton.

Ainscow, M. (1998) Exploring links between special needs and school improvement. *Support for Learning*, 13, 2, 70–5.

Ames, C. and Archer, J. (1988) Achievement goals in the classroom: Students' learning strategies and motivation processes. *Journal of Educational Psychology*, 80, 3, 260–67.

Beard, R. (1998) *National Literacy Strategy: Review of Research and other Related Evidence*. Sudbury, Suffolk: DfEE Publications.

Bell, P. and Fidge, L. (1992) *Ginn Spelling*. Aylesbury: Ginn and Company.

Brooks, G., Pugh, A.K. and Schagen, I. (1996) *Reading Performance at Nine*. Slough: National Foundation for Educational Research.

Broomfield, H. and Combley, M. (1997) *Overcoming Dyslexia*. London: Whurr.

Department for Education and Employment (1998) *The National Literacy Strategy Training Pack*. London: DfEE.

Fernald, J. (1943) *Remedial Techniques in the Basic School Subjects*. New York: McGraw-Hill.

Gillingham, A. and Stillman, B.U. (1946) *Remedial Training for Children with Specific Disability in Reading, Spelling and Penmanship*. Cambridge, MA: Educators Publishing Service.

Goswami, U. (1996) *Rhyme and Analogy as part of the Oxford Reading Tree*. Oxford: Oxford University Press.

Hannavy, S. (1995) *Middle Infant Screening Test and Forward Together Follow-up Programme (MIST)*. Windsor: NFER-Nelson.

Harris, C. (1986) *Fuzzbuzz*. Oxford: Oxford University Press.

Hatcher, P., Hulme, C. and Ellis, A. (1994) Ameliorating early reading failure by integrating the teaching of reading with phonological skills. *Child Development*, 65, 41–57.

Hickey, K. (1992) *A Multisensory Language Programme*. London: Whurr.

Hinson, M. (ed.) (1999) *Surviving the Literacy Hour*. Tamworth, Staffs: NASEN Publications.

Hinson, M. and Gains, C. (Revised 1997) *The NASEN A-Z: A Graded List of Reading Books*. Tamworth, Staffs: NASEN Publications.

Hinson, M. and Smith, P. (Revised 1997) *Phonics and Phonic Resources*. Tamworth, Staffs: NASEN Publications.

Hornsby, B. and Shear, F. (4th edition, 1996) *Alpha to Omega. The A-Z of Teaching Reading, Writing and Spelling*. Oxford: Heinemann Educational.

Johnston, R.S. (1998) The case for orthographic knowledge. *Journal of Research in Reading*, 21, 3, 195–200.

Kulik, J.A. (1991) Mastering Learning. Chapter 4 in K.A. Spencer (ed.) *The Psychology of Educational Technology and Instructional Media*. Liverpool: Manutius Press.

Lazo, M.G., Pumfrey, P.D. and Peers, I. (1997) Metalinguistic awareness, reading and spelling: Roots and branches in literacy. *Journal of Research in Reading*, 20, 2, 85–104.

Linsley, O.R. (1992) Precision teaching: Discoveries and effects. *Journal of Applied Behaviour Analysis*, 25, 1, 51–7.

Lloyd, S. (1992) *The Phonics Handbook*. Chigwell, Essex: Jolly Learning Ltd.

Miles, T.R. and Miles, E. (1990) *Dyslexia: A Hundred Years On.* Milton Keynes: Open University Press.

Norrie, E. (1960) *The Edith Norrie Letter Case.* London: Helen Arkell Word Blind Centre.

Orton, S.T. (1937) *Reading, Writing and Speech Problems in Children.* New York: Norton.

Pumfrey, P.D. and Reason, R. (1991) *Specific Learning Difficulties (Dyslexia): Challenges and Responses.* London: Routledge.

Reason, R. (1998) How relevant is connectionist modelling of reading to educational practice? *Educational and Child Psychology,* 15, 2, 59–65.

Reason, R. and Boote, R. (1994) *Helping Children with Reading and Spelling: A Special Needs Manual.* London: Routledge.

Reason, R., Wilson, J. and Huxford, L. (1998) *Rhyme World.* Oxford: Heinemann.

Reason, R., Frederickson, N., Heffernan, M., Martin, C. and Woods, K. (1999) *Dyslexia, Literacy and Psychological Assessment.* Report by a Working Party of the Division of Educational and Child Psychology, The British Psychological Society. Leicester: The British Psychological Society.

Rego, L.B. and Bryant, P.E. (1995) The connection between phonological, syntactic and semantic skills and children's reading and spelling. *European Journal of Psychology in Education,* 8, 3, 235–46.

Shelton, K. (Revised 1997) *Skill Teach.* Sheffield: PAVIC Publications, Sheffield Hallam University Press.

Snowling, M.J. (1998) Reading development and its difficulties. *Educational and Child Psychology,* 15, 2, 44–58.

Walton, M. (1998) *Teaching Reading and Spelling to Dyslexic Children.* London: David Fulton.

Wasik, B.A. and Slavin, R.E. (1994) Preventing reading failure with one-to-one tutoring: A review of five programmes. *Reading Research Quarterly,* 28, 178–200.

Source

This is an edited version of an article previously published in *Support for Learning,* 15 (2). 2000. Reproduced by permission of Blackwell Publishers Ltd.

Part 3

Individual pupil

Examinations, assessments and special arrangements

Nick Peacey

Introduction

This chapter examines the granting of special arrangements to students in assessments and examinations, particularly in relation to literacy difficulties. It sets out to:

- explain what special arrangements are and how they are regulated;
- place them in the context of the national commitment to inclusion and good assessment practice;
- discuss issues of equity, appropriateness and consistency;
- explain the current approaches to special arrangements in written assessments for pupils with literacy difficulties;
- consider aspects of special arrangements in relation to other than purely written assessments;
- suggest possible developments over the next few years.

Special arrangements are and how they are regulated

The assessments and the authorities

The national Key Stage test systems: the SATs

Since 1988 formal testing systems of one sort or another have been in place across the United Kingdom for pupils at the ages of 7, 11 and 14 (see note 1).

National government agencies set, monitor and regulate these tests. While English and Welsh test systems are very similar, they differ substantially from the Scottish and Northern Irish systems.

GCE, GNVQ, GCSE and VCE

The GCE 'A' level and GCSE examinations are the best known of a range of possible qualifications, including the GNVQ and the Vocational Certificate of Education (VCE) which are available across the United Kingdom. They have traditionally been taken by pupils aged 16 years or more, though it is possible to take them at a younger age. These assessments are overseen by the Joint Council for General Qualifications (JCGQ), a body made up of representatives of the awarding bodies who offer qualifications for these examinations and assessments. The awarding bodies are independent institutions, which are themselves regulated by national government agencies (see note 2).

A rationale for special arrangements

The Joint Council for General Qualifications gives a brief explanation of the rationale for special arrangements in its Regulations and Guidance (JCGQ, 2001):

> The awarding bodies recognise that there are some candidates who have coped with the learning demands of a course but for whom the standard arrangements for the assessment of their attainment may present a barrier.

To put this another way, some sort of modification of the examination or assessment is likely to be appropriate if a candidate can manage the learning demands of a course of study but is likely to be discriminated against by the standard way of assessing what has been learnt.

The Regulations and Guidance continue:

> This applies both in the cases of candidates with known and long-standing learning problems and candidates who are affected at or near the time of assessment. Such barriers may arise as a result of:
>
> - a permanent or long-term disability or learning difficulty;
> - a temporary disability, illness or indisposition;
> - English being a second or additional language;
> - the immediate circumstances of the assessment.
>
> Special arrangements are approved before an examination or assessment and are intended to allow attainment to be demonstrated. They can be provided in respect of [the first three bullet points] above.

Special arrangements and special considerations

Although this chapter does not explore the latter in any detail, we should note the distinction between:

> a special *arrangement,* which seeks to remove a long standing or permanent barrier to assessment; and
>
> a special *consideration* (relevant to the second and fourth bullet point above: to help with something temporary, like an accident shortly before the examination).

The JCGQ guidance states:

> Special *consideration* is given following an examination or assessment to ensure that a candidate who has a temporary illness, injury or indisposition at the time it is conducted is given some compensation for those difficulties and the circumstances.

The national commitment to inclusion and good assessment practice

Regulation and statute

The government has made clear its commitment to inclusive education and has increasingly backed this through legislation, most recently through the SEN and Disability in Education Act 2001, which applies to all UK education provision.

As part of this commitment, schools and colleges have a responsibility to think about arrangements for minorities in all assessments. The most accessible description appears in the general Inclusion Statement of the English National Curriculum (which has statutory force under the provisions of the Education Act 1996): 'teachers are required to have due regard' to the principles of this statement (DfEE/QCA, 2000).

The principles of the Inclusion Statement

Responding to pupils' diverse learning needs

- When planning, teachers should set high expectations and provide opportunities for all pupils to achieve, including boys and girls, pupils with special educational needs, pupils with disabilities, pupils from all social and cultural backgrounds, pupils of different ethnic groups including travellers, refugees and asylum seekers, and those from diverse linguistic backgrounds. Teachers need to be aware that pupils bring to school different experiences, interests and strengths which will influence the way in which they learn. Teachers should plan their approaches to teaching and learning so that all pupils can take part in lessons fully and effectively.

- To ensure that they meet the full range of pupils' needs, teachers should be aware of the requirements of the Equal Opportunities legislation that covers race, gender and disability.

- Teachers should take specific action to respond to pupils' diverse needs by:

(a)   creating effective learning environments;
(b)   securing their motivation and concentration;
(c)   providing equality of opportunity through teaching approaches;
(d)   using appropriate assessment approaches.

The Statement makes clear that all assessments, including informal and formal tests and examinations, need to be part of inclusive good practice. The first paragraph above directs us to a broad concept of the groups needing consideration. The range of minorities mentioned is indicative rather than comprehensive: inclusion is about the appropriate involvement of everyone.

So, while this chapter deals with fair assessment in relation to special educational needs and disability issues, the net needs to be cast wider for a full picture. In particular, we need to consider the issue of equity and culture in assessment.

The Inclusion Statement returns to tests and examinations in its next section:

Overcoming potential barriers to learning and assessment for individuals and groups of pupils

Pupils with special educational needs

• Teachers must take account of these requirements and make provision, where necessary, to support individuals or groups of pupils to enable them *to participate effectively in the curriculum and assessment activities. During end of Key Stage assessments, teachers should bear in mind that special arrangements are available to support individual pupils.*

Pupils with disabilities

• Not all pupils with disabilities will necessarily have special educational needs. Many pupils with disabilities learn alongside their peers with little need for additional resources beyond the aids which they use as part of their daily life, such as a wheelchair, a hearing aid or equipment to aid vision. *Teachers must take action, however, in their planning to ensure that these pupils are enabled to participate as fully and effectively as possible within the National Curriculum and the statutory assessment arrangements.* Potential areas of difficulty should be identified and addressed at the outset of work, without recourse to the formal provisions for disapplication.

> • Teachers should take specific action to enable the effective partic-
> ipation of pupils with disabilities by: 'planning appropriate amounts
> of time to allow for the satisfactory completion of tasks'.

We need to note the careful distinction drawn in these sections.

- The first emphasises the teacher's planning and provision for diversity in
  a teaching group: this will be part of ordinary class preparation.
- The second discusses specific planning and provision for individuals and
  groups.

The better whole group planning and provision can be, the less need there
is for specific planning for the needs of individuals and groups. We should
note, for example, the emphasis on high quality short and medium class plans
to guarantee appropriate provision for many pupils with SEN that appears in
the revision of the SEN Code of Practice (DfES, 2001): this is a shift from
the encouragement of Individual Education Plans for all.

Similarly, well-written, clear tests and examinations for all are less likely to
require special arrangements for individuals than assessments written to a lower
standard. For example, the Qualifications and Curriculum Authority and
organisations, such as the National Foundation for Educational Research, who
write the Key Stage tests for them, employ panels of specialists in inclusion.
These specialists not only advise on possible special arrangements for tests but
also on developing question papers and other assessments to the highest
possible standards of clarity, readability and accessibility.

Equity, appropriateness and consistency

Is there such a thing as fair assessment?

We must not underestimate the difficulty of creating fair assessments. The task
probably seemed easier in the nineteenth century when formal written examinations were enthusiastically endorsed as

- being free from corruption and self interest;
- testing basic abilities as well as attainments or skills.

(Sutherland, 1992)

Gordon Stobart (Stobart, 2000) points out that we are now not so confident
about the fairness of such examinations, though they may have been a
step forward in their day. Challenges over many years, particularly in the
United States, have forced reappraisal of formal assessment in a multi-cultural
society. Even where matters seem fair, for example, because outcomes are
similar, Stobart points out that this may be far from the case: 'It is possible,

Table 13.1 Curriculum and Assessment Questions in Relation to Equity
(from Gipps and Murphy, 1994, after Apple, 1989; cited in Stobart, 2000)

Curriculum questions	Assessment questions
Whose knowledge is taught?	What knowledge is assessed and equated with achievement?
Why is it taught in a particular way to this particular group?	Are the form, content and mode of assessment appropriate for different groups and individuals?
How do we enable the histories and cultures of people of colour, and of women, to be taught in responsible and responsive ways?	Is this range of cultural knowledge reflected in definitions of achievement? How does cultural knowledge mediate individuals' responses to assessment in ways which alter the construct being assessed?

in relation to fairness, to have similar outcomes for two groups and yet to see this as unfair to one of the groups. For example, despite achieving comparable results, the curriculum may have marginalised what was important knowledge or cultural reference for one group and emphasised content that was not easily accessible for this group – thus making it harder to get comparable results.' He points out that material from the Eugenics Movement was incorporated into American biology textbooks right up to 1949 in some states. 'This material legitimated both social inequality and white supremacy – and other ethnic groups had to study and "learn" it' (and we might add, be assessed on it).

Stobart notes that any study of equity and assessment needs to look at the whole system in which it plays its part. 'If assessment represents one of the key outcomes of education (as also do attitudes to learning), then it is also necessary to include both inputs and processes.' The table he quotes (see Table 13.1) sets out some of those curriculum questions, the 'inputs and processes', in the left hand column.

This holistic approach enables Stobart to raise enough questions about equity in assessment to make any conscientious education minister's or examinations watchdog's hair stand on end. He stresses, for example, the impact of decisions:

- about the language of the assessment: 'in monolingual approaches [such as that of England there is] an issue of accessibility of tests for those not using their first language';
- about how deeply assessment agencies involve themselves with the quality of a centre's preparation for the assessment: 'For GCE "A" level and GCSE examinations there has been little intervention other than informing centres about procedures';

- about how assessment is carried out: 'We know that during compulsory schooling (up to 16 years) girls are likely to outperform boys on tasks which involve open-ended writing';
- about the selection of the materials to be assessed: for example, Stobart reminds us of the furious arguments over the culturally-narrow choice of reading texts for public examinations and national tests which marked the Thatcher years.

The 'fair enough' assessment?

Designers of tests and examinations have to decide how to tackle these issues. One approach, for example, has been to offer the possibility of alternative evidence of ability, e.g. in relation to a balance of 'coursework' and other approaches in English examinations. But there are no easy answers and such 'solutions' can be seen as patronising and unwelcome even by those for whom they are devised. As Stobart says, 'fair assessment in multi-cultural settings [and in relation to gender and disability] is something we strive for rather than fully achieve'. Every decision represents a political and cultural choice.

We can perhaps expect, however, that those who make decisions for us on formal assessments follow four principles:

- They are guided by an awareness of the relationship between curriculum (what is to be learnt and how it is learnt) and assessment discussed above.
- They monitor a formal assessment's effects on different groups.
- They build the results of such monitoring into the preparation of future examinations and assessments (including the special arrangements).
- All decisions are taken within a commitment to inclusive principles, such as those set out in the National Curriculum Inclusion Statement.

Pupils for whom English is an additional language

As discussed above, probably the single most important decision affecting pupils for whom English is an additional language is the UK-wide consensus that the languages of examination and test papers will only be in English, Welsh or Gaelic. You will not find many special arrangements for them. The issues, if there are any in relation to literacy, are seen as mostly the same as for other groups. So the devising of the papers is the critical area for scrutiny: the test- or examination-setters have to be aware of all the issues discussed above.

Papers must not either, by implication or by more obvious means, such as failure to represent diversity in illustrations, discriminate against one group or another. It can be contentious, for example, to set an English test in a context which many pupils from ethnic minorities may not have experienced. Is it equitable to use a sheep farm as test context for pupils, most of whom spend their time in the inner city? Will they be disadvantaged in relation to those who live in the country? These questions will usually be resolved (once again) by looking at the test or examination objectives. Is the assessment looking for knowledge of sheep farming? Is it looking for ability in deducing answers from text?

If the latter (usually the case in an English test!) the question then becomes 'Should all candidates, either through pre-study or through material in the paper itself, have sufficient knowledge to answer all these questions appropriately?' The argument will not always end there: people will still feel those who know the context well will have an advantage. The test authors then have to set this concern against the wish to make assessments interesting by providing a good range of contexts.

All these decisions become more straightforward if the authors give enough time to checking previous monitoring exercises, piloting papers and consulting with relevant groups.

Special arrangements for EAL

Specific special arrangements relate to these areas:

- When a pupil has limited fluency in English they may be allowed extra time (national Key Stage Tests).
- Bilingual dictionaries are allowed in subjects other than assessing ability in English (see above).

Current approaches to special arrangements for pupils with literacy difficulties

Special arrangements: the principles

We can now consider special arrangements in relation to pupils with literacy difficulties. These remain the single largest group for whom special arrangements are sought.

In granting any special arrangements there are two dimensions to be considered:

- the assessment demands of the test or examination in question;
- the needs of the candidate in that assessment.

The JCGQ (2001) guidance puts it like this:

> The provision for special arrangements and special consideration is made so that candidates are able to receive recognition of their attainment so long as valid and reliable examinations or assessments can be provided. *Such provision is not intended to alter the assessment demands of the qualifications.*

So (to take a straightforward example of the principle in practice), the KS2 (11-year-olds) English National Test Assessment and Reporting Arrangements for 2002 say, 'electronic spell checkers may be used in any test except the spelling test' (QCA/DfES, 2001a,b). The assessment is testing the candidate's ability to spell, so whatever the literacy difficulty it would be inappropriate to allow the use of a spell-checker.

The JCGQ guidance says: 'Centres should note that a candidate with a Statement of Special Educational Needs does not qualify automatically for special arrangements.' This sentence sometimes puzzles readers. The JCGQ is emphasising the two dimensions of judgement needed in relation to special arrangements. A study for the Schools Examinations and Assessment Council in 1992 put it like this:

> Special education need should be considered in terms of its implications for assessment. It is necessary to show the *direct effects* of a precisely specified disability or learning difficulty *upon a pupil's performance in assessment situations*. Special educational needs do not provide the most appropriate basis for determining *assessment needs*.

This approach represented a substantial shift from earlier approaches to the granting of special arrangements. These had often focused on sensory impairments, like blindness or deafness, or physical disability. In these cases it then seemed reasonable to start from an approach that simply 'diagnosed' the difficulty and then prescribed the arrangements appropriate to that disability. By 1992 it was clear the approach, which was essentially one based on categories, was resulting in inequity at GCSE and A level:

> Examining bodies do not recognise all of the categories, which have tended to form the basis of physical provision in determining the granting of special arrangements, and in the setting of assessment tasks. Pupils described as having Specific Learning Difficulties, Emotional and Behavioural Difficulties and Moderate Learning Difficulties do not have the 'tangible' needs of Visually Impaired, Hearing Impaired or Physically Handicapped pupils. This does not mean that examining bodies do not attempt to meet their needs, but lack of precision in identifying the constraints imposed by some assessment procedures, coupled with anomalies in the treatment of requests, has led to areas of contention.
>
> (SEAC, 1992)

The concerns went well beyond lack of fairness to particular categories of need. They also focused on the inability of any system based entirely on SEN labels to reflect the needs of individuals in relation to the specified objectives of an assessment. So we now have – largely – systems in which attaching a label to the learning difficulty takes second place to considering evidence on an individual's needs in relation to a specific assessment. Gill Backhouse in her authoritative study for PATOSS (Backhouse, 2000) puts the point about dyslexia like this:

> It is not the case, for example, that everyone with a 'diagnosis' of dyslexia is automatically entitled to 25 per cent extra time across the board – or that this in their interests! The quality of their literacy skills may not place them at any disadvantage in practical subjects, 'multiple-choice' papers and so on. They may not know enough to be able to use extra time profitably – or 'shoot themselves in the foot' during extra time by altering responses which were satisfactory.

We can also note that this approach relegates most of the dispute about what constitutes a specific learning difficulty to a back seat. The barriers presented by the assessment process and the objectives of the assessment are the things that count.

A case study: 'A' level English

We can see how different dimensions of the granting of special arrangements can be by considering the case of a young man studying 'A' level English Literature at a Sixth Form College (some aspects of this story have been changed to respect privacy).

Patrick had good verbal reasoning skills, but a problem with linguistic structures that contained a high proportion of figurative language. The impairment was not identified, but had outcomes similar to those of learners with an autistic spectrum disorder. Naturally enough, this meant that unseen poetry was a cause of great stress, though the rest of the 'A' level work was well within Patrick's grasp and 'seen' poetry was not so much of an issue. The first paper in his 'A' level English was unseen poetry and 'seen' poetry was part of the second paper! The college suggested that he should be exempt from the poetry questions and offer a prose alternative. This was not appropriate because poetry was part of the mandatory core specified by the Qualifications and Curriculum Authority for English 'A' level. But detailed examination of the specification showed that the core requirement could be satisfied by a candidate just taking the 'seen' poetry question in Part 2. It was therefore agreed that this was the appropriate approach for this candidate.

The key issues in this case were:

- Patrick's assessment needs could not be defined within a broad brush approach using labels such as autistic spectrum disorder; they required finer understanding.
- The specification for the examination offered a route to an appropriate and fair approach to meeting Patrick's assessment needs, particularly in relation to his differentiated response to seen and unseen poetry. Anyone who had not looked at this specification would not have been in a good position to propose a way forward.

Appropriate entry to a given assessment

Patrick's case raises another issue which must be considered by schools and colleges. His college chose, as his set text for 'seen' poetry, the work of John Donne, a Metaphysical poet who specialised in particularly complex imagery. The college felt it was appropriate for him to join the group, but arguably another poet from the range available should have been selected for study.

All examinations and tests will be inappropriate for some pupils and it is the task of schools and colleges to ensure that candidates are not entered for something for which they are not ready or where failure is likely to be damaging. The situation shows up starkly where there is compulsory testing or assessment for a whole school population, as at 7, 11 and 14 in the English system. Single tests will normally cover most of the age group at 7, because the spread of 'levels of attainment' is relatively small. By 14, the spread on the attainment ladder is very substantial and tiered entry to the tests is often the norm. (At all Key Stages there is an option, where pupils would find written tests beyond them, to use teacher assessment only.)

Examinations (at 16+) are less often tiered, but the different types of examinations and assessments themselves form a hierarchy of choices. By the time a student reaches the public examination stage teachers often encourage alternative accreditation to the 'normal' GCSE if the barriers seem over-whelming. The status of the assessment can be an issue: do employers and other important people think well of the alternative on offer? Does it have 'street cred' among the student's peers?

The institution's attitude to accreditation is important. If the school or college culture supports the validity of a range of formal assessments, and can demonstrate their status, student choices will be less inhibited by peer group (or parent?) pressure and more linked to their own aspirations. The whole issue would in fact seem to be based on the appropriateness of a given assess-ment to student plans.

But once again, there are no easy answers and in worrying about failure we are in danger of lowering expectations. Some students are fired by the status of an assessment and perform well beyond teacher expectations. In other cases, teachers establish a collective culture of high expectations that works to pull entire groups forward together and a choice of examinations seems to become irrelevant. The government has argued since 1997 that challenging targets for all are the way to go. But challenge way beyond someone's reach can be devas-tating. Perhaps the best one can conclude is that the balance of risk should be tilted towards high expectations; if one is not given the chance to succeed, one certainly will not.

Taking time to decide about assessment needs

Sometimes it is not realised that identification of individual assessment needs should take place well before the assessment or examination. Gill Backhouse (2000) notes:

Historically, there has been a rush for candidates with SEN to be assessed during the run-up to the exams. There may be a misconception locally that this is still appropriate. Candidates, their parents, teaching staff need to know that the JCGQ regulations require centres to identify and then support candidates with special assessment needs throughout their exam courses. 'Last-minute' reports – particularly when the centre has been unaware that a learning difficulty is thought to exist – are unacceptable.

An approach based on routine over time will have other benefits. Backhouse spells this out.

The JCGQ Regulations emphasise that not only must there be evidence of need but also 'a history of provision during the course'. The regulations state that 'Centres must ensure that the candidate has experience of, and practice in, the use of any special arrangements which are requested'.

There should be nothing very mysterious about any special arrangements needed. Similar activities to those of the assessment take place in class or lecture room throughout the course of study; teachers can work with the student of whatever age in identifying the issues that affect them and ensuring they practise use of the arrangements. This is not just a matter of preparing for a formal test or examination; anyone taking the Inclusion Statement seriously is under a duty to think about arrangements in relation to every type of assessment (end of module tests, for example).

Gatekeeping special arrangements systems

All this makes matters easier when formal applications for special arrangements are made. The procedures for granting special arrangements still vary substantially. Though substantial work on consistency across special arrangements for England, Wales and Northern Ireland has been done in recent months, there will never be complete consistency between the GCSE 'A' Level, GNVQ and the Vocational Certificate (VCE) and the National Key Stage Tests arrangements because their purposes are different. The former offer employers and society a view of an individual's ability, the latter, while testing the attainment of individuals, are normally only a public resource for making judgements about institutional success.

A comparison can be made by looking at Table 13.2. It summarises the JCGQ and National Test responsibilities for permitting arrangements which are likely to be of most use to students with literacy difficulties. As far as literacy difficulty is concerned the important possibilities are likely to be:

- rest breaks/separating the tests into sections;
- making taped versions for the Mathematics and Science tests;
- photocopying onto coloured paper or using coloured overlays;

Table 13.2

Arrangement	KS1, 2 and 3 tests: authority	JCGQ regulations
Early opening (one school day)	LEA	Not allowed in any circumstances
Extra time	LEA	School or college
Rest breaks/separating tests into sections	School	School or college
Word processor	School	Awarding body
Coloured overlays/paper	School	School or college
Early opening (longer than one school day)	QCA/ACCAC (Wales)	Allowed up to one hour before the start of the examination with permission from awarding body
Readers, communicators, signers, scribes (only for papers where they will not give unfair advantage to candidates)	School	Awarding body
Production of a transcript of responses (where handwriting is really difficult to read)	School	Awarding body
Bilingual dictionaries and spell-checkers (not to be used in English or Welsh assessments)	School	School or college (permission must be sought for modern languages and general studies)

NB: The information on tests applies to maintained schools only.

- use of mechanical and technological aids such as word processors where the pupil normally uses one;
- taking the tests in a separate room or away from the school.

The level of regulation

The level of regulation that surrounds these arrangements has partly grown up because of their status. In England, for example, the Key Stage test and public examination results are published and high stakes for all involved in both schools and colleges. In the rest of the UK earlier formal assessments are somewhat less of an issue (though we should note that the 11-plus examination is still universal in Northern Ireland) but public examinations at 16+ are still of great importance. High stakes assessments are characterised by high demand for scrutiny for fairness. So it is not surprising that a hierarchy of organisations oversees the possibility of inequity in the granting of special arrangements.

Granting special arrangements: the KS1, 2 and 3 national tests

As the table above demonstrates, the Qualifications and Curriculum Authority, local education authorities, schools and colleges are all involved in oversight of special arrangements for English KS1, 2 and 3 tests. In recent years, there has been more delegation of powers to grant special arrangements and many can be applied at the school's discretion.

Granting special arrangements: the GCSE, 'A' Level, GNVQ and Vocational Certificate (VCE)

While the gate-keeping of special arrangements in Key Stage tests is relatively simple, the system is less straightforward for GCSE, GCE 'A' Level, GNVQ and VCE examinations and assessments. Towards the end of the 1990s, a steady rise in the number of applications for special arrangements, as well as developments in national policy and ways of thinking about SEN, made change inevitable. While many commentators have noted the alteration to the rules for writing reports to justify the grant of a special arrangement, fewer people realise the extent to which this represents a broader shift in assessment practice.

The current system for the provision of evidence works as follows:

- Where regulations permit schools or colleges to take the decision, i.e. in the matter of extra time or rest breaks (see Table 13.2), a specialist teacher (normally working in the candidate's school or college) or an educational psychologist can write a report specifying the candidate's assessment needs. This, with evidence of the 'history of provision', can 'validate' a request for special arrangements.
- Where the decision rests with the Awarding Body, a specialist teacher or an educational psychologist will write the report detailing the candidate's assessment needs. Evidence must also include a history of the candidate's individual needs and a history of provision for these needs during the course.

(The professional groups mentioned above are those normally involved in writing reports on candidates with literacy difficulties: but evidence from medical specialists may also be important, for example, if a pupil's slow handwriting is caused by a physical impairment. These reports need to have been written post KS2/Y6, even if secondary transfer has taken place later, as in some LEAs and independent schools.)

Up to a few years ago all reports had to be prepared by educational psychologists. There were several reasons why this practice was modified.

- Increasing numbers of applications stretched educational psychology services.

- Some educational psychology services (e.g. the large Birmingham LEA service) refused to prioritise assessments for special arrangements, believing there were more important elements in their workload.
- Increasing numbers of candidates were going to expensive private psychologists for assessment. This was clearly inequitable and often led to weaknesses in communication between the external practitioner and the school. Many candidates in post-16 education outside school have no access to maintained educational psychology services anyway, and many could not afford to pay for assessment.
- Few educational psychologists have the deep knowledge of syllabus objectives (relatively) easily available to the secondary school teacher or FE college lecturer, let alone an understanding of how a student has performed in assessments over time. They may therefore in one sense bring less knowledge to report-writing than a specialist teacher.
- The shift . . . from the 'diagnosis' of a difficulty and the use of that label alone for assessing the need for special arrangements to matching candidate's needs to the objectives of the assessment ideally takes the school or college as its starting point: it makes the involvement of teachers and lecturers highly appropriate.
- All teachers taking on the report-writing role must have a qualification from a list approved by the JCGQ and published annually.

(JCGQ, 2000).

Extra time in national Key Stage tests

The test regulations require permission from the local education authority for the granting of extra time for completion, the most popular special arrangement. (Independent schools have to seek permission from the appropriate national agency.) There is no reason why a pupil should need extra time for every test or examination they are involved in, though many will do. The reading and writing demands of a multiple choice Science paper, for example, may be very different from those of an English 'response to text' paper which demands long written answers. Whatever the assessment, Gill Backhouse's advice is surely right:

> Assessment should include timed tests of reading and writing in order to identify all those whose difficulties are predominantly to do with speed/fluency, as well as those with more severe problems with regard to accuracy.
>
> (Backhouse, 2000)

Schools also need permission for early opening of test papers. This can become important if something like photocopying numbers of papers is necessary. It is unlikely, however, given current anxieties about malpractice in the tests, that any school will easily get permission to open the tests more one school day before the test.

The independent practitioner

Gill Backhouse raises a concern about the work of assessors working outside the school or college (Backhouse, 2000).

> It is sometimes the case, that candidates present assessment reports from independent practitioners stating that the student has a difficulty about which the school/college is unaware. The guidelines for completion of both the Psychological and Specialist Teacher's Assessment Forms stress the importance of liaison between EPs/Specialist Teachers and centres in these matters. Liaison between assessor and SENCO is therefore necessary in order to meet the examinations boards' requirements.

Looking beyond written assessment

Teacher assessment

We have so far looked largely at written assessments. They form the major element of the UK system. Two other national assessments, however, need consideration. First, the KS1, 2 and 3 test system retains a 'parallel track' duty on teachers (see notes 1 and 3) to make their own assessments of pupils' attainment. The balance between these two tracks varies from country to country. The 'TGAT report' (DES/Welsh Office, 1988) on the design of the English and Welsh test system emphasised the need for a balance of modes of assessment:

> We recommend that a mixture of standardised assessments including tests, practical tasks and observation be used in the national assessment system in order to minimise curriculum distortion.

Published performance tables have tended to downgrade the importance of maintaining such a balance.

Oral assessment: mathematics

The dominance of the written test has also recently been challenged by developments in mathematics education. 'Mental mathematics' is a statutory element of the curriculum now and can only be assessed by an oral test. This in its turn has led to the need for new types of special arrangements and these appear, both for those with sensory impairments and, more relevantly, for this chapter, for those who have problems in getting the answers down on paper quickly. (Only the questions are delivered orally.) Interestingly, test special arrangements for this area in England are still dominated by the disability model. There are arrangements in the current regime for pupils with hearing impairments (see below) which would often be suitable for other minorities, including students with speech and language impairments, but they are not currently permitted.

Modified versions of the mental arithmetic tests for pupils with hearing impairment

Modified materials for the mental arithmetic test are available for pupils with permanent or long-term profound hearing loss who rely on British Sign Language or other sign-supported communication, or who supplement their residual hearing with lip reading. These materials consist of a modified transcript of the test and a set of OHP transparencies or flashcards of the stimulus material. The taped version of the standard test or the teachers' transcript of the standard test **must not** be used with these materials, and the test must be delivered by a communicator or signer on a one-to-one or small group basis.

(QCA/DfES, 2001a,b)

Looking ahead

Increased responsibility given to schools and colleges

Concerns about the JCGQ's changes (above) have concentrated on the danger of schools and colleges being over-generous to their own students and teachers' ability (or otherwise) to write the reports. While these concerns often stem from misunderstandings about the way in which the granting of special arrangements is now organised and conceptualised, there is no doubt that increased scrutiny in terms of inspection of arrangements in centres and tightening of qualifications for the specialist teacher role are likely.

Commitment to all minorities

As we have noted, pressure for special arrangements often relates to the level of anxiety about the outcomes of an assessment. One might prophesy therefore that the shift away from publishing test results in Wales and moves to their abolition in Northern Ireland would lead to a diminution of interest, and therefore development. This would be a pity. Special assessment arrangements are the right of every student in school or college who needs them. Development in this field could atrophy, like any other form of educational progress. In particular, there are two groups, those with Autistic Spectrum Disorder and Speech and Language Impairments still lose out under the surviving 'medical' approach (as we saw above).

But public examinations, including GCSE, 'A' level and GNVQ, seem unlikely to lose status over the next few years. The demand for and the development of, special arrangements in this area will certainly be pushed forward.

Developments in the law

The law is likely to tighten its oversight of special arrangements.

Gill Backhouse now encourages any specialist teachers, not covered by institutional policies, to seek insurance against challenges about the consequences of their advice.

> It is clear from the thrust of the recent opinions of The Lords of Appeal for Judgment in the Cause of *Phelps v. Mayor Etc. of The London Borough of Hillingdon* (see, House of Lords Judgments, Session 1999–2000; which can be downloaded from – www.parliament.the-stationery-office. co.uk/pa/ld199900/ldjudgmt/jd00.../phelp-l.ht) that Specialist Teachers (as well as EPs) have a duty of care to children with SENs with regard to the advice that they give. Therefore, they should ensure that they themselves are fully covered.

This will particularly be the case where a recognised disability is involved. The SEN and Disability in Education Act covers England, Scotland and Wales, and extends inclusive legislation into FE – so there may be more interest in this field.

The challenge is to ensure that planned and effective changes to the system translate such pressures into more inclusive assessment practice for all, rather than litigation-driven fair assessment for some, but not the rest.

Notes

1 The authorities

KS1, 2 and 3 tests arrangements vary from country to country of the UK. The best way to check the arrangements for a given area is to visit the national agency's website.

England	QCA	www.qca.org.uk
Northern Ireland	CCEA	www.ccea.org.uk
Scotland	SQA	www.sqa.org.uk
Wales	ACCAC	www.accac.org.uk

2

Bodies responsible for formal examinations and tests now set out the arrangements for the granting of special arrangements in regulations and guidance booklets which are modified annually (see for example QCA/DfES, 2001a,b and JCGQ, 2001).

3 Teacher assessment

The level descriptions in the National Curriculum are the basis for judging pupils' levels of attainment at the end of the Key Stage. Teachers should use their knowledge of a pupil's work over time, including written, practical and oral work in the classroom, homework and results of other school examinations or tests.

The aim is for a rounded judgement which:

- is based on knowledge of how the pupil performs over time across a range of contexts;
- takes into account strengths and weaknesses of the pupils' performance;
- is checked against adjacent level descriptions to ensure that the level awarded is the closest match to the pupil's performance in each attainment target.

References

Backhouse, Gill (2000) *Providing For Candidates With Special Assessment Needs During GCE (A Level), VCE, GCSE & GNVQ: A Practical Guide.* Patoss.

DES/Welsh Office (1988) *National Curriculum Task Group on Assessment and Testing: A Report,* London: DES.

DfEE/QCA (2000) 'General statement on inclusion' in *Curriculum 2000,* London: QCA.

DfES (2001) *The SEN Code of Practice,* London: DfES.

JCGQ (2001) GCE, VCE, GCSE & GNVQ: *Regulations and Guidance Relating to Candidates with Particular Requirements,* Joint Council for General Qualifications.

QCA/DfES (2001a) *Key Stage 2 2002 Years 3 to 6 Assessment and Reporting Arrangements,* London: QCA.

QCA/DfES (2001b) *Key Stage 3 2002 Years 7 to 9 Assessment and Reporting Arrangements,* Birmingham: JCGQ.

Schools Examination & Assessment Council (SEAC) (1992) Interim Report on Research Project: Special Educational Needs and the GCSE, commissioned from the Centre for Assessment Studies, the University of Bristol.

Stobart, Gordon (2000) Examinations, Formal Qualifications and the Construction of Professional Identities: A British Case Study 1880–1940. IREX-Hungarian Academy of Sciences Conference, Budapest.

Source

This chapter was written especially for this volume.

Chapter 14

Learning to understand written language

Jane Oakhill and Nicola Yuill

We read to gain information and to be entertained. Reading is therefore about understanding, not word recognition.

It cannot be assumed that once children have acquired word recognition and word decoding skills they will then become good readers. Some children appear to decode written words more successfully than they understand them. At its most extreme, occasional children and adults are reported who are able to read aloud irregular words and novel words, and yet are unable to understand the individual words they can read. Such cases are referred to as 'hyperlexia', and are associated with very low IQ.

In this chapter Jane Oakhill and Nicola Yuill discuss the case of children who, unlike hyperlexic children, fall within the normal IQ range and yet nevertheless fail to comprehend fully what they read. The meanings of individual words are not the problem; rather, the difficulty lies in understanding the content of what they read: the structure and point of a story and the inferences necessary to understand points not explicitly made. What is more, investigations conducted by the authors have shown that the problem is not confined to understanding written text, but is apparent in other language-based tasks too, and can even be observed in children's own attempts to structure a story when describing events in a series of pictures. Clearly understanding and recognizing these different levels of language comprehension in children is of vital importance to the teacher and child in the classroom.

Encouragingly, preliminary attempts at remedial teaching of comprehension skills of poor comprehenders have been successful, at least over the short term, suggesting that some children may not have been exposed to narrative sufficiently often to develop these skills unaided. On the basis of further evidence, the authors tentatively propose that reading aloud to children may be one way to develop these skills naturally at an early age.

Introduction

In this chapter, we will be considering the problems of children who have good word recognition, can understand sentences and can read aloud apparently fluently, but who have only a rudimentary understanding of what they have just read. There are many skills needed to understand a text adequately. The meanings of the individual sentences and paragraphs must be integrated, and the main ideas of the text identified. On-going comprehension also needs to be monitored, so that any failures can be corrected. We are going to concentrate on three main areas of comprehension skill, and illustrate the problems of less-skilled comprehenders with some of our own work in each of the areas.

The first area is *Inference skills*. In many cases, inferences will be needed to go beyond what is explicitly stated in a text. Authors, of necessity, leave some of the links in a text implicit, and the reader will need to assess, at some level, which inferences need to be made. Second, readers need to *understand the structure* of the text they are reading. In the case of stories, this might include identifying the main character(s) and their motives, following the plot of the story, identifying the main theme. The third area, *comprehension monitoring*, requires the readers to assess their understanding as they are reading. Not only should they be able to identify any comprehension problems, they should know what to do about them, if they do find them. We shall present some of our own research on children with specific comprehension difficulties and, in particular, work that relates to the three areas outlined above.

Our studies have compared groups of skilled and less-skilled comprehenders. Typical groups of subjects are shown in Table 14.1.

Table 14.1 Characteristics of groups of skilled and less-skilled comprehenders

	Chronological age (years)	Accuracy age (years)	Comprehension age (years)	Gates–MacGinitie (score/48)
Less skilled	7.9	8.4	7.3	38.0
Skilled	7.9	8.4	9.1	38.3

The groups were selected using the Neale Analysis of Reading Ability and the Gates–MacGinitie Vocabulary Test. The Neale Analysis provides measures both of reading accuracy (word recognition) and comprehension (assessed by ability to answer a series of questions about each passage). The Gates–MacGinitie test requires the child to select one of four words to go with a picture. Thus, it acts as a measure of silent word recognition, and provides an index of the child's vocabulary. In all our studies, the groups of skilled and less-skilled comprehenders were matched for word recognition ability (Neale accuracy and Gates–MacGinitie) and chronological age, but differed in Neale comprehension scores. In general, all children were above average at word recognition. One group were also very good comprehenders; the other group were poor comprehenders, particularly with respect to their ability to recognize words.

Some theories of poor comprehension, for example that of Perfetti,[1] have proposed that comprehension problems are really an extension of word recognition problems. Such theorists argue that accuracy of word recognition is not sufficient for good comprehension: recognition must also be fast and automatic so that, in a limited-capacity system, the lower-level (word recognition) processes do not use up the resources needed for higher-level (comprehension) processes. However, we have found no differences between groups as selected above in decoding speed or automaticity (see Yuill and Oakhill[2]) so, although we do not deny that such factors are likely to lead to comprehension problems in some children, we argue that poor comprehenders exist who do not have difficulties at the word level. Another possibility is that poor comprehenders have difficulties at the level of sentences, failing to understand certain syntactic constructions. However, when we tested the children on Dorothy Bishop's *Test for Reception of Grammar*[3] we found no differences between the groups. Let us turn now to the areas in which we have found differences.

Making inferences

One persistent finding in our work is that less-skilled comprehenders have difficulties in making inferences from text. Here, we will outline just one experiment to illustrate the sorts of difficulties that they have. In this experiment, Oakhill[4] explored the children's ability to make inferences about things that were only implicit in texts. The experiment also looked at how the groups responded to the memory demands needed for answering questions about texts. Most measures of comprehension, including the Neale Analysis, require children to answer questions from memory without referring to the text, so one simple, and not very theoretically interesting, explanation of poor comprehenders' problems is that they have a general memory deficit.

To test this possibility, the children were required to answer questions in two conditions: either without referring to the text, or when the text was freely available for them to refer to. They read the passages aloud (and were given help with words as needed) and were then asked two sorts of questions about the text: ones that could be answered from information immediately available in the text (literal), and ones that required an inference. An example text, with questions, is shown below.

Example story, 'John's Big Test'

John had got up early to learn his spellings. He was very tired and decided to take a break. When he opened his eyes again the first thing he noticed was the clock on the chair. It was an hour later and nearly time for school. He picked up his two books and put them in a bag. He started pedalling to school as fast as he could. However, John ran over some broken bottles and had to walk the rest of the way. By the time he had crossed the bridge and arrived at class, the test was over.

LITERAL QUESTIONS (examples)
1. What was John trying to learn?
2. How many books did John pick up?

INFERENCE QUESTIONS
1. How did John travel to school?
2. What did John do when he decided to take a break?

The child first attempted to answer the questions from memory, and then the experimenter re-presented the questions and asked the child to check the answers to the questions in the text. In this second condition, the child was free to re-read the text to find the answers to the questions. The children's responses to the questions indicated that, as expected, it was easier to answer them with, than without, the text and good comprehenders performed better overall. What was of particular interest, however, were the different patterns of performance between the good and poor comprehenders with and without the passage. The performance of the two groups in the different conditions is shown in Table 14.2. When they could not see the passage, the good compre-henders were reasonably good, and better than the less-skilled comprehenders, on both types of question. When the passage was present, the poor compre-henders improved their performance on the literal questions to the same level as that of the good comprehenders in that condition (i.e. near perfect); however, they still made many errors on the questions requiring an inference: over 35 per cent in this condition (the good comprehenders' error rate was 10 per cent). This strikingly high error rate shows that the poor comprehen-ders' difficulties cannot be attributed to a straightforward memory problem – they have great difficulty in making inferences even with the story available to refer to.

Table 14.2 Percentages of errors on literal and inferential questions

	Unseen		Seen	
	Literal	Inferential	Literal	Inferential
Less skilled	29.2	45.8	3.6	35.4
Skilled	10.9	15.6	1.0	9.9

Why might poor comprehenders have such problems? One possibility is that they simply lack the knowledge required to make some of the inferences. We did not test for this possibility explicitly, though it seems likely that 7-year-olds would have available such knowledge as that pedalling implies riding a bicycle. Moreover, some recent (unpublished) work by Kate Cain at Sussex has shown that even poor comprehenders do have such knowledge available to them when they are questioned about it directly. A second possibility is that less-skilled comprehenders may not realize the relevance of inferences to understanding a text – they may be concentrating on 'getting the words right', and may process the text at a superficial level. A third possibility is that the children may know about the importance of inferences for text understanding but may be unable to elicit the relevant knowledge and integrate it with the information in the text itself because of processing limitations. We shall argue later that both the second and the third possibilities apply to some extent.

Understanding text structure

Our research in this area serves to illustrate the generality of the less-skilled comprehenders' problem, as well as their difficulties in understanding a story's structure. Our main work on children's understanding of story structure comes from tasks where the children were asked to *tell* stories, rather than to read them. Their story-telling was prompted by picture sequences which told a simple story. These experiments showed that less-skilled comprehenders did not seem to have an integrated idea of the stories as a whole – they tended to give picture-by-picture accounts rather than connecting together the events in each picture to create a cohesive whole.

One index of story cohesion is the use of connective words, including temporal ones (e.g. *then*), contrastive ones (e.g. *but*) and the most sophisticated ones, causal connectives (e.g. *because*). We told children in the two skill groups a very simple story, with pictures (shown in Figure 14.1) containing only temporal connectives (*and, then, when*). Twelve of the sixteen skilled comprehenders when they retold the story, added new connective terms of all three types, whereas only four of the less-skilled group did so, and none of these additions were causal. The different flavour of the resulting stories is best shown by examples, the first from Anne, a poor comprehender, and the second from Hayley, a good one. The connectives that were not in the original story are in italics.

> (ANNE) Sally was getting up for school. Her mum done her lunchbox. She went to school. She's singing a song. She put her lunchbox down. She's doing her lessons. She's doing her lessons again. She goes and gets her lunchbox. She eats the wrong lunch. Another girl came with hers and they had their lunch together.

> (HAYLEY) One day there was a little girl and she got off . . . out of bed *because* she . . . she forgot school. [Here the child seemed to mean that the girl was rushing because she had forgotten it was time for school.] Her mum has got . . . has got her breakfast ready. And then she took her lunchbox and said goodbye to her mum. Then she went to school with her lunchbox la'ing to herself. Then she put her lunchbox on the table and then she did her lessons. *After that*, she . . . it was lunchtime, she went to get her lunchbox. *But* she got the wrong lunchbox. *So* they went in to the room with different lunchboxes. And then she sat down and she said,

Figure 14.1 The pictures used in the story retelling experiment

'I've got the wrong sandwiches'. Then she went . . . and another girl came along and said, 'You've got my lunchbox'. *So* they had lunch together. Yum!

Notice that Hayley's story is full of false starts and speech repairs, but shows an obvious attempt to add cohesion to a simple story. Anne's story, on the other hand, is list-like. This impression of a list is created by several features of the story in addition to the lack of connectives. First, Anne uses the present continuous tense (*was getting up, is doing*), which gives a 'running commentary' style, while Hayley uses the past. Anne also repeatedly mentions the same event, and this does not contribute to the story line (*she's doing her lessons again*). This phrase also suggests that she is not recounting a story, but describing in turn the contents of each picture as a separate entity. Hayley's production integrates narrative and descriptive information (*she went to school . . . la'ing to herself*), uses various connectives (e.g. *but, so*), and includes phrases conventionally used in stories (*one day there was . . .*).

This evidence, however, is somewhat impressionistic. We therefore looked more systematically at children's narrative productions by asking them to tell their own stories from a series of pictures, and we scored their stories for various features that we found to differentiate between the two stories above. First we looked at the tenses of the verbs used. There was a striking difference between the two groups: only 19 per cent of the poor comprehenders' stories used the past tense, compared with 57 per cent of the skilled children's stories. We are not claiming that past tense is 'better': many talented writers use the present tense to great effect. But poor comprehenders tended to use just this tense, contributing to the list-like quality of their stories, while good comprehenders were more likely to vary the tense used to fit the demands of the story: predominantly past tense but with occasional uses of the present, perhaps for dramatic effect and immediacy.

We also looked at the way children referred to characters in the story: whether the references were appropriately varied and unambiguous (e.g. *the man saw the table . . . he went into the shop*) or whether they were either repetitious (e.g. *the man saw the table . . . the man went into the shop*) or ambiguous (e.g. *he saw the table . . . he went into the shop*, where the referent of 'he' has not been introduced). There was a tendency for skilled children to use the first pattern, which was smoother and clearer, more frequently than the less skilled children did. However, more interesting than this was the way that the children in the two groups were influenced by the conditions under which they told the story. For some of the stories, we presented the pictures one at a time, and the children did not know what would happen next. This makes it quite difficult to plan any coherent strategy for the use of referring expressions, because you do not know who is the main character or who will appear in the next picture. There was little difference between the two groups here: both used the repetitious or ambiguous style about half of the time. In a second condition, we showed the children all the pictures before they told the story. This gave them the opportunity to plan the best way of referring to the characters, for example using pronouns more often for the main character. This mode of presentation gave no advantage to the poor comprehenders: they carried on using the same style they had used in the other condition. But the good comprehenders could derive benefit from this condition: they used the more varied and appropriate pattern of reference for 83 per cent of the stories. The differences between the narratives of the two groups can be seen in these examples, from a poor comprehender, Tina, and a good one, Lucy, respectively:

> (TINA) A man and a lady is walking along and the doggie is behind them and there's some chicken hanging out of their bag and the dog bites it and they have a picnic and all the food is gone.

(LUCY) Once there was a man and a lady and a dog and they went for a walk to have a picnic and they took two legs with them. When they came near the spot they were gonna have their picnic, the dog was trying to get their food because he thought the food was for him so he ate the food, and when they got to their picnic spot they looked in and everything was gone and they were so surprised they went home and got their dinner at home.

Lucy seems to have some general plan in mind, as she mentions the couple's intention to have a picnic, and their approach to the picnic spot, which only appears in the final picture of the sequence. This planning requires her to look ahead, and to modify the description of the current picture with respect to what will be said about subsequent ones. Tina merely describes one or two aspects of each picture, and seems to focus on each picture in isolation, to provide an external place-marker of where she is in the story. Also, notice that the central point of the story is not clear in Tina's story. There is no indication that the couple are surprised at the disappearance of the chicken, and it is not even clear why 'all the food has gone': without seeing the pictures, a listener might assume that the couple ate the food themselves.

These stories bring out a more general issue about how to tell a good story: you need to have an idea of the 'point' of the narrative, otherwise the story has no interest or purpose. We investigated children's understanding of story points in another story-narration study with 8–9-year-old children. After they had told a story from picture sequences, children were asked to choose, from four statements: 'What was the most important thing about the story, the point of it?' So, for example, in a story where a cowboy goes into a cowboy accessories shop, he pretends he wants to examine a lasso, and uses it to tie up the shopkeeper, and robs the till. We asked the children to choose one of the following four statements (adults were unanimous in choosing statement 1):

1.   A cowboy tricks and robs the shopkeeper.
2.   A cowboy buys a lasso.
3.   A cowboy is in the shop.
4.   A kind shopkeeper gives the cowboy some money.

Overall the skilled comprehenders picked the main point of the stories 79 per cent of the time, compared with only 46 per cent for the less-skilled comprehenders. It is clear that the good comprehenders are much better at understanding the main point of a story, and it is interesting that they are better are understanding the point of even picture sequences.

Some other work that is related to this issue has been done recently by Kate Cain at Sussex. She assessed how good and poor comprehenders understood the role of a title. The children were asked what a title could tell the reader about a story. If they seemed unsure, or did not respond, they were asked what a specific title might tell them about a story, e.g. 'Jack and the

Beanstalk'. The children's responses were scored as correct if they said things like the title 'tells you what it's about', or gave an example such as: 'The Princess and the Pea – well, you can tell it's going to be about a princess and a pea'. Other responses, such as 'the words that are in the story' or 'whether it's good or not' were not allowed as correct. Overall, far more skilled than less-skilled comprehenders were able to produce an acceptable answer.

These findings indicate that less-skilled comprehenders have less clear ideas than skilled ones about how stories are typically structured – they tend to produce 'stories' that are less integrated and coherent than those of skilled comprehenders, and do not appreciate the main point of stories, even when the stories are presented as a series of pictures.

Comprehension monitoring

The third skill area we mentioned was that of comprehension monitoring. Some recent work in this area has shown that less-skilled comprehenders have difficulty in detecting problems of various kinds in short texts. Previous developmental studies, for instance by Ellen Markman,[5] have shown that young children generally have difficulty in saying explicitly what is wrong with a text so, in the experiments we report here, we used slightly older good and poor comprehenders (9–10-year-olds).

In the first experiment (an undergraduate project, conducted by Deborah Samols), we explored both 'spontaneous' and 'directed' comprehension monitoring whilst the children were reading short passages which contained misspelt words and jumbled sentences. An example passage is shown below:

Comprehension monitoring: example passage, 'Fortune Tellers'

We all know about events in the past because we can remember them, but we do not know about the future in the same kind of way. The future is uncertain. It is for us to be sure impossible about what will happen.

There are people who say that they know what will take place in the future. Some of these people are called 'fortune tellers'. If you go to see them, they will tell you what they think will happen to you. For example, you might be told that you will be going on a long trep. You might be told that someone who seems to be a friend is really an enemy.

The fortune teller may perp into a crystal ball, where she says she can see pictures of the future. She may tell you that the pictures are incomplete or imperfect, so she can only give you clues. In this a better chance way she has of being right. The more detail she gives, the more likely she is to get it wrong.

To assess spontaneous monitoring, the children were simply asked to read aloud the passages, without any indication that anything was wrong. Their ability to detect the errors was assessed by monitoring their hesitations, repetitions and self-corrections as they read aloud. The children were also asked if they has noticed anything that did not make sense in the texts. We found no differences between the groups on the measures of spontaneous monitoring. However, 67 per cent of the good comprehenders reported noticing that parts of the passages did not make sense when asked if they had noticed anything unusual, whereas only 17 per cent of the less-skilled group reported doing so – a highly significant difference. Disappointingly, however, only one of the good comprehenders could identify the problematic lines in the texts. There were clear differences between the groups when they were told that some parts of the story might not make sense, and they were specifically requested to underline any words or sentences that they did not understand (directed monitoring). The numbers of problematic words and phrases as a proportion of the total numbers of words or phrases underlined was calculated. Surprisingly, even the good comprehenders were not very good at this task: only 51 per cent of their word underlinings and 56 per cent of their phrase underlinings were correct. However, these figures were markedly better than those for the less-skilled comprehenders: 17 per cent and 25 per cent respectively. Thus, there were large differences between the good and poor comprehenders in their ability to detect both problematic words and phrases. The children were also asked questions about the passages, after both the spontaneous and the directed conditions. Overall, the skilled comprehenders were better than the less-skilled comprehenders at answering questions. However, the directed condition did not lead to better performance on the comprehension questions in either group.

In a further study, comprehension monitoring was assessed using an inconsistency detection paradigm (similar to that used by Markman[5] for example). In this study, the children had to detect inconsistencies that depended on the integration of information between two sentences in the text. For example, they might read that 'Moles cannot see very well, but their hearing and sense of smell are good' and, later in the same passage, that 'Moles are easily able to find food for their young because their eyesight is so good'. The passage from which this example is taken is shown below.

Inconsistency detection: example passage, 'Moles'

Moles are small brown animals and they live underground using networks of tunnels.

Moles cannot see very well, but their hearing and sense of smell are good.

They sleep in underground nests lined with grass, leaves and twigs.

Moles use their front feet for digging and their short fur allows them to move along their tunnels either forwards or backwards.

They mainly eat worms but they also eat insects and snails.

Moles are easily able to find food for their young because their eyesight is so good.

_____ This passage makes sense, it does not need to be changed.
_____ This passage does not make sense, it needs to be changed.

In this experiment, there was a further variable: the inconsistencies were either in adjacent sentences, or were separated by several sentences. Thus, for some children, the italicized sentence (which was not, of course, italicized in the texts shown to the children) appeared immediately prior to the final sentence of the passage. In this way, the memory load intrinsic to the task was manipulated. There were also a number of control passages, which did not contain inconsistencies, to ensure that the children were not trying to find problems where none existed. Once again, 9–10-year-old subjects were used in this experiment.

The children were asked to read the passages out loud, and to identify anything that 'didn't make sense'. They were given an example of blatant inconsistency of the sort that they should be looking for. They were asked to read at their own pace, to underline any problems they found in the passage, and then to tick an overall assessment of the passage at the bottom of the page (as shown above). The children were also asked to explain any problems that they identified. If they did not identify a problem on the first reading, testing did not stop immediately. They were told that there was a problem in the passage, and they were asked to re-read the passage and try to identify it. If the child still failed to identify the inconsistency on the second reading, the experimenter underlined the two inconsistent sentences and asked if they made sense together. If a child was still unable to identify the problem at this stage, the experimenter turned to the next passage. The child was allocated a score of 0–3 for each passage, depending on whether or not they identified the inconsistency, and how much prompting they required before they could do so. Thus, a maximum score was obtained if they marked the correct option at the end of the passage and were able to explain the inconsistency.

The results showed that the skilled comprehenders were better at detecting the inconsistencies overall (mean score 5.1 out of 6) than the less-skilled group (mean score 3.7). there was also an effect of the distance between the two inconsistent sentences: when the two sentences were adjacent, the task was much easier. However, the difference was much greater for the poor than for the good comprehenders – good comprehenders' performance was barely affected by whether the sentences were adjacent in the text, or were separated by several other sentences. The performance on the control passages (which did not contain any inconsistencies) was uniformly high in both groups. The performance on the inconsistent passages suggests that the integration of information across sentences in a passage is much more difficult for less-skilled than for skilled comprehenders. We (Yuill, Oakhill and Parkin[6]) found similar results with younger children in a task that required the detection of apparent anomalies in text. The less-skilled comprehenders could readily resolve anomalies in passages (e.g. a boy is *praised* by his mother for not sharing his sweets with his little brother) only if the apparent anomaly and the information that resolve it (in this case, that the little brother was on a diet) were in adjacent sentences. If the two items of information were separated by a few sentences, the less-skilled comprehenders could not seem to integrate them, and performed very poorly. These findings indicate that the performance of children on these tasks may be related to their ability to integrate information in working memory, and we will discuss this issue in the next section.

Working memory and text comprehension

Work with adults, by Meredyth Daneman and Patricia Carpenter,[7] has shown that a variety of comprehension skills are related to performance on a verbal working memory test in adults. These findings led us to assess working memory in our groups of good and poor comprehenders. The children who participated in the anomaly detection study outlined above also had their working memory assessed using a non-linguistic working memory test. In this test, the children were required to read out loud sets of three digits, and recall the final digits in each of the sets without looking back at them. So, for example, they might read the sets.

$$9 \quad - \quad 4 \quad - \quad 1$$
$$5 \quad - \quad 3 \quad - \quad 6$$
$$2 \quad - \quad 7 \quad - \quad 8$$

and have to recall the final digits, 1, 6, 8, in order. The difficulty of the test was increased by increasing the number of sets of digits to be processed and thus the number of final digits to be recalled: the children had to recall either two, three or four digits. We found that the skilled and less-skilled comprehenders performed very similarly on the easiest version of the task, but that the less-skilled comprehenders were worse than the skilled ones on the two harder versions of the task. We have now replicated this pattern of findings many times.

Thus, one plausible reason for the problems of the less-skilled comprehenders might be that their poorer working memories are preventing them from efficient text processing, and limiting their ability to make inferences, integrate information and understand the overall structure of a text. However, other work of ours indicates that deficient working memory cannot provide a complete explanation for the less-skilled comprehenders' problems. For instance, some recent work by Kate Cain at Sussex has been looking into children's reading habits. She has been asking both children and their parents questions about the amount of reading they do at home, the numbers of books owned, and library membership and use. (This study differs from the recent work brought together by Keith Topping and Sheila Wolfendale,[8] which primarily addresses the effects of parents listening to their children read, or actively coaching them in reading, rather than literacy activities more broadly.) Although the numbers of participants in Cain's study are fairly small at the moment, some interesting findings are emerging. For instance, skilled comprehenders are *read* to significantly more frequently than less-skilled comprehenders. Similarly more of the skilled than less-skilled comprehenders said they had visited a library, and more of their parents said they were members of a library, though the latter differences did not reach statistical significance. These findings may mean that the poorer comprehenders have not had the same level of exposure to stories and story structures from a very early age that skilled comprehenders might have had. Thus, they might have missed out on hundreds or even thousands of hours of story reading and book sharing from a very early age, and this experience, if it proves to be crucial to later reading comprehension skill, would be exceedingly difficult to compensate for (even if such compensation were found to be effective at a later age). Of course, it could be that poorer comprehenders are read to less *because* they are poor comprehenders, and perhaps do not enjoy being read to, or are not rewarding to read to. We end this chapter on a more optimistic note, because we have found that even relatively short-term training studies can be very effective in improving comprehension.

Remediation studies

There are three main ways in which comprehension of and learning from text might be improved, only one of which we consider in any detail here. First, additions and changes to the text could be made, to improve its comprehensibility and memorability. Additions might include pictures, subheadings and summaries; other changes might be to improve the organization or coherence of the text. These sorts of changes are ones that are made *for* readers, and do not require any effort on their part. Second, readers can be encouraged to engage in various activities either while they are reading or after reading a text, for example note-taking, underlining or summary-writing (such activities are often called 'study aids'). Research discussed by Oakhill and Graham[9] has also shown that they can be used to improve comprehension. Third, children can be taught to apply processing strategies as they are reading: ways of thinking about the text, whether it relates to what they know, and whether their understanding is adequate. Such strategies differ from the first two types in that they rely on what is going on *in the reader's head*, rather than on external aids to comprehension. Most remediation studies have attempted to train children in such strategies on the assumption that it is most useful to develop procedures that can then be applied to any text.

The aim of the studies we describe in this section was to see if less-skilled readers' comprehension could be improved. The rationale was that, if less-skilled children can be trained in the skills they are supposed to lack, then their comprehension should improve. If the poor comprehenders' understanding is deficient *because* they lack the skill in which they are being trained, then we would expect that the less-skilled comprehnders might improve to the same level as the skilled ones following training, but the skilled ones would not benefit from training (since they already have the skills being trained).

The general idea of the first study (Yuill and Oakhill[10]) we will describe here was to try to make children more aware of, and get them more involved in, their own comprehension: to encourage inferencing and comprehension monitoring. As well as the group who received training (which we will come to in a moment), there were two 'control' groups, who spent the same amount of time with the experimenter but doing activities which we did not expect to improve their comprehension. All three groups spent a total of seven sessions of about thirty minutes each with the experimenter. One of the control groups simply spent their time answering questions about a series of short passages. The other group had training in rapid word decoding. As we mentioned earlier, one theory of poor comprehension suggests that *accurate* word recognition is not sufficient for efficient comprehension, but that words must also be recognized quickly and automatically. If they are not, then the resources devoted to word recognition will not be available for comprehension processes, which will suffer. This group read the same texts as the other group, and practised decoding lists of words from them. Thus, the improvement of the trained group could be compared with that of the control groups.

Like the control groups, the groups who received training were seen in seven separate sessions of about thirty minutes each. There were three components to the training. First, practice in *lexical inferences* was included in all seven sessions. Here, the children were encouraged to say what they could work out about a sentence or story from the individual words. For instance, in the sentence 'Sleepy Tom was late for school again', we can infer from 'sleepy' in that context that Tom has probably only just got up, and perhaps that he went to bed late, or habitually goes to bed late. The name 'Tom' suggests that Tom is a pupil, rather than a teacher, at the school because he is referred to by his first name, rather than being called 'Mr', and so on. The children were given practice in applying this technique, first with sentences, and then with short abstract stories of the sort shown below. Second, in four of the sessions, the children engaged in *question generation*. They were invited to generate questions such as 'Who was crying?' and 'Where was Billy?' for the passage shown (the questions listed were *not* presented in this training condition). The children took turns to generate questions. Third, in one session, they were encouraged to engage in *prediction*. In this session, part of the text was covered and the children were encouraged to guess at what was missing. After they had done so, the text was revealed and the appropriateness of their guesses was discussed with them.

The control group who did comprehension exercises were first told about the importance of accurate comprehension. The children in the group shared the reading of the text, and took turns at attempting to answer the set question on it. A sample text with questions is shown below.

Inference training: example text

Billy was crying. His whole day was spoilt. All his work had been broken by the wave. His mother came to stop him crying. But she accidentally stepped on the only tower that was left. Billy cried even more. 'Never mind,' said his mother, 'We can always build another one tomorrow.' Billy stopped crying and went home for his tea.

EXAMPLE QUESTIONS (exercise group only)
Where was Billy?
Why was Billy crying?
What had the wave broken?
Why did his mother go to him?
Why did Billy cry even more?

The children were given little feedback on their answers by the experimenter, except that obvious errors were corrected. However, the children often discussed the answers amongst themselves which, as we shall see later, may have influenced the results. The children in the other control group, who were given training in rapid decoding, practised reading words, including the most difficult words, from the same texts as quickly as possible.

After a period of about two months, during which the training took place, the children were re-tested on a different form of the Neale Analysis. The improvement scores for the six groups are shown in Table 14.3. As can be seen, the very smallest increase in improvement was six months. However, the absolute differences in improvement mean very little because the different forms of the Neale Analysis may not be exactly parallel, or because the children just happen to make rapid progress in reading at the time of year the testing was done. What is remarkable, though, are the *relative* differences in improvement in the various groups. The less-skilled comprehenders benefited from inference training more than the skilled comprehenders, and the less-skilled group who received inference training improved more than those given decoding practice. However, the surprising aspect of these results, from our point of view, was that comprehension exercises also improved comprehension. Indeed, the improvement of the inference groups was not significantly different from those given comprehension exercises. Training did not differentially affect reading speed or accuracy of word decoding – there were no differences between the groups on these measures. The gains in comprehension scores after this relatively short period of training were impressive. However, it was surprising that the group given inference training did not improve more than those given comprehension exercises. One possible explanation for this result is that children in the latter group discussed their answers, and often argued with one another about what was the correct answer. These discussions may have had the effect of increasing their awareness of their comprehension. In addition, as can be seen from the example text, the texts used were rather abstract and obscure (to provide suitable material for the

Table 14.3 Inference training study: average improvement (months)

	Rapid decoding	Comprehension exercises	Inference training
Less-skilled	6.00	13.71	17.38
Skilled	10.33	5.43	5.92

group given inference training) and this in itself may have encouraged more inferential processing and reflection than would have occurred with more traditional stories.

We have also explored, in collaboration with Sima Patel at Sussex, the effects of training in generating mental images of the events in a text on comprehension. Michael Pressley's work, for example,[11] has shown that imagery can be successful as a way of improving children's comprehension of stories, but it is not until about 8 that children can learn to use self-generated images. We explored whether less-skilled comprehenders might benefit from imagery training, and also addressed the issue of whether imagery might be particularly suitable for aiding memory for particular sorts of information (Oakhill and Patel[12]). We did this by asking the children three different sorts of question. The first type, 'factual' questions, tapped memory for facts that were explicit in the texts. The second type, 'inferential', asked about information that could only be inferred from the story, and the third, 'descriptive', asked about details that might be particularly likely to come to the reader's attention if an image had been formed. An example text, with the three types of question, is shown below.

Imagery training study: example story and questions

The step ladder was put away safely behind the door which was just to the right of the cooker. The three shelves were up at last and, even with a sore thumb, Terry Butcher was happy. The hammer that had caused the pain was put away in the tool box with the other tools.

Linda, Terry's wife, came into the room with a box of crockery. 'The shelves are for my little model aeroplanes,' said Terry, in a stern voice. 'We'll see,' was the reply from Linda.

A little while later, when Terry was putting away the tool box, he heard a loud scream and the sound of breaking glass and china. Terry walked back into the room and was angry. 'I warned you about those shelves,' he said to Linda.

EXAMPLE QUESTIONS
How many shelves had been put up? (factual)
Why did Terry have a sore thumb? (inferential)
Describe the scene in the room when Linda screamed (descriptive)

We selected good and poor comprehenders with a mean age of 9.7. Each group was divided into two subgroups, one of which was given training in imagery. The imagery training took place in small groups (four or five children) over three sessions, on different days. The children were told that they would be learning to 'think in pictures' as they read stories, to help them to answer questions about them. Nine stories were used altogether: four for training, and five in the test session. In the first training session the children read one of the stories, and the experimenter then produced two drawings: one was a cartoon-like sequence of four pictures, which represented the main sequence of events in the story. The other was a single picture, which represented the main event in the story. The children were shown how each of the pictures related to the story, and were encouraged to use these 'pictures in their minds' to help them to answer questions about the stories. For a second story in this session, the children were not shown pictures but were encouraged to formulate their own mental images. They discussed their pictures and received feedback and suggestions from the experimenter. In a second session, a similar procedure was followed. In the final training session, the children were not shown any drawings. The imagery procedure was reiterated, and the children read and answered questions about a new story and a discussion of their 'mental pictures' took place, as in the first two sessions.

The children who did not receive imagery training saw the same stories, also spread over three sessions. They read the stories and answered the questions, and their answers were then discussed with them. The children in these groups spent as long with the experimenter as those in the imagery training groups. In the test phase, the groups who had received the imagery training were reminded of this strategy before they read the test stories, and were reminded to used their mental pictures to help them to answer the questions. The children in the control condition were told to read the stories very carefully and to answer the questions in as much detail as possible.

The results showed that, overall, the good comprehenders answered more questions correctly than poor ones, and that the children given imagery training performed better than the control group. As predicted, the poor comprehenders given imagery training showed a marked improvement in memory for the passages: they performed significantly better on the test questions than did the control group or poor comprehenders. There was no such difference between the groups of good comprehenders. Imagery training did not have a differential effect for the different types of questions: where there was improvement, it was general, and not related to particular question types. These results show that imagery training was especially beneficial for those children who do not possess adequate comprehension skills. Poor comprehenders may show a particular benefit from imagery training because it enables them, or forces them, to integrate information in the text in a way that they would not normally do. Of course, the finding that the comprehension of the good group did not improve with imagery does not necessarily mean that they already use imagery. It may be that they have some equally efficient strategy for remembering information from text, and that training in imagery gives them no additional advantage. Imagery may help poor comprehenders by giving them a strategy to help them to overcome some of the limitations on their comprehension skills. For instance, the ability to use imagery strategies may give poor comprehenders a way to help circumvent their memory limitations by enabling them to use a different, and perhaps more economical, means of representing information in the text.

In conclusion, we have shown that two very different types of training can have substantial effects on the comprehension scores of less-skilled comprehenders, at least in the short term. However, further work is needed to establish the long-term effects of such training. Although these findings give us cause for optimism, we conclude this section with two notes of caution. First, most methods of improving comprehension assume that poor comprehenders will benefit from being taught the skills that good readers use. However, the picture might not be so simple: the fact that poor readers lack some skills might indicate that, at least in some cases, they are unable to use them. Second, some forms of instruction might need to wait until after the beginning stages of learning to read, until decoding skills are fairly well established. A related point is that young readers may find learning to use skills such as imagery and comprehension monitoring very difficult – it is not until about 9, for instance, that children are typically able to understand and use imagery. Of course, these reservations about specific training in comprehension skills should not be taken to mean that reading for meaning should not be encouraged from the very beginning, but just that deliberate training of comprehension skills may need to be delayed.

Conclusions

The general picture that emerges of less-skilled comprehenders is of children who are poor at making inferences and connecting up ideas in a text. Their problem seems not to be restricted to understanding the written word: in general they also have difficulties with listening comprehension and in understanding picture sequences. Working memory may play a part in such skills: our work has shown that less-skilled comprehenders perform poorly on a test of working memory. Such a deficit could readily explain the less-skilled comprehenders' problems in making inferences, understanding story structure and monitoring their comprehension. However, patterns of causality have yet to be established. In any case, this seems very unlikely to be a complete explanation of the less-skilled children's problem, since inference skills can be trained, and one would not expect working memory to be susceptible to training. One possibility that reconciles these two sets of findings is that less-skilled comprehenders do have a basic deficit in working memory which affects their comprehension, but that they can be taught strategies that help them to circumvent their memory limitations. In addition, some findings are emerging to show that extensive experience of being read to may be important. It may be that being read to from an early age turns out to be a crucial factor in the development of comprehension skills.

Notes

1 Perfetti, C.A. 1985: *Reading Ability*, Oxford: Oxford University Press.
2 Yuill, N.M. and Oakhill, J.V. 1991: *Children's Problems in Text Comprehension: An Experimental Investigation*, Cambridge: Cambridge University Press.
3 Bishop, D. 1983: *Test for Reception of Grammar*, Manchester: Department of Psychology, University of Manchester.
4 Oakhill, J.V. 1984: 'Inferential and memory skills in children's comprehension of stories', *British Journal of Educational Psychology*, 54, 31–9.
5 Markman, E. 1977: 'Realising that you don't understand: a preliminary investigation', *Child Development*, 48, 986–92.
6 Yuill, N.M., Oakhill, J.V. and Parkin, A.J. 1989: 'Working memory, comprehension ability and the resolution of text anomaly', *British Journal of Psychology*, 80, 351–61.
7 Daneman, M. and Carpenter, P. 1980: 'Individual differences in working memory and reading', *Journal of Verbal Learning and Verbal Behaviour*, 19, 450–66.
8 Topping, K. and Wolfendale, S. (eds) 1985: *Parental Involvement in Children's Reading*, London: Croom Helm.
9 Oakhill, J.V. and Garnham, A. 1988: *Becoming a Skilled Reader*, Oxford: Blackwell.
10 Yuill, N.M. and Oakhill, J.V. 1988: 'Effects of inference awareness training on poor reading comprehension', *Applied Cognitive Psychology*, 2, 33–45.
11 Pressley, G.M. 1976: 'Mental imagery helps eight-year-olds remember what they read', *Journal of Educational Psychology*, 68, 355–9.
12 Oakhill, J.V. and Patel, S. 1991: 'Can imagery training help children who have comprehension problems?', *Journal of Research in Reading*, 14, 106–15.

Source

This is an edited version of a chapter previously published in E. Funnell and M. Stuart (eds) *Learning to Read: Psychology in the Classroom*. 1995. Reproduced by permission of Blackwell Publishers Ltd.

Chapter 15

Specific developmental dyslexia (SDD)

'Basics to back' in 2000 and beyond?

Peter Pumfrey

Questions addressed in this chapter include:

- Does specific developmental dyslexia (SDD) exist? If so:
- What is the nature of SDD?
- How may SDD be identified?
- What is the incidence of SDD?
- How might SDD be prevented? and
- How may SDD be alleviated?

Preamble

In the Summer of 1998, an American clinical psychologist with extensive experience in the teaching of reading, published in the UK a book (McGuinness, 1998) that had appeared in 1997 in the USA. It contains many challenging statements. For example:

> There is no diagnosis and no evidence for any special type of reading disorder like 'dyslexia' (p. 165); . . . overwhelming evidence that there is no such thing as 'dyslexia' or 'learning difficulty'.
>
> (p. 220)

and

> Clear your minds of notions like 'dyslexia' and 'learning difficulties'. The research data are overwhelming that these terms are invalid.
>
> (p. 226)

The foreword to the book was written by an eminent neuropsychologist, Steven Pinker, Director of the Centre for Cognitive Neuroscience at the Massachusetts Institute of Technology.

In the Autumn of 1998, the Department for Education and Employment (DfEE) issued a pamphlet entitled 'How can I tell if my child may be dyslexic?' (DfEE, 1998b). This was intended to sensitize primary school teachers and inform their practice. Inevitably, its brevity meant that it did not help greatly in improving educational decision-making concerning the literacy difficulties faced by individual children. (As an aside, a spelling mistake on the front page did not inspire confidence in the care with which the document was initially produced and distributed.) Fortunately, more adequate information is available from various of the publications included in this chapter in which the questions with which this chapter began are addressed. The chapter is an abridged and updated version of the 15th Vernon Wall Lecture given at the British Psychological Society's Education Section Annual Conference in 1995. The full 1995 publication is available from the British Psychological Society (Pumfrey, 1996).

Introduction

In the year 2000, the concept 'dyslexia' has a widespread and increasing currency. Etymologically, the word derives from both Latin and Greek. The Latin root is *dis* (difficulty) plus *legere* (to read); the Greek *dys* plus *lexis* (words). In the broadest sense, the term includes acquired dyslexia (AD) resulting from injuries to (and illnesses affecting) the brain, and also ostensibly idiopathic conditions collectively known as specific developmental dyslexia (SDD). This chapter is concerned with SDD and its aims are as follows:

- To identify tensions deriving from a paradox concerning the concept of SDD.
- To specify some basic professional skills pertinent to the resolution of the tensions identified.
- To illustrate the promise and the pitfalls of these basic professional skills in current work on SDD.
- To provide information enabling readers to continue their own professional development thereby improving institutional and individual decision-making in relation to SDD.

Dyslexia comprises distinctive difficulties with various aspects of receptive and expressive language in textual and/or oral modalities (reading, writing/ spelling, listening, talking). Some theorists include other symbolic systems, such as mathematics and music. The concept includes both acquired dyslexia (AD) and specific developmental dyslexia (SDD). It is important to distinguish between them.

Here, we are concerned only with the latter. Nowadays, the words 'specific' and 'developmental' are frequently omitted, even in official documents. The adjectives 'specific' and 'developmental' are important in considering the nature of the syndrome. The appealing convenience of contracting SDD to 'dyslexia', rather than the use of SDD, leads to conceptual confusions, avoidable ambiguities and unnecessary disagreements. Not all pupils with receptive and/or expressive language difficulties have SDD.

Multi-disciplinary context

The medical profession has had a longstanding involvement in the diagnosis and treatment of the aphasias. Identification of a specific aphasic loss of the ability to read, 'word blindness', despite the powers of sight, the intellect and speech remaining intact, is usually credited to a German physician Kussmaul in 1878. He also introduced the concept of 'word deafness'. Such patients are not genuinely deaf and can express themselves in words, but use many words in the wrong places and often distort them (Miles and Miles, 1999). In 1887, Berlin, a German ophthalmologist, used the word 'dyslexia' to refer to a group of patients experiencing problems in reading because of cerebral disease. The condition was an *acquired* one and was viewed as one of the aphasias.

One hundred years ago, the first recorded individual case of congenital word blindness in a schoolboy was reported by a medical practitioner in the *British Medical Journal* (Morgan, 1896). The one-page note describes a 14-year-old boy, Percy F. He is perceived as one of the brightest pupils in the class. In the opinion of his teachers, if all the teaching and assessments had been oral, Percy would have been the top of the class in his achievements. As it was he was struggling at the bottom. To account for this disability, Morgan suggested that the brain region suspected of being structurally damaged by disease/injury in acquired dyslexia was underdeveloped in this adolescent. Morgan also noted that 'the condition is unique so far as I know, in that it follows no injury or illness, but is evidently congenital'. The full text of this article was reprinted in the British Dyslexia Association's 1996 Handbook (Crisfield, 1996).

From an epidemiological standpoint, it is interesting to note that the annual report of the Medical Officer of Health, Dr James Kerr, in the City of Bradford in Yorkshire, England, was published some weeks before the appearance of Morgan's paper. Kerr reported the existence in local schools of some pupils who appeared to show what he described as 'congenital word-blindness'. Kerr was awarded the Howard Medal by the Royal Statistical Society in the same year for an essay based on his work in Bradford. Included in it was the observation that reading and writing difficulties could be found in children having no other apparent cognitive difficulties. The involvement and interest of the medical profession in certain cases of unexpected difficulties in literacy represents a longstanding and continuing involvement (Pumfrey and Reason, 1992; Hulme and Snowling, 1994, 1997; Chase *et al.*, 1996; Stein and Walsh, 1997; Klein and McMullen, 1999; Miles and Miles, 1999).

As professionals working with children mainly in educational settings, educational psychologists and teachers are concerned with both theory and practice. The school, the classroom and the clinic are laboratories within which a wide variety of ongoing and scientifically imprecise 'action research' takes place each day. This research can focus on individuals, small groups, classes, schools, local education authorities (LEAs) and the whole state educational system. Increasingly, technologically sophisticated and systematic studies of the myriad questions raised by SDD are taking place. To date the evidence is that these studies reveal ever-greater complexities, rather than simple answers, concerning SDD.

SDD has been described as 'the hidden handicap'. In its pre-school stages, it is typically *unseen*. Its subsequent early manifestations in difficulties in the acquisition of the skills of literacy, are *unexpected*. The difficulties also prove to be *unusual* in both degree and type and *unremitting* in character. Their cognitive, affective and motivational consequences for the individual can be disastrous (Edwards, 1994; Riddick, 1996). Is such a group of children distinguishable from other pupils who also experience difficulties in becoming literate? Is the concept of SDD valid?

The unexpected intrigues. Explanations are sought. Despite the considerable progress that has been made over the last century, SDD continues to be a controversial topic (Sampson, 1975a, 1976; Pumfrey and Reason, 1992; Hulme and Snowling, 1994, 1997; Miles and Miles, 1999). We remain intrigued, we seek explanations, we discuss and investigate their respective merits, we produce and consider evidence. Agreement, compromise or disagreement concerning the interpretation of evidence occurs. Investigations continue.

Life is filled with paradoxes. A paradox is a statement, seemingly self-contradictory or absurd, though possibly well-founded or essentially true. SDD presents many paradoxes. In an interview given in 1995, Stephen Hawking demonstrated the value of the proposition that 'One of the best places to look for new ideas in theoretical work is in the apparent paradoxes that occur in the existing theory'. With reference to SDD, the following paradoxical statement causes tensions: 'All children are the same: all children are different'.

Put in terms of the tensions between individuals and groups: 'Value and understand my child's uniqueness, but ensure that my child becomes literate at about the same time as his/her peers'.

Tensions

Setting the scene: values, priorities and resources:

- How important is literacy to you?
- How much is literacy worth to our children and to society?
- How much is literacy worth to the individual pupil with SDD?

In our society, literacy enriches both culturally and economically. Whatever its causes, illiteracy isolates and impoverishes. In principle, there is general agreement that illiteracy, irrespective of its causes, should be minimized. In practice, there are many barriers. They may be summarized as:

- Resources finite.
- Priorities contentious.
- Knowledge partial.
- Demands infinite.

Three of these are largely socio-political in nature. One is scientific.

Disagreements within (and between) disciplines provide the challenge of finding resolutions. Hypothesis and antithesis can either identify mistaken ideas or stimulate syntheses. For example, in education, deriving from the earlier 'Top-down' versus 'Bottom-up' positions concerning the development of literacy, its learning and teaching, have emerged more comprehensive interactive formulations (Adams, 1990; Ruddell and Ruddell, 1994; Lazo *et al.*, 1997; Reitsma and Verhoeven, 1998; Klein and McMullen, 1999).

In general, it is constructive to remember that no single profession has a freehold on validity. Similarly, no single research methodology can address adequately all questions concerning SDD. Both qualitative and quantitative approaches have their respective strengths and weaknesses (Hammersley, 1995; Neuman and McCormick, 1995; Pumfrey, 1995a). In their various fields, all professions share equivalent responsibilities to their respective clients and disciplines. *Continuing professional development of one's knowledge, skills and understanding is essential.* [Editor's emphasis.]

Basics to back?

In clarifying contentious areas of theory and practice, it is typically the asking of challenging questions which advances understanding. Productive questions frequently arise when predictions based on one theory are falsified; or when contradictory predictions derived from competing theoretical positions are tested. We have extensive yet still limited and fragmentary understandings of the initial six questions posed.

Distinguishing socio-political barriers from scientific ones is essential. Paradoxically, the wide range of insights from various disciplines into these complex questions, coupled with professional tunnel vision, can restrict the development of more adequate scientific answers. It is difficult enough to keep abreast of developments within even a single field. *The biggest danger to progress is becoming immured in the conceptual concrete of one's own profession. No one profession has sole claim to expertise concerning the nature, identification, prevention and alleviation of SDD.* [Editor's emphasis.] The perspectives of educational, psychological, sociological, medical and ophthalmological professions are complementary.

The six questions cited at the beginning of this chapter are being actively explored by different professions, using distinctive and often highly specialized methodologies and materials, in a variety of contexts, often working from complementary or even contrasting theoretical positions (Ruddell *et al.*, 1994; Gough, 1995). Syntheses of complementary perspective are being sought (Frith, 1995, 1997; DECP, 1999).

In combination with an appreciation of theories of child development in general and human communication in particular, two 'basics' could help a larger proportion of professionals address more constructively, and thus advance understanding of, the questions concerning SDD posed earlier. These 'basics' are the application of research methods and test theory. Through the generation

---

Specific developmental dyslexia (SSD):

Differentiation and labelling

        Differences
        Deviations
        Difficulties
        Disabilities
        Deficits
        Defects

The slippery path from Differences to Defects can lead to the pathologizing of normality

---

Figure 15.1 SDD – differentiation and labelling

and testing of hypotheses concerning the nature of SDD (its identification incidence, prognosis and alleviation in individuals or groups) knowledge is advanced. The scientific basis of individual and institutional decision-making can be improved. The miseries of avoidable educational failure and its concomitant effects on motivation and self-concept can be reduced (Turner, 1997).

Q1 Does SDD exist?

Is SDD a legitimate professional concern for teachers and psychologists (among other professionals)? Does SDD exist or is it a conceptual blind alley? (Figure 15.1).

Acceptance of inter- and intra-individual differences on virtually any structural or functional aspect of development is essential if one assumes that children do not all learn to become literate in the same way. There is a slippery path from the recognition of such differences to the identification of defects.

Does the label SDD lead to the pathologizing of normality? An informed minority of professionals doubt the validity and thus the educational utility of the concept (Tizard, 1972; Young and Tyre, 1983; Presland, 1991; Anon. 1994; Stanovich and Siegel, 1994; Stanovich *et al.*, 1997; McGuinness, 1998). Others, who are equally well-informed, consider SDD an exciting challenge whereby our understanding of the acquisition of literacy and our ability to alleviate children's difficulties will be enhanced (Bakker, 1990, 1994; Miles, 1993; Fawcett and Nicolson, 1994; Bakker *et al.*, 1994; Hulme and Snowling, 1994, 1997; Seymour, 1994; Licht and Spyer, 1995; Nicolson and Fawcett, 1995; Turner, 1997; Pumfrey *et al.*, 1998; Miles and Miles, 1999).

With Mary Warnock as Chair, the Committee of Enquiry on the Education of Handicapped Children and Young People [England and Wales] argued for the abolition of categories of disabilities and the development of the concept of special educational needs (Committee of Enquiry, 1978). This move was reflected in the Education Act 1981. Ten years later, in a House of Lords

Debate held in December 1991, Baroness Warnock publicly renounced her earlier position concerning the value of categories of disabilities and in 1994 became President of the British Dyslexia Association.

There are many definitions of SDD. The following represent the views of the Orton Dyslexia Society (ODS), now the International Dyslexia Association (IDA). These demonstrate a difference in emphasis between the Council and the Research Committee of the ODS appointed to consider a definition based on current scientific evidence.

Definitions: Orton Dyslexia Society 1994

Committee of the Orton Dyslexia Society (ODS) Members Definition (ODS, 1994a):

> Dyslexia is a neurologically based, often familial disorder which interferes with the acquisition of language. Varying in degrees of severity, it is manifested by difficulties in receptive and expressive language, including phonological processing, in reading, writing, spelling, handwriting and sometimes in arithmetic. Dyslexia is not a result of lack of motivation, sensory impairment, inadequate instructional or environmental opportunities, but may occur together with these conditions. Although dyslexia is life-long, individuals with dyslexia frequently respond successfully to timely and appropriate intervention.

ODS Research Committee Definition (ODS, 1994b):

> Dyslexia is one of several distinct learning disabilities. It is a specific language-based disorder of constitutional origin characterised by difficulties in single word decoding, usually reflecting insufficient phonological processing abilities. These difficulties in single word decoding are often unexpected in relation to age and other cognitive and academic abilities: they are not the result of generalised developmental disability or sensory impairment. Dyslexia is manifest by variable difficulty with different forms of language, often including, in addition to problems of reading, a conspicuous problem with acquiring proficiency in writing and spelling.

Following a detailed study of available research evidence and professional consultations, a Working Party of the Division of Educational and Child Psychology (DECP) of the British Psychological Society reached the following definition:

> Dyslexia is evident when accurate and fluent word reading and/or spelling develops very incompletely or with great difficulty. This focuses on literacy learning at the 'word level' and implies that the problem is severe and persistent despite appropriate learning opportunities. It provides the basis for a staged process of assessment through teaching.
>
> (DECP, 1999, p. 18)

Unlike the ODS Research Committee's definition, that of the DECP makes no mention of dyslexia being 'unexpected in relation to age and other cognitive and academic abilities'.

When Rome ruled the world, the saying 'All roads lead to Rome' underlined the then power of the Empire. In the new century, the 'Royal Road' towards specifying a major cause of SDD is increasingly pointing towards phonological processing abilities. Even at the level of single-word decoding, it is unlikely that all workers would agree that this represents a comprehensive analysis of the situation (Fawcett and Nicholson, 1994; Nicolson and Fawcett, 1995; Stein and Walsh, 1997; Jeanes et al., 1997; Scholes, 1998; Robertson, 1999; Coles, 2000). The fact that profoundly deaf children can be taught to read and spell is relevant.

At least one of the following conditions must be demonstrated if the claim for the conceptual coherence and existence of SDD is to be seen as well-founded. There must be a distinctive:

- aetiology; cause / origin of disease
- pattern of presenting symptoms;
- prognosis; or
- response to particular interventions.

Data from studies of twins (DeFries, 1991; DeFries et al., 1997), from behavioural genetics (Olson et al., 1999), psychoneurology (Duane, 1991; Klein and McMullen, 1999), vision science and psycho-ophthalmology (Pumfrey, 1993; Willows et al., 1993; Wilkins et al., 1996) provide important but not conclusive evidence supporting the first three requirements for the existence of SDD. Geneticists are exploring genetic linkages to SDD. Chromosomes 6 and 15 have been the focus of recent work. SDD is unlikely to involve the presence of a single gene defect with the inevitable occurrence of SDD, but a genetically linked susceptibility that may be minimized (or maximized) by environmental contingencies (Olson et al., 1999). On completion of the human genome project, it is likely that the diagnosis of a range of genetically transmitted conditions will be able to be made on the basis of single-cell biopsy.

The following non-genetic but biological processes have been implicated as possible causes of dyslexia: the effects of testosterone being released into the developing foetus during pregnancy; the transference from the mother to the foetus of immune-antibodies; and a wide range of perinatal risk factors.

Even if evidence exists for the first three of the above requirements, it does not follow that unequivocally effective interventions are either known or can be developed. In this field, assertions are easy. Evidence concerning the efficacy of a wide range of interventions is less readily available and more contentious (Pumfrey, 1991, 1993; Pumfrey and Reason, 1992; Wilkins et al., 1994; Rack, 1995; Reid, 1996a, 1996b; Ott, 1997; Turner, 1997; McGuinness, 1998; DECP, 1999; Miles and Miles, 1999).

Increasingly, SDD is being described as 'a variable syndrome'. This highlights the distinction between those who argue that SDD has a single underlying cause, but that this can be manifest in different ways, and other workers who argue that there are qualitatively different subtypes of SDD. This controversy is likely to run for a considerable time (Miles, 1993; Bakker, 1994; Fawcett and Nicolson, 1994; Seymour, 1994; Stanovich and Siegel, 1994; Snowling, 1995, 1999; DECP, 1999). Arguably, considerations of both 'trait' and 'type' are required in a more adequate formulation of SDD.

Q2 What is the nature of SDD?

To address this question, it is essential to clarify our uses of the term SDD. The relationships between a *concept* such as SDD (an abstraction that can never be directly measured) (SDD 'A'), the *observable behaviours* in everyday life from which the existence of the concept is inferred (for example, particular patterns of literacy-related behaviours) (SDD 'B') and *tests/assessments* (techniques that systematically sample defined aspects of such behaviours) (SDD 'C') are essential considerations. If the level at which discussion is taking place is not specified, misunderstandings can readily multiply. SDD 'A', 'B' and 'C' must be differentiated. They must also be considered simultaneously if apparent paradoxes concerning the nature, identification and alleviation of SDD as a complex and variable developmental syndrome are to be addressed. Their formulations vary across disciplines.

As noted earlier, a key issue is whether SDD is a unitary condition. If the former holds, pupils' inter-individual differences in the information-processing abilities required for literacy would vary quantitatively. They would be likely to require help in developing the same skills. Some would require more assistance than others. The concept of SDD would, in effect, become redundant. If common crucial skills underpinned all surface failures in reading and spelling, all children can be helped and in similar ways. Currently, the importance of phonemic awareness is receiving considerable attention (Frederickson and Reason, 1995b; Snowling, 1995; Hulme and Joshi, 1998; Scholes, 1998; Stuart, 1998; DECP, 1999).

Other workers point to qualitative differences between pupils' information-processing strengths and weaknesses. If there are qualitative differences between pupils' abilities, pupils are likely to require different teaching and to use different learning techniques (Gjessing and Karlson, 1989; Bakker, 1990; Tyler, 1990; Bakker, 1994; Ellis *et al.*, 1997a, 1997b; Robertson, 1999). Is a shared theoretical framework possible? (Frith, 1995, 1997; DECP, 1999).

Q3 How may SDD be identified? (Potential versus attainments)

The cry 'Could do better' continues to reverberate through the educational system. The concept of 'underachievement' is a powerful one. It underpinned the pioneer work of the Remedial Education Centre at the University of Birmingham (Schonell and Wall, 1949; Sampson, 1975b). When the Americans were considering how 'Learning Disabilities' (their equivalent to SpLDs) could be operationally defined, the only consensus was that it resulted in a major discrepancy between what, on the basis of pupils' aptitudes, you would *expect* academically of learning-disabled children and the level at which they were *actually* achieving (Reynolds, 1984). In the UK, 80 per cent of educational psychologists considered that some kind of discrepancy was a central attribute of SDD (Pumfrey and Reason, 1992). The DfE also considers discrepancies between abilities and attainment as central to identification (DfE, 1994a). The same is true of the advice given by the DfEE to primary school teachers in a pamphlet issued during the autumn of 1998 on the identification of dyslexic children (DfEE, 1998b).

In general, intellectually able pupils become literate more rapidly than less intellectually able pupils. The ability-attainment discrepancy had a considerable appeal as an initial step in defining underachievement. The selection of particular tests to provide measures of intellectual ability and attainments in literacy is not straightforward (Elliott, 1990, 1994; Stanovich, 1991; McNab, 1994a; Stanovich and Siegel, 1994; Turner, 1997; Pumfrey et al., 1998).

There are also many ways of operationally defining discrepancies (Reynolds, 1984; Frederickson and Reason, 1995a; DECP, 1999). The features of a psychometrically satisfactory method are as follows:

- Age-corrected standard scores are essential to the calculations required to calculate and evaluate differences.
- Account must be taken of the correlation between ability and attainment scores in order to allow for the effects of regression to the mean.
- It is essential to evaluate whether the differences between the ability and attainment scores are significantly larger than could happen by chance.
- The frequency of a difference in the population of differences as large as the one under consideration must be estimated.

This definition of underachievement does not necessarily identify SDD (Dobbins, 1994). Where the cut-off lines indicating 'unusualness' in the discrepancy are drawn, is an arbitrary decision. How severe is a 'severe' discrepancy? (McNab, 1994b). Despite this problem, such an explicit, public, replicable first stage in both institutional and individual decision-making has much to commend it. However, a second consideration is the qualitative characteristics of the pattern of pupils' strengths and weaknesses. Different professionals will bring varying perspectives. The final judgement should be made by a multidisciplinary team. Probability rules. Professional judgement is central.

Stanovich (1991, 1994) has suggested that discrepancy definitions of reading disability, using conventionally measured intelligence as an aptitude benchmark, hide untenable assumptions concerning the concept of potential. He has argued for the use of listening comprehension as a more educationally relevant aptitude measure. Interestingly, a variant of this strategy was introduced in the 1950s by the late J. McNally, when he was Principal Educational Psychologist for the City of Manchester. Over a period of years, it proved increasingly effective in raising teachers' expectations of primary school pupils and the pupils' educational achievements. The approach was particularly effective in raising the reading attainments and success in the 11-plus selection examination used at that time to decide the type of secondary school education for each child within a tripartite school system. The mean reading standards and examination successes of pupils from socio-economically deprived areas of the city increased markedly to approximate the overall levels for the city's schools. The system was not intended to identify SDD but aimed to reduce under-achievement, irrespective of its causes. A Remedial Education Service provided support to schools. The system of testing oral comprehension and reading attainment in Junior School Year 2 was later abandoned as the educational system became comprehensive and pupil selection at the age of 11 did not take place. Currently, in the UK, concern about underachievement by pupils and schools is, once again, a government priority. SDD is perceived as one facet of this political and educational challenge.

By use of a regression approach, Stanovich's subsequent work enabled him to test the phonological skills of older poor readers with and without (somewhat small) IQ achievement discrepancies. No significant mean differences in phonological skills were identified (Stanovich and Siegel, 1994). The phonological-core variable-difference hypothesis was also tested across a range of discrepancy criteria by workers in England by use of the *Phonological Assessment Battery* (PhAB) (Gallagher, 1995). Comparison of the differences between normal, poor readers, SDD and 'garden-variety' poor readers were made. The effects of reading age was partialled out for each of the ten tests in the PhAB. The total sample comprised 244 subjects at three levels 6, 8 and 10 years. In summary, it is suggested that the findings of Stanovich and Siegel (1994) 'may be premature, particularly in relation to pupils with the more severe and complex difficulties' (Gallagher and Frederickson, 1995, p. 66). A later publication at the Fourth International Conference of the British Dyslexia Association presents Stanovich's case more fully (Stanovich *et al.*, 1997). The case is not accepted by all workers (Elbrow, 1998).

Within the context of child development and educational psychology, an understanding of both research design and test theory is central to appreciating the technicalities of such approaches:

> No other contribution of psychology has had the social impact equal to that created by the psychological test. No other body of theory in psychology has been so fully rationalised from the mathematical point of view.
> (Guilford, 1952)

Guilford's concern was with what is currently known as 'normative test theory'. Its limitations in education are considerable, but it remains an important approach to the assessment of children's relative attainments and progress. The increasing popularity of a method test construction known as Rasch scaling, based on item response theory, demands that users of tests developed in this way are aware of the technical strengths and weaknesses of the approach (Pumfrey, 1987). Item response theory also underpins two diagnostic batteries developed by Elliott and colleagues. These are widely used by British and American psychologists respectively: the *British Ability Scales* and the *Differential Ability Scales*.

Much has happened since then in the area of assessment and its links with both instruction and motivation (Elliott and Figg, 1993). Increasing importance is accorded to direct observation of the literacy-related behaviours of pupils with SDD, to domain-referenced assessment, diagnostic batteries based on item response theory and informal inventories which include miscue or error analysis (Pumfrey, 1985, 1987, 1991, 1995b, 1999; Blythe and Faulkner, 1994; Turner, 1994, 1995). A greater awareness of the respective strengths and weaknesses of these approaches to assessment would have helped avoid some of the unnecessary and expensive mistakes made with the introduction of the National Curriculum English Standard Assessment Tasks and Teacher Assessments (Pumfrey, 1995e). To use unreliable, and therefore invalid, instruments for such a profile-based decision-making procedure would be likely to result in a very high numbers of false negative and false positive classifications. Albeit belatedly, Her Majesty's Chief Inspector of Schools has acknowledged the unreliability of the Standard Assessment Tasks used by the Qualifications and Curriculum Authority to monitor standards and progress (Cassidy, 1998). This calls into question the validity of use of the results of SATs to determine educationally important discrepancies that may be indicative of dyslexia.

Considerable concern has been expressed about the misuse of published tests in education. Problems arise largely because many users do not have the knowledge to make informed judgements about the strengths and weaknesses for particular decision-making purposes of the published tests that they are using. Many test users have not been trained in test administration, scoring and interpretation (Pumfrey, 1990). There are also indications that poorly designed tests are being produced.

In order to provide a qualification in psychological aspects of educational testing for professionals wishing to use psychological tests, but not having a background in psychology, the British Psychological Society (BPS) Steering Committee on Test Standards has been developing a certification procedure (BPS, 1992; Boyle *et al.*, 1995). The aim is to ensure that users of published tests do so at an acceptable level of competence and hence have the ability to look more critically at SDD screening tests and assessment procedures that are currently in use.

More recent arrivals meriting consideration, but not necessarily adoption, include the 1994 *Dyslexia Screening Instrument* (DSI) from the USA. It is intended to cover the age range 6–21 years. The DSI is based on a rating scale of 33 items to be completed by the student's teacher. Each item is scored on a five-point scale. Using a computer, the ratings are analysed via the *Scoring Programme* software. DSI capitalizes on the potential of 'expert systems' and information technology (Coon *et al.*, 1994). The use of a four-category classification of pupils as 'Passed' (not SDD), 'Failed' (possible SDD) 'Inconclusive' and 'Cannot be scored' is not particularly illuminative. Information concerning the psychometric characteristics of the individual items is not available in the manual. Currently the validity of the DSI is being investigated in a small-scale study in Manchester.

Available English instruments include the *Phonological Assessment Battery* (PhAB) (Gallagher and Frederickson, 1995), the *Dyslexia Early Screening Test* and the *Dyslexia Screening Test* (6;6 to 16;5 years) (Nicolson and Fawcett, 1996a, 1996b). Additionally, the *Cognitive Profiling System* (CoPS) (Singleton, et al. 1996), a *Graded Nonword Reading Test* (Snowling *et al.*, 1996), Wilkins's *Rate of Reading Test* (Wilkins *et al.*, 1996), the *Phonological Abilities Test* (Mutter *et al.*, 1997), and the *Phonological Battery* (PhAB) (Frederickson *et al.*, 1997) are available and in use.

Intelligent Testing with the WISC-III is the challenging title of an important book on diagnostic assessment (Kaufman, 1994). It is extremely helpful in terms of both the psychometric and psychological evaluation of profiles and discrepancies.

The theoretical assumptions on which all such screening and diagnostic tests are based must be made explicit. Evidence of content, concurrent, predictive and construct validities is important. Its psychometric 'Siamese twin', test reliability, also comes in at least four forms in conventional test theory. These are known as internal consistency, stability (test–retest), equivalence (parallel forms) and stability and equivalence. Reliability is a necessary but not sufficient condition for test validity (Pumfrey, 1977, 1985).

Tests are selected to enable hypotheses to be investigated (Pumfrey, 1999). Despite the limitations of psychological tests, the identification of SDD demands that exceptionality be quantified as a necessary but not sufficient condition for diagnosis.

The validity of a sophisticated psychometric approach in clinical work with dyslexic pupils has been well-demonstrated by the Principal Psychologist of the Dyslexia Institute's Psychological Service. He has published information describing and commenting on basic tools used in testing pupils' reading and spelling that has been well-received by many teachers (Turner, 1993, 1994, 1995). For psychologists, he has made challenging contributions concerning the improvement of professional practice in the assessment of SDD in particular (Turner, 1997). The Dyslexia Index that he has developed is an interesting idea based on individualized objective testing. Both his rationale and methodology are explicit. Whether his seven-point scale of dyslexic severity will be seen as fair depends on the validity of the assumptions on which the diagnostic procedures is based (Turner, 1997, pp. 310–20).

In the USA, State criteria and procedures used in the identification of children with learning disabilities vary markedly (Frankenberger and Fronzaglio, 1991). The same is true in relation to the identification of pupils with SDD in LEAs in the UK. Considering the following question indicates why this is likely to remain the case for some time.

Q4 What is the incidence of SDD?

Exploring the links between SDD 'A', 'B' and 'C', is dependent on quantification. The assertion made by the late R.L. Thorndike merits restating: 'Whatever exists, exists in some quantity and can, in principle, be measured'.

Never forget the 'in principle'. Some aspects of assessment are more soundly based than others. An understanding of the various levels of measurement is pertinent. The strengths and weaknesses of nominal, ordinal, interval and ratio scale-based instruments for particular decision-making purposes needs to be understood by test constructors and users.

The challenges of conceptualizing SDD and of operationalizing the concept, remain crucial concerns (Connor, 1994; Turner, 1997; Rispens *et al.*, 1998). As the former Chief Inspector of Schools for England and Wales, Professor Stuart Sutherland, remarked at an interview held in 1992 concerning education in general, '*If you can't measure it, you can't manage it*'. So, too, with SDD. Herein lies a central dilemma related to the establishment of educational priorities and the provision of resources from the public purse (including professional expertise). How can this be achieved in a way accepted as 'fair' to all pupils?

The incidence of SDD is either 4 per cent (severe) or 10 per cent (mild) according to estimates by some organizations, including the British Dyslexia Association (Crisfield, 1996). Such estimates are both theoretically and technically contentious. Establishing a resource allocation decision-making model that is explicit, open, fair and theoretically defensible, requires considerable professional knowledge. Inevitably, it involves subjectivities of professional judgement and the values and assumptions on which such judgements depend. Making the model accord to the law requires additional sensitivities. The management of provision for SDD requires considerable care (Pumfrey, 1995c).

Measurement has many strengths; it also has considerable limitations. Figures can be used as a smokescreen, deliberately or unwittingly. On balance, Sutherland's comment concerning institutional decision-making that must be seen to be open and equitable in the interests of accountability, acknowledges the value of tests, despite their weaknesses.

In the *Division of Educational and Child Psychology Newsletter*, an article entitled 'Dyslexia, perplexia, mislexia' (Anon., 1994) spelled out some of the serious concerns that many professionals having responsibilities for all pupils and all disabilities will recognize. The issue of preferential help for particular groups of children with special educational needs, is a socio-political one (Cornwall, 1995). Entirely legitimate pressure groups attempt to influence national policies, priorities and resource allocations.

Q5 How might SDD be prevented?

Early identification, though fraught with the many dangers of false positive and false negative identifications, may help. So, too, would raising professional awareness of SDD and more clearly specifying constructive approaches to its identification and alleviation as a part of initial teacher training and INSET (Layton and Deeny, 1995; Pumfrey, 1995d). In relation to children with SpLDs, the Special Education Needs Training Consortium (SENTC) has presented a report which includes a specification of the professional competencies required by the teachers of such pupils (SENTC, 1996). More recently, the Teacher Training Agency (TTA) has issued a consultation paper concerning the standards of knowledge, understanding and skills required of Special Educational Needs Specialist Teachers (TTA, 1998).

It is vital to distinguish between socio-political and scientific considerations in decision-making. In England and Wales, the government accepts that SDD exists and comprises a subset of SpLDs. SDD is acknowledged in law, in the Code of Practice on the Identification and Assessment of Special Educational Needs, in Circular 6/94, and in the beliefs of many citizens (Chastey and Friel, 1993; DfE and Welsh Office, 1994; DfE, 1994a, 1994b; DfEE, 1998a; Smythe, 2000).

Despite this socio-political and legally enshrined confidence concerning the existence of SDD, some professionals disagree concerning the validity of the concept (Presland, 1991; Young and Tyre, 1983; McGuinness, 1998). Those who accept the validity of the concept often differ when methods of identification are considered. It follows that professional opinions currently differ markedly concerning the nature of SDD, its identification, incidence and alleviation. Uncertainties exist and are likely to continue (Pumfrey and Reason, 1992; Miles, 1993; Nicolson and Fawcett, 1995; Seymour, 1994; Ellis et al., 1997a, 1997b; Frith, 1995, 1997; Klein and McMullen, 1999).

In connection with the case of a young person deemed to have SDD, the following comment was made by the Law Lords: 'The failure to treat his condition which would have improved had it been correctly diagnosed and treated, has disadvantaged the individual' (*The Times*, 1995).

There is an interesting circularity in this argument based on the suspect assumption that a suitable treatment was available and would have been effective. It depends on what one means by effective. Does this imply that the individual's attainments in literacy skills should approximate some agreed index of intellectual ability?

Professionals should be aware of what can be regarded as the limits of their reasonable expertise. They should also be extremely careful in what they say, write or recommend in the service of their employers. Technical aspects of assessment and the interpretation of test results are important areas. The Association of Educational Psychologists (AEP) and the Division of Educational and Child Psychology of the British Psychological Society (DECP) have circulated a document providing guidance for educational psychologists concerning the statutory advice that they are required to provide to LEAs (AEP and DECP, 1995). The Division of Educational and Child Psychology of the British Psychological Society Working Party's report entitled *Dyslexia, Literacy and Psychological Assessment* provides a current review of research (DECP, 1999).

In summary, socio-political considerations largely determine the official recognition of SDD. Only in part is such recognition a result of scientific knowledge. The prevention of SDD depends on capitalizing on the promise in existing imperfect knowledge and continuing to expand the existing multi-disciplinary professional knowledge base.

Q6 How may SDD be alleviated?

Moving to the 1990s, promising educational practices are myriad (Pumfrey, 1991; Pumfrey and Reason, 1992; Reid, 1993, 1994; Reason and Boote, 1994; Reid, 1996a, 1996b; Ott, 1997; Reid, 1998; Reitsma and Verhoeven, 1998; Miles and Miles, 1999; Robertson, 1999). Some workers consider that it is possible theoretically to define, identify and remediate the core deficits of SDD. The situation may be summarized as 'Variety: neither consensus nor panacea'. We can learn from studies of the outcomes of interventions with pupils with SDD (Lovett, 1999). When considering such studies, it is essential to consider the quality of the evidence on which the case for a particular intervention is based.

The potential of information technology in facilitating the identification and alleviation of SDD is immense and developing at a rapid rate (Singleton, 1994; Boutskou, 1995; Singleton et al., 1996; Blamires, 1999). Special Educational Needs Information Technology (SENIT) is a computer-based network of individuals interested and involved in using and developing various applications of information technology in addressing obstacles to learning experienced by those with special educational needs in general. The SENIT list is supported by the government. Its address is <senit@ngfl.gov.uk>. The British Dyslexia Association Computer Committee is a helpful source on Information Communications Technology (ICT) for dyslexic individuals (Cotgrove, 2000).

Among the rapidly growing number of commercial suppliers of ICT for dyslexic students, Dyslectech from Iansyst Training Products merits consideration (its web page address is http://www.dyslexic.com). Multidisciplinary interest is considerable as the work of neuropsychologists such as Bakker (1990, 1994, 1997) and teachers (Robertson, 1999) demonstrates. Research by vision scientists such as Wilkins, formerly of the Medical Research Council Applied Psychology Unit at Cambridge and now holder of a Chair in the Department of Psychology at the University of Essex (Wilkins et al., 1996), and Stein of the University Laboratory of Physiology at Oxford, testifies to activity in this field. In the USA the use of drug treatments, for example ritalin, with dyslexic pupils is considerable, growing and controversial (Pumfrey and Reason, 1992). The drug is also increasingly being prescribed for dyslexic pupils in the UK.

At a series of workshops with practising educational psychologists and specialist support teachers, the following information was elicited concerning psychomedical interventions available within their LEAs, albeit not necessarily through the LEA (Table 15.1). No claim for either comprehensiveness or representativeness of this 'convenience' sample of professionals is made. Despite this caveat, some interventions were more frequently reported than others. The table supports the proposition that SDD is not a unitary condition.

Based on earlier work by Stordy of the University of Surrey and published in the *Lancet* on 5 August 1995, a proposal to study the effects of docosahexaenoic acid in a randomized placebo-controlled study with children identified as dyslexic has been suggested. The aim is to test the effects on auditory information processing and phonological abilities in children identified as being dyslexic.

The simultaneous consideration of all children's literacy development must accompany the search for individuals and groups of pupils with SDD. Bakker's Balance Theory of the development of literacy addresses both normal

Table 15.1 Pupils with SpLD (SDD): psychomedical interventions*

	Used in your LEA	
	Yes	Rank order
Neuropsychological interventions		
Perceptual development	26	6
Dominance training	15	= 9
Reprogramming	0	= 20
Neurological impress method	1	= 18
Hemispheric Specific Stimulation (HSS)	1	= 18
Hemispheric Alluding Stimulation (HAS)	3	= 14
ARROW (Aural, Read, Respond, Oral, Written)	5	13
Others	0	= 20
Psycho-ophthalmological interventions		
Occlusion	74	2
Cambridge optical lenses	15	= 9
Flicker distortions	2	= 16
Visual pattern distortions	2	= 16
Irlen coloured overlays	96	1
Irlen lenses	45	3
Binocular stability tracking	18	8
Prismatic lenses	3	= 14
Others	0	= 20
Dietary and psychopharmaceutical interventions		
Vitamins	43	4
Trace elements	19	7
Antihistamines	12	11
Food additives	40	5
Psychostimulants (including ritalin)	8	12
Nootropics	0	= 20
Others	0	= 20

*Replies from 81 educational psychologists and 291 specialist teachers (opportunity samples).

development and the identification of groups of pupils showing important vari-ations based on differential hemispheric development. Bakker is the former Head of the Research Department at the Paedological Institute and Professor of Child Neuropsychology at the Free University, Amsterdam. According to his Balance Theory of reading development, reading is initially mainly perceptual. If right-hemisphere strategies fail to shift to predominantly left-hemisphere strategies, children remain using right-hemisphere strategies. Such children remain particularly sensitive to the perceptual features of text and make characteristic mistakes when reading. These include a high frequency of fragmentation errors. Such pupils are called P- (Perceptual) type dyslexics. In contrast, other pupils generate mainly left-hemisphere strategies when starting to learn to read. They show a high frequency of substantive errors such as omissions and additions. These pupils are called L- (Linguistic) type dyslexics. Bakker argues for the stimulation of the underused hemispheric func-tions. He has developed two interventions. The first is called hemispheric-specific stimulation (HSS); the second, hemispheric-alluding stimulation (HAS). The former is achieved by presenting reading materials in the left visual half-field of L-types and in the right visual half-field of P-types. This can be done by use of a specially devised computer program called HEMSTIM (Moerland and Bakker, 1991) or by the use of a tactile training box. HAS for L-type dylsexics is based on the presentation of perceptually demanding text: for P-type dyslexics, a range of linguistically challenging materials is used (Licht and Spyer, 1995).

Bakker's work in developing intervention programmes provides one of the better examples of a theoretically based identification of potentially important Aptitude Instruction interactions. What works for subjects of perceptual dyslexia (P-type) differs from interventions of value to subjects of linguistic dyslexia (L-type) (Bakker, 1990, 1994; Bakker et al., 1994; Licht and Spyer, 1995; Robertson, 1999; Robertson and Pumfrey, in press). The results from one of Bakker's major studies using a tactile training box are summarized below (Figure 15.2).

The findings are promising. Work in this field is currently being carried out in Manchester (Robertson, 1999; Robertson and Pumfrey, in press).

Conclusion

SDD is a complex syndrome and its manifestations change as the child matures. There are no easy answers to understanding the complexities of SDD; no single agreed approach to its identification; no unequivocal method of estimating incidence, no unambiguous agreement on methods of either prevention or alleviation. On the positive side, there are many promising practices. Central to all of these is the importance of making explicit and replicable whatever is done. Measurement matters.

The nature of research is hydra-headed: one question answered raises others to be addressed. This suggests that pupils, parents, politicians and professionals

56 remedial teachers; 98 pupils; IQ > 80	
L-type (N = 59) Mean chronological age 10;06 years Mean reading-age 7;05 years HSS to right hemisphere Use left hand to palpate letters (out of sight) on board Use words with concrete meanings (e.g. bike)	P-type (N = 49) Mean chronological age 9;04 years Mean reading age 7;02 years HSS to left hemisphere Use right hand to palpate letters (out of sight) on board Use more abstract words (e.g. cold, love)
Single letters, words, sentences	
20 sessions, 2 sessions per week	
Experimental group (N = 28) Predict decrease in substantive errors Control group (N = 21)	Experimental group (N = 26) Predict increase in fluency Control group (N = 23)
RESULTS	
L-type relative to control subjects: larger improvement in accuracy of reading P-type relative to control subjects: larger improvement in fluency	

Figure 15.2 Effects of hemisphere-specific stimulation (HSS).

would be well-advised to learn to live with legitimate doubts concerning the nature, identification, incidence, prognosis and alleviation of SDD. Acknowledging and accepting uncertainties is an essential prerequisite to addressing them. In this respect, the paradoxes identified and the tensions they represent hold promise for the extension of knowledge in all the questions posed earlier. Parents say 'Neither we, nor our children, can afford to wait'. In my judgement, they are correct.

The socio-political dimensions of values, resources and priorities in a democratic society, including the involvement of the legal system in decisions concerning SDD, are ones in which individually and collectively citizens have a powerful voice. What type of society and educational system would we wish for our children and ourselves? How much are the citizens of our respective countries willing to pay in taxes to reduce the undoubted adverse effects on individuals of SDD?

Legitimate professional disagreements concerning the nature, identification, incidence and alleviation of SDD are viewed with great impatience by many parents. Simple solutions to complex learning difficulties are often, albeit unrealistically, expected. In England and Wales, an increasing number of cases of pupils with SDD are being taken by parents before the courts, to the Ombudsman and to SEN Tribunals in the quest for additional resources. If class sizes for pupils over seven years of age increase, as advocated publicly by the current Chief HMI Woodhead in November 1995, this is unlikely to make it easier for teachers to provide the support that pupils with SDD require. Woodhead acknowledges that small classes do benefit pupils with special educational needs and also lower-attaining pupils in secondary schools. In 1995, reducing class size to a maximum of 30 for pupils under the age of seven was estimated to cost about £180 million per annum. In 2001 this class size reduction should be achieved. If, however, the resources required to reduce class size were used to improve teachers' skills in identifying and alleviating literacy difficulties in general, and SDD in particular, there could be benefits to many pupils. Raising public awareness concerning the antecedents, concomitants, consequences and costs of SDD inevitably increases parental expectations of the public services whose existence is to facilitate children's learning. Psychologists' and teachers' expertise, is central. So, too, is that of many other professions.

The answer to the question 'How much should the nation invest in improving the literacy of pupils deemed to have SDD?' lies in citizens' collective hands. It is a responsibility of all citizens, not solely that of experts.

In terms of professional knowledge, 'If a man begin with certainties, he shall end in doubts; but if he will be content to begin with doubts, he shall end in certainties'. Thus wrote Bacon 395 years ago in *The Advancement of Learning*. Forgiving the sexist anachronism, the maxim stands the test of time. Even though the horizon of 'certainties' in relation to SDD is unlikely to be reached in the near future, there is considerable evidence to show that progress is being made. There *are* professional basics to back.

References

Adams, M.J. (1990) *Beginning to Read: Thinking and Learning about Print*. Cambridge, MA: MIT Press.

Anon. (1994) Dyslexia, perplexia, mislexia. *Division of Educational & Child Psychology Newsletter* 62: 37–8.

Association of Educational Psychologists and the Division of Education and Child Psychology of the British Psychological Society (1995) *Statutory Advice to the LEA: Guidance for Educational Psychologists*. Leicester: British Psychological Society.

Bakker, D.J. (1990) *Neuropsychological Treatment of Dyslexia*. New York: Oxford University Press.

Bakker, D.J. (1994) Dyslexia and the ecological brain. *Journal of Clinical and Experimental Neuropsychology* 16: 734–43.

Bakker, D.J. (1997) Dyslexia in terms of space and time. *Abstracts*. Fourth World Congress on Dyslexia, Halkidiki, Macedonia, Greece, 23–26 September; 7.

Bakker, D.J., Licht, R., Kappers, E.J. (1994) Techniques in children with dyslexia. In: M.G. Tramontana, S.R. Hooper (eds). *Advances in Child Neuropsychology*, Vol. 3. New York: Springer Verlag; 144–47.

Blamires, M. (ed.) (1999) *Enabling Technology for Inclusion*. London: Paul Chapman Publishing.

Blyth, C., Faulkner, J. (1994) To test or not to test, that is the question. *Division of Educational and Child Psychology Newsletter* 62: 27–35.

Boutskou, E. (1995) Computers and Specific Learning Difficulties (Literacy) in the Primary School. Unpublished MEd dissertation, Centre for Special Needs, School of Education, The University of Manchester.

Boyle, J., Dinham, H., Rust, J.N., Williams, T., Bland, S. (1995) Checklist of Competences in Educational Testing: Foundation Level. Consultation document. Leicester: British Psychological Society Steering Committee on Test Standards, September.

British Psychological Society Standing Committee on Test Standards (1992) *Psychological Testing: A Guide*. Leicester: British Psychological Society.

Cassidy, S. (1998) 'Tests are unreliable' says chief inspector. *Times Educational Supplement* 18 December.

Chase, C.H., Rosen, G.D., Sherman, G.F. (1996) *Developmental Dyslexia: Neural, Cognitive and Genetic Mechanisms*. Parkland, MD: York Press.

Chastey, H., Friel, J. (1993) *Children with Special Needs, Assessment, Law and Practice – Caught in the Act* (second edition). London: Kingsley.

Coles, G. (2000) *Misreading Reading. The Bad Science that Hurts Children*. Portsmouth, NH: Heinemann.

Committee of Enquiry into the Education of Handicapped Children and Young People (1978). Special Educational Needs (Warnock Report) Cmnd. 7212. London: HMSO.

Connor, M.J. (1994) Dyslexia (SpLD): assessing assessment. *Educational Psychology in Practice* 10: 131–9.

Coon, K.B., Waguespack, M.M., Polk, M.J. (1994) *Dyslexia Screening Instrument*. San Antonio, CA: The Psychological Corporation.

Cornwall, J. (ed.) (1995) Psychology, disability and equal opportunity. *The Psychologist* (Special Issue) 8: 396–418.

Cotgrove, A. (2000) Voice activated systems. In: I. Smythe (ed.) *The Dyslexia Handbook 2000*. Reading: British Dyslexia Association; 189–96.

Crisfield, J. (1996) *The Dyslexia Handbook 1996*. Reading, British Dyslexic Association.

DeFries, J.C. (1991) Genetics and dyslexia: an overview. In: M. Snowling, M. Thomson (eds). *Dyslexia: Integrating Theory and Practice*. London: Whurr Publishers; 3–20.

DeFries, J.C., Alarcon, M., Olson, R.K. (1997) Genetic aetiologies of reading and spelling deficits: developmental differences. In: C. Hulme, M. Snowling (eds). *Dyslexia: Biology, Cognition and Intervention*. London: Whurr Publishers; 20–37.

DfE (1994a) *The Organisation of Special Educational Provision*. Circular No 6/94. London: DfE.

DfE (1994b) *Special Educational Needs Tribunal: How to Appeal*. London: DfE.

DfE and the Welsh Office (1994) *Code of Practice on the Identification and Assessment of Special Educational Needs*. London: Central Office of Information.

DfEE (1998a) *The National Literacy Strategy Framework for Teaching, including additional guidance for children with English as an additional language (EAL) and children with Special Educational Needs (SEN)*. London: DfEE.

DfEE (1998b) Pamphlet: *How Can I Tell if a Child may be Dyslexic? Handy Hints for Primary School Teachers*. London: DfEE.

Division of Educational and Child Psychology of the British Psychological Society (DECP) (1999) *Dyslexia, Literacy and Psychological Assessment. Report by a Working Party Chaired by Dr R. Reason.* Leicester: British Psychological Society.

Dobbins, A. (1994) Expected reading scores of pupils in Years 3 to 6. *British Journal of Educational Psychology* 64: 491–6.

Duane, D.D. (1991) Neurobiological issues in dyslexia. In: M. Snowling, M. Thomson (eds). *Dyslexia: Integrating Theory and Practice.* London: Whurr Publishers; 21–30.

Edwards, J. (1994) *The Scars of Dyslexia: Eight Case Studies in Emotional Reactions.* London: Cassell.

Elbrow, C. (1998) Reading–listening discrepancy definitions of dyslexia. In: P. Reitsma, L. Verhoeven (eds). *Problems and Interventions in Literacy Development.* London: Kluwer; 129–46.

Elliott, C.D. (1990) The definition and identification of specific learning difficulties. In: P.D. Pumfrey, C.D. Elliott (eds). *Children's Difficulties in Reading, Spelling and Writing* (third edition). Basingstoke: Falmer Press; 14–28.

Elliott, C.D. (1994) *British Ability Scales: A 'G-enhanced' Short-form IQ.* Windsor: NFER-Nelson.

Elliott, J., Figg, J. (1993) Assessment issues. *Educational and Child Psychology* 10: whole edition; 80 pp.

Ellis, A.W., McDougall, S.J.P., Monk, A.F. (1997a) Are dyslexics different? III. Of course they are! *Dyslexia: An International Journal of Research and Practice* 3: 2–8.

Ellis, A.W., McDougall, S.J.P., Monk, A.F. (1997b) Are dyslexics different? IV. In defence of uncertainty. *Dyslexia: An International Journal of Research and Practice* 3: 12–14.

Fawcett, A., Nicolson, R. (eds) (1994) *Dyslexia in Children: Multidisciplinary Perspectives.* Hemel Hempstead: Prentice Hall.

Frankenberger, W., Fronzaglio, K. (1991) 'A review of states' criteria and procedures for identifying children with learning disabilities. *Journal of Learning Disabilities* 24: 495–500.

Frederickson, N., Reason, R. (1995a) Discrepancy definitions of specific learning difficulties. *Educational Psychology in Practice* 10: 195–205.

Frederickson, N., Reason, R. (1995b) Phonological assessment of specific learning difficulties. *Educational and Child Psychology* 12: whole edition; 88 pp.

Frederickson, N., Frith, U., Reason, R. (1997) *Phonological Assessment Battery (PhAB).* Windsor: NFER-Nelson.

Frith, U. (1995) Dyslexia: Can we have a shared theoretical framework? *Educational and Child Psychology* 12: 6–17.

Frith, U. (1997) Brain, mind and behaviour in dyslexia. In: C. Hulme, M. Snowling. *Dyslexia: Biology, Cognition and Intervention.* London: Whurr Publishers; 1–19.

Gallagher, A. (1995) The development of a phonological assessment battery: research background. *Educational and Child Psychology* 12: 18–24.

Gallagher, A., Frederickson, N. (1995) The phonological assessment battery (PhAB): an initial assessment of its theoretical and practical utility. *Educational and Child Psychology* 12.

Gjessing, H.J., Karlson, B. (1989) *A Longitudinal Study of Dyslexia.* New York: Springer-Verlag.

Gough, P.B. (1995) The New Literacy: caveat emptor. *Journal of Research in Reading* 18: 79–86.

Guilford, J.P. (1952) *Psychometric Methods.* New York: McGraw-Hill.

Hammersley, M. (1995) Opening up the quantitative–qualitative divide. *Education Section Review* 19: 2–9.

Hulme, C., Joshi, R.M. (1998) *Reading and Spelling: Development and Disorders*. London: Lawrence Erlbaum.

Hulme, C., Snowling, M. (eds) (1994) *Reading Development and Dyslexia*. London: Whurr Publishers.

Hulme, C., Snowling, M. (1997) *Dyslexia: Biology, Cognition and Intervention*. London: Whurr Publishers.

Jeanes, R., Martin, J., Lewis, E., Stevenson, N., Pointon, D., Wilkins, A.J. (1997) Prolonged use of coloured overlays for classroom reading. *British Journal of Psychology* 88: 531–48.

Kaufmann, A. (1994) *Intelligent Testing with the WISC-III*. New York: Wiley.

Klein, R.M., McMullen, P.A. (eds) (1999) *Converging Methods for Understanding Reading and Dyslexia*. Cambridge, MA: MIT Press.

Layton, L., Deeny, K. (1995) Tackling literacy difficulties: can teacher training meet the challenge? *British Journal of Special Education* 22: 20–23.

Lazo, M., Pumfrey, P., Peers, I. (1997) Metalinguistic awareness, reading and spelling: the roots and branches of literacy. *Journal of Research in Reading* 20: 85–104.

Licht, R., Spyer, G. (1995) *The Balance Model of Dyslexia: Theoretical and Clinical Progress*. Assen: Van Gorcum.

Lovett, M.W. (1999) Defining and remediating the core deficits of developmental dyslexia: lessons from remedial outcome research with reading disabled children. In: R.M. Klein, P.A. McMullen (eds). *Convening Methods for Understanding Reading and Dyslexia*. Cambridge, MA: MIT Press; 111–32.

McGuinness, D. (1998) *Why Children Can't Read and What We Can Do About It. A Scientific Revolution in Reading*. Harmondsworth: Penguin.

McNab, I. (1994a) *The Benefits of the British Ability Scales 'g-enhanced' Short-form IQ*. Windsor: NFER-Nelson.

McNab, I. (1994b) *Specific Learning Difficulties: How Severe is Severe?* British Ability Scales Information booklet. Windsor: NFER-Nelson.

Miles, T.R. (1993) *Dyslexia: The Pattern of Difficulties* (second edition). London: Whurr Publishers.

Miles, T.R., Miles, E. (1999) *Dyslexia: A Hundred Years On* (second edition). Buckingham: Open University Press.

Moerland, R., Bakker, D.J. (1991) *Hemispheric Stimulation (HEMSTIM). A computer based treatment program for children with P-type or L-type dyslexia*. Netherlands: Centrum Informatica voor Gehandicapten.

Morgan, W.P. (1896) A case study of congenital word blindness. *British Medical Journal* 2: 1378.

Mutter, V., Hulme, C., Snowling, M.J. (1997) *Phonological Abilities Test*. San Francisco, CA: The Psychological Corporation.

Neuman, S.B., McCormick, S. (eds) (1995) *Single Subject Experimental Research: Application for Literacy*. Newark DE: International Reading Association.

Nicolson, R.I., Fawcett, A.J. (1995) Dyslexia is more than a phonological disability. *Journal of Dyslexia* 1: 19–36.

Nicolson, R.I., Fawcett, A.J. (1996a) *The Dyslexia Early Screening Test*. New York: Psychological Corporation.

Nicolson, R.I., Fawcett, A.J. (1996b) *The Dyslexia Screening Test (6;6 to 16;5 Years)*. New York: Psychological Corporation.

Olson, R.K., Datta, H., Gayan, J., DeFries, J. (1999) A behavioural genetic analysis of reading disabilities and component processes. In: R.M. Klein, P.A. McMullen (eds). *Converging Methods for Understanding Reading and Dyslexia*. Cambridge, MA: MIT Press; 133–52.

Orton Dyslexia Society (ODS) (1994a) Dyslexia: definition by ODS members. *Perspectives in Dyslexia*, 3015.

Orton Dyslexia Society (ODS) (1994b) Dyslexia: definition by ODS Research Committee. *Perspectives in Dyslexia*, 3015.

Ott, P. (1997) *How to Detect and Manage Dyslexia. A Reference and Resource Manual.* London: Heinemann.

Presland, J. (1991) Explaining away dyslexia. *Education Psychology in Practice* 6: 215–21.

Pumfrey, P.D. (1977) *Measuring Reading Abilities: Concepts, Sources and Applications.* London: Hodder & Stoughton.

Pumfrey, P.D. (1985) *Reading: Tests and Assessment Techniques* (second edition). Sevenoaks: Hodder & Stoughton in association with the UK Reading Association.

Pumfrey, P.D. (1987) Rasch scaling and reading tests. *Journal of Research in Reading* 10: 75–86.

Pumfrey, P.D. (1990) Testing and teaching pupils with reading difficulties. In: P.D. Pumfrey, C.D. Elliott (eds). *Children's Difficulties in Reading, Spelling & Writing.* Basingstoke: Falmer Press; 187–208.

Pumfrey, P.D. (1991) *Improving Reading in the Junior School.* London: Cassell.

Pumfrey, P.D. (1993) Focus on dyslexia: coloured overlays and tinted spectacles. *Special!*: 44–6.

Pumfrey, P.D. (1995a) Open dialogue: peer commentary on 'Opening up the quantitative–qualitative divide' by M. Hammersley. *Education Section Review* 19: 13–15.

Pumfrey, P.D. (1995b) Assessing and teaching children with specific developmental dyslexia (SDD): issues and promising practices. In: G. Shiel, U.N. Dhalaigh, B. O'Reilly (eds). *Reading Development to Age 15.* Dublin: Reading Association of Ireland; 3–12.

Pumfrey, P.D. (1995c) The management of specific learning difficulties (dyslexia); challenges and responses. In: I. Lunt, B. Norwich, V. Varma (eds). *Psychology and Education for Special Needs: Recent Developments and Future Directions.* London: Ashgate; 45–70.

Pumfrey, P.D. (1995d) Specific learning difficulties: implications of research findings for the initial and in-service training of teachers. In: P. Mittler, P. Daunt (eds). *Teacher Education for Special Education Needs in Europe.* London: Cassell; 94–105.

Pumfrey, P.D. (1995e) Reading Standards at Key Stage 1: aspirations and evidence. In: P. Owen, P.D. Pumfrey (eds). *Children Learning to Read: International Concerns* Vol. 2. *Curriculum and Assessment Issues: Messages for Teachers.* London: Falmer Press; 135–54.

Pumfrey, P.D. (1996) *Specific Developmental Dyslexia: Basics to back?* Leicester: British Psychological Society.

Pumfrey, P.D. (1999) Reading: testing. In: B. Spolsky (ed.). *Concise Encyclopedia of Educational Linguistics.* Amsterdam: Elsevier; 459–62.

Pumfrey, P.D., Reason, R. (1991) Emotional and social factors, specific difficulties. In P.D. Pumfrey, R. Reason (eds). *Specific Learning Difficulties (Dyslexia): Challenges and Responses.* London: Routledge; 64–74.

Pumfrey, P.D., Reason, R. (1991) *Specific Learning Difficulties (Dyslexia): Challenges and Responses.* London: Routledge.

Pumfrey, P.D., Elliott, C.D., McNab, I., Turner, M., Tyler, S. (1998) Reactions to 'Understanding and managing dyslexia: guidelines for educational psychologists' by R.J. (Sean) Cameron. *Division of Educational and Child Psychology Newsletter* 81: 19–31. *DECP Newsletter* 84, April: 42–55.

Rack, J. (1995) Steps towards a more explicit definition of dyslexia. *Dyslexia Review* 7: 1–13.

Reason, R., Boote, R. (1994) *Helping Children with Reading and Spelling: A Special Needs Manual*. London: Routledge.

Reid, G. (ed.) (1993) *Specific Learning Difficulties (Dyslexia). Perspectives on Practice*. Edinburgh: Moray House Publications.

Reid, G. (1994) Dyslexia and Metacognitivie Assessment. Paper presented at the Third British Dyslexia Association International Conference on Dyslexia, Manchester University, and in *Links* II 1: 38–44.

Reid, G. (1995) *Specific Learning Difficulties (Dyslexia): A Handbook for Study and Practice*. Edinburgh: Moray House Publications.

Reid, G. (ed.) (1996a) *Dimensions of Dyslexia Volume 1: Assessment, Teaching and the Curriculum*. Edinburgh: Moray House Publications.

Reid, G. (ed.) (1996b) *Dimensions of Dyslexia Volume 2: Language and Learning*. Edinburgh: Moray House Publications.

Reid, G. (1998) *Dyslexia: A Practitioners Handbook* (second edition). Chichester: Wiley.

Reitsma, P., Verhoeven, L. (eds) (1998) *Problems and Interventions in Literacy Development*. London: Kluwer.

Reynolds, C. (1984) Critical measurement issues in learning disabilities. *Journal of Special Education* 18: 451–76.

Riddick, B. (1996) *Living with Dyslexia. The Social and Emotional Consequences of Specific Learning Difficulties*. London: Routledge.

Rispens, J., van Ypern, T.A., Yule, W. (1998) *Perspectives on the Classification of Specific Developmental Disorders*. London: Kluwer.

Robertson, J. (1999) *Dyslexia and Reading: A Neuropsychological Approach*. London: Whurr Publishers.

Robertson, J., Pumfrey, P.D. (in press) Differential teaching of pupils with dyslexia: bye-way or highway? *British Journal of Special Education* 27.

Ruddell, B.R., Ruddell, M.R. (1994) Language acquisition and literacy processes. In: B.R. Ruddell, M.R. Ruddell, H. Singer (eds). *Theoretical Models and Processes of Reading* (fourth edition). Newark, DA: International Reading Association; 83–103.

Ruddell, B., Ruddell, M.R., Singer, H. (eds) (1994) *Theoretical Models and Processes of Reading* (fourth edition). Newark DA: International Reading Association.

Sampson, O.C. (1975a) Fifty years of dyslexia: a review of the literature, 1925–75. I: Theory. *Research in Education* 14: 15–32.

Sampson, O.C. (1975b) *Remedial Education*. London: Routledge & Kegan Paul.

Sampson, O.C. (1976) Fifty years of dyslexia: a review of the literature, 1925–75. II: Practice, *Research in Education* 15: 39–54.

Scholes, R.J. (1998) The case against phonemic awareness. *Journal of Research in Reading* 21: 177–88.

Schonell, F.J., Wall, W.D. (1949) Remedial education centre. *Education Review* 2: 3–30.

Seymour, P. (1994) Variability in dyslexia. In: C. Hulme, M. Snowling (eds). *Reading Development and Dyslexia*. London: Whurr Publishers; 65–85.

Singleton, C.H. (ed.) (1994) *Computers and Dyslexia: Educational Applications of New Technology*. University of Hull: Computer Resource Centre.

Singleton, C.H., Thomas, K.V., Leedale, R.C. (1996) *Cognitive Profiling System (CoPS)*. Beverley: Lucid Research.

Snowling, M.J. (1995) Phonological processing and developmental dyslexia. *Journal of Research in Reading* 18: 132-8.

Snowling, M.J. (1999) Reading difficulties. In: B. Spolsky (ed.). *The Concise Encyclopedia of Educational Linguistics*. Amsterdam: Elsevier; 451–2.

Snowling, M.J., Stothard, S.E., McClean, J. (1996) *Graded Nonword Reading Test*. Bury St Edmunds: Thames Valley Test Company.

Special Educational Needs Training Consortium (1996) *Professional Development to Meet Special Education Needs*. Report to the Department for Education and Employment. SENTC: Institute of Education, University of London.

Stanovich, K.E. (1991) Discrepancy definitions of reading disability; has intelligence led us astray? *Reading Research Quarterly* 36: 7–29.

Stanovich, K.E. (1994) Annotation: does dyslexia exist? *Journal of Child Psychology and Psychiatry* 21: 7–9.

Stanovich, K.E., Siegel, L. (1994) Phenotypic profile of children with reading disabilities: a regression-based test of the phonological-core variable-difference model. *Journal of Learning Disabilities* 21: 590–612.

Stanovich, K.E., Siegel, L.S., Gottardo, A. (1997) Progress in the search for dyslexic subtypes. In: C. Hulme, M. Snowling (eds). *Dyslexia: Biology, Cognition and Intervention*. London: Whurr Publishers; 108–30.

Stein, J.F., Walsh, K.E. (1997) To see; but not to read. The magnocellular theory of dyslexia. *Trends in Neuroscience* 20: 147–51.

Stuart, M. (1998) Response to Scholes (1998). Let the Emperor retain his underclothes. *Journal of Research in Reading* 21: 189–94.

Teacher Training Agency (TTA) (1998) *National Standards for Special Educational Needs (SEN) Specialist Teachers*. London: Teacher Training Agency.

The Times (1995) *Law Report*. 30 June.

Tizard, J. (1972) *Children with Specific Reading Difficulties. Report of the Advisory Committee on Handicapped Children*. London: HMSO.

Turner, M. (1993) *Testing Times* (a two-part review of tests of literacy). *Part 1: Special Children* 65, April; *Part 2: Special Children* 66, May.

Turner, M. (1994) Quantifying exceptionality: issues in the psychological assessment of dyslexia. In: G. Hales (ed.). *Dyslexia Matters*. London: Whurr Publishers; 109–26.

Turner, M. (1995) Assessing reading: layers and levels. *Dyslexia Review* 7: 15–19.

Turner, M. (1997) *Psychological Assessment of Dyslexia*. London: Whurr Publishers.

Wilkins, A., Evans, B.J.W., Brown, J.A., Busby, A.E., Wingfield, A.E., Jeanes, R.J., Bald, J. (1994) Double-masked placebo-controlled trial of precision spectral filters in children who use coloured overlays. *Ophthalmic and Physiological Optics* 14: 365–70.

Wilkins, A.J., Jeanes, R.J., Pumfrey, P.D., Laskier, M. (1996) Rate of reading test: its reliability, and its validity in the assessment of the effects of coloured overlays. *Ophthalmic and Physiological Optics* 16: 491–7.

Willows, D.M., Kruk, R.S., Corcos, E. (eds) (1993) *Visual Processes in Reading and Reading Disabilities*. Hillsdale, NJ: Lawrence Erlbaum.

Young, P., Tyre, C. (1983) *Dyslexia or Illiteracy? Realising the Right to Read*. Milton Keynes: Open University Press.

Source

This is an edited version of a chapter previously published in M. Hunter-Carsch (ed.) *Dyslexia: A Psychological Perspective*. 2001. Reproduced by permission of Whurr Publishers Ltd.

Chapter 16

Multisensory teaching of reading in mainstream settings

Mike Johnson

Introduction

As Johnson and Phillips (1999) note, research has consistently indicated the importance of phonological awareness as a prerequisite for reading acquisition. In addition, interventions focusing on phonics are the most successful when they relate directly to the reading process. This chapter aims to summarise and discuss an evaluation study of three published schemes designed to promote phonological awareness through a structured, multisensory approach against the author's understanding of the national literacy curriculum context within which individual programmes or strategies have to operate.

Developments in the national literacy curricular context

For many years there has been an almost annual debate about pupils' reading standards and methods of teaching. Some very dubious comparisons have been made and partisan positions taken up. Callaghan's 'Great Debate' and the subsequent 'Black Papers' (e.g. Cox, 1970) are dramatic examples of these confrontations. However, little co-ordinated action resulted. Even the introduction of the National Curriculum was more concerned with content than pedagogy.

The establishment of the Special Educational Needs (SEN) Tribunals as part of the mechanisms underlying the SEN Code of Practice (DfEE, 1994) had a greater effect and has provoked considerable discussion and concern relating to the rising number of pupils being given the protection of Statements of Special Educational Needs, many of whom are diagnosed as dyslexic. Appeals to the SEN Tribunal are costly in terms of both specialist time and resources. Further concern has been generated by successful litigation against schools and LEAs for inappropriate teaching and subsequent awards of significant damages and costs.

The results are that:

- LEAs sometimes seek to discontinue existing statements or are reluctant to assess for them in the first place;

- specialist services are overburdened and pupils do not get the individual attention awarded to them in the statement;
- schools and teachers may feel abandoned;
- parents become concerned that their child's needs are not being met;
- many children with significant, but not severe needs are not being allocated the resources to meet their needs.

The National Literacy Strategy

In a proactive approach to this situation David Blunkett, the then Shadow Secretary of State for Education and Employment, set up the Literacy Task-force in May 1996. With the change of Government in 1997 the National Literacy Strategy (NLS) was developed from its work. The aim was to raise the standards of literacy in English primary schools over a five- to ten-year period and naturally attracted a great deal of comment. Some was both provocative and inaccurate: 'Scots throw down literacy gauntlet' (*Times Educational Supplement*, October 1998); 'Literacy Hour is "too long"' (*Times Educational Supplement*, November, 1998). The former refers to the distinction between analytic and synthetic phonics in the teaching of reading and spelling (Watson and Johnston, 1998), the latter to the Early Reading Research Project (ERR) (Solity *et al.*, 1999).

In *Analytic phonics* reading teaching starts with whole words. This was sometimes referred to as 'Look-and-Say'. The child's attention is drawn to letters and sounds within the words taught, i.e. *analysing* a word for sounds. Children are then taught to 'sound out' and blend unfamiliar words, e.g. 'cuh-ah-tuh' for cat. In the *Synthetic phonics* method letter sounds are taught and pupils shown how they can build words from independent sounds. They learn to form words from these sounds as soon as possible. Watson and Johnston concluded that, 'The synthetic phonics method leads to fewer underachieving children', stating that:

> Children have to be shown that the sequence of the phonemes in the spoken word maps on to the sequence of letters in the printed word. . . . This should be reinforced by teaching them to sound and blend letters in order to pronounce words and to spell words using magnetic letters.
>
> (p. 11)

In their study there was a clear advantage for the group taught using methods based on synthetic phonics.

Solity advocates teaching strategies 'interleaved' throughout the day rather than in an intensive hour as originally mandated in the Literacy Hour. For lower attaining pupils Solity recommends direct teaching of synthesis skills, segmentation skills, phonic skills and a sight vocabulary with the addition of small group sessions for two to three minutes three times a day to review the content of the main sessions. Second 'the goals of teaching, purposes of reading and instructional strategies' should be explained and made explicit to the pupils. Finally, they should be given a wide range of books to read. Literacy teaching in the ERR Project is both structured and systematic. For lower achievers 'overlearning' is also built in. There is an emphasis on immediate use of new learning in supervised reading activities.

The major literature digest underpinning the National Literacy Strategy is by Beard (1998). He cites Crévola and Hill's (1998) Early Literacy Research Project in Melbourne, Australia. This recognises three 'waves' of teaching. The First Wave with 'good teaching in the first year of school' sees 80 per cent of pupils having reading and writing 'underway'. (This is very reminiscent of Aylott Cox's (1983) dictum that whatever teaching methods were used 80 per cent of pupils well taught using them would begin to learn to read. Some of the 80 per cent would be different pupils depending on the methods used.) The Second Wave needs more specialised teaching that in Melbourne was Marie Clay's 'Reading Recovery' method (Clay, 1993). This takes care of another 18 per cent leaving a Third Wave needing 'further referral and special support'. Whilst this may well be an accurate reflection of Crévola and Hill's results it has been our experience that only some children respond successfully to the Reading Recovery methods as the challenge to a pupil's visual memory is such that those with even mild to moderate dyslexia soon stop making progress. As we shall see later these three 'waves' are now articulated within the NLS.

Beard (1998) also points to the classroom policy factors characterising effective schools detailed in *School Matters*, a longitudinal study of 50 primary schools by Mortimore *et al.* (1988). These include structured sessions within which there is an 'audit' of tasks achieved, the use of 'higher-order questions and statements', sessions having 'limited focus' organised around one curricular area with differentiation and, finally, maximum communication between teachers and pupils.

Finally, he notes that Adams' claims that teaching approaches including systematic code instruction result in superior reading achievement overall both for low readiness and better prepared pupils. He concludes by quoting:

Recent research-based models of early reading and fluent reading suggest that reading is neither 'top-down' nor 'bottom-up' in nature. Sources of contextual, comprehension, visual and phonological information are simultaneously interactive issuing and accommodating to and from each other.

(Adams and Bruck, 1993)

Also in 1998 HMI produced an evaluation report on the implementation of the NLS in a pilot cohort of 250 schools (HMI, 1998). Whilst basically very positive in its findings certain less successful areas were noted:

Statemented pupils and those at Stages 3 to 5 of the Code of Practice made less progress than those with no defined SEN or those at Stages 1 and 2.

Many teachers reported increased confidence in their teaching of literacy, as they became more familiar with the requirements of the Framework. However, gaps remained in teachers' knowledge, particularly about the teaching of phonics, and this must be remedied as quickly as possible.

The skill of questioning is one which a number of teachers have had to improve particularly in their whole-class teaching.

The Literacy Strategy itself has been a model of pragmatic innovation. It has been introduced in stages with each one taking into account the effects of the preceding part. Stage 1, the Framework File (DfEE, 1998), was meant to ensure 'Quality Teaching' for all children. As part of the monitoring of the Strategy, Manchester Metropolitan University (MMU) in collaboration with the British Dyslexia Association (BDA) did a 'snapshot' study of the effects of the NLS on pupils with SEN (including dyslexia) (Johnson and Peer, 1999). Our findings were very similar to those of HMI above. We pointed to the danger of the 'social inclusion' of pupils with SEN within the Literacy Hour masking the insecurity of their learning in some areas of work, to some lack of coherence in the sequencing of experiences and activities and to the failure of some teachers to recognise clear indications of specific learning difficulties. We also demonstrated that in their attempts to differentiate questions for pupils with SEN some teachers revert to closed questions rather than more carefully articulated open ones. It was also clear that literacy teaching was neither structured nor sequential enough for pupils with difficulties. There rapidly followed the Additional Literacy Support materials for use at Key Stage 2 including the video 'Progression in Phonics' (National Literacy Strategy, 1999, 2000). These went some way to helping some pupils who previously were struggling but still left some for whom Literacy remained a problem area.

However, the NLS team recognised that it would be far better if intervention took place much earlier. They also wished to address a problem that has been inherent in the implementation of the Framework – the potential 'culture clash' between the emphases on whole-class teaching from the NLS Team and the more open, play-centred pedagogy of the early years world. The Framework contains the curriculum for Key Stage 1 that includes the Reception Year. It presents the full hour's structured full-class teaching as the way to deliver that curriculum. Nowhere does it even imply that teaching methods in Reception can be different. However, this seems to have been resolved and the final part of the Strategy, the 'Early Literacy Support Programme' (ELSP) (NLS, op. cit.) arrived in LEAs in September 2001.

This can be downloaded from the Literacy Web Site. It states that:

- In Term 1 *all* children in Year 1 will receive high quality teaching in the literacy hour. A training programme, an assessment package and a trained Teaching Assistant (TA) will support the teaching. In that first Term it is expected that Quality First Teaching and assessment will identify and address any difficulties or gaps in learning for the majority of children. Towards the end of Term 1 the teacher and Teaching Assistant will identify those children who need a more intensive programme of support – research indicates this may be about 20 per cent of an average class (that is, a group of about 6 children).
- In Term 2 all children will continue to be supported as in Term 1 but in addition the identified group will receive a daily planned programme of support from the Teaching Assistant.
- By Term 3 it is expected that most children will no longer need daily additional support although some may need continuing group support whilst others may be identified, through assessment, as needing individual support.

The Programme is in addition to the work in the Literacy Hour and intended to take place outside the classroom. In the Pilot schools:

> the best examples were found when the intervention sessions took place in a dedicated space – usually away from the class. However, this is not always possible and a corner or space in the classroom can work well. Wherever the sessions are located it is important to display work and give the Teaching Assistant a base from which to work.

Importantly, the programme also considers what should be done if any pupils are still having difficulties. This is referred to as the 'Exit Strategy'.

> The programme aims to significantly reduce the number of children who fail to make good progress in Key Stage 1. At the present time, too many children leave this stage with poor literacy skills. However, it is recognised that a small minority of children will continue to need support even after high quality teaching and ELS additional support in a group. Further (Wave 3) support could include one-to-one programmes.

What these 'one-to-one' programmes might be is still (November 2001) under discussion. Informally LEA representatives and individual members of the NLS Team have said they believe that this 'small minority's' lack of significant reading progress in spite of taking part in the 'Three waves' indicates, without the need for multi-professional assessment, that they would benefit from being provided with specialist teaching from a qualified 'dyslexia specialist'.

However, in the term currently being used we believe that there is a 'middle way'. The Centre for Inclusive Education and Special Educational Needs at the Manchester Metropolitan University is a major provider of courses for specialist teachers of pupils with dyslexia. A significant part of our research efforts are, therefore, related to the professional concerns of such teachers and their mainstream colleagues. Peer (2002) estimated that at least 4 per cent of pupils (at least one in each class on average) have severe dyslexia. In each class there will also be pupils with mild to moderate dyslexia, which might have been overcome with appropriate teaching methods started early enough. There may be other pupils whose literacy development is hindered by the methods used in their infant classrooms. These could be accurately described as 'instructional casualties'. There is a danger that the reasons for their difficulties may be seen as in the environment (poor homes, economic conditions, etc.) or within the child (slow learner, emotional problems, not 'settled' yet, etc.) rather than in the teaching methods. However, Project Read in the USA and more recently, as detailed above in the UK, Watson and Johnston (1998) and Solity *et al.* (1999) demonstrated that successful methods with all these pupils were, as had been pointed out many years earlier by Cox (1983), 'basically synthetic and multisensory as opposed to the analytic technology (methods) of the whole word-meaning approach'.

Multisensory approaches to phonological awareness

Synthetic phonics introduces the 44 sounds of English in an order that allows them to be combined to make up as many words as possible right from the start. I,T,P,N,S are usually the first. This enables the words it, pit, pin, pits, pins, sip, sit, snip, snips etc. to be read. The pupil is never asked to read any words containing letters not yet taught, and certainly not to read them aloud. Some 'instructional casualties' may well have lost confidence in their ability to deal with print at all. Use of synthetic phonics with the early introduction of words can re-establish their self-confidence through its emphasis on teaching as opposed to learning.

The USA has used 'synthetic', direct teaching methods for some time partly due to the influence of the work of Samuel Orton (1925, 1937) and the Orton Society, now the International Dyslexia Association. Early programmes were 'clinical' and based on individual instruction by teachers who had undergone special training. However, Margaret Smith in Texas, a student of Aylott Cox at the Scottish Rite Hospital in Dallas, developed a programme for group use in mainstream schools, the 'Multisensory Teaching System' (MTS) (Smith, 1993). MTS is broken down into short, self-contained lessons and what the teacher says to the pupils and their likely replies are given. Thus the scheme is fully 'scripted' with all equipment provided so that the only demands on the teacher are that s/he reads and understands the lesson ahead. It intersperses the direct teaching of phonics with that of morphology and word structure. The lessons follow the sequence and structure developed within the Orton, Gillingham and Stillman (e.g. Gillingham and Stillman, 1969) and Aylott Cox (e.g. Cox, 1983) tradition. They use a multisensory teaching approach to maximise their effectiveness with pupils finding the attainment of literacy difficult.

Multisensory teaching is teaching done using all the learning pathways in the brain (visual, auditory and kinaesthetic–tactile) in order to enhance memory and learning. It is crucial that whatever pathways are being addressed in a particular exercise are directly focused upon by both teacher and child. For example, they look at, feel, move and say the names of the wooden letters they are using to compose a word. When 'writing' a word in the air the left hand holds the right elbow and the eyes follow the pointing finger. A tray with salt or sand on it or the reverse side of a piece of hardboard can be used to 'write on' with a finger. The rough surface maximises the sensory input and in both cases the letters and the final word are said out loud. Any white-board or desk used for teaching must be kept clear of 'clutter' so that only the stimuli intentionally put before the child are in sight so that very clear signals are received. There are several sources of such activities, e.g. Croydon (1999) and Kelly (1999, 2001)

Teachers in today's classrooms are more 'accountable' than ever before. Much of this accountability results in record keeping and report writing. Lesson preparation is more detailed and comprehensive. 'Advice' arrives regularly from the DfES. Using a new and different method with a small number of pupils will clearly provide an additional challenge. If this challenge is to be minimised the method must be self-contained, not require significant amounts of preparation, and have all the materials needed complete and included.

Today's classrooms also have more adults working in them. There are learning and special support assistants (LSAs and SSAs) and parent-helpers. Our survey of Literacy Hour teaching referred to earlier showed that these assistants tended to be used to teach lower attaining pupils. It would seem wise, therefore, to ensure that an assistant under the direction of a teacher could use any proposed methods safely and effectively.

With a grant from the then DfEE MMU in collaboration with the BDA mounted a project to identify methods of identification and assessment of specific learning difficulties (dyslexia) and effective intervention strategies which can be used by classroom and subject teachers in mainstream schools. The project went on to evaluate three published teaching schemes, 'Phonological Awareness Training' (Wilson, 1994), 'Beat Dyslexia' (Stoane, Franks and Nicolson, 1993) and the 'Multisensory Teaching System' (Smith, 1993) and develop materials appropriate to the UK classroom.

Key findings

- The literature review identified phonological awareness as a prerequisite for all pupils when learning to read and that interventions which focus on phonics are most effective if directly related to the reading process.
- A questionnaire to specialist teachers showed that the methods they use all:

- promote phonological awareness, ensure 'over-learning' and give time for review and attainment of mastery;
- are based on cumulative, structured, sequential multisensory delivery with frequent small steps; and
- encourage independent learning and improved self-esteem.

- In the evaluation of the three published schemes based on these principles, all produced significant gains in reading and spelling attainments and enhanced the pupils' understanding of how to learn to read.
- The most effective and accessible of these was the 'Multisensory Teaching System' (MTS) scheme.

Key recommendations

Teaching methods for pupils who do not acquire literacy easily should:

- be structured, sequential and multisensory and ensure 'over learning'; and
- provide an effective screening method to identify pupils who do not find the attainment of literacy easy and require further assessment.

Whilst MTS even in its American form produced clear gains in both reading and spelling in pupils previously having made very little progress in even engaging with reading there were elements of it that required modification for UK schools. Thus the 'Multisensory Teaching System for Reading' (MTSR) was developed.

The MTS comprises six books, including one on Phoneme Awareness. The UK edition, *A Multisensory Teaching System for Reading* (MTSR) (Johnson, Phillips and Peer (1999), consists of two books based on the first three American books. Each book contains easy-to-follow short lessons and practice activities (in the form of photocopiable worksheets) which are contained in the appendix of each book.

The most frequently recurring graphemes (letters and letter clusters) together with their varying pronunciations are taught in MTSR. A fundamental principle is that about 85 per cent of the English language follows predictable rules of pronunciation. Teaching about what is *consistent* and *predictable* will help pupils gain confidence in tackling the reading process. At the same time, they are not misled and do learn about 'irregular' words, particularly those which are used frequently.

The concept of phoneme awareness is reinforced every time a letter is taught. A sound is first represented in the context of spoken words; the sound is analysed, then the letter that represents that sound is shown. Finally the pupil sees the letter in written form, reinforcing the idea that letters in written words represent sounds in spoken words. As soon as pupils have been taught 'i' and 't', they read the word 'it'. As new letters are taught they read more words that can be formed with those letters. After nine letter sounds have been presented, they begin reading phrases and short sentences. Since some graphemes (letters or letter clusters) have more than one pronunciation, pupils are taught how to make the appropriate choice from possible multiple pronunciations of the same grapheme, such as how to tell if a vowel is short or long, or when 'c' is pronounced (k) or (s). In addition to teaching letter–sound correspondence and related concepts, there is a systematic study of basic syllable types, suffixes and prefixes. The goal is to teach pupils the science and structure of the written English language, together with processes for applying their knowledge, so that they will have lifelong skills for independent reading.

The MTSR is a cumulative, structured, multisensory programme designed to be delivered by a teacher (or assistant under a teacher's guidance) in a normal primary classroom. The programme is taught to groups of up to six children, and all the materials required are contained in the published package. Lessons normally take 10 to 20 minutes and should be delivered daily for four or five days each week. The lessons are fully scripted and a Handbook provides details about the teaching methods. Each course book also contains a copy of the essential instructions for teaching the lessons.

The DfEE sent two copies of MTSR to every English LEA. One was addressed to the Literacy Strategy Manager, the other to the Adviser for SEN. Since then a considerable number of schools and services in both England and Ireland have adopted it and there have been two independent evaluations of it in use.

Moore and Tansley (2001) working in Rutland with Year 1 pupils compared its use with that of Phono-Graphix (McGuiness and McGuiness, 1998). They write:

> Pre- and post-testing did not indicate a significant difference between the groups in terms of gains in scores; but there was a highly significant difference overall between pre- and post-scores. This confirms the impact of regular small-group teaching in Y1 in addressing difficulty in developing reading skill.
>
> (p. 1)

However, if multisensory methodology is to be used in mainstream classrooms, as we indicated earlier, it must be made available in a 'teacher-friendly' format. Qualitatively Moore and Tansley report:

> The MTSR teachers were relatively cautious about the rationale: one felt that the use of jargon to label the various concepts was confusing for some children; the other found personal difficulties with it, although she reported that the children seemed to remember it quite easily! They both stressed the need to make time to read lesson plans carefully as a preparation for each session. They were, however, very enthusiastic about the materials. They felt that the lesson plans were user-friendly and helped them to prepare lessons effectively, particularly in the list of resources and

in the element of built-in revision which, they felt, help to build children's knowledge and, hence, confidence. Both praised the lesson scripts as a means of building their own confidence, so that eventually they could personalise them for their own use. One felt, however, that the lessons were too long, so divided each lesson and followed it scrupulously for each session. The other laboured particular parts as appropriate for those children who were showing difficulty then faded her support as they made progress. Both teachers also praised particular techniques, particularly the use of mirrors for visual feedback when articulating the various sounds, and the use of pictures as cues for key terms.

(p. 9)

This illustrates the point well. Pupils, not having preconceptions about terminology readily, indeed enthusiastically, accept correct, precise terms. (Look how they respond to the names of dinosaurs!) The teachers' comments here are typical. In our own evaluation we found that parents of pupils not in the special group came to complain that their children were not getting as good teaching because they couldn't talk about their reading in the same way as the group members!

Moore and Tansley further report:

All teachers expressed delight and surprise at the progress made by most of the children, and felt that the project had effectively differentiated needs: it had dramatically accelerated learning for some children, so that some had overtaken classmates; it had given others a grounding in phonological skill so that they were beginning to generalise this skill in beginning to read; and it had identified those children who needed longer term help. The MTSR children in one school spontaneously prepared themselves for their lesson without supervision; in the other school, their teacher felt that they would have enjoyed a lesson every day if allowed one. All MTSR children loved using the mirrors.

The comments of the MTSR teachers bore strong witness to the value of well-designed materials, coherent, detailed and scripted lesson plans within a clearly structured programme, the use of a predictable structure which incorporated on-going revision, and techniques attractive to children.

Again we see the value of synthetic phonics, structure and sequence. The pupils are quite clear what has to be learnt and get sufficient practice to ensure that they have learnt it. The skill then generalises to *how* to learn to read. As one of the pupils put it in our own study,

I now know that reading is something you can learn to do, not just something that happens to you!

In Ireland similar results were found in a very small rural school with mixed age classes. This study evaluated MTSR against a control group of pupils of similar age – 7+ (Johnson, 2001).

Project Group pupils showed superior gains in Spelling and Reading Comprehension. Differences in gains in Reading Accuracy were either comparable with those of the Control Group or superior. The attainment of the Project group in Reading Comprehension was quite startling, being a full nine standard score points over the year whilst the Control Group gained only three. It would seem that modest increases in ability to decode single words results in quite significant gains in ability to comprehend connected prose. There are likely to be a number of factors operating. Two that come immediately to mind are enhanced confidence in approaching text and a greater willingness to engage with the detail of it.

Conclusion

Overall both the work that led up to the development of MTSR and the subsequent evaluations of it have demonstrated clearly the effectiveness of both the Literacy Strategy 'Three Wave' model and the value of using multisensory methods sooner rather than later. The comments from the schools point to the value of regarding the teaching of reading as similar to that of learning a skilled activity. It is beyond the scope of this chapter but Nicolson and Fawcett (e.g. Nicolson and Fawcett, 1990, 1994; Nicolson, 1996) write of language skills as being comparable in a real sense to physical skills and their development to automaticity controlled by the cerebellum. It is therefore interesting to note the work of Pascual-Leone *et al.* (1995) in their study of mental and physical practice on the same five-finger exercise. They report that:

> Over the course of five days mental practice alone led to significant improvement in the performance of the five finger exercise though the performance was significantly less than that produced by physical practice alone. However, mental practice alone led to the same plastic changes in the motor system as those occurring with the acquisition of the skill by repeated physical practice.

They conclude:

> Mental practice alone seems sufficient to promote the modulation of neural circuits involved in the early stages of motor skill learning. This modulation not only results in marked performance improvement but also seems to place subjects at an advantage for further skill learning with minimal physical practice.

(p. 1037)

It would be interesting to see if similar effects are obtained with language skills.

The clinical insights of Orton, Gillingham and Stillman, Aylett Cox and their students are gradually being clarified and, for the most part confirmed by the latest work at brain level.

References

Adams, M.J. and Bruck, M. (1993) Word recognition: the interface of educational policies and scientific research, *Reading and Writing: An Interdisciplinary Journal*, 5, 113–39.

Beard, R. (1998) *National Literacy Strategy: Review of Research and Other Related Evidence*. London: DfES.

Clay, M.M. (1993) *Reading Recovery: A Guidebook for Teachers in Training*. Auckland, New Zealand: Heinemann Education.

Cox, A.R. (1983) Programming for teachers of dyslexics, *Annals of Dyslexia*, 33, 221–33.

Cox, C.B. (1970) *Goodbye Mr Short*. London: Critical Quarterly Society (Black paper, 3).

Crévola, C.A. and Hill, P.W. (1998) Evaluation of a whole-school approach to prevention and intervention in early literacy, *Journal of Education for Students Placed At Risk*, 3, 2, 133–57.

Croydon (1999) *Literacy Games*. Croydon: London Borough of Croydon.

DES (1975) *Special Educational Needs* (The Warnock Report). London: HMSO.

DfEE (1994) *Code of Practice. On the Identification and Assessment of Special Educational Needs*. London: HMSO.

DfEE (1998) *The National Literacy Strategy: Framework for Teaching*. London: DfEE.

Early Literacy Support Programme (ELSP) (2000) *Phonics – Progression in Phonics for Whole Class Teaching*. Reading: National Centre for Literacy and Numeracy.

Early Literacy Support Programme (ELSP) (2001) *Materials for Teachers Working in Partnership with Teaching Assistants*. Reading: National Centre for Literacy and Numeracy.

Gillingham, A. and Stillman, B. (1969) *Remedial Training for Children with Specific Disabilities in Reading and Penmanship*. Cambridge, MA: Educators Publishing Service.

HMI (1998) *National Literacy Project – HMI Evaluation*. London: HMSO.

Johnson, M. (2001) Report on results of monitoring of introduction of Multisensory Teaching System for Reading into four schools in Ireland. Personal communication to the Irish Board of Education.

Johnson, M. and Peer, L. (1999) Pupils with SEN and the Literacy Hour: difficulties and possible solutions. Unpublished report to DfEE.

Johnson, M., and Phillips, P. (1999) *Specific Learning Difficulties (Dyslexia): Early Identification, Assessment and Intervention Strategies*, London: DfEE.

Johnson, M., Phillips, S. and Peer, L. (1999) *A Multisensory Teaching System for Reading (MTSR)*. Manchester: Manchester Metropolitan University.

Kelly, K. (1999) *Multisensory Teaching: A Practical Guide*. Manchester: MMU.

Kelly, K. (2001) *Multisensory Teaching: Workbook One*. Manchester: MMU.

McGuiness, C. and McGuiness, G. (1998) *Reading Reflex*. London: Penguin Books.

Moore, L. and Tansley, J. (2001) An evaluation of structured teaching programmes for reading with Year One children. Personal communication.

Mortimore, P., Sammons, P., Stoll, L., Lewis, D. and Ecob, R. (1988) The effects of school membership on pupils' outcomes, *Research Papers in Education*, 3, 1, 3–26.

National Literacy Strategy (1998) *Framework for Teaching YR to Y6*. Nottingham: DfES Publications Centre.

National Literacy Strategy (1999) *Additional Literacy Support (ALS)*. Reading: Centre for School Standards.

National Literacy Strategy (2000) *Progression in Phonics*. London: DfES.

National Literacy Strategy Website: www.standards.dfes.gov.uk (The Standards Site).

Nicolson, R.I. (1996) Developmental dyslexia: past, present and future, *Dyslexia*, 23, 190–207.

Nicolson, R.I. and Fawcett, A.J. (1990) A new framework for dyslexia research? *Cognition*, 35, 159–82.

Nicolson, R.I. and Fawcett, A.J. (1994) Comparison of deficits in cognitive and motor skills among children with dyslexia, *Annals of Dyslexia*, 44, 147–63.

Orton, S.T. (1925) Word blindness in school children, *Archives of Neurology and Psychiatry*, 14, 581–615.

Orton, S.T. (1937) *Reading, Writing, and Speech Problems in Children*. New York: W.W. Norton.

Pascual-Leone, A., Nguyet, D., Cohen, L.G., Brazil-Neto, A.C. and Hallett, M. (1995) Modulation of muscle responses evoked by transcranial magnetic stimulation during the acquisition of new fine motor skills, *Journal of Neurophysiology*, 4, 3, 1037–45

Peer, L. (2002) What is dyslexia? in M. Johnson and L. Peer (eds) *The Dyslexia Handbook 2002*. Reading: British Dyslexia Association.

Smith, M. (1993) *Multisensory Teaching System*. Forney, Texas: Edmar Publishers.

Solity, J., Deavers, R., Kerfoot, S., Crane, G. and Cannon, K. (1999) Early reading research: an overview, *DECP Newsletter* 91.

Stoane, C., Franks, E. and Nicolson, J. (1993) *Beat Dyslexia (Bks 1–4)*. Wisbech: LDA.

Watson, J.F. and Johnston, R.F. (1998) Accelerating reading attainment: the effectiveness of synthetic phonics, *Interchange 57*. Edinburgh: The Scottish Office.

Wilson, J. (1994) *Phonological Awareness Training*. London: Educational Supply Publishers.

Source

This chapter was written especially for this volume.

Chapter 17

Researching the social and emotional consequences of dyslexia

Barbara Riddick

> It was traumatic for him, incredibly traumatic, every morning I had to pull him up screaming 'I don't want to go to school' and then I had to pull him all the way down to the school.

There is little research on the social and emotional consequences of dyslexia. Pumfrey and Reason (1991) in their comprehensive report *Specific Learning Difficulties (Dyslexia)* state that more research on this area is essential. Despite the paucity of research, concerned clinicians and educationalists have consistently pointed to the devastating effects that dyslexia or specific learning disabilities can have on some children's lives. Concern can be traced from Orton's early clinical work through both the Bullock (1975) and Warnock (DES, 1978) Reports to the recent report by Pumfrey and Reason. It appears that, whatever the debate about terminology and identification, at a global level there is agreement that such difficulties can have a detrimental effect on both the lives of children and their families. Despite this agreement this is a difficult and complex area to research. To start with both dyslexia and social and emotional difficulties have to be clearly defined and identified before the relationship between them can be examined. To date much of the research has looked at children with reading disabilities or more generally at children with learning disabilities. This research has generally used a group comparison design so that, for example, the self-esteem of a group of reading-delayed and non-reading-delayed children would be compared. The problem with this approach is that individual differences between children can be masked and it doesn't relate the individuals' specific experiences to their level of self-esteem. We might expect for example that a dyslexic child who has been well supported at home and at school would be more likely to have a reasonable level of esteem than a child who has not been supported well at either home or school. Another difficulty in researching this area is that dyslexia is a developmental disorder which changes in its manifestations over time. It may be that social and emotional experiences change or fluctuate considerably over time and that circumstances, cumulative experiences and maturation all affect the likely outcome at a given point in time. If for example a study looked at

10-year-old dyslexics who had learnt to read and were well supported in the classroom and compared their self-esteem to that of their classmates no significant difference might be found. If this were the case this would be an interesting and valid finding in its own right. The danger would be in over-generalising this finding and saying that dyslexic children don't have lower self-esteem than other children or even that 10-year-old dyslexic children don't have lower self-esteem than other children. These same children at 7 years of age before they were identified as dyslexic and offered support may have had very low self-esteem compared with their classmates. So as with all cross-sectional research the age and stage at which a child is studied is of key importance. Yet another difficulty is in selecting the right measures to tap into any difficulties or differences that dyslexic children display compared with their peers. A study by Porter and Rourke (1985) found that 10 per cent of a sample of 100 learning disabled children had somatic problems such as migraines or stomach upsets despite scoring normally on an inventory of social and emotional functioning. These kinds of difficulties may account for some of the mixed findings to emerge from this area. Porter and Rourke found for example that 50 per cent of the children in their sample did not show social or emotional difficulties and in a study by Speece et al. (1985) one third of the learning-disabled children showed no social or emotional difficulties. The problem with these studies is that they are not specific to children with dyslexia, but they do underline the point that it is important not to assume that all children with dyslexia will automatically have social or emotional difficulties.

Because of the difficulties involved in following the ups and downs of children's lives and understanding the complexities of them, interest has more recently focused on different more qualitative methods of research such as ethnography, case studies, interviews and grounded theory. Whilst case studies and interviews are scarcely new to the scene, the more recent focus on trying to see things from the individual's perspective has probably informed and influenced how they are likely to be carried out. Quantitative and qualitative methods are sometimes seen as being in opposition to each other, whereas Mittler (1985) in reviewing research methods in special education states that, 'it would be dangerously misleading to polarize or stereotype these methods as lying at opposite ends of a continuum'. He goes on to point out that these methods are often used in combination by researchers and that a study might, for example, start with a broad quantitative survey and then move into detailed qualitative case studies of individuals. At present the main body of evidence on the social and emotional concomitants of dyslexia comes from personal accounts and life histories. Probably the best known personal account in Britain is recounted by Susan Hampshire the actress in her book entitled Susan's Story (1981). As well as detailed individual accounts, several collections of interviews with parents of dyslexic children, and adults with dyslexia have been published (Osmond, 1993, Van der Stoel, 1990, Melck, 1986). Although these books have included some comments by dyslexic children, the views of parents have predominated. Kavanaugh (1978) in the USA published a book entitled *Listen to Us!* which was based entirely on the views of dyslexic children, which were first aired during discussions between them. Much of this work has been produced by lay people often with first-hand experience of dyslexia. The aim has been 'to tell it how it is' and not to answer theoretical questions or provide highly systematic accounts. But in their own right they have provided an important level of description about how individuals live with dyslexia and they have raised numerous questions for further research. In particular it can be argued that they have challenged some of the more dogmatic ideology surrounding dyslexia and have provided compelling accounts of how dogmatism and ignorance can combine to provide poor and in some cases atrocious educational practice. In addition to this single case studies have occasionally appeared in books and journals, but these have often focused on reading failure rather than dyslexia. Edwards (1994) provides detailed personal case studies on eight boys attending a residential school for children with dyslexia. Despite the enormous diversity of these various accounts, consistent themes, issues and experiences can be identified and these will be discussed in more detail later in the chapter. Because of the limited amount of research on the social and emotional consequences of dyslexia a number of overlapping areas of research relevant to this issue will be briefly reviewed.

Self-esteem/self-concept

Although the terms self-esteem, self-concept and self-image are sometimes used interchangeably they do have different but interrelated meanings. Self-concept is defined as an umbrella term that encompasses an individual's evaluation of themselves at a cognitive (thinking), affective (feeling) and behavioural level. Self-esteem is taken as a measure of how far an individual's perceived self (self-image) matches up to their ideal self. Burns (1982) in an extensive review of the literature relating to self-concept and education argued that there are clear links between an individual's self-concept and school performance. He suggests that where an individual has poor academic performance and low motivation in school this is often linked to a poor self-concept. Lawrence (1987) and Huntington and Bender (1993) make similar claims for the link between poor school performance and low self-esteem. Drawing on the work of Rogers (1951) many writers have suggested that in order to develop a positive self-concept an individual needs a sense of acceptance, competence and worth. It is postulated that these are learnt through social interaction firstly within the family, then school and the wider environment. This is seen as an interactional process with the child influencing the environment and the environment influencing the child. Both Burns and Lawrence in their overviews of the area stress that, although families have an important role in the fostering of good self-concept or self-esteem, teachers also have a vital role in this process. Lawrence states that, 'whenever the teacher enters into a

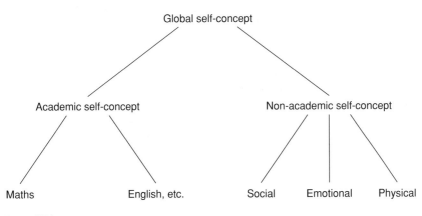

Figure 17.1

relationship with a student a process is set into motion which results either in the enhancement of self-esteem or in the reduction of self-esteem'. Lawrence goes on to suggest that many good teachers intuitively enhance the self-esteem of their pupils, but even so they might benefit from more explicit knowledge of the factors that help to enhance self-esteem.

One of the problems in reviewing the literature on self-concept and self-esteem in relation to academic performance is that it is unclear if poor self-esteem leads to poor performance or if poor performance leads to poor self-esteem. A third possibility is that some kind of interactional process takes place. Lawrence (1985) in reviewing research in this area favours an inter-actional explanation and argues that on this basis it is important to work on a child's self-esteem and skills in tandem. Most researchers agree (Battle, 1990; Coopersmith, 1967) that self-esteem and self-concept are developmental in nature and move from a global, relatively undifferentiated state in young children to a more complex hierarchical state with a number of clearly differentiated components feeding into global self-esteem as a child gets older. There is still much debate as to the precise nature of any hierarchical model and the developmental history underpinning it. Marsh (1992) has carried out extensive research in this area and gives a simplified outline of how such a model might look. [See Figure 17.1.]

What is also uncertain is the degree of individual difference in the way that the self-concept is structured and operates. It may be that some individuals operate more heavily on the basis of a global self-concept whereas others operate more heavily on the basis of differentiated aspects of self-concept. Battle (1990) claims that once an individual's level of self-esteem is well estab-lished it becomes difficult to alter and remains relatively stable over time. Studies that attempt to measure self-esteem run into a number of method-ological difficulties. The first is in selecting a valid and reliable means of assessing self-esteem: this is usually done by means of a self-esteem inventory which relies on the subject responding to a set of specific questions. This raises questions about how honestly and accurately the subject responds to the questions. More recent well designed self-esteem inventories try to get round this problem: the *Culture-Free Self-Esteem Inventories* (Battle, 1992) for example include a lie scale. Given that we know that a number of variables such as the gender, colour and role of the tester can affect children's performance differentially on various tests of ability it might also be the case that the role of the self-esteem tester and the context in which the test is carried out might affect the children's responses differentially. It has been suggested that some children with learning disabilities might defend themselves by denial and that this might in turn influence how they respond to a self-esteem inventory. Self-esteem inventories vary in accordance with the model of self-esteem that they are based on. The major difference is between those that simply give a global self-esteem score (Coopersmith, 1967; Lawrence, 1982) and those that in addition to a global score divide self-esteem up into a number of contributing areas (Battle, 1992; Marsh *et al.*, 1991) such as academic, physical and social self-esteem. Children's self-esteem scores may therefore vary depending on the sensitivity and appropriateness of the instrument used. Another difficulty in assessing self-esteem is that little is known about the way in which day-to-day events may influence children's self-perceptions. A study by Callison (1974) found that children's self-concept could be altered by a single incidence of feedback. In this study he first gave 8-year-old children half of the Piers-Harris Self-Concept Scale followed by a maths test. Half of the group of 28 were told that they had performed badly on the test and half were told that they had performed well. They were then given the second half of the self-concept scale to complete. It was found that children who had been given negative feedback scored significantly lower in their self-concept scores on the second part of the test. This suggests that events immediately prior to a self-esteem or self-concept inventory or scale could significantly influence the results. Despite these methodological difficulties there is general agreement that a number of behaviours are characteristic of children with high self-esteem and a number of other behaviours are characteristic of children with low self-esteem. Children with high self-esteem are said to display more confidence in their own ability, to be more willing to volunteer answers and try out new learning situations, whereas children with low self-esteem show little confidence in their own ability, give up easily and are often fearful of or avoid new learning situations. A crucial difference appears to be that, whereas children with high self-esteem generally expect to succeed, children with low self-esteem generally expect to fail. Butkowsky and Willows (1980) in a study comparing children with reading difficulties with children of average or good reading ability found many of these characteristics. The poor readers in their study had lower expectations of success not only on a reading task but also on a drawing task. They responded more negatively to failure and were more likely to give up thus increasing the likelihood of future failure. They also differed in their attribution style to good readers. Poor readers tended to 'blame them-selves' by attributing failure to their own incompetence and success to environmental factors such as luck, whereas good readers attributed success to their own ability. Again the question can be raised as to whether attribution style is a cause or an effect of poor reading or both. Pumfrey and Reason (1991) suggest that this style of thinking fits well with Seligman's notion of learned helplessness. Seligman claims that individuals who have been put in a nega-tive situation from which they cannot escape and feel that they have no control over will become apathetic and demoralised. More importantly when these individuals are put in a more positive situation they persist in their apathetic behaviour and thus display learned helplessness. In a similar vein Bannister and Fransella (1971) in extending Kelly's (1955) work on personal construct theory argue that in order to change an individual's behaviour you need to change their personal constructs (self-beliefs). Although some empir-ical evidence has been presented to support this point of view, behaviourists can equally present evidence that changing behaviour can lead to a change in self-concept. [Some theorising] (Beck *et al.*, 1979) attempts to reconcile these positions by arguing for a cognitive behavioural approach that recog-nises the interrelated nature of cognition (thinking) and behaviour. This gets back to Lawrence's point that in the absence of more convincing evidence it's safest to assume that we need to work on both children's self-beliefs and their learning skills. Lawrence (1971, 1973, 1985) found that an individual coun-selling approach focused on children's self-beliefs was consistently more successful than a traditional remedial reading approach alone in improving the performance of poor readers. Lawrence found that counsellors did not need to be highly trained professionals and that anyone with a warm sympathetic approach could with limited training fulfill the role. Pumfrey and Reason (1991) argue that at a commonsense level working on individual skills in combination with personal support would seem the best option. They suggest that this support doesn't need to be in the form of formal counselling sessions and that what is required is an interested adult who gives the child support and encouragement.

Self-esteem in children with dyslexia or specific learning difficulties

The studies mentioned so far focus on backward or reading-delayed children and not on children defined as having dyslexia or specific learning difficulties. Whilst the groups are likely to have included such children they were not differentiated from other children and it is therefore impossible to say if these children responded in the same way as other children to specific interven-tions. A longitudinal study (Gjessing and Karlsen, 1989) of 3,000 children in Norway did distinguish a sub-group of children with specific learning disabil-ities from the cohort. It was found that these children all responded differently to the same instruction with some making very good progress and others making poor progress. This suggests that it is important not to over-generalise in talking about children's responses to intervention and to be alert to individual differences. Nonetheless it was found in this study that dyslexic children along with reading-retarded children in general had a poor self-concept which was reflected in their lack of self-confidence and poor peer relationships. Several earlier studies (e.g. Rosenthal, 1973, Thomson and Hartley, 1980) have found that dyslexic children have low self-esteem compared to non-dyslexic children. Thomson (1990) used the Battle (1981) *Culture-Free Self-Esteem Inventories* to test the self-esteem of three groups of children with dyslexia. The first group were tested when they were first interviewed for a place at a specialist school for dyslexia, the second group had already attended the school for 6 months and the third group had attended the school for 18 months. Thomson found there was a significant increase in self-esteem over this period of time which he attributed to the benefits of specialist schooling. The results from this study would have been stronger if the same group of children had been followed and tested at each of these time intervals but, despite this, several interesting points emerged from the study when the four subscales for general, social, academic and parental self-esteem were compared. On the first test children's lowest area of self-esteem was for social (32 per cent). By the third test their social esteem was 84 per cent and their academic was 77 per cent and their parental remained at 87 per cent. This would suggest that the major source of low self-esteem for these children was the mainstream school environment and especially children's sense of failure in comparison to their peers. Studies by Chapman *et al.* (1984) and Fairhurst and Pumfrey (1992) have found that reading-disabled children score lower on their perception of academic ability compared to non-reading-disabled children. Chapman *et al.* found that children's perception of ability was closely related to success in school and was relatively independent of intelligence as measured by the WISC-R, a standard IQ test. They suggest that although it can be argued that children are being realistic about their level of ability in terms of school performance these kinds of beliefs may set up a self-fulfilling prophecy of expecting to fail. Whereas Chapman *et al.* were looking at 9-year-olds, Fairhurst and Pumfrey were looking at third year pupils in three secondary schools. They found that in addition to the lower self-concepts as learners the poor readers had a significantly higher rate of absence than the competent readers. They suggest that this high rate of absenteeism combined with their low self-concept and poor performance in school can all combine in a negative downward spiral for some of these children. Another factor that they found contributing to this overall picture was that the poor readers also scored lower on a sub-scale designed to look at their perceptions of their role in the classroom; it showed that they felt less valued and less important than the better readers. Casey, Levy, Brown and Brooks-Gunn (1992) studied a group of middle-class pre-adolescent children with reading disabilities. They found that these children had low self-esteem and were more anxious and less happy with school than a control group of non-reading-disabled children. The problem with cross-sectional studies like these is that they only give us a snapshot of the child's self-concept at a given point in time, they say nothing directly about how the child came to acquire their particular self-concept or what sort of developmental history it might have followed. This is a more difficult area to research as a number of complex and interacting variables are likely to be involved. These include the child's temperament, cognitive abilities, and social and educational experiences. Burns (1982) argues that despite these complexities there is clear evidence that children's self-concepts as learners are strongly influenced by their teachers. One particularly important question that arises is what the long-term effects of such negative attributions might be. Kosmos and Kidd (1991) carried out a study on the personality characteristics of adult dyslexics. They found that dyslexic women scored high on the pleasing others scale and dyslexic men showed a lack of self-confidence, a tendency to self-defeating thoughts and questioning of their own ability to reach goals. These findings, it could be argued, fit with a poor self-concept or low self-esteem. Even if these results are replicated it still doesn't demonstrate that poor self-concept in adulthood is a result of earlier schooling, as it could be an outcome of difficulties that the adults are still facing especially in the work situation. Susan Hampshire, the actress, recounts what happened when she was asked at the height of her fame and success to read a story on children's television. She had spent four days trying to learn this story word for word as she knew she would not be able to read it directly from the book whilst on camera. Despite her strong reservations because of her dyslexia her protests were waved aside and she started to be filmed reading from the book with the following consequences:

> I was now not only sweating, blind, uncoordinated and laughing inanely, but started to shake as well. . . . In the pit of my stomach lay the pain of frustration and humiliation.

But methodologically these kinds of experiences are difficult to disentangle in terms of causation and Susan Hampshire herself relates these feelings in part to her childhood:

> Once inside the studio, the feeling of emptiness in my head that I had as a child returned. I looked at the book and I couldn't see it. The more I panicked the less I could see.

A danger of case studies is that as with astrology just the bits that fit the story might be picked out. But if they are used judiciously in conjunction with more empirical research they can add life and insight to bare figures. In the Kosmos and Kidd study for example it was claimed that dyslexic women scored higher than non-dyslexic women on the 'pleasing others' scale. More research would be needed to verify this but it does fit with Susan Hampshire's claim that as a child and to a lesser degree as an adult she desperately wanted to please others. The following three quotations on this issue are all from her auto-biography.

> I desperately wanted to be liked and I assumed that no one could like someone as stupid as me.

> I wanted to please.

> If you are inventive, loving, always smiling and laughing, people will forget that you are stupid.

Another methodological problem is that because the majority of studies have focused on reading delay and not dyslexia they have only examined self-esteem in relation to reading competence. There is increasing evidence that the cognitive deficits underlying dyslexia are long term for more severely affected individuals and that spelling and writing are equally if not more difficult areas for them to master. This being the case, studies that look at the self-concept or self-esteem of dyslexics over the time period when they are struggling with these skills would add to our understanding of the relationship between self-concept and academic performance.

Although there is a large literature on parenting styles and the development of self-esteem in children within the context of the home environment there is almost no research on how parents respond to the kind of low self-concept or esteem which appears to be related to learning difficulties at school. In the study to be described in this book concern over low self-esteem and how to improve it was a major preoccupation of the majority of mothers in the study.

Teacher expectations

In looking at the relationship between teachers and their pupils and the way that this might affect pupil's self-concept, a body of research on how teachers' expectations of individual pupils can affect their performance has grown up. Although it's been heavily criticised on methodological grounds probably the best known study is the one carried out by Rosenthal and Jacobson (1968). In this study teachers were told that certain children were going to 'bloom' over the following year on the basis of their IQ scores. These children were in fact picked at random and the teachers were given false information on their IQ scores. It was claimed by the researchers that these selected children did increase significantly in IQ compared to non-selected children. Rosenthal and Jacobson suggest that this might have been brought about by the teachers treating these children differently to other children and for example giving them more positive attention. Because of the wide amount of interest that this study attracted and the serious doubts over its validity several better designed studies were carried out. These came up with conflicting results.

In 1974 Brophy and Good reviewed nearly all the work on teachers' expectations. They suggested that whereas it was difficult to demonstrate this effect in experimental studies there was clear evidence from more naturalistic studies that teachers' inaccurate expectations of pupils could have an effect on their performance commensurate with the teachers' beliefs. Hargreaves (1972) has suggested that one reason for the mixed results obtained in this area is that, for teacher expectations to have an effect on the child, the teacher must be seen by the child as a significant other, and the teacher's and the child's perceptions of ability must be congruent. So, where a child has a poor academic self-concept, the teacher views the child's ability as poor and as the child regards the teacher as a significant other the child is most likely to be affected by the teacher's negative expectations. Both Rogers (1982) and Good and Brophy (1987) in reviewing this area conclude that although the potential is always there for the influence of teacher expectations they only influence children sometimes and to a relatively small degree. But on the other hand the effect of this in interaction with other factors especially if it is compounded by more than one teacher may have a significant influence on a child's performance and self-concept as a learner. Good and Brophy (1987) in their review also looked at all the research on how teachers' expectations were transmitted. They concluded that there tended to be consistent differences in the way that some teachers responded to low and high achieving pupils. The low achieving students were less often chosen to answer questions even when they volunteered to answer. When it came to giving verbal feedback some teachers praised everything that low achieving children contributed whereas others were overly harsh and critical of their contributions. It was also found that in comparison to high achievers low achievers were given less time to answer questions and were seated further away from the teacher. All the studies mentioned so far are aimed at children in general and say nothing specific about children with specific learning disabilities or dyslexia. But if it is assumed that these children are often viewed as low achievers then presumably the kind of expectancy effects described so far may well take place. More empirical research is needed to see if this is the case and, if so, how the particular nature of the learning difficulties affects teachers' expectancies. One particular issue for dyslexic children is the extent to which their slow and poor written work influences teachers' expectations of them.

Burns (1982) suggests that there are four areas that teachers should concentrate on if they want to ensure that they aren't unwittingly transmitting different expectations to high and low achieving students. These include:

Interacting evenly with all pupils

Give all pupils the same amount of attention and the same degree of positive feedback. Burns suggests that because this is difficult to keep track of it helps to be systematic and keep records of seating plans, assembly contributions, project supervision and so on. The important point is that all children get an equal amount of attention and are equally invited to participate in the life of the classroom and for that matter the school in general. Evidence from personal accounts suggests that a significant proportion of dyslexic children become quiet and withdrawn in school and try not to draw attention to themselves. They may therefore be easier for the teacher to overlook. In the interviews carried out for the study reported in this book many of the secondary school pupils in particular felt that they were ignored and overlooked by teachers. Younger children as well sometimes felt overlooked partly because the poor standard of their work meant that it was less often displayed in prominent places and they were less often picked to carry out special tasks and their work was less likely to be read out in class.

Talking to all pupils

Although it can be very difficult, especially in large classes, it is important to ensure that all children are spoken to on a personal basis however briefly and that teachers should whenever possible be receptive to any contact that the child makes. As most teachers are only too aware it is particularly important that quiet and unforthcoming children do not miss out. Given what is already known about the risks of poor self-concept in children with a range of learning disabilities it would seem particularly important that they get this kind of personal contact. Several children [in a study] said that they tried to make themselves as invisible and unnoticed as possible in the classroom.

Realistic praise

Getting the balance right between being over critical or indiscriminately lavish in praise can be difficult and the ideal balance will vary from child to child. It can be argued that whereas the effects of harsh criticism are easy to identify and understand the effects of overpraising are less obvious especially as it is often done with the best of intentions. What seems important (Rowe, 1974) is that praise is linked systematically to the child's performance so it provides an effective form of feedback and is valued by the child. What also seems important is that any negative feedback is given in a positive context and the child is given constructive advice on how to improve their perform-ance. This is basic good practice that many teachers already follow, but keeping the right balance when faced with a piece of written work where the hand-writing is almost indecipherable and the spelling atrocious can be more difficult. One experienced and sympathetic classroom teacher recounted to a dyslexic boy's mother her bewilderment when faced with his first piece of free writing of the year. There were so many errors in letter formation, sentence construction and spelling for a child of 10 years that she felt unsure about where on earth to begin. She decided after some thought to praise various aspects of the content and to pick up on a few of his most consistent and basic errors. Several classroom teachers in informal interviews recounted similar problems. Some of them felt that because of their own lack of knowledge about dyslexia and the fact that they were not following a specific intervention plan with the child their feedback tended to be rather random and idiosyncratic and they were dubious about its long-term effectiveness. This suggests that praise will be most effective in enhancing learning when a teacher has a clear understanding of the underlying difficulties and how they can be helped. Gross (1993) suggests that because of the tendency of children with learning difficulties to 'blame' themselves for failure and to attribute success to 'luck' it is important that negative feedback is aimed only at specific external and changeable aspects of their performance (for example, 'I think you were so involved in writing this really exciting story that you forgot your capital letters today') and that when giving positive praise for performance this is linked to general attributes of the child ('you've done really well to remember capital letters, it shows what a hard worker you are and how much you are helping yourself to improve').

Matching tasks to individuals

Much has been written about the need to individualise learning and match tasks to individuals and many would argue that this has become a basic tenet of good practice. Even so many would also point out that environmental factors such as class size, amount of extra support for special needs and possibly the requirements of the National Curriculum can all impinge on a teacher's ability to individualise learning. Burns emphasises that what is important is that children are set realistic rather than arbitrary goals and that being successful at tasks they find challenging but not overwhelming will help to improve their self-esteem. Again the problem arises that if teachers have little understanding of the learning problems involved in dyslexia it will make it difficult for them to set appropriate goals. Under the Code of Practice they should be able to get advice from the special needs co-ordinator and, if required, outside agencies. Given the wide range of responsibilities and tasks already required of classroom teachers they should feel entitled to receive adequate training and support on individualising learning for children with specific learning difficulties.

Behavioural and emotional difficulties

Along with low self-esteem there is a general consensus from a mixed body of research that children with reading disabilities are more likely to have behavioural or emotional difficulties (Tansley and Panckhurst, 1981; Gentile and Macmillan, 1987; Hinshaw, 1992; Huntington and Bender, 1993). Evidence would suggest that overlap exists between these areas and that many of the methodological problems encountered in researching self-esteem are also evident in researching behavioural and emotional difficulties. Again much of the research has focused on children with a range of reading disabilities and not on children with specific reading difficulties. This is not to imply that the experiences of all reading-delayed children are not of concern but without looking at different sub-types we cannot tell if the commonalities in their reactions outweigh any specific differences. Differences in the criteria for identification, the sensitivity and appropriateness of the measuring instruments and the sampling strategy used probably account for the variability found in estimates of the prevalence of behavioural and emotional difficulties in children with reading difficulties. Some of the available data has come from samples of children referred for special educational or clinical intervention and the reliability of prevalence estimates based on these samples is open to question. Maughan (1994) provides a useful review of much of the research in this area in terms of both methodology and data. She suggests that the most reliable estimates of prevalence rates generally come from epidemiological (whole population) studies although these are still open to problems of measurement and definition. The large scale Isle of Wight epidemiological study found that a quarter of 10-year-old children with specific reading retardation also displayed antisocial behaviour (Rutter, Tizard and Whitmore, 1970). This immediately raised the question of whether poor reading led to antisocial behaviour or antisocial behaviour led to poor reading or if some common underlying factor such as social deprivation or cognitive deficits was related to both sets of difficulties. They found that the reading-retarded children with antisocial behaviour were similar in many respects to the reading-retarded children without behavioural difficulties and bore less resemblance to the children who just displayed antisocial behaviour. This was taken as evidence that behavioural difficulties were generally secondary to reading difficulties. This kind of study says little about the processes that lead from reading to behavioural difficulties so more recent studies of a prospective longitudinal design have been used to look at the development over time of behavioural and emotional difficulties as well as provide further evidence on prevalence rates. These studies have followed children from before they enter school or on entry to school over a number of years (Jorm et al., 1986; McGee et al., 1988; Pianta and Caldwell, 1990). Overall these studies have found an increasing correlation between reading difficulties and behavioural problems over the primary school period. They also found that in the early and middle primary school years that these difficulties mainly took the form of inattentiveness and restlessness and that overt behavioural difficulties in the form of conduct disorders were less frequent at this age although they increased somewhat by late primary. These findings fit well with accounts by dyslexic children and their parents of their experiences at school.

'I want to be like invisible, I just cut myself off.'

(Riddick study, 1995)

Eventually I'd sort of turn off and dream my way through the day. Actually that's quite easy to do if you're undisturbed for long enough. You get almost catatonic. I don't think that it helped that I was always very well behaved, very quiet. So no one took any notice.

(Osmond, 1993)

So I just used to sit there and sort of dream and look out of the window. . . . Nothing was interesting to me. I became withdrawn and bored and sort of put my mind on hold. I felt very isolated and alone.

(Osmond, 1993)

She told me he sometimes deliberately broke the point of his pencil 10 times a day.

(Van der Stoel, 1990)

I was for ever being told off and was the laughing stock of the class. Turns at reading aloud were a disaster. Well then I really threw in the towel! I'm quite a spitfire and my self-control went completely.

(Van der Stoel, 1990)

In the Bruck (1985) inner-London study which looked at a clinical sample of learning-disabled children from socially disadvantaged backgrounds, it was found that 85 per cent were rated as having poor adjustment during the school years when compared to a control group of non-learning-disabled children. Spreen's 1987 study reported similar findings. In both cases it was found that adjustment problems had significantly decreased by adulthood suggesting that they were closely related to children's experiences in school. It was found in these studies that learning-disabled girls were particularly vulnerable to adjustment problems and that especially in adolescence problems of with-drawal were common. In adulthood it was found that the reading-disabled women tended to score higher on measures of anxiety and depression. Hales (1994) also found that by young adulthood levels of anxiety were particularly high in dyslexic women. As yet no clear-cut explanation is available for these differences and more research is needed to look at a wide range of factors such as possible differences in amount of self-blame, sensitivity to criticism or expectations of others which might lead to these findings.

Another finding from the longitudinal studies is that some reading-disabled children show behavioural difficulties before they enter formal schooling. Whether these behavioural difficulties are a concomitant of the pre-reading linguistic difficulties that a proportion of reading-delayed children have or whether they are due to other factors such as adverse social environment is as yet not clear. What is apparent is that the linkage between reading and behavioural difficulties is a complex one, which will probably reveal multiple causation and interactional effects. Nonetheless the evidence in general, corroborated by personal accounts, suggests that some primary age children will present with overt behaviour problems but that more are likely to present as well behaved, quiet and compliant although they have detached themselves from much of the learning process. It is these unengaged children, many would claim, who are easier to overlook especially in large or demanding classes.

Hales (1994) suggests that in the past the social and emotional consequences of dyslexia have been underestimated and that research that has treated dyslexics as 'broken learning machines' has only given us a partial under-standing of what dyslexia entails. Hales administered a personality question-naire (16 PF, Cattell *et al.*, 1970) to a group of 300 people with dyslexia aged from 6 years to 18 plus years with the majority being of school age.

He cautions that it would be naive to expect there to be a specific dyslexic personality but he argues that this research can give us some indications of how individuals with dyslexia develop over time. He found that infant age children had scores which indicated that they were tense and frustrated, in the middle school years scores indicated low motivation and high anxiety and at secondary school scores indicated a desire to keep in the background. Hales also found that during the middle school years there was a noticeable drop in confidence and optimism especially among girls. One of the most striking find-ings overall was the inverse relationship between anxiety and IQ with low IQ children from middle school years onwards tending to have higher levels of anxiety. This counters the myth that is sometimes subscribed to that 'intelli-gent' children suffer more and underlines the importance of not having assumptions about how particular groups of children will respond to dyslexia. Hales speculates that more intelligent children may be more sympathetically treated by the world or they may be able to develop better coping strategies. Further research is needed to corroborate these findings but they do show that we need to know more about how children with dyslexia develop over time.

The effect of emotion and mood on thinking

Given the low self-esteem and high anxiety in literacy tasks that is often reported for individuals with dyslexia, it is surprising that cognitive psychol-ogists researching in this area haven't looked at this issue more closely. Research by Zatz and Chassin (1985) for example found that high test anxiety impaired the performance of children and Darke (1988) found that working memory was particularly affected by anxiety. As poor working memory is already considered to be a key part of the processing difficulties that dyslexic children encounter it seems likely that anxiety will further impair their perfor-mance. Yasutake and Bryan (1995) give a useful review of some of the research in this area and conclude that positive affect (emotion) can enhance chil-dren's performance on tasks like learning new vocabulary and doing maths and that negative affect can detract from their performance. They claim that for learning-disabled (US term closest to specific learning difficulties) chil-dren, the benefits of positive affect are particularly large and suggest that simple strategies to increase positive affect could be used in the classroom. In two studies by Bryan and Bryan (1991) it was claimed that simply getting children to close their eyes and think of something 'wonderful' for 45 seconds improved their performance on 50 maths sums compared to children who were asked to count to fifty. It may well be that some teachers already use similar strategies in the classroom. One particularly good and positive teacher of top infants explained how she attempted to make spelling tests less stressful by trying to convince all the children in her class that they really enjoyed them!

Looking in detail at life histories, case studies and interviews

The great strength of these approaches is that they can give a holistic and long-term account of an individual's life. A criticism can be that they empha-sise a within-person perspective, but examination of these accounts reveals that much of the focus is on how individuals see environmental factors impinging on them. Cognitive deficits are usually only raised in relation to various environmental demands such as learning to read and spell. Miles and Miles (1990) have warned against the danger of confusing primary and secondary difficulties. If a child with a primary cognitive impairment has diffi-culty learning to read and in response to this goes on to develop behavioural difficulties, it is important that the behavioural difficulties are not then seen as the primary cause of the child's reading difficulties, although by now they may well be a strong contributory factor. On the uncluttered world of the page this might seem an insultingly obvious point but in the messier world of the classroom such issues can become more confused. One mother [in a study] recounted a clear example of this. She was a primary school teacher herself and was aware that her son was having immense difficulty learning to read and write, although at that point he had not been identified as dyslexic. At 7 years of age he had a new teacher who was not sympathetic to his problems, he became very distressed and his behaviour at school deteriorated.

> It got to the stage where I heard myself saying as my little boy cried himself to sleep at night, 'It's not long now' (to the end of term).

He started wetting the bed, and came home shaking if he had a spelling test to revise for the following day. His bad behaviour at school was frequently reported to his mother.

> The problem was by then you couldn't see the wood for the trees because the behaviour problems had become paramount.

Harry's mother suggested to the teacher that Harry's behaviour might partly be a response to a learning difficulty of some kind and was told:

> Rubbish he's just very immature, when he learns to behave properly and knuckles down to the work he'll be OK.

The following year when Harry was 8 years old he had a teacher who was more sympathetic in her outlook. She realised in conjunction with Harry's mother that something underlay the bad behaviour that he was displaying in class. By half-term she had identified him as dyslexic and appropriate support was set in place. From this point Harry's behaviour started to improve again.

Although a life history approach cannot be used in an empirical sense to 'prove' cause and effect it can suggest what might be happening and guide teachers and parents in checking out their suspicions or hunches. It can be argued that a life history approach is a useful adjunct to a curriculum based approach that focuses on the learning difficulties that a child is having at a specific point in time. Children bring to a learning situation their past experiences and expectations and by understanding these it is easier to get a wider picture of what might be happening. The problem for many teachers is that they don't automatically have access to a child's life history and what they do know may be second-hand and filtered through the school's perceptions of the child's past experiences. Harry, for example, had an August birthday and therefore was a little immature for his year group. In addition some of the cognitive deficits underlying dyslexia such as problems with sequencing led to difficulties with tasks like tying up shoe laces which added to the picture of a somewhat immature child. The problem was that this was then used exclusively to account for his disruptive behaviour whereas a fuller picture which showed that he was reasonably well behaved in the infants and responded well to supportive and encouraging teaching would have suggested that immaturity alone was not a sufficient explanation for his behaviour. In addition his mother's reports of his specific difficulty with reading tasks and the distress that they were causing him would suggest that this area needed investigating.

Life history inevitably involves bias and self-selection of what is presented and this can cause problems of validity and believing for both teachers and parents. This is made more difficult because they are observing children in totally different environments to which children may respond in different ways. Many of the parents in the study reported in this book and in other case studies said that their dyslexic child became quiet and withdrawn when they entered school. But this was often not noticed by the school because they had not seen the child before school or in the home environment so from the school's point of view the child's behaviour was normal and not a cause for concern. Again many parents reported that their child was showing distress at home as a direct consequence of going to school but it was difficult for the school to take this on board as the child was not showing this distress to a noticeable degree at school. The old adage 'seeing is believing' seems to apply and can perhaps explain some of the difficulty parents and especially teachers have in believing one another. The following is a typical account given by many parents on the difference in their child at school and at home.

He became a withdrawn, frightened, timid child at school. But once he was at home he was completely different. He'd be full of confidence and happy once he was outside, playing with his motorbike.

(Osmond, 1993)

Edwards (1994) documents in detail the lives of eight teenage boys attending a boarding school for children with dyslexia. In a sense it can be argued that these boys ended up in boarding school because they were extreme cases in terms of their reactions to mainstream school, with all eight displaying behaviour problems and seven out of the eight truanting. Edwards points out that she originally chose these boys as examples of 'successful dyslexics' who'd developed well in their special school and was shocked herself when she started interviewing them to find the degree of pain and humiliation these boys still felt over their past experiences. They all felt they had been neglected, humiliated and teased in their mainstream schools and five of them felt they had been treated unfairly or punitively by teachers. In all eight cases this had led to lack of confidence, self-doubt, and sensitivity to criticism and in five cases boys reported that at the worst points in their school career they had felt extremely isolated and despairing often wanting to hide or die. These same themes of distress and humiliation run through the interviews reported by Osmond and Van der Stoel and these sorts of experiences were not uncommon in the study to be described in this book. Whilst the degree and the range of such difficulties can be debated it is clear that how dyslexic children and their families cope with dyslexia is closely related to how such children are treated in school.

Summary

1. Both quantitative and qualitative methods have a role to play in researching the social and emotional consequences of dyslexia.
2. For dyslexic children reading, writing and spelling are their primary problems but these can lead to secondary problems such as inattentiveness, low motivation, restlessness or disruptive behaviour.
3. Reading-disabled children do as a group have lower self-esteem than non-reading-disabled children.
4. Teachers have a strong influence on a child's self-concept as a learner.
5. Systematic strategies can be employed to improve a child's self-esteem and self-concept as a learner.
6. Dyslexic children need specific help for their literacy difficulties allied to general help for their social and emotional well being.

References

Bannister, D. and Fransella, F. (1971) *Inquiring Man: The Theory of Personal Constructs*. Harmondsworth: Penguin.

Battle, J. (1990) *Self-Esteem the New Revolution*. Edmonton: James Battle Associates.

Battle, J. (1992) *Culture-Free Self-Esteem Inventories* (2nd edn). Austin, Texas: PRO-ED.

Beck, A. T., Rush, A. J., Shaw, B. F. and Emery, G. (1979) *Cognitive Therapy of Depression*. New York: Guildford.

Brophy, J. E. and Good, T. L. (1974) *Teacher–Student Relationships: Causes and Consequences*. New York: Holt, Rinehart and Winston.

Bruck, M. (1985) 'The adult functioning of children with specific learning disabilities: a follow-up study'. In I. Siegal (ed.) *Advances in Applied Developmental Psychology*. Norwood, NJ: Ablex.

Bryan, T. and Bryan, J. (1991) 'Positive mood and math performance'. *Journal of Learning Disabilities*, 24, 490–4.

Bullock, Lord A. (Chair) (1975) *A Language for Life*. London: HMSO.

Burns, R. (1982) *Self-Concept Development and Education*. London: Holt, Rinehart and Winston.

Butkowsky, T. S. and Willows, D. M. (1980) 'Cognitive-motivation and characteristics of children varying in reading ability; evidence of learned helplessness in poor readers'. *Journal of Educational Psychology*, 72 (3), 408–22.

Callison, C. P. (1974) 'Experimental induction of self-concept'. *Psychological Reports*, 35, 1235–8.

Casey, R., Levy, S. E., Brown, K. and Brooks-Gunn, J. (1992) 'Impaired emotional health in children with mild reading disability'. *Developmental and Behavioural Paediatrics*, 13 (4), 256–60.

Cattell, R. S., Eber, H. W. and Tatsuoka, M. M. (1970) *Handbook for the Sixteen Personality Factor Questionnaire*. Champagne, IL: Institute for Personality and Ability Testing.

Chapman, J., Silva, P. and Williams, S. (1984) 'Academic self-concept: some developmental and emotional correlates in nine year old children'. *British Journal of Educational Psychology*, 54, 284–92.

Coopersmith, S. (1967) *The Antecedents of Self-Esteem*. San Francisco: Freeman Press.

Darke, S. (1988) 'Anxiety and working memory capacity'. *Cognition and Emotion*, 2.

DES (Department of Education and Science) (1978) *Special Educational Needs (Warnock Report)*. Cmnd 7271. London: HMSO.

Edwards, J. (1994) *The Scars of Dyslexia*. London: Cassell.

Fairhurst, P. and Pumfrey, P. (1992). 'Secondary school organisation and the self concepts of pupils with relative reading difficulties'. *Research in Education*, 47.

Gentile, L. M. and Macmillan, M. M. (1987) *Stress and Reading Difficulties: Research Assessment and Intervention*. Newark, DE: International Reading Association.

Gjessing, H. J. and Karlsen, B. (1989) *A Longitudinal Study of Dyslexia*. New York: Springer Verlag.

Good, T. L. and Brophy, J. E. (1987) *Looking in Classrooms* (4th edn). New York: Harper and Row.

Gross, J. (1993) *Special Educational Needs in the Primary School*. Buckingham: Open University Press.

Hales, G. (1994) 'The human aspects of dyslexia'. In G. Hales (ed.) *Dyslexia Matters*. London: Whurr Publishers.

Hampshire, S. (1990) *Susan's Story*. London: Corgi.

Hargreaves, D. H. (1972) *Interpersonal Relations and Education*. London: Routledge and Kegan Paul.

Hinshaw, S. P. (1992) 'Externalising behaviour problems and academic underachievement in childhood and adolescence'. *Psychological Bulletin*, 111, 127–55.

Huntington, D. D. and Bender, W. D. (1993) 'Adolescents with learning disabilities at risk? Emotional well being, depression and suicide'. *Journal of Learning Disabilities*, 26, 159–66.

Jorm, A. F., Share, D. L., Maclean, R. and Matthews, R. (1986) 'Cognitive factors at school entry predictive of specific reading retardation and general reading backwardness'. *Journal of Child Psychology and Psychiatry*, 27, 45–54.

Kavanaugh, D. (ed.) (1978) *Listen to Us!* New York: Workman Publishing.

Kelly, G. A. (1955) *The Psychology of Personal Constructs*. New York: W. W. Norton.

Kosmos, K. A. and Kidd, A. H. (1991) 'Personality characteristics of dyslexic and non dyslexic adults'. *Psychological Reports*, 69, 231–4.

Lawrence, D. (1971) 'The effects of counselling on retarded readers'. *Educational Research*, 13 (2), 119–24.

Lawrence, D. (1973) *Improved Reading Through Counselling*. London: Ward Lock.

Lawrence, D. (1982) 'Development of a self-esteem questionnaire'. *British Journal of Educational Psychology*, 51, 245–9.

Lawrence, D. (1985) 'Improving self-esteem and reading'. *Educational Research*, 27 (3).

Lawrence, D. (1987) *Enhancing Self-Esteem in the Classroom*. London: Paul Chapman.

Marsh, H. W. (1992) 'Content specificity of relations between academic achievement and academic self-concept'. *Journal of Educational Psychology*, 84 (1), 35–42.

Marsh, H. W., Craven, R. G. and Debus, R. (1991) 'Self-concepts of young children 5 to 8 years of age: measurement and multi-dimensional structure'. *Journal of Educational Psychology*, 83 (3), 377–92.

Maughan, B. (1994) 'Behavioural development and reading disability'. In C. Hulme and M. Snowling (eds) *Reading Development and Dyslexia*. London: Whurr.

McGee, R., Share, D., Moffitt, T. E., Williams, S. and Silva, P. A. (1988) 'Reading disability, behaviour problems and juvenile delinquency'. In D. H. Saklofske and S. B. G. Eysenck (eds) *Individual Differences in Children and Adolescents*. London: Hodder and Stoughton.

Melck, E. (1986) 'Finding out about specific learning difficulties'. Available from 2, Manor House, Church Lawford, Warwickshire, CV23 9EC.

Miles, T. R. and Miles, E. (1990) *Dyslexia: A Hundred Years On*. Milton Keynes: Open University Press.

Mittler, P. (1985) 'Approaches to evaluation in special education: concluding reflections'. In S. Hegarty and P. Evans (eds) *Research and Evaluation Methods in Special Education*. Windsor: NFER-Nelson.

Orton, S. T. (1937) *Reading, Writing and Speech Problems in Children*. New York: Norton.

Osmond, J. (1993) *The Reality of Dyslexia*. London: Cassell.

Pianta, R. C. and Caldwell, C. B. (1990) 'Stability of externalising symptoms from kindergarten to first grade and factors related to instability'. *Development and Psychopathology*, 2, 247–58.

Porter, J. and Rourke, B. P. (1985) 'Socio-emotional functioning of learning disabled children. A subtype analysis of personality patterns'. In B. P. Rourke (ed.) *Neuropsychology of Learning Disabilities: Essentials of Subtype Analysis*. New York: Guildford.

Pumfrey, P. D. and Reason, R. (1991) *Specific Learning Difficulties (Dyslexia): Challenges, Responses and Recommendations*. London: Routledge.

Riddick, B. (1995) 'Dyslexia and development: an interview study'. *Dyslexia: An International Journal of Research and Practice*, 1 (2).

Rogers, C. R. (1951) *Client Centred Therapy*. Boston: Houghton Mifflin.

Rogers, C. (1982) *A Social Psychology of Schooling*. London: Routledge and Kegan Paul.

Rosenthal, J. (1973) 'Self-esteem in dyslexic children'. *Academic Therapy*, 9 (1), 27–39.

Rosenthal, R. and Jacobson, L. (1968) *Pygmalion in the Classroom*. New York: Holt, Rinehart and Winston.

Rowe, M. B. (1974) 'Wait time and rewards as instructional variables'. *Journal of Research in Science Teaching*, 2, 81–9.

Rutter, M., Tizard, J. and Whitmore, K. (eds) (1970) *Education, Health and Behaviour*. London: Longman and Green.

Speece, D.L., McKinney, J. D. and Appelbaum, M. I. (1985) 'Classification and validation of behavioural sub-types of learning disabled children'. *Journal of Educational Psychology*, 77, 67–77.

Spreen, O. (1987) *Learning Disabled Children Growing Up: A Follow Up into Adulthood*. Lisse, Netherlands: Swets and Zeitlinger.

Tansley, P. and Panckhurst, J. (1981) *Children with Specific Learning Difficulties: A Critical Review*. Windsor: NFER-Nelson.

Thomson, M. (1990) *Dyslexia and Development* (3rd edn). London: Whurr.

Thomson, M. and Hartley, G. M. (1980) 'Self-esteem in dyslexic children'. *Academic Therapy*, 16 (1), 19–36.

Van der Stoel, S. (ed.) (1990) *Parents on Dyslexia*. Clevedon: Multilingual Matters.

Yasutake, D. and Bryan, T. (1995) 'The influence of affect on the achievement of behaviour of students with learning disabilities'. *Journal of Learning Disabilities*, 28 (6), 329–44.

Zatz, S. and Chassin, L. (1985) 'Cognition of test anxious children under naturalistic test taking conditions'. *Journal of Consultancy and Clinical Psychology*, 53, 393–401.

Source

This is an edited version of a chapter previously published in *Living with Dyslexia*. 1996. Reproduced by permission of Taylor & Francis Ltd.

Chapter 18

An examination of the relationship between labelling and stigmatisation with special reference to dyslexia

Barbara Riddick

In this chapter it is argued that although labelling can lead to stigmatisation this is not always the case. Evidence is presented to demonstrate that stigmatisation can take place in the absence of formal labelling or stigmatisation can precede labelling. Most of the evidence presented is from two interview studies, one with 27 children and the other with 16 adults. It is suggested that further deconstruction of the labelling process is necessary, and that factors such as whether labels are formal or informal, private or public need to be taken into account. Finally, it is proposed that labelling can be considered at many levels of analysis from the personal to the political and that a coherent framework that integrates these different levels of analysis is needed.

Labelling is sometimes treated as a unitary construct as something that can be simply described as good or bad. However, as soon as it is inspected in any detail it becomes apparent that there are many aspects to this process and that there can be negative and positive consequences of labelling or not labelling. Gallagher (1976) provides a useful summary of the possible positive and negative outcomes of a label. He described the positives as:

1. Diagnosis and appropriate treatment and alteration to the environment.
2. To enable further research which may lead to better understanding, prevention and treatment.
3. To act as a positive way to call attention to a particular difficulty and obtain better resources through funding and legislation.

The negatives were:

1. The professionals labelling for its own sake, without suggesting any form of treatment or support.
2. As a way of maintaining the status quo by keeping minority groups at the bottom of the social hierarchy.
3. To maintain focus on within-child problems and not address the environmental factors which have produced or exacerbated the problems.

In this chapter it is suggested that the process can be broken down into a number of key areas:

1. The nature and content of the label.
2. What this label signifies to various social groups.
3. The relationship of the label to other labels.
4. The context in which it is applied.
5. Who applies/owns the label.
6. The purpose of labelling.
7. The developmental history associated with a label.

These various factors will be considered in relation to the label 'dyslexia'.

Beliefs about labelling

Among some educationalists there is a strong belief that 'labelling' children is harmful. The basic argument is that labelling can lead to stigmatisation, and give the child and adults involved negative expectations. A further argument is that each child is an individual and as such has an individual profile of educational needs which will not be fully identified if they are simply assumed to have the needs that are held to go with a particular label. In examining these beliefs it is apparent that a number of implicit assumptions are involved. The first is that labelling automatically leads to stigma. This is perhaps not a surprising assumption because there are many instances where labelling has led to stigma. The Spastics Society in Britain has recently changed its name to Scope because of the negative connotations surrounding the word 'spastic'. 'Spastic' started as a legitimate medical term to describe one of the major types of movement difficulty in individuals with cerebral palsy and only through inappropriate usage came to have negative connotations. However, this assumes that before the label 'spastic' was coined people with this and similar types of movement difficulty were not stigmatised. Christy Brown (1954) who had athetoid cerebral palsy describes in his autobiography his first awareness of stigmatisation at the age of 10.

> I hid my face whenever anybody strange passed me by, but I couldn't help seeing how they'd glanced at my face and then down at my hands, nodding their heads significantly to whoever was with them as they went up the road, glancing back at me till they passed out of sight.

At this point Christy Brown had no label for his severe motor difficulties and it is unlikely that many of his onlookers did either, but the effects of being perceived as having a negative difference from others were already being experienced by him.

> They went right through me, those looks from people in the streets. My brothers didn't think I took any notice, but I did. Even in the space of a

few weeks since my old go-cart broke down, I had become as different in mind as I now knew I was in body. I had become more sensitive, more apprehensive to those I met outside the home.

This shows quite clearly how stigmatisation can take place without a formal label. This is an important point because it suggests that labels on their own do not necessarily lead to stigma, but that labels can encapsulate or distil the stigmatisation that already exists. It can also be argued that the particular form of a label relative to the cultural context in which it is being applied can increase or decrease the existing level of stigmatisation attached to it. So it can be argued that mentally handicapped, by it's very terminology, is seen by some to emphasise the negative whereas describing someone as an exceptional learner is thought to give a more positive perspective. A particularly important point has been to try and change the way in which labels are used so that instead of a person being described solely in terms of their label, e.g. she is deaf, the shift has been towards emphasising that someone is an individual first who happens to have certain special attributes, e.g. she has a hearing impairment. Szivos (1992) points out the tension between labels that can be seen to devalue or highlight negative differences and labels that are used as a positive assertion of difference such as 'gay' or 'black'. In a similar vein some individuals with perceived impairments use this form of terminology to assert a positive difference such as 'deaf' or 'dyslexic'.

Labelling and stigmatisation

The assumption that labelling leads to stigmatisation or, indeed, that the two are virtually interchangeable terms drew heavily on the writings of Szasz (1961), Becker (1963), Lemert (1967) and Goffman (1968). However, Goffman (1968) in his book entitled *Stigma* makes not a single reference to the term labelling. The whole book is concerned with the direct effects that peoples reactions to disabled individuals has on them. Although recent critics (Barnes *et al.*, 1999) suggest that Goffman gave too negative an account of individuals' responses to stigmatisation, his work based on direct observations did raise some important points. For example, Goffman distinguished between the experience of having a visible disability such as a withered hand and a hidden disability such as illiteracy. He proposed that in terms of stigmatisation the former were already discredited, whereas the latter were discreditable in that the potential was there for their disability to be found out. He also pointed out that those with a hidden disability may have already been discredited in certain circumstances, and may therefore have to face difficult issues of when or when not to disclose their disabilities.

Labelling and categorisation

Closely allied to the concerns about labelling were concerns about the categorisation of children. These concerns were identified in Britain by the

Warnock report (DES, 1978), which abolished statutory categories, such as physically handicapped or maladjusted, and introduced instead the concept of a continuum of special educational needs. However, as Pumfrey and Mittler (1989) have pointed out, what has happened in effect is that a number of diverse categories have been replaced by two superordinate categories of special educational needs or non-special educational needs. In 1989 Pumfrey and Mittler argued that:

> The concept of SEN (special educational needs) has served its useful awareness raising function and should now be abandoned and replaced with a more precise formulation and quantification of inter- and intra-individual differences.

Jordan and Powell (1992) argue that 'An educational dogma has developed that discredits the labelling of children'. What these kinds of comments express is disquiet from highly experienced special needs researchers and practitioners about the vagueness and lack of clarity in understanding some children's special educational needs. In theory, the concept of special educational needs meant that for each child their particular needs would be identified and addressed. However, the idea that each child's needs could be identified without reference to a body of knowledge arranged around an existing label or category was an optimistic and idealistic one, based on the assumption that highly experienced and trained professionals with plenty of time to investigate each child would be available. At the teaching level, it was assumed that much of this could be done by closely observing children's behaviour. However, this assumes that simply observing behaviour is a reliable way of identifying children's difficulties. One of the problems with this is that children can display the same behaviour for a variety of reasons. So a junior age child who is restless and disruptive in class may have personal difficulties at home, may have problems of attention, may have a poor teacher, may have general problems in learning or may be having specific difficulties in learning to read and write among a number of possible explanations. It is only by being able to accurately identify the cognitions (thinking) and the emotions behind the behaviour as well as the more self-evident environmental factors that a reliable and accurate conclusion can be reached. The important point is that the teacher has a variety of possible explanations available which focus on both environmental and within-child factors, and the interaction between them. The teacher in collaboration with others also needs to know how to effectively carry out preliminary investigations to identify more clearly what a child's special needs are. Many educationalists would say that these points are obvious and hardly need reiterating, but evidence from practice would suggest otherwise. Riddick (1995, 1996) found that half the parents in her study were offered solely environmental explanations such as moving school to account for the marked difficulties their children were having in learning to read and write. These children were all later clearly identified as having dyslexia, and many of these children went through considerable distress and unhappiness because their difficulties were not correctly identified and addressed sooner. In some cases teachers stated quite clearly that they did not believe in the concept of dyslexia so in having no intention of looking for specific within-child factors and their interaction with the educational environment they inevitably made incorrect attributions of negative environmental factors at home or within-child factors, such as slowness or laziness. Other teachers were neutral about the concept of dyslexia or specific learning difficulties in that they didn't know what it was or how to identify it. Although some of these teachers were sympathetic to the child's problems, they said they were mystified by them and unsure what to do. In this case it was found that without some prior knowledge of specific learning difficulties teachers were not able to construct an accurate model for themselves which would effectively inform their mode of intervention.

> They did try for him they really did, but they basically didn't know what was wrong, they didn't know what to do.
>
> (Riddick, 1996)

A particular difficulty in the case of dyslexia is that it is a hidden impairment where there are no obvious physical markers which will identify the child. In addition, different children present with very different behaviours, both because the nature and the degree of their difficulties vary and also because different children respond to them in very different ways. Some children respond with disruptive behaviour whereas probably many more respond by becoming quiet and withdrawn in the classroom. Many children also expend considerable energy in covering up their difficulties.

> I asked him what on earth this ERIC was. It stood he told me for enjoyable reading in class, apparently they had to choose a book and sit and read it silently to themselves. At this time he couldn't read at all so I was curious to know what he did during these sessions. He said what he did was to take a book and sit with it and stare at the pictures so he could try and work out what was going in case the teacher should ask him. He said he also watched the other children and turned a page when they did to try and give the impression he was reading the book. These sessions were quite long and he said the worse thing was they were very boring and he was also terrified of being found out.
>
> (Riddick, 1996)

Goffman uses the term passing to describe these kinds of strategies where a person tries to hide some aspect of themselves for which they think they might be stigmatised.

Evident and hidden disability (1)

Goffman (1968) suggests that even more critical than the notion of visibility is the notion of how evident a certain impairment is. Experience to date would indicate that dyslexia is not an evident impairment unless you already have some understanding of it and some willingness to look for the appropriate evidence. The interesting point is that once someone understands the construct and the signs that alert one to it they appear to have little difficulty in identifying individuals with dyslexia. Several dyslexic children in the Riddick (1995, 1996) study commented that they thought they knew of other children in their class or school who were dyslexic, and that if they could spot them then teachers should be able to as well. It is also important to note that the majority of children in this study thought that other children were aware that they had difficulties with their work even though the label dyslexia had not been publicly used. In other words, children felt stigmatised by other children because of visible signs like their poor spelling or handwriting or because they always finished last, not because of the label dyslexia. Many of them also internalised these negative evaluations of themselves and described their feelings of shame and self-denigration in the school environment before they had been identified as having dyslexia.

> I felt like I was not like one of them, and when you don't know anything and the other kids know more than you, you think like you are the lowest thing on earth.

A student in a later study by Riddick *et al.* (1997) made the following response when asked if he'd ever been ridiculed about his dyslexia:

> No one has ever really ridiculed me for my dyslexia, but I have been ridiculed for not being able to read things.

This student was making the point that he hadn't been ridiculed or stigmatised because he had the label dyslexia, but because of specific aspects of his performance that others picked up on that were quite independent to the labelling process. Other students reiterated this theme and several students who were not identified as dyslexic until after school gave clear accounts of stigmatisation at school.

> At school a lot of teachers ridiculed it constantly. . . . I keep dreaming about being back at school and being told I am lazy, stupid and silly and if I don't learn to read and write I won't be anything, I won't get a job, I'll never learn to drive, I'll probably be on the streets sleeping rough.

In a similar vein some of the mature students in the study who had either not known they were dyslexic or had not disclosed that they were dyslexic at the time talked about past incidences of stigmatisation at work.

I had to leave a note for my boss's husband and it was the only occasion I ever did it and the man was absolutely foul with all the staff not just me, but eventually I did become singled out because he took to reading things I had written and he used to ring red lines round them, and he kept saying you're so stupid you should be neater, he would actually be so silly, wretched little mistakes, how can you do that and it doesn't give a good impression, it wasn't going out to anyone other than him, it wounded my self-esteem appallingly.

So it is quite clear that stigmatisation can go on independent of any formal labelling. In both the Riddick (1996) and the Riddick *et al.* (1997) study it was found that the majority of adults and children with dyslexia found the label helpful at a private level and many were quite emphatic about the importance of having such a label.

I'd rather know I've got dyslexia than think I was an idiot.

(School age child)

It helps me understand.

(School age child)

I remember after I had seen the educational psychologist and got the results back, it was like a massive weight had lifted off my shoulder and suddenly I wasn't stupid any more.

(Student)

It had a name, I wasn't stupid, the psychologist said I wasn't stupid, and it was a lovely feeling.

(Student)

Another student on being asked if he got anyone to proof read his work had replied 'no, never'. He was then asked why not.

I'm not embarrassed to admit I'm dyslexic but I know it's going to be riddled with mistakes. . . . The spelling mistakes that I make are really stupid, I don't want anyone to see them.

This illustrates that for this individual it is not the label dyslexia that is stigmatising for him, but his actual spelling that he is ashamed of and wants to hide. Some children and adults felt that since they had been given the label dyslexia they no longer needed to feel ashamed of various aspects of their literacy.

Definitely because beforehand (before he knew he was dyslexic) . . . you don't want people to see your handwriting and this sort of stuff whereas now it doesn't really matter and they know it's not my fault rushing it or anything like that.

Here, the label is seen as conveying a positive message in preventing negative attributions of carelessness or laziness. It was similarly felt by many of the children and students that having the label dyslexia countered the more general negative attribution that they were slow or stupid and they were therefore positive about the label at both private and public level of usage.

> No teacher now brands me as thick, 'cause I've told them I was dyslexic.

> I don't care I tell everyone with a big neon flashing light, it's a good thing actually to be labelled it, than not being labelled it, because you've still got the same problems whether labelled or not. It's perceived in a better way knowing you're dyslexic than not knowing you're dyslexic, if you just can't read they thought I was thick, (dyslexia is) actually a reason for not being able to read.

Gerber et al. (1996) have suggested that one of the key features of successful adults with learning disabilities[1] is that they have been able to reframe their earlier learning difficulties and put them into a more positive context. For many individuals with dyslexia a label that adequately explains their difficulties appears to be an important first step in this process.

Having said this approximately half the children and adults in these studies (Riddick, 1996; Riddick et al., 1997) expressed concern about others outside the family knowing about their difficulties. Among both children and adults their concern about publicly using the term dyslexia was that others would ridicule them and think less of them.

> I've always been so scared of saying it is dyslexia. I don't tell people because I'm so scared of being called stupid.
>
> (Mature student)

> I don't want to tell anyone, because I think they'll tell everyone else, and then everybody might tease me.
>
> (Primary age child)

However, even in cases like this it was the difficulties embodied by the word dyslexia that these individuals were particularly concerned to hide or had come to feel ashamed of.

> It often happens when I'm halfway down the first page when everyone has read it and taken it in and I feel totally out of it, and I think if I can't read I shouldn't be here.
>
> (University student)

I try and cover my writing with my hand so the boy next to me can't see it.

(School child)

The critical question is whether public usage of the label dyslexia increases or decreases an individual's experience of stigmatisation. Not surprisingly, those children and students who thought that dyslexia was perceived negatively by others were reluctant to use it in public, whereas those that saw it as having basically positive connotations were willing to use it in public. Another factor interacting with this appeared to be how ashamed or unashamed of their difficulties an individual was and how this, in turn, influenced the degree to which they were reticent or forthcoming about their difficulties. Sophie a 16-year-old school girl was ashamed and frustrated by her severe literacy difficulties, and said she had told none of her friends at school about them. When, at the age of 13, she had first been told she had dyslexia she had been upset and shocked, but now, at the age of 16, she was positive about the label at a personal level, especially as a way of feeling she was not the only one with the problem. She was critical of the negative attitude of her school towards dyslexia.

Well people think you're stupid to be quite honest, that's the whole attitude of it.

(Riddick, 1996)

Sophie felt that the school should be promoting better understanding and a more positive attitude towards dyslexia.

Just to make people more aware of it so you don't feel like you've got some horrible disease. People just jump to the wrong conclusion and they should be educated about what dyslexia means. It's just been one of my dreams to tell them all what it means.

In cases like this the argument is that rather than not using the label in public because of its negative connotations, individuals would like the public to have a more informed and positive view of the label so that it can be used. Several of the students interviewed endorsed this argument, and some took it further in suggesting that it was up to other people to be informed about dyslexia, and if they were not it was their problem and not one that the person with dyslexia should feel they need to take responsibility for.

It didn't bother me . . . telling someone I was dyslexic. Why not, I mean what is their problem?

Barga (1996), in a qualitative study of nine students with learning disabilities[1] in the USA, found that students experienced labelling as positive when it helped them to make sense of the academic difficulties they were encountering and enabled them to get the help that they needed. Labelling was seen as negative when it set students apart from their peers and meant that they received different provision from other students. However, it can be argued that this is really a criticism about how support and intervention are arranged in response to a particular label or category. At one time in Britain, very young visually impaired children were sent away from home to receive specialist schooling. This has not been used as an argument to invalidate the label of visual impairment, but has led to changes in practice and provision in response to the needs of individuals with visual impairments. As noted by one of the students earlier in this chapter you have still got the same problems whether you are labelled or not; the key question is whether the label enhances or detracts from the way you perceive yourself and are perceived by others. Barga cites the case of a student who is dissuaded from taking a particular course as an example of labelling and consequent stigmatisation. However, this student does not have the required grades and has a history of failing classes, so it is unlikely that, label or no label, he would have been allowed to do the course. It is true that certain labels especially when applied inappropriately lead to a person being stigmatised, but this is not always the case and the question has to be asked how would this person be treated in the absence of a formal label and will a formal label increase or decrease stigmatisation. It may also be important to distinguish between the private and public functions of a label or construct. In some instances, a label may be perceived as helpful at the level of personal understanding and control, but not be perceived as helpful in the public arena or vice versa.

Formal and informal labels

The implicit assumption behind criticising labels appears to be that in the absence of formal labels there will be no labelling taking place. However, it can be argued that in numerous instances negative informal labelling takes place (Gottlieb et al., 1986; Knight, 1999). Many children and adults with dyslexia reported being informally labelled as lazy, careless or stupid before they were given a formal label (Van der Stoel, 1990; Osmond, 1993; Edwards, 1994; Riddick, 1996; Riddick et al., 1997). Despite the difficulties of formal labels they do have the advantage that evidence has to be produced to justify their usage. This evidence may well be contested, but it does mean that the assumptions supporting the use of a label are made explicit and are open to serious examination. The implicit assumptions behind informal labels or attributions are rarely open to public scrutiny or debate. It can be argued that when someone gets to the point of saying about a child 'I don't want to label him or her' they are already informally labelling the child as a worry, troublesome, odd, vulnerable, puzzling, etc. Riddick and Hall (2000) found that some practitioners of children as young as 3 years were already using informal labels such as lazy or spoilt to describe children who were having perceived difficulties with the nursery curriculum. The legitimate concerns surrounding formal labels have been well rehearsed over a number of years and include for children the dangers of a self-fulfilling prophecy, inappropriate or stigmatising labels, and premature labelling for transitory difficulties either of an environmental or developmental nature. However, there has been less examination, in an educational context, of the informal labels and attributions that invariably precede the labelling process. In the absence of a formal label these can continue in some cases for the whole of a child's school career.

Specificity of labels

There are often difficult issues about the degree of specificity that a label should have and this, in turn, will depend on the purpose for which the label is being used, and the context in which it is being applied and who is doing the applying. The arguments in the 1970s and 1980s against specific labelling have led to the adoption of very broad labels such as learning disabled in the USA and special educational needs in Britain. The difficulty is that the labels are so broad and inclusive and include such a heterogeneous group of individuals that they end up conveying little more than the fact that a child is thought to have a problem of some kind. Three out of the four students in Barga's study who were identified as having a problem whilst at school resented the fact that they had been placed in educational classes with a wide range of disabled students, including students with emotional and behavioural difficulties. The following comment by one of the mothers in the Riddick (1996) study typified the view of many of the mothers of children with dyslexia.

> And I think when they do say 'special needs', I think that's a big umbrella, and they can sort of fit everything into it.

Critics sometimes construe this as elitism and a wish to distance yourself from a group you perceive to have a greater negative difference than yourself. However, an alternative view is that what people are objecting to is misattributions being made about their impairment which have consequences for the way they are responded to. It was understandable that people who were deaf objected to also being seen as 'dumb', and people with severe movement and speech difficulties objected to being treated as severely 'mentally handicapped'. It might be appropriate to speak more slowly or simply to someone who processes speech more slowly and needs time to comprehend what is being said, but it is obviously not appropriate for individuals who do not have such difficulties. To create responsive environments we have to be clear about the abilities of the individuals the environment is responding to.

Ownership of labels

Bogdanowicz (1996) in Poland found that, when she systematically surveyed the understanding of the term dyslexia by different members of the public including various professional groups, the best informed group were parents of dyslexic children, rather than educationalists. This finding may not seem surprising, but it does highlight an issue over the ownership of labels and who has the right to suggest their usage. Tomlinson (1993) suggests that over the last 20 years professionals have gained unprecedented power in the area of special needs and that the voices of other groups such as parents are rarely heard.

Tomlinson goes on to argue that most of these professionals in Britain would claim that they are working in the best interests of the child following an ideology of benevolent humanitarianism. The problem with this is that it obscures the fact that many of the professionals are working for the state as part of the system by which troublesome groups are controlled, and scarce or inadequate resources are apportioned out. In the case of dyslexia parents and voluntary associations have argued for its existence, whereas a significant proportion of educational professionals have denied or ignored its validity. Interestingly, as evidence for a cognitive and biological basis to dyslexia (albeit in interaction with environmental factors) has increased professionals antagonistic to the construct have shifted their argument away from complete denial to criticising the way that the label is used by parents and voluntary organisations to identify and support children. There is nothing inherently wrong with this, but when on best estimates 4 per cent (Miles and Miles, 1999) of children are struggling with severe specific learning difficulties often without adequate acknowledgement and support it seems odd that these professionals are not vigorously campaigning for improvements for all these children as a priority before criticising more specific aspects of the support process. It is also interesting that almost none of this criticism is aimed at schools or educationalists for failing to identify and support children with dyslexia, but is aimed at those who are asking for more support for such children. It can be argued that the kind of questions asked by researchers reflects their own priorities and assumptions. Riddell et al. (1994) in Scotland in one of the first major surveys of specific learning difficulties made it a priority to ask whether children with dyslexia were getting preferential treatment compared to other groups of children with learning difficulties. Not an unreasonable question to ask, but one that would be expected to be asked when more fundamental questions such as whether all children with dyslexia were being identified and supported had been asked. What some educationalists seem to be objecting to is parents asking for a previously unmet need to be met. In doing this they are seen to be arguing with professionals about how a problem is defined and dealt with. This is not simply an argument about resources, but an argument about the right to define a problem in a certain way.

Many educational professionals prefer the term specific learning difficulties to dyslexia because they argue it places such children on the continuum of special educational needs. They tend to see the term dyslexia emanating from a medical model of disability with its purported emphasis on within-child factors and an exclusive category of children. However, the educational model of dyslexia which terms it specific learning difficulties can also be criticised. This is a term coined to fit the conceptualisations of educationalists and has not been negotiated with individuals with dyslexia. It may be that this term fits into the notion of a continuum of special educational needs within the school context. However, this assumes that school is the focal point for understanding and negotiating the nature and experience of such difficulties. It places power firmly in the hands of educational professionals and allows for a narrow curriculum-focused conception of such difficulties. Dyslexia does not stop at the school gate or at school leaving age and the difficulties encountered span a wide range of situations. Riddick *et al.* (1997) found that writing cheques was the situation most frequently mentioned by university students as highly stressful. The term 'dyslexia' despite its medical roots is seen by many dyslexics and their families as a more socially valid label which allows them to access a diverse range of support from specialist societies, support groups, positive role models, specialist literature, etc. It also allows individuals the chance to identify with the culture of dyslexia and, in doing so, start to empower themselves. It may be the empowerment that the term dyslexia signifies that threatens some members of the educational establishment. Oliver and Barnes (1998) note that there are often two distinct definitions of disability, with an official one used by professionals and academics, and a separate one used by disabled people and their organisations.

Evident and hidden disability (2)

An interesting question is whether labels have a developmental history of their own. It may be that, in the case of hidden impairments such as dyslexia, autism and dyspraxia, one of the first functions of a label is to prove the legitimacy of the impairment by demonstrating its constitutional origins to those who are sceptical of the construct. In cases like this people with such impairments may choose a strong form of label that emphasises their differences in order to explain the nature of their difficulties and prevent what they see as negative or dismissive attributions of their difficulties. Most disabled individuals are only too aware of the environmental factors that help to create difficulties for them, but with hidden disabilities you first have to prove that you have a disability before you have the legitimacy to go on and challenge the society that is helping to produce your difficulty. Dyslexia in many ways exemplifies the social model of disability in that before mass literacy dyslexia was not a widespread problem and it is societal changes that have created dyslexia. Alongside the more traditional impairment model of dyslexia the newer conception of dyslexia as a positive difference is gaining ground (West, 1991). Although at one level dyslexia can be seen as a relatively trivial impairment at another level it poses a strong challenge to society for two reasons. One is that a considerable proportion of the population have dyslexia type difficulties (up to 10 per cent; Peer, 1994; Miles and Miles, 1999) and the second is that it challenges many implicit and explicit assumptions about literacy (people who cannot spell are careless, people who cannot spell should not be teachers). At a practical level it poses a challenge to the way literacy is taught and assessed in schools. It also challenges the implicit assumptions held by many educationalists of a highly positive correlation between literacy skills and overall ability to learn.

It may be that in the case of hidden or not evident impairments labelling serves the function of explaining why specific aspects of a person's behaviour should not be judged negatively by the prevailing cultural standards. Paradoxically, in this case labelling can be seen as having a positive role in pointing up differences which are not visible, whereas for evidently disabled people the problem is that they are often visually perceived as different. In this instance labels can be seen as having a negative role in underlining the differences, rather than the overriding similarities that they have to the wider culture. Low (1996) suggests that disabled individuals are trying to negotiate interconnected, and sometimes contradictory, non-disabled and disabled identities depending on their environmental circumstances.

Concluding comments

What do these discussions about labelling and dyslexia have to say about the wider issues of labelling and future models of disability/ability?

One is that we need a more careful deconstruction of the role of labelling. Some (Johnstone, 1998) have seen labelling as an unnecessary and wholly destructive process. The assumption from this perspective appears to be that abolishing labelling will abolish stigmatisation and discrimination. Dyson and Millward (1998) suggest that a *millennialist* deconstruction of special needs however valuable may be based on the false assumption that an ideal state where inequality and discrimination do not exist can be reached.

Another point of view would be to see formal labelling as an historical process which can be dispensed with when it has served (at best) certain awareness raising and educative functions and is no longer seen as a productive part of the lives of disabled people. Whether formal labelling is an inevitable part of this process or with newer models of disability/difference can be largely circumvented is as yet unclear.

A third point of view is for ownership of the labelling process by disabled people, and a move towards self-definition with personal understanding and control at the centre. We all have multiple identities and roles in life, and may wish to have several overlapping identities that are relative to context and time. Several writers have stressed that a social or rights model of disability does not preclude medical considerations where they are relevant to an individual's experience of disability. Others (Zola, 1994; Crow, 1996; Williams, 1996) argue that a social model alone is not sufficient in explicating people's experiences of disability. They argue for a more interactionist analysis which allows for individual variation in how physical impairments/differences are experienced, to be considered in relation to social, economic, environmental and political forces. Quicke and Winter (1994) suggest that, from an inter-actionist perspective, labelling can lead to either positive or negative discrimination depending on the context and the nature of the label. They also posit that there is often a tension between these two outcomes. Oliver and Barnes (1998) express concern that 'post'-theorising 'plays down the materiality of disabled people's lives' and that discourse analysis although important is only part of a wider analysis. Analysis at this level may be furthered by considering some of the social-psychological factors that mediate the experience of disability and influence the reactions of others to disability. Leyens *et al.* (1994) in an overview of the literature on stereotyping conclude that it is intrinsic to human interaction and can be seen as a way of managing complex information systems to facilitate communication. In this scenario, stereotyping is neither inherently good or bad, it depends on what is being communicated and the power relationship between the communicators. They also contend that a set of naive meta-theories prescribe a number of rules that people must apply when making such judgements. In relation to labelling this would suggest we need to know more about the social psychological factors that influence it and their reciprocal interaction with wider cultural influences. Theories based on wishing and hoping are not good enough, some rapproche-ment between everyday pragmatics and social construction must be reached if disability theory is to represent the diverse experiences and perceptions of disabled people. Rorty (1998) suggests that 'disengagement from practice produces theoretical hallucinations'.

Note

1   Learning disability is the US term closest to the British term specific learning difficulties, and is used in this chapter where research is reported under this label. Both are educational terms that primarily include dyslexia.

References

Barga, N.A. (1996) Students with learning disabilities in higher education managing a disability, *Journal of Learning Disabilities*, 29, pp. 413–421.

Barnes, C., Mercer, G. and Shakespeare, T. (1999) *Exploring Disability: a sociological introduction* (Cambridge, Polity Press).

Becker, H.S. (1963) *Outsiders: studies in the sociology of deviance* (New York, Free Press).

Bogdanowicz, M. (1996) Awareness of dyslexia in Poland, Keynote speech, Dyslexia in Higher Education, 2nd International Conference, Dartington Hall, Devon, UK.

Brown, C. (1954) *My Left Foot* (London, Mandarin Books).

Crow, L. (1996) Including all our lives: renewing the social model of disability, in: J. Morris (ed.) *Encounters with Strangers: feminism and disability* (London, Women's Press).

DES (Department of Education and Science) (1978) *Special Educational Needs (Warnock Report)*, Cmnd 72771, London, HMSO.

Dyson, A. and Millward, A. (1998) Theory and practice in special education, in: P. Haug and J. Tossebro (eds) *Theoretical Perspectives on Special Education* (Norway, Norwegian Academic Press).

Edwards, J. (1994) *The Scars of Dyslexia* (London, Cassell).

Gallagher, J.J. (1976) The sacred and profane uses of labels, *Exceptional Children*, 45, pp. 3–7.

Gerber, P.J., Reiff, H.B. and Ginsberg, R. (1996) Reframing the learning disabilities experience, *Journal of Learning Disabilities*, 29, pp. 98–101.

Goffman, E. (1968) *Stigma: notes on the management of spoiled identity* (Harmondsworth, Pelican Books).

Gottlieb, J., Alter, M., Gottlieb, B.W. and Wishner, J. (1994) Special education in urban America: it's not justifiable for many, *Journal of Special Education*, 27, pp. 453–465.

Johnstone, D. (1998) *An Introduction to Disability Studies* (London, David Fulton Publishers).

Jordan, R. and Powell, S. (1992) Stop the reforms, Calvin wants to get off, *Disability and Society*, 7(1), pp. 85–88.

Knight, B.A. (1999) Towards inclusion of students with special needs in the regular classroom, *Support for Learning*, 14(1), pp. 3–7.

Lemert, E.M. (1967) *Human Deviance, Social Problems, and Social Control* (Englewood Cliffs, NJ, Prentice Hall).

Leyens, J.P., Yzerbyt, V. and Schadron, G. (1994) *Stereotypes and Social Cognition* (London, Sage Publications).

Low, J. (1996) Negotiating identities, negotiating environments: an interpretation of the experiences of students with disabilities, *Disability and Society*, 11, pp. 235–248.

Miles, T.M. and Miles, E. (1999) *Dyslexia: a hundred years on*, 2nd edn (Buckingham, Open University Press).

Oliver, M. and Barnes, C. (1998) *Disabled People and Social Policy* (London, Longman).

Osmond, J. (1993) *The Reality of Dyslexia* (London, Cassell).

Peer, L. (1994) *Dyslexia: the training and awareness of teachers* (Reading, British Dyslexia Association).

Pumfrey, P. and Mittler, P. (1989) Peeling off the label, *Times Educational Supplement* 3842, pp. 29–30.

Quicke, J. and Winter, C. (1994) Labelling and learning: an interactionist perspective, *Support for Learning*, 9, pp. 16–21.

Riddell, S., Brown, S. and Duffield, J. (1994) Parental power and special educational needs: the case of specific learning difficulties, *British Educational Research Journal*, 20, pp. 327–344.

Riddick, B. (1995) Dyslexia: dispelling the myths, *Disability and Society*, 10(4), pp. 457–473.

Riddick, B. (1996) *Living with Dyslexia: the social and emotional consequences of specific learning difficulties* (London, Routledge).

Riddick, B. and Hall, E. (2000) Match or mismatch: the perceptions of parents of nursery age children related to those of the children's main nursery workers, *International Journal of Early Years Education*, 18(2), pp. 115–130.

Riddick, B., Farmer, M. and Sterling, C. (1997) *Students and Dyslexia: growing up with a specific learning difficulty* (London, Whurr Publishers).

Rorty, R. (1998) The dark side of the academic left, *Chronicle of Higher Education*, 3, pp. 134–136.

Szasz, T. (1961) *The Myth of Mental Illness* (New York, Harper Row).

Szivos, S. (1992) The limits of integration, in: H. Brown and H. Smith (eds) *Normalisation: a reader for the nineties* (London, Routledge).

Tomlinson, S. (1993) Conflicts and dilemmas for professionals in special education, in: L. Apelt (ed.) *Social Justice, Equity and Dilemmas of Disability in Education* (Brisbane, Queensland Department of Education).

Van der Stoel, S. (ed.) (1990) *Parents on Dyslexia* (Clevedon, Multilingual Matters).

West, T. (1991) *In the Mind's Eye* (New York, Prometheus Books).

Williams, G. (1996) Representing disability: some questions of phenomenology and politics, in: C. Barnes and G. Mercer (eds) *Exploring the Divide: illness and disability* (Leeds, Disability Press).

Zola, I. (1994) Towards inclusion: the role of people with disabilities in policy and research in the United States – a historical and political analysis, in: M.H. Rioux and M. Bach (eds) *Disability is not Measles: new research paradigms in disability* (North York, Ont., Roeher Institute).

Source

This is an edited version of an article previously published in *Disability and Society*, 15 (4). 2000. Reproduced by permission of Taylor & Francis Ltd.

Chapter 19

The long-term effects of two interventions for children with reading difficulties

Qualifications and Curriculum Authority

In 1997 the government launched the National Literacy Strategy which has as its aim that, by 2000, 80 per cent of all 11-year-olds will reach the standards expected of their age (i.e. Level 4) in the Key Stage 2 National Curriculum tests. This follows analyses of literacy standards in English which suggested a 'long tail of underachievement'. The National Literacy Strategy Framework and the structure of the Literacy Hour address what is to be taught and how. Within this major initiative there are likely to be some children who, in the short term at least, find it hard to catch on to reading and writing. The interventions studied here are intended to offer help to such children. This evaluation, which is of international significance, offers evidence as to their effectiveness.

Introduction

This study, a long-term evaluation over six years, was set up to consider the effectiveness of intervention programmes aimed at very poor or non-readers at the age of six. Some of the approaches used in the interventions are relevant to all pupils and there are clear links between these approaches and those advocated in the National Literacy Strategy. The work reported [. . .] is, however, limited to specific programmes for a particular group of children, and shows the value of longitudinal studies in this area.

In the context of concern over achievements in literacy, there has been both interest and debate about interventions which might prevent later problems.

Traditionally, children in England have been offered additional help with reading problems when they have been in the school system for several years. However, in the last decade evidence has been growing to suggest that early intervention may be advisable. This study considers the effectiveness of two such interventions aimed at preventing reading failure.

Aims of the research study

The aim of the present study was to investigate practical ways of helping children who had made a slow start in their reading, and to establish whether or not early intervention was effective over the longer term. Two programmes were evaluated, both with a proven track record, but with very different approaches. The first, Reading Recovery, is one of the most successful early interventions with a broad model of reading. The second, a phonological intervention closely based on that of Bradley and Bryant,[1] has a narrower focus but has been found effective in a research setting.

The effectiveness of the programmes was assessed in the short term, in the medium term and in the long term. In addition programme costs were monitored. We also investigated whether either of these programmes was particularly suited to certain groups of children, as such information could be useful in planning targeted intervention.

The interventions

Reading Recovery

Reading Recovery is an intervention designed to help children who are in the bottom 20 per cent of their class after one year of schooling. It is best characterised as a preventative intervention, rather than a remedial programme, as many of the children who are offered Reading Recovery are barely reading at all. The aim is early correction of inadequate strategies used by these children so that they will go on to be independent readers.

One feature of Reading Recovery which is different from other interventions is its attention to implementation issues. To work effectively, Reading Recovery aims to achieve change along four dimensions:[2]

- behavioural change on the part of teachers;
- child behaviour change achieved by teaching;
- organisational changes in schools achieved by teachers and administrators;
- changes in financing by controlling authorities.

The full implementation of Reading Recovery requires in-service training and support of teachers consistent with its emphasis on the quality of instruction. Experienced teachers are selected for training as tutors. The training takes one year and includes fortnightly seminars where teachers acquire skills in observational, diagnostic, and assessment techniques and are taught about the model of reading underpinning Reading Recovery. Additional training is required for tutors who are certified to train and support Reading Recovery teachers in their Education Authority and the continuing support and monitoring role of the tutor is seen as crucial to maintain the quality of implementation in the post training years.

Reading Recovery training is expensive and some have argued that such extensive training is unnecessary. However, Pinnell and her colleagues (1994) found that the programme ceased to be effective when implemented by teachers who had been trained in a much shorter course. The longer course is likely to raise theoretical understanding to ensure a more accurate delivery of the programme and to gain the commitment of the teachers, elements which have been identified as hallmarks of a successful intervention.

Reading Recovery: the model of reading and learning

According to Clay, reading is defined as a 'message-gaining, problem solving activity which increases power and flexibility the more it is practised'.[3] She suggests that children make use of a variety of strategies to help them in this problem solving activity, the most central of which are: understanding of the concepts of print, phonological awareness (both of the sounds in words and of the letters and letter strings on the page), understanding of the meaning of the text and also knowledge of syntax. Meaning is not derived from the print alone but also from the knowledge of the world that readers bring to the task, for example, their knowledge of the language of books and language in general, their prior knowledge of the subject matter of the text and their ability to make inferences. The goal of Reading Recovery is to help children to use all the skills or strategies that they have at their disposal. An important aspect of this is to encourage children to monitor their own reading, detecting and correcting errors by checking responses against all the possible sources of information.

Reading Recovery: structure of the sessions and discontinuation

Children who have been in school for one year (aged around six years old in New Zealand and the UK) and who are the poorest readers in their class are considered eligible for Reading Recovery where it is available. Selection is made on the basis of a battery of tests which cover concepts about print, letter identification, word reading, word writing and dictation, and the text reading level.[4] The precise selection is a professional judgement, made on the basis of a child's profile of scores. It is recommended that the bottom 20 per cent of readers in the age band be offered the programme.

Once selected, children are withdrawn from their class for individual tuition of half an hour daily until they have reached the average reading level of their classmates. For the first two weeks the teacher and pupil 'roam around the known', reading and writing together in an unstructured supportive fashion, to build a positive relationship and to give the teacher information on which to build a structured sequence of activities.

In Reading Recovery a typical tutoring session would include each of these activities, usually in the following order, as the format of the daily lesson:

- re-reading two or more familiar books   text
- re-reading yesterday's new book and taking a running text
  record

- letter identification (plastic letters on a magnetic board) words and
  and/or word-making and breaking   letters
- writing a story (including hearing and recording sounds   text and
  in words)   sounds
- cut-up story to be rearranged   text
- new book introduced   text
- new book attempted   text[5]

Children graduate or are 'discontinued' from the programme when they have reached the average reading level for their class. Some children fail to reach a satisfactory reading level and it is recommended that they be referred to a remedial service. In any case the maximum number of weeks recommended is between 20 and 26 weeks. The average number of weeks varies but appears to be around 16 weeks in mature programmes.

Phonological Training

The Phonological Training grew out of the work of Peter Bryant and Lynette Bradley, who were interested in the observed relationship between poor phonic awareness and subsequently delayed reading.[6] They devised an experimental intervention for six-year-olds with poor phonic awareness which was closely based on Lynette Bradley's experience as a teacher.[7] The circumstances surrounding the development of the Phonological Intervention differ from those of Reading Recovery, and implementation issues were not considered, beyond ensuring that the researchers delivered the intervention adequately.

The Bryant and Bradley intervention

The intervention designed by Bryant and Bradley was based on their research into the normal developmental stages of phonological awareness. They had already found that pre-school children who could not read were nonetheless able both to hear and produce rhymes with evident relish. Bradley and Bryant argued that the most natural division of words into smaller sound units was that of onset and rime, i.e. 'b' + 'at'; 'r' + 'ing'. Thus their training placed emphasis on an awareness of various methods of sound categorisation, starting with rhyme and initial sounds. Its aim was to develop the awareness of sound, concentrating at the outset on alliteration and rhyme but moving towards more sophisticated phonic distinctions in response to the child's progress. Each child was given 40 ten-minute, individual sessions, spread over two years. Typically they would be shown three or four pictures of familiar objects, where all but one showed objects with a common sound, and would then be asked to identify the 'odd one out', in terms of rhyme, alliteration, etc. For example, the odd one out for the words CAT, MAT, PEN and BAT would be PEN. Children were also asked to think of examples in their heads, especially as their training progressed. Plastic letters were used to make explicit connections between letters/letter groups and sounds.

In the Bryant and Bradley study, the children who received this intervention made significantly more progress than the control children, with reading and spelling ages at least 10 months in excess of the control groups. They did particularly well in spelling.

The phonological in the present study

In the present study the content of the intervention was very similar to the sound and plastic letters intervention of Bradley and Bryant. However, it was not suitable to give the intervention over two years, as in the case of the original successful experiment. So, the 40 ten-minute sessions were retained but spread over seven months instead of two years.

The phonological tutors, all of whom were experienced primary teachers, were given three days of training in the techniques required to teach the Phonological Intervention, spaced over three months, together with a training manual. They were also given an opportunity to rehearse their newly acquired skills with children not involved in the study. The tuition was given by those who administered the phonological programme in the original Bradley and Bryant studies (Bryant and Bradley, 1985; Bradley and Bryant, 1985; Kirtley et al., 1989).

Research methods

In order to evaluate the effectiveness of these interventions, children who had received the programmes were compared with similar children who received no special programme.

Sampling

Schools sample

Reading Recovery programmes were evaluated in seven Local Education Authorities: Bexley, Greenwich, Hammersmith and Fulham, Islington, Surrey, Wandsworth and Westminster. The number of Reading Recovery schools sampled was 22. For each Reading Recovery school, the LEA was asked to identify two other similar schools, which were then randomly assigned to the Control (18 schools) or Phonological Training (23 schools) condition.

Children in the sample

Six children were included in the study from each selected school. The six poorest readers in each school in the age range six years to six years six months were selected on the basis of their performance on a battery of reading assessments (the Diagnostic Survey; Clay, 1985, described below). In the Reading Recovery schools these six children were allocated to the Reading Recovery or Control group on the basis of their reading scores: the bottom three or four entered the intervention programme in September and October 1992; the remaining two or three, who had the next lowest scores, formed the within-school Control group. In the Phonological schools, four of the six poorest readers in each school were randomly assigned to the Phonological training. The remaining two children formed the within-school Control group for the Phonological schools. In the Control schools all six of the bottom readers constituted the Control group.

At the third, long-term follow-up in 1996, in addition to testing the original cohort of children, 1,398 of their classmates were also tested. Year 6 classmates of children attending 57 of the original 63 schools or their feeder junior/middle schools were assessed, in order to establish the average proficiency in reading and spelling for this population of children.[9]

Procedure

The reading abilities of all the children in the study were assessed on a battery of reading tests in September/October 1992, before the start of either of the two interventions. The children were then re-tested in June and July 1993 after the interventions were completed. There were further follow-ups in May/July 1994 and September/December 1996. At each follow-up children were tested 'blind', in other words the tester did not know to which experimental group children belonged.

On the basis of this research design four comparisons can be made:

1. Reading Recovery children with Control children in the same school (within-school Controls).
2. Reading Recovery children with Control children in other schools (between-school Controls).
3. Phonological children with Control children in the same school (within-school Controls).
4. Phonological children with Control children in Control schools (between-school Controls).

Marie Clay's stated aim in her early New Zealand research was that most children who participated in Reading Recovery would 'catch up' with their classmates and continue their literacy careers in the 'average range'. To explore this, we carried out follow-up assessment of the children in the original sample and also their classmates and compared their reading attainment in Year 6.

Measures

Measures used at pre-test and in the 1993 follow-up

Measuring reading ability of six-year-olds with limited reading skills is a challenge especially since many of these children were unable to read much at all. Two standard reading tests, the British Ability Scale Word Reading Test (Elliot *et al.*, 1984) and the Neale Analysis of Reading Ability (1988), and various other tests which assess lower order reading skills, such as the child's knowledge of the alphabet, were employed. The standard reading tests – a word recognition test (BAS Word Reading), and a test of prose reading with both reading accuracy and comprehension components (Neale Analysis of Reading) – were valuable since they offer the possibility of comparisons with broadly established norms, their reliability and validity have been rigorously established and they are widely used and understood. Although they were not the most sensitive measures at the outset of the study, they were more suitable as the children's skills improved and it was necessary to establish baseline scores on both measures. More sensitive to early reading skills is the Diagnostic Survey (Clay, 1985), a battery of five tests, which takes about 30 minutes to administer and includes:

1. *Letter Identification*
    The child is asked to identify all upper and lower case letters. This has been found to be a powerful predictor of subsequent progress in reading of Reception Year children (e.g. Tizard *et al.*, 1988).

2. *Concepts about Print*
    The child's knowledge of early reading skills is explored, such as the fact that print contains a message, directionality of print, what is a letter and what is a word.

3. *Word Test*
    This is a word recognition test suitable for children with a very small reading vocabulary.

4. *Written Vocabulary*
    The child is simply asked to write as many words as he/she can in the space of 10 minutes.

5. *Dictation*
    The child is asked to write down a short, simple, dictated passage. Incorrect spellings are acceptable as long as they show an appropriate phonic analysis, for example 'skool' instead of 'school'.

Written Vocabulary and Dictation are both measures of writing.

The resulting scores are referred to subsequently in this report as the Diagnostic Survey and represent the combination of all five sub-tests.[10]

In addition to the Diagnostic Survey, a Book Level was established for each child, as in the Reading Recovery. This entailed establishing which of a series of texts, graded from 1 to 26 according to the Reading Recovery levels, children could read with 90 per cent accuracy or above.[11]

Phonological awareness was also assessed. Like letter identification, it is an ability measurable in pre-readers which has been found to predict subsequent reading progress. Phonological awareness was measured at all follow-up points, using the Rhyme, Initial and End Schools Oddities Test (Kirtley et al., 1989). In this test, children are given three words and asked to identify, the 'odd one out'. (In the rhyme condition the odd one does not rhyme with the other two. In the initial and sound conditions, the odd one does not start or end with the same letter sound). Children are given ten tasks in each of the three conditions. Scores range from 0 to 21.[12]

At pre-test, the children's IQs were estimated using the BAS Short Form IQ Test. Information was also collected on age, sex, whether the children spoke English as a first or additional language and free school meal status.

Measures used in the 1994 follow-up

The BAS Word Reading Test and the Neale Prose Reading Test were repeated at second follow-up but the Diagnostic Survey and Book Level were dropped as they were too easy for many of the children by this stage. Instead, as a measure of spelling ability, the British Ability Scale Spelling Test was used.

Phonological awareness was measured using the Oddities Test and the Snowling Non-Word Reading Test. In the non-word reading test, children are presented with non-words of three levels of difficulty and awarded points for each word read within appropriate phonological representation. Scores range from 0–30.[13] As children have never seen these words before, their ability to read them relies entirely on their ability to decode phonologically.

Information was again collected on free school meal status.

Data collected for the 1996 follow-up

Details of age, sex and free school meal status were collected for the total sample (i.e. the original cohort of poor readers plus some of their classmates in 1996).

All children's reading levels were tested using the NFER-Nelson Group Reading Test 6–12. Spelling was tested using the Young Parallel Spelling Test.

Cost of extra tuition for poor readers

For the school years 1992/93 and 1993/94 and for the autumn term 1996, information was collected on the amount of paid extra help given to children in each of the groups. Also details of any extra help provided to poor readers in intervention and control conditions within their school were collected.

The results

Findings for the short- and medium-term effects of Reading Recovery and Phonological Training have already been published in greater detail (Sylva and Hurry, 1995a, 1995b). However, the key findings for short-, medium- and long-term effects are summarised below.

Children's reading and writing at the beginning of the study

At the outset of the study in 1992, many of the original cohort of children could barely read, but on average the children selected for the interventions were doing slightly worse then the Control groups.

The implication of this difference is that subsequent comparisons between experimental groups must take account of children's initial reading levels.

Because there were differences in the average reading abilities of children in the three groups at the beginning of the study, their performances were compared, after taking these into account. This was done using a regression analysis where the Diagnostic Survey and BAS Word Reading Test at pre-test was taken as the measure of initial reading ability.

Key findings

This study is the third follow-up assessment of children's reading and spelling progress after intervention at the age of six years. The original research evaluated the effectiveness of Reading Recovery and a specifically phonological training up to 15 months post-intervention (Sylva and Hurry, 1995b). We now seek to establish the long-term effects of both interventions.

The study commenced in September 1992, when 390 six-year-old children who had made a slow start in their reading were selected from 63 schools in London and Surrey. There were three broad and comparable groups:

- the *Reading Recovery* group (95 children);
- the *Phonological Training* group (97 children); and
- the *Control* group (198 children).

Findings

During the school year 1992/93, according to their assigned group, children received Reading Recovery (half an hour daily for an average of 20 weeks), the Phonological Training (40 × 10 minute sessions over two terms) or the normal school programme, which often included additional reading support.

In the summer of 1993:

> *Reading Recovery* children had made twice as much progress in their reading and spelling than the other two groups (17 months progress as compared to 9 months progress in the other two groups).

Phonological Training only improved children's phonological skills and to some extent spelling but not their reading.

In the summer of 1994:

Reading Recovery children were still significantly ahead of the Control children in their reading and spelling (approximately a six-month advantage). For children on free school meals and for children who were complete non-readers in 1992, Reading Recovery was particularly effective.

The *Phonological Training* group were reading and spelling significantly better than controls, though their reading advantage was only three months compared with the six-month advantage of the Reading Recovery group.

In the autumn of 1996, at the top of the primary school, 342 of the children were retested on reading and spelling.

Reading Recovery children had about a three-month reading age advantage over their controls but this difference did not reach statistical significance. There was no effect on spelling. For children who received free school meals (about 50 per cent of the sample) Reading Recovery gave them a significant six-month reading age advantage over their controls. For about half the children in the original cohort, who could not read at all when they were six years old, Reading Recovery had a significant long-term effect (six-month reading age advantage).

The *Phonological Training* group, similar to the Reading Recovery group, had a three-month (non-significant) reading age advantage over their controls. However, the children who had received Phonological Training were significantly better spellers, with an approximately six-month spelling age advantage. Selecting only those children who were eligible for free school meals the Phonological Training had a significant benefit on children's reading (about six-month reading age advantage) and spelling (six-month spelling age advantage). However, for children who were non-readers at six years old the Phonological Training had no significant effect on reading or spelling.

A comparison was also made between these groups and their classmates in 1996. The average reading age of the classmates was nine years, well below their chronological age of ten and a half, but typical of children living in socially disadvantaged areas. In terms of reading, 70 per cent of the Reading Recovery group were within the average band (+ or − 1 standard deviation) of their classmates, as opposed to about 60 per cent of the Controls and 56 per cent of the Phonological Training group.

The issue of whether or not it is reasonable to expect interventions to have a measurable impact on children's educational attainment years after the intervention has ceased is a complex one.

Overall, despite short- and medium-term effects, neither of the interventions appears to have had a significant long-term effect on reading, though the Phonological Training significantly improved spelling. However, both interventions were useful for specific groups of the children studied.

Both interventions, in the long term, significantly improved the reading of children who took free school meals. It is likely that the school will play a particularly vital role in the support of children with reading difficulties who come from homes with an impoverished literacy environment.

For children with minimal reading skills at six years, it would appear that reading progress without individual tuition is very limited and Reading Recovery is the most suitable programme for this group. It may be that children who are total non-readers, and those who are very poor, cannot benefit from ordinary classroom instruction. Children with some literacy skills or from better-off homes, are more able to cope in the classroom.

Phonological Training

In the comparison between schools, children who had received Phonological Training one year previously had now made significantly more progress in reading and spelling, as well as in the phonological skills measured. However, comparing the Phonological children with the Control children attending the same schools (the within-schools comparison) there were no statistically significant effects.

Summary and discussion

In the light of current concerns about the standards of literacy in the UK, the evidence presented here may have implications for both national policy and local practice.

Reading Recovery

Soon after children had completed the programme, the effect of Reading Recovery was clearly positive. The Reading Recovery children had made significantly greater progress than Control children in reading across a wide range of measures, double the progress that would usually be expected in one school year. However, at second follow-up one year later, although the Reading Recovery children were still significantly ahead of Control children in other schools, they were not significantly better than non-Reading Recovery children in the same schools. The developers of the Reading Recovery programme acknowledge that children's rate of progress will be reduced once the intensive help is withdrawn. All children participating in the study had made progress in this second year, but the rate of progress of the Reading Recovery children was not as great as that of the Controls, indicating that the Controls had caught up to some extent. This 'catching up' was greatest in Reading Recovery schools suggesting 'leakage' of the programme into ordinary classrooms which improved their practice overall.

Assessments at the third follow-up, at the top of the primary school, show that the Reading Recovery group held on to their absolute gains, although these were no longer statistically significant. There are two sub-groups of children, however, who showed lasting and statistically significant gains from Reading Recovery. One sub-group who came from socially disadvantaged homes scored significantly higher than matched Control children at all three follow-ups. Many children who fail to make progress in reading do so because their school reading is not supported at home by books, electronic media and literacy 'toys'. When such children encounter the richness of the materials in Reading Recovery, their reading improves quickly and this group scored consistently higher than Control children throughout the rest of primary school.

The second group of children for whom Reading Recovery led to lasting gains were those who could not read at all when they entered Year One. Although there is some overlap between this and the disadvantaged group, this second group had lower entry scores than the children from poorer homes who were scattered throughout the entire sample. Non-readers need very intense intervention if they are to 'catch on' to reading. Their matched controls, who also began as virtual non-readers, were never able to catch up with the Reading Recovery group because neither classroom instruction nor the special needs help offered by their schools was intensive or systematic enough to meet their very great needs.

For these two important sub-groups, it is clear that without intensive extra help at school 'the poor become poorer' (Stanovich, 1986). The children in this study who were non-readers at six and who attended the Control schools had an average reading age of seven years eight months in Year 6. In over four years at school they had only made about two and a half years' progress, and they had started well behind their peers.

Children who are total non-readers, and those who come from impoverished homes find it difficult to benefit fully from school work. Children with some literacy skills, or from better-off homes, are more able to cope in the classroom and so slowly narrow the gap with their peers who received Reading Recovery. Stanovich (1986) described an ever widening gap which is seen graphically in this study where the poorest readers in the Control groups made little progress over the five years.

Phonological Training

Immediately post-intervention, the effect of the Phonological Training was narrowly confined to phonological awareness and had no significant effect on reading. By the end of the second year, however, the children who had received the phonological intervention were reading and spelling significantly better than the Control children in other schools.

The pattern of progress made by the children in the Phonological group differs from those who received Reading Recovery. The Reading Recovery children made great gains during the intervention year but their progress slowed down in the year following intervention. In contrast, the Phonological children made less dramatic progress in reading during the intervention year, but their reading and spelling improved considerably in the year after their training. The Reading Recovery children were still 'ahead' but the gap had narrowed. It is possible that the phonological skills children had developed during the programme were gradually integrated and put to use as they encountered more text.

Despite the fact that the Phonological Training was less intensive than Reading Recovery and less effective in the short- and medium term, in the long term it had significant effects on spelling. Comparing the children who received Phonological Training with similar children in Control schools, we found evidence of significant spelling gains, maintained in Years 5 and 6. The impact of phonological training on reading just missed statistical significance, although these results were not replicated in the within-schools comparison. It may be that the Phonological Training, though slow to show an impact, had a lasting effect on spelling and to a lesser extent reading, as it focuses on a skill that underpins the process of learning both to read and spell. The long-term success of the Phonological Training offers more evidence to support the importance of teaching children phonological skills (Adams, 1990).

As with Reading Recovery, Phonological Training was more effective in the long term for children receiving free school meals, where it gave them a significant advantage in both spelling and reading. However, for children who were non-readers at six years old the Phonological Training was not significantly effective. It appears that children with such minimal skills need more than help with decoding, important though this is, and so need a broader programme of intervention such as Reading Recovery.

Costs

Educating children with reading difficulties is costly. For time-limited and intensive early interventions such as Reading Recovery, these costs are concentrated at a particular time, but taken over the whole of the primary school cycle the cost is little more than for current alternatives. The less intensive early intervention, Phonological Training, is slightly cheaper than standard special needs provision.

However, to consider the cost of specialised reading help in a vacuum is insufficient since it must be weighed against the effectiveness of the provision. It would be inadvisable to reject intensive early intervention on the basis of short-term costs, especially in view of the potential long-term costs to society of such a 'tail' of low achievers. The Phonological Training, followed by routine school provision, was the most cost effective, producing significantly better spellers and marginally better readers at the lowest cost. For children who were complete non-readers at six, however, Reading Recovery was significantly better at a minimally higher cost. This study shows that short-term programme costs should be taken in the longer-term context.

The costs of teacher training and programme maintenance, which in the case of systems such as Reading Recovery can be considerable, cannot be ignored. The costs of professional development for teachers in Control schools were not investigated systematically, but we know that many of these teachers did attend special courses. The benefits of Reading Recovery teacher training are likely to go beyond the children included on the Reading Recovery programme. Hints of this are seen in the superior performance of Control children in Reading Recovery schools and classroom teachers' reports of adopting methods from the Reading Recovery programme. Elsewhere, Reading Recovery teacher training has been found to be an effective form of professional development in terms of raising classroom levels of literacy, where children taught by a class teacher with Reading Recovery training outperformed their peers (Rowe, 1995). Research has shown that children taught by specially trained, well motivated teachers make more progress (Wasik and Slavin, 1993; Adams, 1990).

The costs of all forms of specialised help go beyond the school-based cost of the teacher. Training, management and monitoring are invariably involved. Although these costs are fairly visible for Reading Recovery they are not readily available for standard LEA provision, and this may give the false impression that Reading Recovery is uniquely expensive. However, in every LEA special needs provision must be managed. The quality and value for money of special needs provision is affected by LEA management. The Audit Commission (1992) on the provision for children with special educational needs specifically identified management as a problem, in particular lack of clarity in aims, monitoring and accountability. In evaluating the cost effectiveness of particular interventions the full costs over the longer term must be taken into account.

Implications of these findings

For reading development

These findings suggest that the causes of reading difficulties may vary between children from disadvantaged and more affluent homes. Both interventions were more successful in raising reading scores of impoverished children and this suggests that the difficulties of these children may be related to lack of materials and literacy activities in the home. Interventions which produce differential effects for sub-groups of children may be of considerable theoretical significance.

The study also contributes to theory about early interventions. Shanahan and Barr (1995) have questioned the expectation that reading interventions should have effects that are sustained over years without any additional support. 'To use a medical analogy, early interventions are supposed to operate like a vaccination, preventing all future learning problems, no matter what their source or severity. It appears, however, that early interventions, no matter how successful, are more similar to insulin therapy. That is, substantial treatment effects are apparent right away, but these gains can be maintained only through additional intervention and support' (p. 982). From another perspective, it is argued that early intervention might be expected to have far reaching effects by stepping in to prevent a downward spiral. Our findings lend some support to both these positions. On the one hand, early intervention with the very poorest readers and those from socially disadvantaged homes did make a long-term difference. Those that received the specific programmes did significantly better than children being given the standard provision. However, for children who had made some progress in reading at six and for those not taking free school meals, early intervention failed to have a significant long-term impact.

What should we make of these findings? Are children from better-off homes and the children who can read a little at six unable to benefit from early intervention? This is not the case. In fact these children made better progress in reading than the less advantaged groups, even in the intervention conditions. In the short term, Reading Recovery made a substantial difference to both groups of children. But for the more advantaged children there was another route to reading. They made slow but steady progress without intervention and so in time they nearly caught up with the children given planned early intervention. Presumably they received sufficient support from home or were not so behind their peers that they could not keep abreast in the classroom. However, for the others early intervention appears to be vital.

The difference in the effectiveness of Reading Recovery and Phonological Training for children who were non-readers at six has potentially theoretical importance for reading development. It suggests that intensive work with books is necessary to help these children and that Phonological Training alone is insufficient. It was certainly the case in the present study that the Phonological Training took longer than Reading Recovery to show significant impacts on children's reading. Phonological awareness is important in the early stages of learning to read but it may be that it is a necessary but not sufficient element. In the early stages of reading development children with difficulties may require considerable support to make the links between phonological awareness and the process of reading and extracting meaning. Alternatively, it could be argued from the evidence of the present study that the more intensive nature of Reading Recovery (on average one hour weekly over the year, as opposed to 10 minutes weekly for Phonological Training) was responsible for the better results for poor readers. However, the work of Hatcher, Hulme and Ellis (1994) lends support to the first interpretation, that intensive experience with books is crucial. Hatcher and his colleagues compared children who received one-to-one tuition in a broad range of reading skills, including a specific and explicit phonics element, with children who received tuition in the phonics area alone. In this study both groups of children received the same amount of tuition. Those who received the broader programme made significantly greater progress in reading than those on the narrow phonics programme.

For Reading Recovery

The results of this study strongly suggest that Reading Recovery should be targeted at the very poorest readers. The policy of targeting schools with a high proportion of socially disadvantaged children was first proposed by Plowden (1967) and led to supplementary resourcing of schools in educational priority areas (EPA schools). However, as Barnes and Lucas (1974) demonstrated, this approach was inefficient for two reasons: the majority of socially disadvantaged children did not attend EPA schools and the better-off children in the EPA schools appeared to reap greater benefits from this targeting than the disadvantaged group. Even with direct remedial support these children have been found to be particularly difficult to help (Carter, 1984; Kennedy et al., 1986). Reading Recovery offers a method of helping those six-year-olds who make up the bottom 10 per cent of readers.

This study suggests the need to make the effects of Reading Recovery last longer so that the very strong effects seen in the year or two following the programme are maintained. Some of the evidence from Reading Recovery evaluations in Australia supports the hypothesis that appropriate early intervention, which encourages independent learning, can have dramatic long-term effects. Why might there be positive effects in Australia for all the children in the programme while in the UK the long-lasting effects were found for sub-groups only? One factor related to the maintenance of effects may lie in the wider school system. The Australian classroom offers a literacy programme which is probably more consistent with the Reading Recovery approach than is generally found in the UK. Children's post-intervention classroom experience is likely to have a substantial impact on their progress and the extent to which any gains can be sustained. Indeed, Glynn and his colleagues found in New Zealand that the quality of the classroom programme was a significant factor in children maintaining the gains they made in Reading Recovery. It seems that classroom programmes which build on the specialised help offered to struggling readers are likely to maximise children's learning.

The Reading Recovery trained teacher in the school and the Reading Recovery Tutor in the LEA have a potentially valuable role in raising the standards of classroom teaching and hence literacy standards in schools as an additional consequence of their intensive training and of the clear management and monitoring system working at school, LEA and national level.

Phonological Training

This intervention was less successful than Reading Recovery in the short term, but like Reading Recovery it led to significantly better reading scores for children from impoverished homes at third follow-up and to better spelling scores for the entire group. It would be worthwhile to explore further the effects of Phonological Training targeted at children from poorer families. The evidence reported here suggests that children who are non-readers will not benefit from a narrow phonological intervention, and that the selection of suitable interventions is important.

One practical issue needs consideration. This research compared a fully-fledged intervention system with a pilot intervention carried out by a small team of teacher-researchers trained by Oxford psychologists and working together as a 'specialist team' at the Thomas Coram Research Unit. Unlike Reading Recovery, the Phonological Training evaluated here cannot be offered to teachers as an intervention straightaway. It is necessary to develop an educational programme to prepare teachers to use Phonological Training, to put suitable procedures in place for identifying children likely to profit from it and to monitor the ongoing programme.

Further development and choice of intervention

There are no other time-limited early educational programmes (including training schemes, support and monitoring), that we know of, that have demonstrated long-term effects in literacy for children experiencing great difficulties. The only other programme involving early intervention that has demonstrated effects higher up the school (Year 4) is Success for All (Wasik and Slavin, 1993). However, in Success for All, children receive input which extends beyond the intervention year and this continuing intervention is not directly comparable with either Reading Recovery or Phonological Training. A recent evaluation of Success for All suggests that the one-to-one tutoring of Reading Recovery is superior to that of Success for All, though the whole-school and follow-through aspects of Success for All are valuable (Ross et al., 1995). It is possible that both Reading Recovery and Phonological Training may also benefit from follow-up sessions as children move through the primary school. Since the children in the present study received specialist teaching throughout their primary schooling, such a strategy could be managed at no increased cost. It would allow teachers to teach higher-order reading skills, such as skimming, scanning and comprehension monitoring, within a programme consistent with the early intervention and may produce more powerful long-term results. This, in tandem with a consistent classroom programme, might help more children who have benefited from Reading Recovery and Phonological Training to maintain their gains. Such an extension to the existing interventions would need to be developed.

In terms of immediately available choices for schools, Reading Recovery is the only intervention with proven long-term results on children's literacy that is currently being implemented in the UK. For children who are non-readers at six, and for those from socially disadvantaged backgrounds, it offers significantly better outcomes at the top of the primary school than other standard specialist provision, at only marginally greater costs. There may also be spin-offs for the school in having a member of staff highly trained in the area of literacy. Phonological Training looks very promising for children with reading difficulties and underscores the importance of explicit phonics tuition but would need to be developed as a programme for school use. It would be wise to build on the positive results shown here which offer a strategy for helping the groups of children who are most difficult to help.

Notes

1 Bradley and Bryant, 1985.
2 Clay, 1987.
3 Clay, 1979.
4 Clay, 1985.
5 Clay, 1993.
6 e.g. Bryant and Bradley, 1985.
7 Bradley, 1984, 1981.
8 [. . .]
9 The other six of the 63 schools would not allow us to test the whole class for a variety of reasons.
10 Each of these tests generates a raw score and, of course, the magnitude and variance vary considerably between tests. In order to derive a total score across all the sub-tests, the raw scores were transformed so that each one had a mean of 0 and a standard deviation of 1. They were then summed and transformed again so that these total scores also had a mean of 0 and a standard deviation of 1.
11 Level 1 texts are the simplest caption books suitable for a child with very limited reading skills. Level 26 equates to a reading age of between 8 and 9 (Glynn et al., 1989, p. 11).
12 Raw scores of 3 or less in each condition are deemed poorer than chance and have been adjusted to 0. Scores of 4 or more per condition indicate increasing phonological awareness and have been adjusted to range from 1 to 7. They are then summed across the three conditions.
13 There are five three-letter, one syllable words at the first level, ten four or five-letter one syllable words at the second level and ten two-syllable words at the third level. A score of 30 is obtained by awarding 2 points for a correct answer on level 1 and 1 point for correct answers on levels 2 and 3.

References

Adams, M. (1990). *Beginning to Read: Learning and Thinking about Print.* Cambridge, MA: MIT Press.

Audit Commission (1992) *Getting in on the Act: Provision for Pupils with Special Educational Needs: the National Picture.* HMSO, London.

Barnes, J. H. and Lucas, H. (1974). Positive discrimination in education: individuals, groups and institutions. In T. Leggatt (eds), *Sociological Theory and Survey Research.* Sage.

Bradley, L. (1981). The organisation of motor patterns for spelling: an effective remedial strategy for backward readers. *Developmental Medicine and Child Neurology*, 23, 83–91.

Bradley, L. (1984). *Assessing Reading Difficulties: A Diagnostic and Remedial Approach* (2nd edn). London and Basingstoke: Macmillan.

Bradley, L. and Bryant, P. (1985). *Rhyme and Reason in Reading and Spelling*. Ann Arbor, MI: University of Michigan Press.

Bryant, P. and Bradley, L. (1985). *Children's Reading Problems*. Oxford: Blackwell.

Carter, L. F. (1984). The sustaining effects study of compensatory and elementary education. *Educational Researching*, 13(7), 4–13.

Clay, M. M. (1979). *Reading: The Patterning of Complex Behaviour*. Portsmouth, NH: Heinemann.

Clay, M. M. (1985). *The Early Detection of Reading Difficulties: A Diagnostic Survey with Recovery Procedures* (3rd edn). Auckland: Heinemann.

Clay, M. M. (1987) Implementing Reading Recovery: systemic adaptations to an education innovation. *New Zealand Journal of Educational Studies*, 22, 35–58.

Clay, M. M. (1993). *Reading Recovery: A Guidebook for Teachers in Training*. Auckland: Heinemann.

Elliot, C. D., Murray, D. J. and Pearson, L. S. (1984). *British Ability Scales*. London: NFER-Nelson.

Glynn, T., Crooks, T., Bethune, N., Ballard, K. and Smith, J. (1989). *Reading Recovery in Context*. Wellington, NZ: Department of Education.

Hatcher, P., Hulme, C. and Ellis, A. W. (1994). Ameliorating early reading failure by integrating the teaching of reading and phonological skills: the phonological linkage hypothesis. *Child Development*, 65, 41–57.

Kennedy, M., Birman, B. F. and Demaline, R. F. (1986). *The Effectiveness of Chapter 1 Services*. Washington: Office of Educational Research and Improvement, US Department of Education.

Kirtley, C., Bryant, P., McLean, M. and Bradley, L. (1989). Rhyme, rime and the onset of reading. *Journal of Experimental Child Psychology*, 48, 224–245.

Neale, M. D. (1988). *Neale Analysis of Reading Ability* (revised edn). Windsor: NFER-Nelson.

Pinnell, G. S., Lyons, C. A., DeFord, D. E., Bryk, A. S. and Seltzer, M. (1994). Comparing instructional models for the literacy education of high-risk first graders. *Reading Research Quarterly*, 20(1), 9–39.

Plowden, B. (1967) *Children and their Primary Schools (The Plowden Report)*. London: HMSO.

Ross, S., Smith, L., Casey, J. and Slavin, R. E. (1995). Increasing the academic success of disadvantaged children: an examination of alternative early intervention programs. *American Education Research Journal*, 32, 773–800.

Rowe, K. J. (1995). Factors affecting students' progress in reading: key findings from a longitudinal study. *Literacy, Teaching and Learning*, 1(2), 57–110.

Shanahan, T. and Barr, R. (1995). Reading Recovery: an independent evaluation of the effects of an early intervention for at-risk learners. *Reading Research Quarterly*, 30, 958–997.

Stanovich, K. E. (1986). Cognitive processes and the reading problems of learning disabled children: evaluating the assumption of specificity. In J. Torgesen and B. Wong (eds), *Psychological and Educational Perspectives on Learning Disabilities* (pp. 87–131). New York: Academic Press.

Sylva, K., and Hurry, J. (1995a). *Early Interventions in Children with Reading Difficulties*. School Curriculum and Assessment Authority.

Sylva, K., and Hurry, J. (1995b). *The Effectiveness of Reading Recovery and Phonological Training for Children with Reading Problems*. School Curriculum and Assessment Authority.

Tizard, B., Blatchford, P., Burke, J., Farquhar, C. and Plewis, I. (1988). *Young Children at School in the Inner City*. Hove and London: Lawrence Erlbaum Assocs.

Wasik, B. A., and Slavin, R. E. (1993). Preventing early reading failure with one-to-one tutoring: a review of five programs. *Reading Research Quarterly, 28*(2), 179–200.

Source

This is an edited version of an article previously published in 1998. Reproduced by permission of the Qualifications and Curriculum Authority.

Chapter 20

Teaching spelling
Some questions answered

Diana Bentley

Introduction

English spelling is famous for its complexity and although this adds both interest and information to many words it also presents numerous writers with a problem. The twenty-six letters of our alphabet produce fifty-two major spelling units, thirty-two for consonants and twenty for vowels. Some letters represent many different sounds so that writers cannot rely on writing a word as it sounds. This was not always the case. Before 1500 AD English words were spelled as they were pronounced and as local dialects changed the sound, so also the spelling varied from place to place. Professional scribes made some attempt to standardise words but they were also responsible for some very unusual spellings. In order to combat the confusing repetition of up and down strokes found in such words as wimin and munk the scribes changed them to women and monk! When Caxton's printing press was first developed he used Dutch printers, many of whom were unsure of how English was pronounced. Hence the ch found in yacht!

Later came the spelling reformers who wanted to attribute most English words to a classical background and insisted that such words as dette should be spelled debt from the Latin debitum and scissors should contain the 'c' as they argued that it owed its origin to scindere (to cleave). Fascinating as this is it has resulted in considerable problems for writers ever since.

Spelling – developmental approach

It has to be accepted that some people will have difficulty with spelling all their lives but we believe that the teacher can bring about substantial improvement with the majority of children.

(Bullock, 1975: 11.42)

Traditionally the teaching of spelling consisted of correcting and testing. However since the 1970s research has concentrated on the *teaching* of spelling and an examination of children's spelling seems to indicate that most, if not all, children progress through recognisable *stages of development* on the road to becoming proficient spellers. Teachers who are able to identify where the child is within these stages are more likely to be able to help the child effectively. These stages have now been generally described as the following.

The pre-communicative stage

In this stage the children's understanding of the written form is limited and adults are generally unable to 'read' what the child has written. However the child does demonstrate considerable knowledge about the purpose of writing and this should be recognised by the teacher. The child knows that invented shapes or letter forms represent a message. The salient feature of this stage is that the child has no knowledge of letter–sound correspondence. They may or may not be aware of the left to right directionality of English writing. In many instances upper case letters, lower case letters and numbers are mixed indiscriminately.

The semi-phonetic stage

In this stage children make the first approximations towards an alphabetic orthography and unlike the previous stage it represents letter–sound correspondence. Where possible the speller will try to represent words, sounds or symbols with letters that match their letter name (as in R = are, U = you) instead of representing the vowel and consonant sounds separately. In some cases they may identify one or two phonemes in a word and finish with a random string of letters because they already know the words contain more letters but are unable to identify them. Children in this stage know that writing goes from left to right, that there are spaces between the words and rarely muddle letters and numbers. In many cases children begin to have a small sight vocabulary which they tend to use excessively.

The phonetic stage

In this stage all surface sound features are represented and children begin to apply phonic knowledge from one word to another, e.g. rat, cat, hat. They begin to put some vowels into the syllables but rely heavily upon the sound of the letter rather than the look of the word, e.g. monstur, yor, cum. The children often tend to use known words in great abundance, e.g. Then they went out and played and played and played . . .

The transitional stage

Here children move from relying upon the sound of the word towards a much greater reliance upon the visual appearance of words. Children begin to recognise acceptable letter patterns, put vowels in every syllable but although all the letters may be included they may be reversed, e.g. huose, freind. This transitional stage may last a very long time. It has been suggested that it is not unusual for children to be at this stage for five or six years before they can confidently claim to be 'correct' spellers.

The correct stage

The identifying feature of this stage is that children say 'it doesn't look right' and when asked to write a word they are unsure about immediately try to write down alternative spellings until they recognise the correct one, e.g. speshal, special, special.

Children in this stage are usually prepared to use longer words when writing and tend to break polysyllabic words into their syllables in order to master the spelling pattern. These writers become interested in words and can use a logical application of spelling patterns to unknown words.

Any model of spelling development is necessarily limited as children progress through these stages at different rates. In particular many children move through these first three stages very rapidly. There is a great temptation for teachers to constantly correct children's attempts in these stages without any recognition of the thought processes a child is demonstrating in his writing. The child who has been allowed the freedom to explore how a word may be represented begins to understand possible letter combinations and is far more likely to grasp the correct form when they eventually achieve that stage of development. The best help the teacher can offer throughout these stages is to encourage children to write. Too often children become daunted by the prospect of acquiring the correct form and feel the gulf between their attempt and the correct spelling is so great that the struggle is too much and they lose confidence and settle for a simple word they can spell. A key feature of the teacher's role at this stage is to boost children's confidence and to value all their efforts.

In the transitional stage teachers may be inclined to label children as poor spellers when in reality they are wavering between adopting the visual approach and relinquishing the phonic stage. This necessarily results in children writing words which are very nearly in correct form and yet the error seems glaring to the experienced speller. These 'mistakes' can offend the reader and distract them from responding to the content of the writing. It is worth remembering that when a writer arrives at the correct stage this does not mean that all words are spelled correctly (anyone can make a spelling mistake), but those mistakes are easily ironed out.

It is not always easy to instantly assess the stage a child has reached because for any individual child their spelling will not fall entirely within the scope of any one stage, e.g. they will spell some words correctly; make some good phonic representations of words and yet still misspell some simple words. Teachers need to analyse the spelling errors children make and decide whether they are a slip of the pen, a mislearned spelling they have written so often that it appears 'correct' to their eyes, or evidence of the stage they are in.

An outline of recent research in spelling

Much of the thrust of recent spelling research has focused upon the relationship between the developmental stages and specific characteristics of spelling behaviour. The following researchers have highlighted certain aspects of the spelling process.

Bradley and Bryant, in *Children's Reading Problems* (1985), looked at older children who made numerous bizarre spelling errors. An examination of the kinds of errors these children make would seem to indicate that they are in the semi-phonetic stage and need to be encouraged to move into the phonic stage.

The following extract describes the method Bradley used in order to help these children.

The method consists of a series of steps in the following order:

1. The student proposes the words he wants to learn.
2. The word is written correctly for him (or made with plastic script letters).
3. The student names the word.
4. He then writes the word himself, saying out loud the alphabetic names of each letter of the word as it is written.
5. He names the word again. He checks to see that the word has been written correctly: this is important, as less able readers are often inaccurate when they copy (Bradley, 1979). Repeat steps 2 to 5 twice more, covering or disregarding the stimulus word as soon as the student feels he can manage without it.
6. The student practises the word in this way for six consecutive days. The procedure is the same whether or not the student can read or write, and whether or not he is familiar with all the sound/symbol relationships, but it must not deteriorate into rote spelling, which is an entirely different thing.
7. The student learns to generalise from this word to similar words using the plastic script letters.

This method was used in a controlled training study, details of which were published in *Developmental Medicine and Child Neurology*, 1981, by Lynette Bradley.

Uta Frith (1980) became interested in those children who are good and rapid readers but who are weak spellers. Many parents and teachers believed that there was a high correlation between spelling and reading competence and were unsympathetic to those children who could read well but who were 'careless' when it came to writing.

Frith argues that these children only use partial clues when reading and use a different process when they are spelling. She clarifies this hypothesis by calling listening to speech and reading as in 'input process' and writing as an 'output process' between which lies 'our internal representation of language'.

She maintains that the requirements for the input and output processes are not only independent but in some cases incompatible. The 'unexpected poor speller' when reading does not take in the constituent letters of the words but uses prediction, and confirmation of the prediction, by almost scanning the text. However this same reader when writing reproduces the sounds of the word rather than the look of it, that is they 'read by eye but spell by ear'. This hypothesis, while explaining the problems of the good reader who cannot spell, also clarifies the limitations of the phonetic speller as Peters (1985) maintains that between one and three words in every ten are not phonically regular.

Margaret Peters (1967) described spelling as being 'unlike reading in that it is encoding a familiar and meaningful sound into a strange and unpredictable code'. Good spellers have a good visual perception of word forms. They often see words within words, perceive letter sequences and patterns and almost subconsciously recognise when they have spelt a word correctly after writing down some possible alternatives. To enable children to become good spellers she maintains that they have to become sensitive to the coding system of our orthography.

Peters recommends the following as a strategy that will help children to become more confident spellers.

LOOK at the word carefully and in such a way that you will remember what you have seen.
COVER the word so that you cannot see it.
WRITE the word from memory, saying it to yourself as you are writing.
CHECK the word. If it is not correct then go back and repeat the steps.

She emphasises that children should never copy words but always be encouraged to write them from memory. Her method links with those spellers who are moving from the phonetic stage into the transitional, and it should be remembered that this stage is one that many children remain in for some considerable time.

In conclusion it must be said we still do not know all the answers but at least we can give children credit for the stage they have reached and then fine tune our teaching strategies to enable them to acquire the next developmental stage.

Questions about spelling

During 1988–1989 teachers were asked to submit any questions about spelling that concerned them. The following are a sample of those questions that arose most frequently.

Spelling and reading

Why are avid readers sometimes poor spellers?

The children who do read fast but appear to be poor spellers are often referred to as the 'unexpected poor speller'. Most primary classes will have a fair number of these children. The work of Uta Frith mentioned in the introduction has offered an explanation as to why this occurs. These children generally need to pay close attention to the way words look and the approach devised by Peters is helpful.

Do word cards displayed around the classroom help children to spell them?

The importance of any display or print is dependent entirely on the use made of it by the individual child or the teacher. Alerting children to look for the word and then to write it from memory, or drawing attention to the letter pattern within it may help children to acquire a correct visual recall. However Frank Smith has described words left decorating the walls as 'teacher's wall-paper' and there is always a danger of this becoming the case.

Do you use words from a reading scheme or reading test for giving children a basic spelling list?

No. When children begin to read and write it often appears that they need a core of 'high usage' words but selecting these for testing in any way is the quickest way to persuade some children that they can neither read nor write. Each child has a different need and these need to be recognised. Trying to short cut the needs of children by inflicting a core of words spells disaster not success.

How do you help a lower junior child who persistently gets letters in the wrong order, e.g. paly, dwon?

If we look at the developmental approach to spelling then putting down letters in the wrong order would indicate that the writer is still in the pre-phonetic stage. This child may be helped by a careful phonic programme. Doing such activities as tracking letter blends, marking digraphs or blends in a page of print, playing phonic dominoes, snap or Pelmanism can help the child to consolidate this stage. However this may not be the only reason. If the letter order is constantly incorrect in certain words it could be that this child has 'learned in his hand' the wrong order and, although he knows how to *say* the correct order, when *writing* his hand automatically puts down his usual spelling. It can help if the child is encouraged to write the word correctly using his index finger onto a tactile surface. A short daily practice doing this appears to help to rub out the incorrect order and replace the correct one.

When do you draw the line between a bad speller and dyslexia?

Whether the child is 'just' a bad speller or has specific learning difficulties is unimportant against the fact that both desperately need help and understanding. However it is very unlikely for spelling ability to be the *only symptom* of specific learning difficulties and if you feel that the child also displays a marked discrepancy between intellectual verbal intelligence and reading and writing, then obviously professional assessment should be requested. Children do *not* deliberately misspell words and an understanding and recognition of the effort they make can be the first step towards overcoming their difficulties.

Spelling and phonics

Can phonics be useful when learning spelling?

When children write 'invented spellings' it is generally a phonetic representation that they produce. It is interesting to look at these words to try to diagnose what they have absorbed and where they need help, e.g. a child who writes *becos* is further along the spelling road than a child who writes *bzaus* (a bizarre spelling) but not as advanced as the child who writes *becuase*. For the bizarre speller a phonic awareness would indeed be useful but the other two children are ready to move into a visual approach. Indeed the child who wrote *becuase* may have just made a slip of the pen and it is often worth checking to see if this was the case.

Does too much phonic input complicate spelling for the poor speller?

Too much of anything quickly leads to boredom and disillusionment and must be avoided. However if the poor speller has not yet become aware of how letter sounds help with spelling – that is the spelling is so poor as to appear bizarre – then a careful systematic presentation of phonics will help with communication. If children can already do this then more of the same is likely to undermine their confidence and they need to be introduced to the 'Look' at the word; 'Cover' the word; 'Write' the word; 'Check' the word routine that will move them towards becoming 'correct' spellers.

Do children need to know initial sounds before they can begin to learn to spell?

No. In fact many young writers write words and could not tell you the initial letter sound of the word they have written. In contrast some adults find shorthand very difficult because they cannot isolate sounds from the visual letter combinations. Some children seem to be able to 'see' how a word looks and reproduce it effortlessly, while others spend a long time inventing spellings for words in their vocabulary which bear little resemblance to English orthography. Look carefully at each child and try to assess what strategy would help them.

How can I help children spell problematic words in English, e.g. definite, friend etc.?

Many children find some words cause them problems. Breaking the word down or deliberately mispronouncing it, e.g. con-science (conscience) can enable them to conquer these problems but this obviously can't be offered for too many words. Getting children to work out their own way of 'tagging' the word is often effective. One young girl who constantly missed out the 't' in catch suddenly said 'I know, I don't want the cat to catch the mouse' and indeed now spells it correctly.

Is it true that the use of a local dialect can hinder spelling accuracy?

It seems fairly certain that spelling is influenced by speech production, so we get 'somefink' and 'are' for 'our'. Dialects can both help and hinder spelling but what is certain is that it would be entirely wrong to denigrate a child's accent and this should never be done. It is only necessary to point out the correct spelling and to try to instil a visual representation of the word so that the child comes to write in the conventional form.

Spelling tests

Are spelling tests necessary?

They become *unnecessary* if the teacher is able to monitor the child's progress in other ways and if the children are able to demonstrate that they are achieving success within their capabilities. A test is only valuable if it enables a teacher to diagnose a problem. Most set 'Friday' spelling tests are a waste of time. Some children could already spell the words selected, others only remember the spellings for that day. The following week they appear to have forgotten them and for the very weak spellers tests are a nightmare. They know they will make mistakes and can easily develop a phobia about their spelling weaknesses.

Is there any value in using a published spelling test?

Justification for testing lies in what you do with the results. If the test was diagnostic and helped to clarify areas of strength and weakness in the pupil, enabling you to plan a more effective teaching programme, then the time and cost are surely well spent, but if the test was purely to measure one child against another then its value is open to question.

So far all the tests which claim a 'spelling age result' are open to strong criticism and there appears to be little correlation between them. This means that a child can appear to do well on one test and badly on another and means none of them do justice to the child's spelling ability. However keeping a careful record of a child's progress over a year is valuable.

Is there any way in which testing can assist the child?

If children each have an individual list of spellings that they want to get right then the only practical way of 'testing' is child with child. There are many 'games' which two children can play which enables them to test each other. In most cases it is useful for each child to have each word on a small piece of card. The 'tester' can then select a word to be spelt from his partner's pile and this has to be correctly written before any action can take place, e.g. going up a ladder in Snakes and Ladders or placing the cross in Noughts and Crosses. For a weekly record children could sit side by side and swop their spellings and test each other. If they notice a word 'going wrong' they could stop their partner and allow them a second look at the word before trying again. This 'cheating' however means that this word would have to be kept in the word list for the following week.

Spelling and parents

Do you think parents can and should help their children with spelling, especially if they are very weak?

Parents who are able to take a concerned and sympathetic view of their child's spelling problems can certainly help and should be encouraged to do so, but it is very easy for parents to become over-anxious and lose patience. They need to be given firm guidelines and if you want them to do any activities these should be easily within the capability of their child.

How can you set up a spelling programme involving parents?

This is only possible if there is a whole school spelling policy and teachers are prepared to hold meetings not only to explain the school's approach but also to devote time to making sure the parents continue to understand what is happening.

Schools who manage this are adamant that it is worthwhile and find that parents are happier about the marking of their children's work. In a small experiment, using parents in Oxfordshire, it was felt to be more effective if the class teacher spoke only to the parents of her class rather than the school holding an open meeting or inviting in eminent speakers to explain their approach.

Spelling and attitude

How do you get a child out of the habit 'Oh I always spell that wrong?'

Not by suggesting they write it out correctly three times or a hundred times! This is most unlikely to result in future correct spelling of the word. The trouble with these kinds of errors is that they seem to have almost become a motor skill of the hand rather than a lack of cognitive awareness. The child needs to 'rub out' the incorrect and substitute the correct spelling. One way of tackling this is to use a multisensory approach.

1. The child identifies the word and the teacher writes it out in print script.
2. The child says the names of the letters and then the whole word.
3. The child uses the index finger of his writing hand to write out the word onto a tactile surface, e.g. carpet, sandpaper or baize fablon.
4. He practises this three times and then, using a pencil, writes it into his word book.
5. He does this each morning for one week (auditory, tactile, visual) and hopefully this will have become a motor skill of correct spelling rather than incorrect.

NB: Up to two words per day is usually successful. Doing more words tends to be less effective and can lead to children sometimes writing them correctly, sometimes incorrectly.

How can spelling confidence be developed for those who find spelling difficult?

Confidence can only grow when the task presented to the child is something they recognise that they *can* achieve. It is very easy to 'overload' the child who has weak spelling with *all* the words they constantly get wrong. It is far better to underestimate and choose, say, five words per week to concentrate upon, rather than twenty which may never be properly controlled. When commenting and marking use *only* the chosen words.

Finally *show* the child the progress they have made – point out that in September they could not spell certain words but that by January they had such-and-such number under their belt. Remember nothing succeeds like success.

At what age should one worry about a child's spelling?

If you show obvious worries about a child's spelling what you are really saying is that you don't think the child will ever succeed and this, in time, can lead the child to believe that they will never become a 'good' speller. Remember spelling is *only* important when the writing is going to be read by someone else. Today this is often loosely described as 'when the work will be published', i.e. for display, for reading by parents, for showing to other pupils. Therefore it is important to ensure that the child takes it upon himself/herself to get spelling, punctuation and handwriting legible and correct for *this* stage. The genuine worry comes if they do not appear to care; then it surely implies the task is of no interest, too great or their own self-image is such that they do not believe they *can* write correctly. This obviously can be at any age and then it *is* the task of the teacher to give the child strategies to overcome their errors.

When a child has learnt a spelling, why doesn't he/she relate it to his/her work?

This is really a back-to-front question. There is ample evidence to show that exercises done in isolation are not transferred to 'real-life' situations. Children may get every page with every phonic blend or every letter string correct but when encouraged to 'write freely' this completely disappears. The way forward is to go from the children's natural writing and to encourage them to (a) identify; (b) choose the words they want to get right. This will mean an individual list for each child *but* it will be a relevant list with a real purpose for getting it correct. At this stage it can be helpful to show a child that if they learn how to spell 'believe' they can find a similar letter string in relieve, field, relief and yield. Getting children to become fascinated by words and their spellings is more effective than any sheet of aimless exercises.

Why can some people spell naturally and some people can't? How much is natural? Does it depend on intelligence?

If you are a poor speller this seems so unfair, but remember it is possible for almost everyone to make progress.

Although we do not know exactly how people become 'natural spellers' the work of Margaret Peters established that these spellers have certain things in common.

1. They have good verbal intelligence.
2. They have good visual discrimination.
3. They have swift handwriting.
4. They are 'careful' children, i.e. they pay attention to detail and often do not read as rapidly as some weaker spellers.
5. They know they are good spellers.

She found that if any three were missing from this list then it was unlikely that the child/adult would be 'naturally good'. How these children acquired these characteristics is impossible to know but encouragement in taking an interest in words does achieve improvement.

What do you do to/with a child who does not seem to care whether spellings are correct or not? I.e. how can we alter attitude?

Most of our 'poor' attitudes are to cover up a sense of failure. Many people boast that they are poor spellers trying to imply that they are therefore good readers but unconcerned about their spelling! The only way to achieve a change in attitude is for the individuals to decide to change – and this seems only possible when they see that they could be successful. Genuine praise and achievable goals are more likely to achieve this than constant cajoling, anger, bribery or corruption! Talking to the individuals to try to find out where they feel they want to help can open the door to changing attitude and encouragement but in the final analysis this has to be taken on by the individual.

Spelling and creative writing

Should spelling accuracy be sacrificed for imaginative and creative writing?

Yes, in the drafting stages. When an author is planning, creating, thinking through the 'story' spelling should not be allowed to get in the way of the writing but when the material is ready for publication – and this can be anything from displaying on the classroom wall to being presented in a bound book format – then attention to all the skills of proof reading can come into play. It is important for spellings to be correct so that the readers are not distracted by the surface structures such as spelling, punctuation and handwriting but can concentrate on the message that the writer wished to convey.

If children are in a situation where they are expected to write straight into their notebooks then leaving a space for words they cannot spell often eases congestion at the teacher's desk and enables the writer to finish the sentence or essay without too much interruption. Junior children quickly adapt to this approach and far prefer it to having wrong spellings 'marked' on their work. It is possible for children to put the first letter or letters to remind themselves of the missing word and for the teacher to write in pencil the correct spelling in the margin near the 'space'.

Teaching spelling

Should you teach spelling as a separate activity?

If you decide to set aside a 'special time' when children are expected to concentrate on spelling then it is the ways in which children can be encouraged to explore words and how to write them that should be emphasised and not a list written on a board to be copied and learnt by Friday. Hopefully the days of twenty spellings per week regardless of a child's needs or ability are over. There is no evidence to show that these lists have any lasting effect – hence the usual complaint 'you got it right on Friday but why is it wrong again here?' Spelling ability is developmental and children need to progress along this path, so in any class there will be children in very different stages (see the introduction). Children need to become responsible for their own learning and it is the words they want to get under their belt that are important.

By all means set aside a time to enjoy and explore words but try to ensure that all the children are allowed to become autonomous in their learning.

Can spelling be taught by learning the rules of spelling?

Some rules give a writer something to fall back upon when all other strategies fail, e.g. 'ent' is a more common ending than 'and', 'able' is more common when the suffix is added to a whole word, but most rules are very complex to learn and let you down. In an experiment a computer was fed over three hundred spelling rules then produced spellings of seventeen thousand words, half of which were unconventional! (Jorm, 1980).

Spelling and handwriting

Should all schools have a spelling and handwriting policy?

Schools which have clear policies to which the staff have both contributed and are committed offer children security and direction which is undoubtedly supportive to learning. However a totally rigid policy will exclude some children and the nurture of a child towards achieving his/her best must take precedence over any policy.

Does joined-up writing help spelling?

Peters (1970) found that the better spellers had a swifter handwriting style than poor spellers, but whether this was because they could spell and were therefore quicker or because they had mastered a swift hand early in their school life was not known. Certainly when writing familiar words it often feels as though the hand takes over so that the writer automatically puts certain letter strings together, e.g. ing, tion, and if the joined hand helps with this then it certainly helps spelling. Bradley (1980) strongly advocates a running, joined hand which she believes helps weak spellers master letter strings more quickly. She found that 'bad handwriting itself does not teach poor spelling but failure to establish motor patterns – elegant or inelegant – could hamper the normal development of spelling'. There is a growing interest in children being introduced to a joined hand as early as possible in the belief that it helps with the automatic production of correct letter combinations but there is no conclusive research to say that all children benefit from this.

Spelling and the National Curriculum

How can I deal with spelling in the National Curriculum?

The developmental approach to spelling is directly reflected in the programmes of study for writing and spelling. If children are given the opportunity to write for a range of purposes and audiences which they have instigated then they will take risks as learners and in doing so will develop as writers and spellers.

How can I assess children's spelling in the terms of the National Curriculum?

The developmental model can be seen to correlate to the statements of attainment (Key Stage 1) for spelling. In order to attain level one the child will have progressed from mark making to writing recognisable letter shapes, some of which represent words. This child would be in the semi-phonetic stage of development.

In order to attain level two the child should be moving from the semi-phonetic stage into the phonic stage and for level three the child would need to be firmly established in the transitional stage (see the Introduction for a fuller description of these stages).

General comments

Inevitably more questions arise about spelling than it is possible to answer here. Perhaps the most important fact to hang on to is that children are moving through stages before they achieve the correct form of many words. As teachers our role is to identify the stage a child has reached and then adapt our teaching techniques to enable that child to progress along the road to becoming a confident and competent speller. Spelling can be taught very successfully but the most successful teaching occurs when teachers recognise the specific help a child needs at any time.

References and further reading

Bradley, L. (1981) The organisation of motor patterns for spelling: an effective remedial strategy for backwards readers. *Developmental Medicine and Child Neurology*, 23, 83–91.

Bradley, L. and Bryant, P. (1985) *Children's Reading Problems*, Blackwell.

Bullock, A. (1975) *A Language for Life*, DES.

Frith, U. (1980) *Cognitive Processes in Spelling Education*, Academic Press.

Peters, M. (1967) *Spelling Caught or Taught?* Routledge and Kegan Paul.

Peters, M. (1970) *Success in Spelling*, Cambridge Institute of Education.

The following are highly recommended for anyone wanting to read more:

Cripps, C. (1989) *Joining the ABC*, LDA.

Gentry, R. (1987) *Spel is a Four Letter Word*, Scholastic.

Torbe, M. (1977/1989) *Teaching Spelling* and *Genys at Work*, Ward Lock.

Source

This is an edited version of a chapter previously published in *Teaching Spelling: Some Questions Answered*. 1990. Reproduced by permission of the University of Reading.

Chapter 21

Spelling

Rea Reason and Rene Boote

The learning of reading and spelling complement and support each other but need a different emphasis in teaching. This chapter covers the following areas of spelling:

- Selecting words to learn.
- Planning help in spelling.
- Developing personal strategies.
- Regular and irregular words.
- Learning to correct spelling.
- The use of dictionaries and other aids.
- Spelling games and activities.

What do we need to teach?

Encouragement, enjoyment and understanding are as important in spelling as they are in reading. Encouragement and enjoyment come from success, and a feeling of being in control of the words. Children who feel in control of only a few words may limit their writing to what they think they can spell. Conversely, poor spellers who have something they urgently want to say may find that no-one can read it, not even themselves.

Against this background, the teacher's task is more complex than just to tell the child which spellings to learn. In this chapter we shall consider seven aspects of the teaching of spelling:

1. Deciding which words the child needs to learn next.
2. Planning help in spelling.
3. Helping the child to develop a personal strategy for learning spellings.
4. Teaching both regular words and less predictable words in such a way that they are retained.
5. Encouraging the child to take responsibility for making sure spellings are correct.
6. Helping the child to work towards independence in spelling by teaching the use of dictionaries and word lists.
7. Games and activities for learning spelling.

Deciding where to start

Deciding where to start teaching is the same in spelling as it is in reading: we look at the child's current work. This is easier in spelling, as we can quickly survey several pieces of independent writing, and decide what are the most pressing needs. It is important to have in mind a limited number of criteria here. It serves no positive purpose to note every spelling mistake in a piece of writing. This would in many cases give too much information, and make effective planning more difficult.

We have devised Table 21.1 to help you to make planning decisions appropriate to the child's stage of development. By referring to it while examining the children's writing, you can decide what are their strengths, and what are their most immediate needs. Because *Stage One* is concerned with the development of concepts rather than actual reading and writing, progress in both aspects usually runs hand-in-hand.

The 'stages' include levels 1 to 3 of National Curriculum English. We have preferred to use the term 'stages' for two reasons. First, the 'stages' reflect our theoretical stance of how children learn to spell which is not identical with national requirements of what should be taught. Second, Stage One is much easier to achieve than Level 1.

Table 21.1 Stages in learning to spell

Stage One
    Recognises rhymes and rhyming words.
    Blends spoken sounds into words.
    Makes some representations of phonic structures in writing the beginnings of
       words.

Stage Two
    Can write:
    • Single letter sounds.
    • Words such as *at, in, hat, sun, dog, lid, net.*
    • Some common harder words (e.g. *have, went, likes*).
    Can analyse words into constituent sounds (e.g. ch-ur-ch, re-mem-ber).

Stage Three
    Can write words with:
    • Consonant digraphs (e.g. ch, sh, th).
    • Consonant blends (sl-, fr-, sk, st, -nd, etc.).
    • Vowel digraphs (ea, au, ow, etc.).
    • Magic e (came, mine, etc.).
    Spells most common words.

Stage Four
    Spells most words accurately.
    Knows when to use a dictionary.

Note: We have preferred the term 'stages' to National Curriculum 'levels' as the 'stages' reflect our theoretical orientation and are not identical to the 'levels'.

Examples illustrating the 'stages'

Each of the examples is from the work of a child who is on the way to achieving the Stage specified.

Stage One

James has not yet understood the nature of sound–symbol correspondences. His writing is largely restricted to the letters of his name.

Figure 21.1 The fairy tripped and lost her shoe

Stage Two

Six months later, James is at the early phonic stage. He can write the prominent consonants in a word, and knows some common easy spellings.

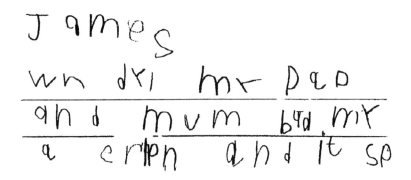

Figure 21.2 One day my dad and mum bought me an aeroplane and it snapped

Stage Three

Yasmin knows many spelling rules, but sometimes over-generalises, e.g. *wighting* for *writing*; *whachin* for *watching*

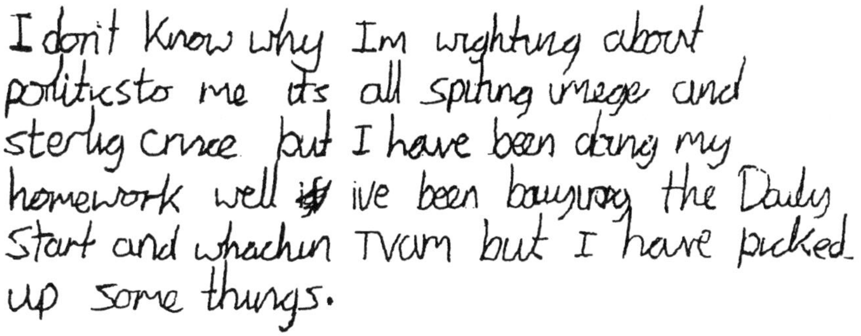

I don't Know why Im wrghting about politicsto me its all spltng image and sterlig crnce but I have been dtng my homework well if ive been baujung the Daily Start and whachin TVam but I have picked up some things.

Figure 21.3

Moving on from Stage One

Before the child grasps the principles of phonic synthesis at Stage Two, her attempts at spelling will probably be based on rudimentary phonic analysis. This may take one or more forms, for example:

- prominent consonants – **wz** (was), **Bt** (bought);
- letter *sounds* – **erpln** (*e-ruh-pl-en* makes aeroplane);
- letter *names* – **Is** (eyes), **nrg** (energy).

It becomes clear that, in order to prevent the development of spelling difficulties, children at these early stages need to be taught to spell the words they want to use in writing (see James at Stages One and Two above). They are unlikely to pick them up from their reading, or from copying under the teacher's scribing of their dictated sentences. They need to be familiar with syllables and vowels, and to develop techniques for learning spellings. And it is important to remember that a child may be at Stage One or Two in spelling not only in the Infant Department, but at the age of nine or ten, having made satisfactory progress in reading.

Games and activities for learning about syllables and vowels are to be found at the end of this chapter.

The importance of word analysis (Stage Two)

Spelling difficulties are compounded if the child does not 'hear' the component parts of a word. For learning to distinguish syllables, games of tapping out rhythms, or clapping each syllable in a name, are popular.

Further activities for learning syllables may be found at the end of this chapter.

The other important component parts of a word are consonant-strings. It is necessary to be able, for example, to analyse **spring** into **spr-ing,** to know the spelling of **ing,** and then further to analyse **spr** into **s-p-r.** This may require extensive practice.

Planning help in spelling

To plan your teaching, look at one or more pieces of the child's writing with reference to Table 21.1. For example, Martin, aged 8, has written the piece below. We can see that Martin has achieved a few aspects of Stage Three, but is still unsure of all of Stage Two. We can list his strengths and needs in spelling.

'ALIEN'

Title given: Alien

Transcript

An Alien is scary
He has 6 eyes
and big teeth to eat
people up.
He has a friend
in space. He
lives in mud.
He likes talking.
His eyes flash
all the time. His eyes
are veiny.

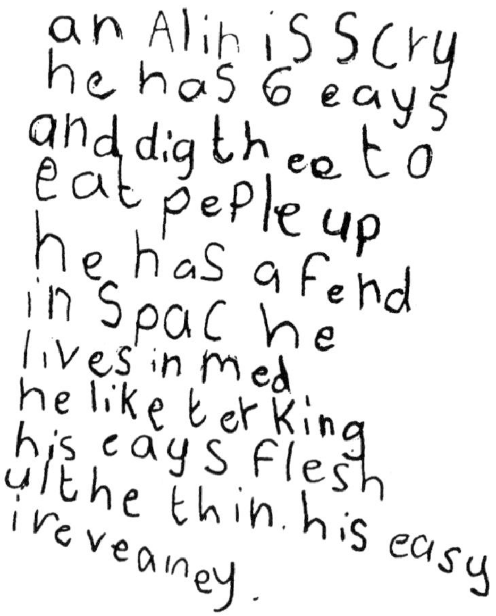

an Alih iS Scry
he haS 6 eays
and dig th ee to
eat pePle up
he haS a fend
in Spac he
lives in med
he like tetKing
his cays flesh
ulthe thin. his easy
i ve vea iney.

Figure 21.4

Strengths	Needs
Stage Two	**Stage Two**
Knows most consonant and short vowel symbols; some short-vowel words (*his, in*);	Revise oral word analysis (t-ee-th, fr-ie-nd)
Common words: knows *are, like*	Consolidate all short vowel sound–symbol correspondences.

Stage Three	Stage Three
Knows some digraphs (sh, th) and blends (fl, sc)	Extension of blends, digraphs, magic e
	Common words: eyes, friend

Initial plan of action

Even from this brief analysis, there is enough evidence for weeks of spelling lessons, but the teacher has to decide on her first priority with Martin. Noting his spellings of **mud, flash**, she chooses to help him to consolidate the short vowel sounds. She does this by introducing the Medial Vowel game (see p. 371), which he can play not only with her, but with anyone who has already acquired this skill, including other children. Martin's difficulties with **eyes** and **friend** are common to many other children in the class, so the teacher decides to use these words for a 'five-minute focus' with the whole class.

Developing a strategy for learning to spell

A strategy for learning to spell is not usually acquired incidentally. It is safer to teach it. Traditional methods like copying out the word a set number of times, or spelling out in letter-names, are inefficient for some people. Most good spellers know when a word looks right, but some go by the feel of their hand writing the letters in sequence (the kinaesthetic approach). Others remember some rules, whether conventional or personal. Different combinations of approaches may be used by one person at different times.

In the past few years, since the publication of the first edition of this manual, many schools have adopted the Look-Cover-Write-Check routine, with mixed results. The biggest complaint is that children learn the drill, and then forget to make use of it when trying to copy or learn spellings. This is not surprising if children do not understand the purpose and value of the routine, and if it has not been practised sufficiently often to be automatic. It is best if children are helped to find their own most successful method of remembering spellings, which may well include some elements of Look-Cover-Write-Check. To do this, and to help those who find spelling exceptionally difficult, a Multisensory Approach is often advocated.

A multisensory approach

This means that the learner concentrates every possible faculty to imprint the spelling on his memory. It requires an act of will, and a belief that the effort is worthwhile. Because it seems laborious to learn at first, it is important that the teacher praises every small advance in acquiring the technique. It is helpful to the learner if the teacher explains:

Let's try to learn this word in every way we can possibly think of. You can learn it with your ears, when you listen to yourself pronouncing the parts separately; with your voice, when you spell it out. Your hand can learn it when you write, and your eyes can be a camera to take a picture of it for your brain to remember. You can look for the bit of the word that tries to trick you, and make sure it doesn't. Let's see what your best way is of learning to spell. (Demonstrate each process.)

- Look at the word, read it, and pronounce it in syllables or other small bits (**re-mem-ber; sh-out**).
- Try to listen to yourself doing this.
- Still looking at it, spell it out in letter-names.
- Continue to look, and trace out the letters on the table with your finger as you spell it out again.
- Look at the word for any 'tricky bits'; for example, **gh** in **right.** (Different pupils find different parts of a word 'tricky'.)
- Try to get a picture of the word in your mind: take a photograph of it in your head!
- Copy the word, peeping at the end of each syllable or letter-string.
- Highlight the tricky bits in colour (or by some other means).
- Visualise the word again.
- Now cover it up and try to write it, spelling it out in letter-names.
- Does it look right?
- Check with the original.
- Are there some tricky bits you didn't spot (i.e. the parts that went wrong)?
- Repeat as much of the procedure as necessary to learn the word thoroughly.

This is an exceedingly lengthy routine. Encourage those who are having some success to slim the procedure down, so that they use only the parts relevant to themselves. This may take a little time to discover, but by thinking about the procedure, and experimenting to find out which parts are useful, pupils are more likely to develop a learning strategy suitable for themselves.

In the example quoted above, Martin reduces this fifteen-point procedure to six, and works out a routine, as shown in Figure 21.5.

He enjoys practising his spellings now that they have a personal challenge. To do this, he takes a long strip of paper, half the width of an exercise page, and copies the word accurately at the top. After studying it by Look-Read-Visualise, he folds the word out of sight, and attempts to write it. Checking is done by unfolding the paper. At the end of several practices, the paper is folded over and over as in the game of consequences, with the word written on each section.

- Look and Read
- Visualise
- Look again
- Cover
- Write (peep if necessary)
- Check

Figure 21.5

Teaching regular and irregular words

Choosing or adapting a spelling scheme

Many schools have adopted a published spelling scheme as an easy source of regular spellings. Children follow this at their own level, learning the weekly word lists and rules assigned to their group. The learning is often followed by a test. Make sure that the scheme you are using is suitable for your learners. Children who find spelling difficult need:

- words they are likely to find useful in their next pieces of writing;
- groupings that emphasise similarities in both sound and spelling, for example, **right**, **night**, **fight**, **sight**, but not **height** or **weight** until the others have been consolidated;
- both regular words in 'families', and less predictable but common words;
- opportunities to use the target words in context.

Features of some schemes may contradict your own policy, for example:

- anagrams and crosswords emphasise constituent letters in a word, but do not encourage learning the letters in sequence;
- word searches should preferably run from left to right and from top to bottom, not backwards;
- in a scheme featuring joined script, the handwriting style may be incompatible with the school's chosen style.

The important thing is to be comfortable with any scheme you use, whether published or self-made. This may mean selecting and adapting to suit individuals, or the whole class. You may, for example, decide to ask some children to learn fewer spellings than the rest of the group, or enhance a sense of success by including in a child's list words that she already knows.

Testing spellings

Tests can give children an aim and a time limit and, if used supportively, can lead to a real sense of achievement. Of course, the ultimate test of success in learning to spell is when children have occasion to use the target word in spontaneous writing. It is disappointing to teacher and learner alike when, despite conscientious effort, the child fails to remember the spellings correctly in continuous writing or, worse, does not achieve full marks in the test. There are several ways of approaching this problem.

To test children on their individual spellings arrange for them to dictate the words to each other. The teacher can then spot-check progress or mark the tests. Children may enter the score on their own bar-charts and follow their weekly progress, without undesirable competition. Some children may learn five spellings, and some twenty, but they can all aim to achieve 100 per cent of their target. With this kind of testing, the child and you can personally select the words to be learnt by any individual, with or without reference to a spelling scheme.

Dictating sentences

To give children practice in using their target words in context, many teachers dictate sentences with the words embedded. This gives the child a 'halfway house' between writing the word in isolation, and using it accurately in continuous writing. Many children, however, are slow to write sentences to dictation. They fail to remember the sentence, or have difficulty with handwriting, or cannot keep pace with the rest of the group. The teacher has to use her judgement to decide when a child will profit from writing dictated sentences, how many of the target words to include in one session, and how to organise the group of children.

Irregular words

Learning to spell cannot follow a completely phonic programme. Children need spellings right from the beginning that are either exceptions to general rules (e.g. **they, people**) or follow complex rules (**knew, brought**). It is advisable for children to learn these words as soon as they begin to make much use of them, since they will otherwise be in danger of consolidating wrong spellings.

Some teachers like to compose a list of commonly used words which they teach systematically, and have available to the children for quick reference. *Our own compilation of a basic spelling vocabulary appears at the end of this chapter.*

One problem with spelling schemes is that they must make assumptions about the words that children will want to spell, based on the child's age or reading level. This can be frustrating for a child like Martin who has an extensive vocabulary. If he wishes to write, for example, about a rocket **accelerating** into space, his teacher will supply the word, but it will not be at his level in the spelling scheme, and she may not have time to point out that **accept, access, accident** and **success** all follow the same rule. So although **accelerate** is not an irregular word, in this case it may have to be treated as one, and an opportunity to generalise is lost.

With truly irregular common words, such as **eyes** and **friend,** which all children need, and many learn to spell consistently wrong, Martin's teacher decided to highlight them with the whole class. She asked the children to consider the 'tricky bits', and invent ways of remembering the spellings.

No memorable ways of remembering **friend** were put forward, until the teacher suggested a sentence she had seen in a book:

'I **fri** ed my **fri** end on **Fri** day.'

This appealed to the class's sense of the ridiculous, and was adopted immediately.

With **eyes**, the children devised a face as mnenomic. This was particularly successful, as it emphasised the symmetry of the word **eye**, the **y** forming the nose between the two **e**'s.

Figure 21.6

Where children persistently misspell the same word, or confuse reversible letters like b and d, they can be given a 'search card' as illustrated below. This is stored in a pocket inside the cover of the child's exercise book, or some other handy place. After finishing a piece of writing, the child turns detective, and searches every line to find any examples of these words which have managed to *misspell themselves*.

This approach makes correcting spelling into a game. It shifts the blame for the misspelling from the child to the word. It then becomes more acceptable to the child to try to control the 'uncooperative' word, rather than feel defeated yet again at having committed the same old misspelling. [See Figure 21.7.]

Taking responsibility for checking own spellings

In an interactive classroom, spelling is not confined to studying the week's lesson on the appointed day. It is a topic that arises out of reading and writing

Figure 21.7

throughout the week. If there is an odd five minutes to fill, the teacher may set the whole class to think of a word family, and find examples of it in books or their own writing. One Y3 class was asked to look out for words beginning with **some**, the teacher having in mind compound words like **something**. One girl got so carried away that she looked in the *Little Oxford Dictionary*, and found all the words, including **Somerset**!

Magic Lines

Teachers of children at early stages of spelling have found the use of Magic Lines helpful. When engrossed in the content of what they want to say, children are encouraged to draw a Magic Line to represent a word with a difficult spelling, and return to it later to write in the correct spelling. Below is an illustration of Laura's use of the Magic Line. It works better if the child can at least put down the initial sound. Some teachers have had to ration the number of Magic Lines per piece, as the writing otherwise becomes completely incomprehensible! [See Figure 21.8.]

Writing with the intended reader in mind

It is now generally acknowledged in schools that creative writing, as distinct from copying, is a messy process. The first draft is unlikely to be totally satis-

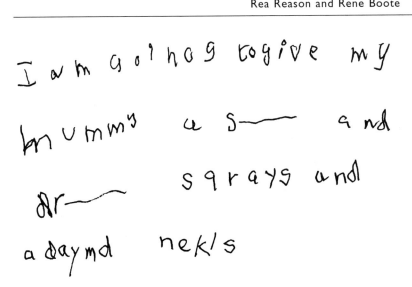

Figure 21.8 I am going to give my mummy a special and brilliant surprise and a diamond
         necklace

factory. With each piece of writing, a decision has to be made about its purpose,
and the intended audience. This will help to determine the standard of presentation necessary. For example, notes needed for future revision must be easy
to read, but planning notes which will soon be scrapped do not need such
care.

This situation is difficult for some people to accept. Fastidious children may
hate to make mistakes, and will limit what they write to words they know.
Their books are often smudged with eraser marks, and the idea of crossing out
horrifies the child. Adults, too, may find the idea of a less-than-best presentation unacceptable.

But established authors feel free to cross out, scribble, cut, and rewrite.
Writing is their medium, not their master. Children are interested to learn
that Real Authors often scrap far more paper than they eventually send to the
publisher in the finished typescript. It helps, too, if they see other children's
work at various stages of development.

The teacher has to decide, with respect to each piece of writing, how much
responsibility the child should take for checking and correcting the spellings,
and which, if any, the teacher is going to correct herself. Her decision will be
influenced by the child's competence in spelling, but also the interest the child
can be encouraged to show in 'publishing' the writing for others to read.

A case example

Paying attention first to meaning, teachers comment on the content of the
writing before going on to help children edit their work. The work of Ben has

been chosen to illustrate how the child gradually takes over responsibility for checking and correcting the spellings. His progress has been monitored from the time he was eight. Ben has followed a systematic spelling programme for four years, and his spelling to dictation, although not perfect, is much improved.

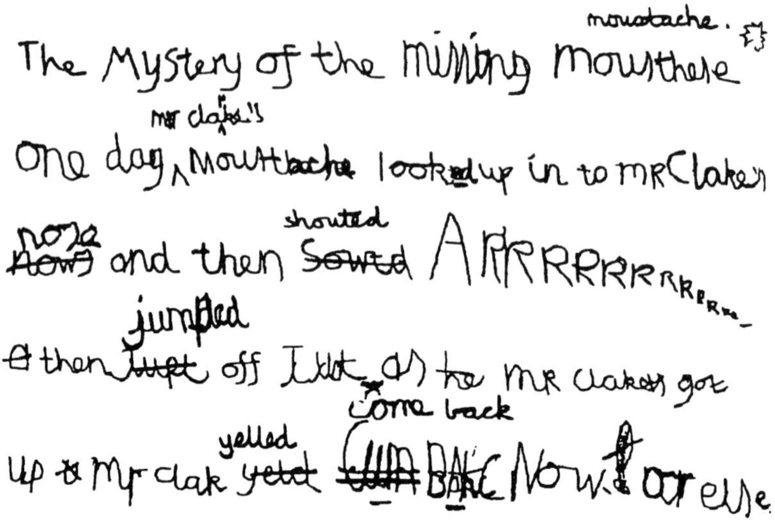

Figure 21.9 Extract from a long story by Ben, aged 10

Teacher's comments:

I'm sure Mr Clarke will be interested to read your story and find out what happened to his moustache! . . .

One of your ways of spelling his name is correct. Can you tell me which one it is? Perhaps you can find it written up somewhere in school.

Check the first five lines and make sure you have spelt all your basic words correctly.

If you like, I will read through the rest of your writing and put in the important words that people might not understand.

(Teacher's Note: revise magic e, final ed.)

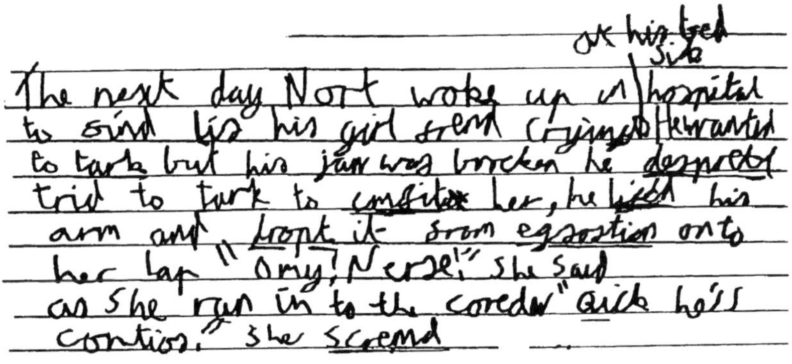

Figure 21.10 Extract from an even longer story by Ben, now aged 12

Memore

. . . The next day Nort woke up in hospital
to find Liz his girl frend crying at his bed side.
He wanted to <u>tark</u> but his jaw was brocken.
he <u>despretl</u> trid to <u>tark</u> to <u>cmfit</u> her. He <u>liftd</u> his
arm and <u>dropt</u> it from <u>egsostion</u> on to her lap.
'Oh my! Nerse!,' she said.

Teacher's comments:

This looks like an exciting story. Do you know how it is going to end?
. . .
    I see you have already started to check the spellings and underline the
ones that don't look right for you.
    Read through the rest of your first draft.
    Correct all the spellings you know to be wrong.
    Put a line under the words you would like me to check, and I will tell
you which ones it's worth looking up in the ACE dictionary. I'll edit the
rest of it for you if you like, so that you can write up your final draft neatly.

The teacher also notes word groups still needing teaching or revision. It will
be observed that the tone of these comments is supportive to the child, and
objective about the spellings. The teacher is not saying, 'You produce, and I
will judge', but 'You have something worthwhile to say, and I will try to help
you to make your meaning clearer'.

A personalised spelling programme

The teacher's comments above show how it is possible to base the child's
spelling tasks on the words he wants to use. To enable the child to classify

words, and make the learning efficient, the teacher needs access to lists of words in the same spelling family.

Constructing individual word lists

Once the spelling rule or word family to be learnt has been decided, it is necessary to select words that are meaningful, and if possible, useful, to the individual child. For example, if the target word is **car**, the teacher could select **bar**, **far**, **star**, **hard**, **start** to be learnt in addition.

The obvious approach would be to give the child the list, and ask him to learn the words by his chosen method. Our experience shows that it is far more effective not to present the list to the child, but to get him to construct it, for example:

> 'We are going to look at the word **car**, and other words in the same family. Let's say the word **car**, and listen to the sounds in it.
>   Yes, it goes **k-ah**.
>   Now let's write it.'
>
> (*Teacher spells out, child writes.*)
>
>   The **k** sound is spelt **C**, and the **ah** sound is spelt **A-R**.
>   Underline the **ah** sound in **car**, and tell me the rule.
>   (**AR** *spells the sound* **ah**.)
>   'Now tell the sounds in **bar (b-ah)**, and show me how you can write it' (etc.).

This approach gives you a quick check on how firmly the child has grasped the principle of spelling rules and families. We are in effect asking whether he can generalise from the rule to construct words he has not already seen.

The personal word book

A personal alphabetic word book helps children take responsibility for their own spelling. In it, they can put words from their own writing which are likely to prove useful in future. It is also a good source of words to learn, if children are invited to construct their own weekly spelling lists.

Where children know in advance what editing their writing is likely to receive, and their own probable share in it, they are often more willing to consult their personal spelling book, and any other word lists or dictionaries they can use easily. Easy reference is vital. Nobody wants to interrupt their flow of ideas by struggling with difficult reference books, or making numerous unsuccessful attempts to spell the word for themselves.

Tape recorders and word processors

For the child who is unable to read her writing even immediately after the whole piece is finished, a small dictaphone may be useful. She can then periodically read into it her last sentence or line of writing, much as an adult writer constantly reviews what she has just written. The recording will be a help to both child and teacher in recalling what the writer meant.

The use of a word processor is of obvious assistance, particularly if it has a spellcheck facility. The Franklin Spellmaster, sold together with the *Oxford Children's Dictionary*, has proved to be another useful tool for helping children correct their spelling.

Learning to use word lists and dictionaries

Independence in spelling is achieved when the writer uses word lists and dictionaries successfully. The irony is that the writer must know enough about the beginning of a word to locate it in the dictionary, and poor spellers find this difficult. Picture dictionaries and topic-based word books are useful in the early stages, but their limitations are obvious. Many of the most difficult spellings are of words that cannot be illustrated.

Learning to use a dictionary requires more than a knowledge of the alphabet and the ability to put words in alphabetical order. There are many skills to be learnt, but these can be made enjoyable if they are incorporated into games.

The steps in learning how to use a word list or dictionary are set out below.

Learning to use a dictionary

The child can:

1. Recite the alphabet.
2. Read the names of all letters, and write the letter for each name.
3. Locate each initial letter in an alphabetic list quickly, looking for example towards the beginning for **D**, the end for **T** and the middle for **Q**.
4. Quickly locate known words in a simple word list; for example, in the 500 Word Book, find **you, have, went, going**.
5. Put short lists of recognised words into alphabetical order, starting with easy lists with different initial letters.
6. Locate known words in a bigger dictionary.

Games for practising these skills are to be found at the end of this chapter. Two useful publications for the early stages are Breakthrough 'My First Word Book' (Longman), which lists very basic words, and has lines for writing the child's personal spellings, and the *500 Word Book* (Remedial Supply Co., Dixon Street, Wolverhampton WV2 2BX). This includes more words, and has space, but no lines, for the child's own words.

A spelling dictionary

The ability to use a dictionary to confirm a spelling depends on having at least some idea how the word starts. For children of ten or older who are still finding this difficult, the *ACE Dictionary* (LDA, Duke St., Wisbech, Cambs. PE13 2AE) may be useful. This lists spellings according to their initial consonant(s), number of syllables, and the sound of the first vowel.

The child needs to be able to analyse the sounds in words. If, for example, he wishes to write the word **gymnastics**, he must know that:

> it has three syllables;
> the first sound is **J**;
> the first vowel sound is short **i**.

He would then be able to find **gymnastics** on the page of words beginning with the sounds **ji**, in the three syllable list. The procedure is laborious at first, but persistence pays off.

Games and activities for learning spelling

Once introduced, many of these activities can be supervised by other adults or children who have already firmly acquired the skill.

A set of small wooden letters, or letters printed on stout card, is needed for many of these games. Some teachers have found it helpful to paint the vowels red, to distinguish them from the consonants.

1 Analysing and blending the sounds in words

This is a spelling version of a word building game.

Procedure

1. Select a limited number of letters according to the words you are going to build. (For example below, you need a, b, c, g, h, i, m, n, o, p, r, t, u.) Check that the child knows all the sounds. If not, teach them with a flip-card alphabet.
2. The procedure is to make a three-letter word like **cat,** and by changing one letter at a time, make a succession of new three-letter words. Start by varying the first letter, and when you are sure that the child has mastered the process, switch to changing the final letter. Proceed to changing the medial vowel only when the child is fluent with consonant changes, for example:

> I am taking a word that I think you know. Can you tell me what it says?
> Yes, cat. Which letters have I used for cat?
> Yes, c-a-t (using sounds, not letter-names). Can you hear that cat is made
>   of c-a-t?

Now I'm going to change the first letter to h, and that will make . . . ?
   . . . Yes, hat.
Tell me the sounds in hat.
Show me how you can change it back to cat.
Now jumble up the letters, and see if you can make cat again.

Make changes as follows:

Change first letter	Change final letter	Change medial letter
cat	man	bag
hat	map	big
bat	mat	bog
rat	cat	bug
mat	cap	rug
	can	rig
	ban	rag etc.

2 The medial vowel sound game

Materials

A set of the five vowels, either plastic letters, or written on cards.
A set of pictures illustrating one-syllable words, each with a medial vowel, for
   example:

   cat, bag, hat, van, bat;
   bell, pen, bed, hen, net;
   pig, fish, zip, witch, pin;
   cot, dog, box, mop, frog;
   bun, cup, gun, nut, sun.

Pictures are provided on page 378.

Procedure

Here are the vowels. Tell me the sound of each one.
Vowels are very important, because each word has to have at least one.
Let's look at the picture cards, and say what each one is.
We are going to say the word for each picture card and put it in the
   column under the vowel we can hear in the middle. Let's see which
   vowel can win by getting five pictures first. So hen is made of h-e-n.
   It has e in the middle, so it goes in the e column (etc.).

3 Learning about syllables

At Stage One Reading, children learn to blend syllables spoken by the teacher into words. For spelling, they need to be able to analyse the words they want to write into syllables. Analysis of words into syllables is a more advanced skill than recognition of words pronounced in syllables by someone else. It may therefore require more preliminary work before the concept is grasped.

For syllables, collect a list of names from the class or school with varying numbers of syllables. It is not necessary at this stage to go into technical details about syllable boundaries. Start with a polysyllable, if possible the child's own name, or that of her friend. Show her how to count the parts or beats in the word, for example:

Mark/ Har/ri/son
John/ Smith
Va/nes/sa/ Bar/tu/lo/vic

You can tap the rhythms on the table, or sing the syllables, giving a different note to each. The important thing is for the child to be able to separate syllables and count the beats for himself. Children need to learn the difference between vowels and consonants in connection with syllables, because every syllable must have at least one vowel.

4 The newspaper game

The aim of this game is to raise awareness of grammatical usage and homophones, or difficult letter groups in common words, for example:

1. Grammatical usage – where/were; there/their.
2. Question-words beginning with wh – where, when, why, what, who, whether.

Materials

Sheets from newspapers or newspaper magazines, one for each child.
A highlighter pen or bright fibre tip for each child.

The game is best played in a group of two or three children.

Procedure

1. Decide on your target spelling combination.
2. Make sure that the news-sheets contain at least some examples of the target spellings!
3. Ask the children to highlight as many target examples as they can in a given time. You can give extra credit for reading the words in context at the end.

4. Players then check with each other that all the highlighted words conform to the set target. If you haven't time to discuss their findings with the children they can be asked to write two or three sentences using and spelling them correctly, either copying from the newspaper, or in their own words. The newspaper examples provide a model, so there must be no wrong usages or misspellings of target words.

The advantages of the game are:

- Children enjoy being 'detectives'.
- They see the words in context.
- They learn to use print as a resource for correct usage.
- The resources are easily available.

5 Dictionary games

All the skills of learning to use a dictionary benefit from separate practice, away from the pressure of needing to find a particular word in the middle of writing a sentence. Once introduced, most of the games do not require teacher supervision.

As far as possible, materials for the games include the dictionaries and word lists in use in the classroom. This should prevent difficulties with transferring the skills from practice to the real situation.

6 Activity for accurate location of initial letters

Materials

Small lower case letters on card or of wood, one of each.

Procedure

1. Two children, or a child and an adult can play.
2. The child arranges the letters, in alphabetical order, in an arc on the table, so that each letter can easily be reached.
3. Each player takes it in turn to name a letter, which the other player has to touch as quickly as possible.

Variations

1. The player closes her eyes, and her partner tells her when she is 'warm' (close to the letter).
2. The partner says a word, not a letter, and the player must find the initial letter.

Extension

The game is played with a publication such as the *500 Word Book*, which has one page for each letter, and a thumb index for easy location.

It can be further extended by using a thicker dictionary in which to locate initial letters.

Locating known words

Materials

A *500 Word Book* (Remedial Supply Company), or *My First Word Book* (Longman Breakthrough) for each participant.

Procedure

Each partner takes turns to ask the other to:

1. Find the page with the word (e.g. **went**).
2. Find the word (**went**).

7 Alphabetical order activity

It is easier to start with sets of words written on individual cards, so that they can be physically manipulated, before asking the child to work with a list of words on paper.

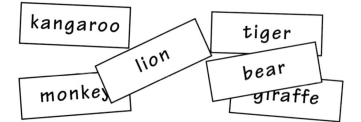

Figure 21.11

Materials

An alphabet for reference. Sets of words:

1. Initial letters in sequence (e.g. Carol, Brian, Anna, David → Anna, Brian, Carol, David – A, B, C, D).
2. Initial letters all different, not in sequence (e.g. plum, banana, orange, grapefruit, apple → apple, banana, grapefruit, orange, plum – A, B, . . . G, . . . O, P).

3. Initial letters all the same, second letters different (e.g. **skip, stop, save, send, shout**).
4. A mixture.

Procedure

1. Place the cards in a column in alphabetical order, checking whether each one precedes or follows those already placed.
2. Where the initial letter is the same, cover it, and continue as in (1), arranging the cards in a column according to the second letter (initial S covered):

    kip
    top
    ave
    end
    hout.

Some children may need to continue using this more concrete method of physically manipulating cards or slips of paper, before they manage to progress to the more abstract way of examining lists of words on paper. They can make their own cards or slips once they have grasped the principle of the activity.

8 Locating known words in a bigger dictionary

Many children would benefit from practice in this skill. It has the advantage, once the procedures have been learnt, of not needing direct teacher supervision.

The teacher can introduce the game to large groups. When working without the teacher, two or three children can play together, taking it in turn to be the Question Master.

Materials

Identical dictionaries for each member of the group.
Pencil and paper.

Procedure

First make sure that everyone understands how to find the head words (target words). They are usually printed in bold characters.

The Question Master writes down a word for the players to locate. When playing in a group, the players write down the word and the page number. Those who locate it first help the rest to find the word. When only two players are involved, writing down is less necessary.

Progression

If the dictionary has 'catch-words' printed at the top of each page, indicating the first or first and last words on the page, these are a good starting point. Words near the top of the page, and in the first column of a double-column page, are easiest to find.

Variations

Find the first word beginning with . . . .
What word comes after _____ ?
Find the word beginning *ho* . . . meaning an animal you can ride on.
What page is it on?

9 The reading–spelling game

This is played by an adult and a child, or two children reading the same book.

Materials

A set of alphabet letters.
A book that both children enjoy reading.

Procedure

1. Arrange the alphabet in a line across the table, with duplicate letters underneath:

    ```
    a  b  c  d  e  f  ...
    a     c  d  e
    a        e
    ```

2. After reading two or more pages and discussing the content, the child
    (i)   goes back and selects a word to spell (e.g. wanted);
    (ii)   reads the word in context;
    (iii) using Look-Cover-Spell-Check, makes the word with the printed letters;
    (iv)   spells the word by letter-names, tracing the letters on the table with a forefinger;
    (v)   when sure of the spelling, scrambles the letters, remakes the word, and checks with the word in context;
    (vi)   the partner checks the spelling, then attempts to spell it with the plastic letters herself.

The advantage of this game is that the child sets his or her own challenge. A surprising number of children select long and complex words, whether playing with a child or adult. The game gives practice in remembering letter-strings but it does not ensure that the word is retained for later spelling.

BASIC SPELLING VOCABULARY

A
about
across
after
afternoon
again
always
and
another
are
ask
auntie
away

B
baby
back
because
been
before
behind
best
birthday
bought
boy
bring
brother
brought
buy
by

C
called
came
can't
car
catch
children
Christmas
come
could

D
daddy
day
do
does
doesn't
don't
down
draw

E
each
eat
end
ever
every

F
family
far
father
find
finish
first
for
found
friend
from
front

G
game
gave
girl
give
go
goes
going
good
grandma

H
had
have
haven't
head
help
her
here
high
his
holiday
home
hospital
house
how

J
just

K
keep
kept
knew
know

L
ladies
lady
last
learn
left

like
little
live
look
looked
lost
love

M
made
make
many
may
me
minute
money
morning
mother
Mr
Mrs
Ms
much
mummy
must

N
name
near
never
new
next
nice
night
nobody
nothing
now
nowhere

O
o'clock
of
off
old
once
one
only
open
or
our
out
over
own

P
people
picture
place
play

played
please
police

Q
quick
quickly
quiet
quite

R
ready
right
round
running

S
said
same
saw
say
school
she
should
show
sister
so
soon
stay
stopped
stopping
street

T
take
taking
talk
teacher
television
than
thank
that
the
their
then
there
they
thing
think
this
those
thought
through
time
to
today

told
too
two

U
uncle
under
use
used
using

V
very

W
walk
walked
want
wanted
was
watch
watched
water
way
we
week
went
were
what
when
where
which
while
who
why
will
wish
wished
woman
women
won't
work
worked
would
wouldn't
write
writing

Y
year
yes
yesterday
you
your

Figure 21.12 Basic spelling vocabulary

Figure 21.13

References and further reading

Adams, M.J. (1991) *Beginning to Read*. Cambridge, Massachusetts: The MIT Press.

Alexander, R. (1992) *Policy and Practice in Primary Education*. London: Routledge.

Branston, P. and Provis, M. (1986) *Children and Parents Enjoying Reading*. London: Hodder and Stoughton.

Butkowsky, I.S. and Willows, D.M. (1980) Cognitive-motivational characteristics of children varying in reading ability: evidence of learned helplessness in poor readers. *Journal of Educational Psychology, 72* (3), 408–22.

*Centre for Language in Primary Education (1990) *Shared Reading and Shared Writing*. London: CLPE.

*Clay, M.M. (1979) *The Early Detection of Reading Difficulties: A Diagnostic Survey with Recovery Procedures*. Auckland: Heinemann.

*Clay, M.M. (1991) *Becoming Literate: The Construction of Inner Control*. London: Heinemann.

*Cline, T. and Frederickson, N. (1991) *Bilingual Pupils and the National Curriculum*. London: University College Educational Psychology Publications.

Cline, T. and Reason, R. (1993) Specific learning difficulties (dyslexia): equal opportunities issues. Research section of *British Journal of Special Education, 20* (1), 30–4.

*Coles, M. (1992) Developing and extending the concept of apprenticeship: sharing reading in the classroom. In C. Harrison and M. Coles (eds) *The Reading for Real Handbook*. London: Routledge

Cooke, A. (1993) *Tackling Dyslexia: The Bangor Way*. London: Whurr.

France, L., Topping, K. and Revell, K. (1993) Parent-tutored cued spelling. *Support for Learning, 8* (1), 11–15.

Galton, M. and Williamson, J. (1992) *Groupwork in the Primary School*. London: Routledge.

Goswami, U. and Bryant, P. (1990) *Phonological Skills and Learning to Read*. Hove, East Sussex: Erlbaum.

*Great Britain, Department for Education (1989) *English in the National Curriculum*. London: HMSO.

Great Britain, Department for Education (1992) Curriculum organisation and classroom practice in primary schools: a discussion paper. London: HMSO.

*Great Britain, Department for Education (1993) *English for Ages 5 to 16*. Proposals of the Secretary of State for Education and the Secretary of State for Wales. London: HMSO.

*Great Britain, Department for Education (1994) *Code of Practice on the Identification and Assessment of Special Educational Needs*. London: HMSO.

*Haring, N.G., Lovitt, T.C., Eaton, M.D., Hansen, C.L. (1978) *The Fourth R – Research in the Classroom*. Columbus, Ohio: Charles Merrill.

Harrison, C. and Coles, M. (eds) (1992) *The Reading for Real Handbook*. London: Routledge.

Hartas, C. and Moseley, D. (1993) Say that again, please: a scheme to boost reading skills using a computer with digitised speech. *Support for Learning, 8* (1), 16–21.

Hornsby, B. and Shear, F. (1990) *Alpha to Omega*. London: Heinemann.

Johnson, G., Hill, B. and Tunstall, P. (1992) *Primary Records of Achievement*. London: Hodder and Stoughton.

Letterland (1993) *Picture Dictionary*. Barton, Cambs.: Letterland Ltd.

Martin, A. (1989) *The Strugglers*. Milton Keynes: Open University Press.

Miles, T.R. and Miles, E. (1990) *Dyslexia: A Hundred Years on*. Milton Keynes: Open University Press.

Pearce, L. (1989) *Partners in Literacy*. Wisbech, Cambs.: LDA.

Peters, M. and Smith, B. (1993) *Spelling in Context: Strategies for Teachers and Learners*. Windsor: NFER-Nelson.

Pumfrey, P.D. (1991) *Improving Reading in the Junior School*. London: Cassell.

*Pumfrey, P.D. and Reason, R. (1991) *Specific Learning Difficulties (Dyslexia): Challenges and Responses*. London: Routledge.

*Reason, R. (1986) Specific learning difficulties: the development and evaluation of an INSET manual on intervention. *Educational and Child Psychology*, 3 (1), 45–58. Leicester: Division of Educational and Child Psychology of the British Psychological Society.

*Reason, R. (1990) Reconciling different approaches to intervention. In P.D. Pumfrey and C.D. Elliott (eds) *Children's Reading, Spelling and Writing Difficulties*. Lewes: Falmer Press.

Reason, R. (1991) Learning to cooperate and cooperating to learn. In *Developing Self-Discipline*. University College London: Educational Psychology Publications.

Reason, R. (1993) Primary special needs and National Curriculum assessment. In S. Wolfendale (ed.) *Assessing Special Educational Needs*. London: Cassell.

Reason, R., Brown, B., Cole, M. and Gregory, M. (1988) Does the 'specific' in specific learning difficulties make a difference to the way we teach? *Support for Learning*, 3 (4), 230–6.

Smith, B. (1994) *Through Writing to Reading*. London: Routledge.

Snowling, M. (1987) *Dyslexia: A Cognitive Developmental Perspective*. Oxford: Blackwell.

Stanovich, K.E. (1991) Discrepancy definitions of reading disability: has intelligence led us astray? *Reading Research Quarterly*, 26 (1), 7–29.

Sterling, C.M. and Robson, C. (eds) (1992) *Psychology, Spelling and Education*. Clevedon, Avon: Multilingual Matters.

Stradling, R., Saunders, L. with Weston, P. (1991) *Differentiation in Action: A Whole School Approach to Raising Attainment*. London: HMSO.

Thomson, M.E. and Watkins, W. (1990) *Dyslexia: A Teaching Handbook*. London: Whurr.

*Wallace, C. (1986) *Learning to Read in a Multicultural Society*. Oxford: Pergamon Press.

*Wasik, B.A. and Slavin, R.E. (1993) Preventing early reading failure with one-to-one tutoring: a review of five programs. *Reading Research Quarterly*, 28 (2), 179–200.

Watt, J.M. and Topping, K.J. (1993) Cued spelling: a comparative study of parent and peer tutoring. *Educational Psychology in Practice*, 9 (2), 95–103.

*Young, P. and Tyre, C. (1983) *Dyslexia or Illiteracy? Realizing the Right to Read*. Milton Keynes: Open University Press.

* Referred to in the text

Source

This is an edited version of a chapter previously published in *Helping Children with Reading and Spelling*. 1994. Reproduced by permission of Taylor & Francis Ltd.

Index

action research *see* Soft Systems
   Methodology
Adams, M. J. 8–10
Additional Learning Support (ALS)
   200
adult education *see* 'family literacy'
   restricted programmes
Adult Literacy and Basic Skills Unit
   (ALBSU) 91–2, 100; evaluation of
   'family literacy' programmes 103;
   flawed findings on 'cycle of
   underachievement' 96–8
Alpha to Omega scheme 87, 197
Apprenticeship Approach 13
assessments: appropriate entry into 215;
   of ability–attainment discrepancies
   252–5, 256; concern over misuse 254;
   equity in 209–11; GCE, GNVQ,
   GCSE, VCE 205–6, 215, 216, 218;
   inclusion and good practice 207–9;
   Key Stage tests 205, 215, 216–18,
   219, 220, 222; oral 220; special
   arrangements 205–7, 208–9, 212–22;
   by teacher 220, 222–3
autonomy-building 181

Bakker, D. J. 259–60
Balance Theory of reading development
   259–60
'barking at print' 12
behaviour: and dyslexia 73, 293–8,
   307
Blackstone, T. 68
British Ability Scale (BAS) tests 254,
   326
British Dyslexia Association 86–7
Brown, Christy 304–5

Checkland, Peter 138, 140, 145, 146–7,
   148–9
classroom assistants, multilingual
   153–4
Clay, Marie 60
comprehension failure 224–5;
   connectives, use of 228–30;
   inconsistency detection paradigm
   233–5; imagery, use of 239–41; and
   inference skills 225, 226–8, 238–9;
   and memory 226, 235–6; and
   monitoring skills 225, 232–5;
   referents, use of 230; remediation
   studies 236–7; tense, use of 230; text
   structure skills 225, 228–32; theories
   of 225–6
construction of meaning, reading as
   11–14, 61
cues, use of in reading 11–12, 60–2,
   191, 343; overreliance on 13
cultural contexts 7–8, 27
curricula: nationally controlled 4, 15,
   269–74; *see also* National
   Curriculum
'cycle of underachievement': flawed
   research findings on 96–8;
   rhetorical claims concerning 94–5,
   102

decoding, reading as 8–10
Diagnostic Survey 326–7
Differential Ability Scales 254
differentiation 169–70, 172, 180, 181,
   190, 248
distance learning 129–30
Division of Educational and Child
   Psychology (DECP) 249–50

dyslexia 176, 243, 244–51, 256, 260–2, 283–4, 346; alleviation 258–60; and behaviour 73, 293–8, 307; causes 111–12, 116, 118, 250; coping strategies 82–7, 117; effects on families/parents 71–8, 117, 282; and environment 112, 117; genetic susceptibility 111–15, 121, 250; as 'hidden handicap' 246, 305, 307, 308–12, 315–16; identification 251–5, 257; labelling 74, 248, 303–6, 309–16; 'life history' approach 297–9; management 79–81; official recognition 257–8; and positive affect 296–7; precursors 112, 115–16; prevention 256–8; and self-esteem 76, 117, 282–3, 287–90, 292–3, 299; and stigmatisation 304–5, 308–9, 312; teaching materials/methods 193–200, 275–9; as 'variable syndrome' 250–1; see also Special Educational Needs; specific learning difficulties
Dyslexia Index 255
Dyslexia Screening Instrument (DSI) 254–5
Dyson Debate 136, 138, 149

Early Literacy Research Project (Australia) 271
Early Literacy Support Programme (ELSP) 272–3
Education Act (1981) 30
Education Action Zones (EAZs) 22, 28
educational psychologists: and special assessment arrangements 218–19
'emergent literacy' 14
English as an Additional Language (EAL): equity in assessments 211–12; special arrangements 212
Even Start programmes 100, 103
examinations see assessments
Excellence in Cities 28

Fairground families see Traveller communities
'family literacy' restricted programmes 89–92; accessibility 100; adult basic education 90–1, 94, 99, 101, 106–7; ALBSU evaluation 103; alternatives to 106–7; effectiveness 101; and

research 92, 93–4, 102–3, 107; and rhetoric 89, 91–3, 94–5, 98, 101–2, 105–6; socio-economic claims 104–5; take-up 99–100; targeting 94–9; see also parental involvement
Frith, Uta 343–4
Fuzzbuzz scheme 196

Gates–MacGinitie Vocabulary Test 225
genetic susceptibility to dyslexia 111–15, 121, 250
Ginn Spelling scheme 195
Goodman, Kenneth 11–12
group reading 167
Gypsies see Traveller communities

Hampshire, Susan 289–90
Haringey project 6, 40–52; implications 52–6
Helping Children with Reading and Spelling scheme 196
hemispheric-alluding stimulation (HAS) 260
hemispheric-specific stimulation (HSS) 260, 261
Her Majesty's Inspectorate (HMI) progress report (1978) 174–5; assumptions behind 175–6
Her Majesty's Inspectorate (HMI) report on NLS (1998) 271–2
Hickey Multisensory Language Course 197
'hidden handicaps' 246, 305, 307, 308–12, 315–16
home–school policies 23–6
home–school relationships 7, 21–2, 25–6, 35–6, 58–9; and family structure 28, 29; implications for services 29–35; national studies 25; OFSTED inspection 23–4; partnership/collaboration distinction 28–9; and teacher visits 27–8; and Travellers 121, 124; see also learning environments; parental involvement; parents
hyperlexia 225

ICT see information technology
Inclusion Statement, National Curriculum 207–9

'independent parental supporters' *see* 'named persons/officers'
individual letter recognition 9–10
information technology (IT) 166–7; and SDD 258; and Traveller access 129–30
Interactive Compensatory model of reading 15
International Dyslexia Association (IDA) 249–50, 274
intra-subject research designs 63

Joint Council for General Qualifications (JCGQ): guidance for special arrangements 206, 212–13, 216, 217
Jolly Phonics scheme 195

Kauffman, J. M. 137–8
Kenan model of family literacy 90, 101, 102
Kerr, James 245

L-type dyslexia 260
labelling of disabilities: and categorisation 305–6; formal and informal 312–13; and ownership 313–15, 316; pros and cons 74, 248, 303–6, 309–17; specificity 313; and stigmatisation 304–5, 308–9, 312, 316
'learned helplessness', notion of 287
learning environments: classroom case studies 153–71; literacy-deficient 6; literacy-rich 14; multilingual 153–4; and social class 5–6; of Travellers 121, 123–4; *see also* home–school relationships
learning support *see* whole-school approach
LEAs *see* Local Education Authorities
libraries 158, 159
'life history' approach to dyslexia 297–9
Literacy Hour 190, 200, 272
literacy level targets 4
Local Education Authorities (LEAs): and parent partnerships 31–2; and SEN Tribunals 33–5, 269–70
'Look-and-Say' *see* phonics, analytic

Matthew effect 15
McNaughton, S. 60
meaning-construction, reading as 11–14, 61
mental mathematics: special assessment arrangements 220–1
Middle Infant Screening Test (MIST) scheme 196
Morgan, W. P. 245
multiracial contexts 55, 59–60, 153–4; fair assessment in 209–12
Multisensory Teaching System (MTS) 274–6
Multisensory Teaching System for Reading (MTSR) 276–9

'named persons/officers' 30–2
National Center for Family Literacy (NCFL) 91, 104
National Curriculum: Inclusion Statement 207–9; and spelling 352–3
National Literacy Strategy (NLS) 190–1, 270–4, 320; HMI evaluation report 271–2; Literacy Hour 190, 200, 272; MMU/BDA 'snapshot' study 272; and phonics 191–3, 194–5, 270; word level targets 191, 192–3, 194; teaching materials/methods 194–200, 270–1
Neale Analysis of Reading Ability 225, 226, 238, 326
New Age Travellers *see* Traveller communities
NFER survey of parental involvement 25, 26, 28
NLS *see* National Literacy Strategy
normative test theory 253
Norway: parent/child dyslexia study 113–15

Occupational Travellers *see* Traveller communities
OFSTED inspection framework for parental involvement 23–4
oral language, as precursor of dyslexia 112
Orton Dyslexia Society (ODS) *see* International Dyslexia Association
Overcoming Dyslexia scheme 197
Oxford Reading Tree scheme 195

P-type dyslexia 260
Paired Reading 8, 13
parent partnership officers (PPOs)
   32–3
parental involvement 5–8, 21–2, 27, 32,
   58–9, 68, 100, 106, 159, 348; effects
   of on reading 39–40; Haringey
   project 40–56; and LEAs 31–2;
   models of 7–8; NFER national survey
   25, 26, 28; OFSTED inspection
   framework 23–4; and parents' rights
   29–30, 33–4; see also 'family literacy'
   restricted programmes; home–school
   relationships; parents; Pause, Prompt,
   Praise
parents: dyslexic 111–13; effects of
   dyslexia on 71–8; lack of teacher
   training with 23; and use of 'named
   persons' 30–2; as partners 25–6, 31–3,
   35, 159; and the SEN Tribunal 33–4;
   of Traveller children 124, 125;
   'unreachable' 22, 25, 26–7, 28–9;
   see also home–school relationships;
   parental involvement
Parents' Charter (1995) 22
Pause Prompt Praise (PPP) 6, 7–8;
   effectiveness of 63–4; in Maori 66–7,
   68; procedures 59–61; tutor training
   66, 67–8; tutors' benefits from 64–6;
   use of 61–3; see also parental
   involvement
peer tutoring 64, 65, 66–7
personal construct theory 287
Peters, Margaret 344
phonics 8–10, 15, 157, 164, 341;
   analytic 270; criticism of 12, 13, 14;
   in the NLS 191–3, 194–5, 270;
   schemes/materials 194–200, 274–9;
   and spelling 346–7, 357; synthetic
   270, 274; v. whole-book approach
   13–14, 15; see also Phonological
   Training
Phonological Assessment Battery
   (PhAB) 253
Phonological Training 323–4; costs
   332–3; v. Reading Recovery study
   324–37; see also phonics
psycholinguistics: 'guessing game' of
   reading 11–13
psychomedical interventions for SDD
   259

Qualifications and Curriculum
   Authority (QCA): special
   arrangements 209

Rasch scaling 253–4
reading: ability measurement 326–7;
   as constructive process 11–14, 61;
   cues 11–13, 60–2, 191, 343; as
   decoding process 8–10; in groups 167;
   as 'guessing game' 11–13; Haringey
   project 40–56; as 'input' process
   343–4; multisensory teaching 274–9;
   parental involvement 27, 39–40,
   55–6, 159; phonological awareness
   327
reading, models of 8–15; 'bottom-up'
   8–10, 13, 14; Interactive
   Compensatory 15; 'top-down' 11–13,
   14
reading programmes/schemes 87, 100,
   103, 163, 167, 193–200, 270–1,
   274–9; problems with choosing 4–5,
   8, 15–16, 336–7; see also 'family
   literacy' restricted programmes;
   Pause Prompt Praise; Phonological
   Intervention; Reading Recovery
Reading Recovery 271, 321; aims 322;
   Australia/New Zealand success 335;
   costs 332–3; structure 322–3; teacher
   training 321–2; v. Phonological
   Training study 324–37
Regular Education Initiative (REI)
   136–7; opponents v. proponents
   137–8
remedial model of SEN 175
research: qualitative v. quantitative
   283
rhetoric: and 'cycle of
   underachievement' 94–5, 102;
   definition 89; and 'family literacy'
   restricted programmes 89, 91–3,
   94–5, 98, 101–2, 105–6
Rhyme, Initial and End Schools
   Oddities Test 327
Rhyme World scheme 195
rich pictures 141–3
Romani 125

Scarborough, H. 112
school reputation 22
SDD see dyslexia

self-correction 12–13, 61–3; failure in 60; in spelling 363–7
self-esteem/concept 55, 180, 181, 284–5; and academic performance 285, 287, 288; and dyslexia 76, 117, 282–3, 287–90, 292–3, 299; high v. low 286–7; 'learned helplessness' 287; measurement of 285–6, 288; personal construct theory 287; and 'pleasing others' 289–90; and teacher expectations 290–3; of Travellers 123
semantic cues 10–12, 191
SEN see Special Educational Needs
Skill Teach scheme 196
skills-development 181
Snowling Non-Word Reading Test 327
social class: relation to achievement 5–6, 333
social exclusion 21, 22, 26–7, 34, 35; see also Traveller communities
socio-economic effects of literacy 105
Soft Systems Methodology (SSM) 136, 138–9, 149; action research 136; conceptual models 146–7; relevant systems 144; root definitions 145; Special Needs application 145–6, 147, 149–51; stages 139–48; usage 149; Weltanschauung 145, 149
Special Educational Needs (SEN): 'appropriate' teaching 175, 176; assessment arrangements 205–9, 212–22; Dyson Debate 136, 138, 149; policy 30–5, 186–7, 306; Regular Education Initiative 136–7; remedial model 175; SSM approach 145–6, 147, 149–51; and technical rationality 4–5, 136; see also dyslexia; specific learning difficulties
Special Educational Needs (SEN) Code of Practice 31–3, 209
Special Educational Needs Information Technology (SENIT) 258
Special Educational Needs (SEN) Tribunals 32, 35, 269; critical review of 33–4; and LEAs 33–5, 269–70
specific developmental dyslexia (SDD) see dyslexia

specific learning difficulties (SpLDs) 175–6; conceptualisations 179–80; definitions 176; dilemmas for schools 177–8, 183; models for provision 174, 177, 178–9, 181–7; rationales for provision 180–1; and self-esteem 287–90; v. whole-school approach 175, 177, 182, 183–4; see also dyslexia; Special Educational Needs
spelling 157, 340, 354; and attitude 348–51; and creative writing 351, 364–5; developmental approach 340–2, 353; and dialect 347; and dictionaries 369–70, 373–6; and dyslexia 346; games 348, 370–8; and handwriting 352; multisensory approach 349, 359–61; and the National Curriculum 352–3; and parents 348; and phonics 346–7, 357; research 343–4; schemes 361; self-checking 363–7; stages in learning 355–7; strategies 344, 345, 351–2, 358–9, 362–4, 367–9; tests 347–8, 362; 'unexpected poor spellers' 345; word analysis 357–8, 372; word lists 361, 362, 368, 369, 377
SSM see Soft Systems Methodology
Stanovich, K. E. 252–3
stigmatisation: and dyslexia 304–5, 308–9, 312
Success for All programme 336
syntactic cues 11–12, 191

targets for raising literacy levels 4
Tatari Tautoko Tauawhi see Pause Prompt Praise
Taylor Report (1977) 56
teacher training: lack of with parents 23, 27; in Reading Recovery 321; for SpLDs 257
teachers: case studies of literacy strategies 153–71; and effective literacy strategies 171–2; and home–school liaison 27–8, 29
Teaching Reading and Spelling to Dyslexic Children scheme 197
technical rational approach 4, 136; criticisms of 4–5
testing 44, 196, 225, 253, 326–7;

British Ability Scale 254, 326; Neale Analysis 225, 226, 238, 326; spelling 347–8, 362; *see also* assessments

Traveller communities: aural skills 126; distance learning 129–30; history 122, 125; and home-learning 123–4; and ICT access 129–30; importance of keeping records 128–9; lack of continuity in education 121, 122, 128; learning difficulties 121, 128–9; oral skills 125–6; racism and bullying 123, 125, 126; reading materials 127; relevance of literacy 126–7

Traveller Education Services (TES) 127

Turner, M. 255

'unexpected poor spellers' 345

Warnock, Mary 248–9

Warnock Report (1978) 29, 30–1, 56, 306

Weltanschauung 145, 149

whole-book/whole-language approach 11–13; conflict with phonics 13–14, 15

whole-class interactive teaching *see* National Literacy Strategy

whole-school approach 135, 138, 175, 177, 182, 183–4

word blindness/deafness *see* dyslexia

word lists 157, 191, 193, 361, 362, 368, 369, 377

writing, as 'output' process 343–4